The Cultural Production of the
Educated Person

SUNY Series, Power, Social Identity, and Education
Lois Weis, editor

The Cultural Production of the Educated Person

Critical Ethnographies of Schooling and Local Practice

edited by

Bradley A. Levinson
Douglas E. Foley
Dorothy C. Holland

State University of New York Press

Published by
State University of New York Press, Albany

© 1996 State University of New York

Printed in the United States of America

For information, address the State University of New York Press,
State University Plaza, Albany, NY 12246

Library of Congress Cataloging-in-Publication Data

The cultural production of the educated person : critical
  ethnographies of schooling and local practice / edited by Bradley A.
  Levinson, Douglas E. Foley, Dorothy C. Holland.
      p. cm. — (SUNY series, power, social identity, and
  education)
    Includes bibliographical references and index.
    ISBN 0-7914-2859-1 (alk. paper). — ISBN 0-7914-2860-5 (pbk. :
  alk. paper)
    1. Educational anthropology—Case studies. 2. Educational
  sociology—Case studies. 3. Critical pedagogy—Case studies.
  4. Ethnicity—Case studies. I. Levinson, Bradley A., 1963–
  II. Foley, Douglas E. III. Holland, Dorothy C. IV. Series.
  LB45C83 1996
  370.1'92—dc20   95-8931
                                                         CIP

10 9 8 7 6 5 4 3 2 1

CONTENTS

For students everywhere who
struggle to make sense of school.

PREFACE

Several of the contributors to this volume first met to discuss the project and share early paper drafts at a session Levinson organized for the International Congress of Anthropological and Ethnological Sciences, held in Mexico City in the summer of 1993. Since then, the intellectual dialogue which has informed and sustained this project took place largely through phones, faxes, and electronic mail. Over great distances, manuscripts were exchanged along with critical comments and friendly exhortations to perservere. The list of contributors fluctuated over time, as other commitments intervened. We appreciate the input of several colleagues who, connected to the project at an earlier stage, helped us to formulate it, even as they eventually went their own ways.

Our debts, both intellectual and personal, are numerous. Levinson would like to thank his colleagues in the Department of Sociology, Anthropology, and Social Welfare at Augustana College for their support and understanding (especially of phone bills which often exceeded all others combined!). A special thanks to Peter Kivisto for his critical acumen, to Elizabeth Walsh for her practical help and good humor, and to student assistants Teresa Winstead, Audrey Yakin, and Carrie Leslie. Another special thanks to Elsie Rockwell, friend and mentor, as well as her colleagues at the Departamento de Investigaciones Educativas in Mexico City (Rafael Quiroz, Ruth Mercado, Justa Ezpeleta, among others) who have always given Levinson a warm welcome in Mexico, and have helped him to broaden his perspective on educational reality. Thanks also to Linda Beine, Roman Bonzón, Jon Clauss, América Colmenares, Tamara Felden, David and Joan Levinson, Gary Mann, Kim McNally, Ben Nefzger, Yesenia Rodríguez, Nancy Smith, Marsha Smith, Vicki Sommer, Narendra Subramanian, Debra Unger, and Rebecca Wee for numerous favors and kindnesses. Levinson would like to acknowledge the help of the Augustana Faculty Research Fund in compiling the book. Levinson and Holland together thank William Lachicotte and Susan Shaw.

For their support and critical feedback on the book, especially the introduction, the editors would like to thank Gary Anderson, Richard Blot, R. W. Connell, Marjorie LeCompte, Aurolyn Luykx, Rolland Paulston, Laura Rival, Elsie Rockwell, and Thomas Shaw. Finally, thanks to Priscilla Ross at SUNY Press for her confidence and support throughout the project.

viii

FOREWORD

During the past twenty years there has been a vibrant research agenda regarding the interplay among culture, the economy, and schooling. Fueled by theoretically driven U.S. scholars such as Michael Apple (1979, 1982a, 1982b), Henry Giroux (1983), Samuel Bowles and Herbert Gintis (1976), Jean Anyon (1981, 1983), Philip Wexler (1987), Martin Carnoy and Henry Levin (1985), Peter McClaren (1986), Doug Foley (1990), and many others, the relationship between education, culture, and the economy has been the site for intense intellectual debate. Debates in Europe and Australia have been no less intense, and the work of Basil Bernstein (1977), Pierre Bourdieu and Jean Passeron (1977), Geoff Whitty (1985), Madeleine MacDonald (later Arnot, 1980), R. W. Connell (1982), Michael F. D. Young (1971), and numerous others has stimulated lively discussions within and across continents. Conferences which I have attended in England, for example, exhibit the passion with which these topics are handled. For none of us went into this area without a sense of social justice, without a sense that the world, and particularly schools, could not be left better places as a partial result of our intellectual presence. For we were all deeply committed to a more just and egalitarian society, a society where the rights and privileges of the historically disenfranchised could be expanded. This was our praxis—this was the space in which we thought we could make a difference. None of us went in bereft of passion—all of us were attracted to the theories of reproduction, contestation, resistance, because of our politics.

Like all times, the early 1970s offered numerous intellectual frameworks with which to work. We gravitated to those which enabled us to explore and express our passions, dreams and desires. Having been trained quantitatively, and using Parsonian-driven frameworks, I found the emerging debates in the sociology of education to be a breath of fresh air. It was as if I could breathe again—that something could be connected with my growing sense that all was not right with the world. The swirling debates around feminism and anti-racism quickly fueled further research and politics. The underlying assumption that class inequality is the only inequality worth focusing upon was roundly attacked by white feminists, feminists of color, men of color, as well as white men who desperately wanted to live in a less racist world. The literature which explored gender and race, as well as social class, in relation to the economy, culture, and society literally exploded. Excellent work in the United States by Cameron McCarthy (1993, 1990), McCarthy and Warren Critchlow (1993), Leslie Roman and Linda Christian-Smith (1988), Catherine Raissiguer (1994), Patrick Solomon (1992), Mwalimu Shujaa (1994), Kathleen Weiler (1988), Michelle Fine (1991), Linda Valli (1986), Nancy Lesko (1988), and Dorothy Holland and Margaret Eisenhart (1990), among others, literally forced us to confront the assumed class-based struggle of our earlier formulations. The struggle over cultural and economic space could no longer be seen as one in which white working-class men are the vanguard. Certainly, white working-class men are one such group poised for struggle, but there are others.

While there has been excellent research on various groups as they struggle for emotional, intellectual, cultural, and economic space, we have not spent enough time focusing on the ways in which these groups struggle in relation to each other. Rather than target elites, Michelle Fine and I are finding that poor and working-class people across racial and ethnic groups construct and target the "other," thus leaving the system basically intact.[1] It is the relational component to the construction of identity that we have not paid enough attention to until now. Sadly enough, it is my sense that we too, in the academy, construct and target the "other," the "other" group which we feel is gaining more space, leaving a growing rightist movement increasing freedom to maneuver. Like the people with whom Michelle and I are working, we also leave the power base essentially intact as we attack across constructed borders of gender and race, hampering the much needed struggle against rightward movement in this country. This is, in my opinion, the ultimate in poststructuralist fracturing—leaving the right all the space they need to cut budgets which we would all agree need expansion.

A number of years ago, Michael Apple said to me that critical ethnographic research, if it is to push current intellectual boundaries, must be comparative. In other words, those of us who do such research must be willing to move across national and international borders in order to probe further the meaning of our conceptions of schooling as related to the economy, society, and culture.

Until this volume, however, the idea did not take root. Here, Levinson, Foley, and Holland have assembled scholars whose research is comparative. As such, they are the first to my knowledge to put together a volume which takes seriously the global dimensions of issues under consideration in critical cultural studies. This is not to say, of course, that work has not been done across national borders. Clearly, such work has been done, as noted earlier. However, the authors specifically probe issues of cultural production in a wide vareity of economic and cultural contexts, making a major contribution to the literature. The essays span Taiwan, Ecuador, Mexico, Bolivia, the United States, and Nepal. The potential for engaging with these essays in a variety of ways is truly exciting and I urge readers to work across essays in order to probe theoretical issues of importance.

In their introduction, Levinson and Holland recenter cultural production as an important concept. Cultural production enables us to use the insights of structuralists as well as culturalists as we probe how it is that groups construct identities inside specified sites. In the mid-1970s, structuralists such as Louis Althusser (1971) and Bowles and Gintis stressed the ways in which institutions such as schools served to reproduce inequalities in the larger society. Paul Willis' now classic volume, *Learning to Labour* (1977), challenged this highly deterministic view by suggesting that the British "lads," through their own culture, helped to reproduce the conditions of capitalist society. Willis took seriously culture as it is produced "on the ground," so to speak, and explored fully the production of working-class culture and the ways in which the "lads" help to reproduce the conditions of their own existence. This led to a series of excellent studies largely grounded in what became known as the "culturalist" tradition, that is, those scholars who tended to focus more on culture as it is produced in ongoing interactions and in relation to class, gender, and race antagonisms in the larger society.

Unfortunately, however, what happened was that structuralists lost the insights of the culturalists, and vice versa. In other words, those who focused on the ways in which schools distribute messages to students depending on social class location ignored the fact that students do not necessarily passively absorb these messages, but, rather, interact with them in highly creative ways. On the other hand, those who focus on the production of culture tended to ignore that such production takes place inside sites that are already differentiated by the type of capital distributed to students, already bounded, in other words, by social structure. Paul Willis, for example, wholly ignores the nature of knowledge itself, and the ways in which knowledge as distributed to working-class lads may be linked in fundamental ways to the located culture which the lads produce. The lads do not only draw upon class culture as expressed outside of the school. Perhaps if the school, for example, had not been so ignoring of their culture to begin with, the cultural production process would have looked somewhat different. This is not to suggest that culturalists have overplayed agency in their studies. Frankly, I do not think this is the case. However, our tendency to place ourselves in little theoretical camps often means that we ignore the insights of other camps, and have a difficult time working across intellectual borders. It is here where the present volume makes a second important contribution. The authors are clear that processes of cultural production must be seen as lodged in that space *between* structure and agency, in that space *between* culture and structure. It is the dialectical interaction between structure and culture that we really must explore across racial, ethnic, class, and gender groupings in a wide variety of national contexts. Agency is not enacted without reference to social structure (of which the school is only one part); indeed, it is absolutely enacted in relation to such structure, and it is here that some postmodernist work worries me. We must recenter the economy and social institutions as they are dialectically related to the production of culture and identity, and Levinson, Foley, and Holland take this very seriously. I could not agree more with their theoretical stance on these issues. We must look at the messages distributed through structure, and the ways in which such messages are dialectically related to the production of culture. It is here, in this space, that we will find much room for future research and action.

Levinson, Foley, and Holland have assembled an exciting volume for yet another reason. They have absolutely stated—in the anthropological but not critical culturalist studies tradition—that education takes place in a wide variety of contexts, and that the school is only one of these contexts. Indeed, it is in these "free spaces," to use Evans and Boyte's (1992) term, that much education takes place, that people become free to imagine what could be, what might be. It is here where passions explode, much as our own exploded years ago when we found space to engage theoretically our politics. In the United States, it is in sites like Headstart, the African-American church, activist shelters, shelters for battered women, multiethnic arts agencies, and numerous others, that people create and sustain a sense of possibility, a sense which is often in direct opposition to the ways in which schools shape people. These sites, constructed by, through, or for local community interests, seem to nurture a sense of hope and possibility, and exist both within and outside of schools. It is important to understand these pockets and reimagine how policies and community life could be constituted to incorporate and multiply such energy. While the authors of this volume do not necessarily do this, the very fact that they pry open the space outside of schools as a space for community-based education, means that they entice us into thinking about these issues. They ask us to engage our energies in these directions. People are not cultural dupes of old structuralist frameworks. They do, indeed, exhibit agency, struggle, and imagination as they grapple with structures wrapped around their located lives. However, they do this in a variety of sites, and the editors open this important door and encourage us to imagine what research surrounding these issues could look like in the future. This volume is exciting and important. It is with great pleasure that I now invite you into the text.

LOIS WEIS

NOTE

1. Michelle Fine and I are currently engaged in a two-city study which examines how young, working-class and poor adults from across ethnic and racial groups narrate their educational, familial, and economic biographies, and how they project their parental involvement within their children's schools. Over one hundred and fifty adults were involved with us in individual and/or focus-group experiences. The research is supported by the Spencer Foundation. Results will be forthcoming.

REFERENCES

Anyon, Jean. 1981. Social Class and School Knowledge. Curriculum Inquiry. 11, 3–42.

———. 1983. Ideology and U.S. Textbooks. *In* Michael Apple and Lois Weis, eds., Ideology and Practice in Schooling. Boston: Routledge and Kegan Paul.

Apple, Michael. 1979. Ideology and Curriculum. Boston: Routledge and Kegan Paul.

————. 1982. Education and Power. Boston: Routledge and Kegan Paul.

Bernstein, Basil. 1977. Class Codes and Control, vol. 3. London: Routledge and Kegan Paul.

Bowles, Samuel and Herbert Gintis. 1976. Schooling in Capitalist America. New York: Basic Books.

Bourdieu, Pierre and Jean-Claude Passeron. 1977. Reproduction in Educating Society and Culture. Beverly Hills: Sage.

Carnoy, Martin and Henry Levin. 1985. Schooling and Work in the Democratic State. Stanford: Stanford University Press.

Connell, R. W. 1982. Making the Difference. Sydney: George Allen and Unwin.

Evans, Sara and Harry Boyte. 1992. Free Spaces. Chicago: University of Chicago Press.

Foley, Doug. 1990. Learning Capitalist Culture. Philadelphia: University of Pennsylvania Press.

Giroux, Henry. 1983. Theories of Reproduction and Resistance in the New Sociology of Education: A Critical Analyses. Harvard Educational Review 53(3):257–93.

Holland, Dorothy and Margaret Eisenhart. 1990. Educated in Romance. Chicago: University of Chicago Press.

Lesko, Nancy. 1988. The Curriculum of the Body. *In* Leslie Roman and Linda Christian-Smith, eds., Becoming Feminine. London: Falmer Press.

McCarthy, Cameron. 1990. *Race and Curriculum*. Bristol, PA: Falmer Press.

————. 1993. "Beyond the Poverty of Theory in Race Relations." *In* Lois Weis and Michelle Fine, eds., Beyond Silenced Voices. Albany: SUNY Press.

McCarthy, Cameron and Warren Critchlow, eds. 1993. Race, Identity and Representation in Education. New York: Routledge.

McClaren, Peter. 1986. Schooling as Ritual Performance. London: Routledge and Kegan Paul.

MacDonald (later Arnot), Madeleine. 1980. "Schooling and the Reproduction of Class and Gender Relations." *In* Roger Dale, Geoff Esland, and Madeleine MacDonald, eds., Education and the State. London: Routledge and Kegan Paul.

Raissiguer, Catherine. 1994. Becoming Women, Becoming Workers. Albany: SUNY Press.

Roman, Leslie and Linda Christian-Smith, eds. 1988. Becoming Feminine. London: Falmer Press.

Solomon, Patrick. 1992. Black Resistance in School. Albany: SUNY Press.

Shujaa, Mwalimu, ed. 1994. Too Much Schooling: Too Little Education. Trenton, N.J.: African World Press.

Valli, Linda. 1986. Becoming Clerical Workers. Boston: Routledge and Kegan Paul.

Weiler, Kathleen. 1988. Women Teaching for Change: Gender, Class and Power. South Hadley, Mass.: Bergin and Garvey.

Willis, Paul. 1977. Learning to Labour: How Working Class Kids Get Working Class Jobs.

Wexler, Philip. 1987. Social Analysis of Education. Boston: Routledge.

Whitty, Geoff. 1985. Schooling and School Knowledge. London: Methuen.

Young, Michael F. D., ed. 1971. Knowledge and Control. London: Collier-Macmillan.

1

BRADLEY A. LEVINSON AND DOROTHY HOLLAND

The Cultural Production of the Educated Person:
An Introduction

Around the world, modern schools are central to the social and cultural shaping of the young. Relatively new to history, especially for those people situated on the margins of industrialization, institutions of mass schooling often remove children from their families and local communities, encouraging mastery of knowledges and disciplines that have currency and ideological grounding in wider spheres. As articulated early on by Durkheim (1956) and others, these schools have served to inculcate the skills, subjectivities, and disciplines that undergird the modern nation-state. No matter how the knowledgeable person is locally defined, regardless of the skills and sensibilities that count as indicators of "wisdom" and intelligence in the home and immediate locale, schools interject an educational mission of extra-local proportions.

Thus, set in the space between the local and the national, modern schools provide a contradictory resource to those students who might benefit from their teachings and credentials. Ironically, schooled knowledges and disciplines may, while offering certain freedoms and opportunities, at the same time further draw students into dominant projects of nationalism and capitalist labor formation, or bind them even more tightly to systems of class, gender, and race inequality. On a more personal level, subjection to the school's ministrations can yield a sense of self as knowledgeable, as "somebody" (Luttrell, this volume), but it also may encourage a sense of self as failure. Encounters with formal education can result in a feeling of responsibility for one's lowly social standing.

Schools have also proven themselves a contradictory resource for those who would fit the young to a particular vision of society. Not surprisingly, schools and education often become sites of intense cultural politics. Local educational practices and ideologies may be pitted against those of national priority. Groups identifying themselves perhaps by ethnicity, perhaps by moral orientation, may feel unfairly subjected to the educational values of a more powerful group. Struggles, sometimes submerged and virtually invisible, sometimes clear and dramatic, erupt. Politics can engulf the curriculum. Coalitions form and reform trying to appropriate the schools to their own ends. And students, often the voiceless objects of educational reform, may become recalcitrant.

1

The Cultural Production of the Educated Person explores these conflicts and contradictions. The volume comprises eleven original case studies addressed to the social and cultural projects of modern schools, and to the contestations or accommodations, dramatic and not, that emerge in and around and against them. Our definition of the "school" is broad, yet specific: a state organized or regulated institution of intentional instruction. We include not only formal educational programs for the young, but also "nonformal" government training schemes, adult education, and the like.

Education is even more broadly defined. We follow the usual anthropological practice of distinguishing education from schooling. Anthropologists have long recognized the existence of culturally specific and relative definitions of the educated person (e.g., Hansen 1979:28, 39, 244; Borofsky 1987; Lave in press). Although the degree to which cultural training is formalized, situated at a remove from activities for which the training is intended, and provided on a mass scale may vary, anthropologists recognize all societies as providing some kind of training and some set of criteria by which members can be identified as more, or less, knowledgeable. Distinct societies, as well as ethnic groups and microcultures within those societies, elaborate the cultural practices by which particular sets of skills, knowledges, and discourses come to define the fully "educated" person. In this volume, for instance, Shaw shows how the "great tradition" of Chinese Confucianism helped define a notion of educated person in terms of filial devotion and service, while Rival describes the Huaorani educated person as constituted by certain culturally salient activities, such as chanting and toolmaking.

Regardless of whether they are legitimized by formal institutions, we consider local forms of education significant. Some educators may have difficulty treating these forms seriously or considering them alongside those enshrined by schools. Yet such a vision is necessary. Otherwise, there is no vantage point from which to appreciate the shape and degree of contestation that goes on around schools, even in places where modern schools have been in place for over a century. Nor is there ample scope to recognize that, despite what may seem to be the homogeneity of a group, cultural production is ongoing, and hegemonic definitions of the educated person may be contested along lines of gender, age, and, in stratified societies, ethnicity and class.

The case studies in this volume chart a new direction for "critical"[1] educational research. Such research is fundamentally local and ethnographic, yet moves beyond the school to examine links between local cultural practices and the community, the region, the state, and the economy. Along with this broadened interpretive perspective, we also urge a more extensive comparative base. Challenging the Eurocentrism of most prior critical research, we draw on studies of schooling in a variety of locales in order to address the global dimensions of educational process and change. Moreover, in carrying forward this process of interpretive and empirical broadening, we urge a consideration of two key terms.

We argue that the concept of "cultural production" allows us to better understand the resources for, and constraints upon, social action—the interplay of agency and structure—in a variety of educational institutions. We also argue that a culturally specific and relative conception of the "educated person" allows us to appreciate the historical and cultural particularities of the "products" of education, and thus provides a framework for understanding conflicts around different kinds of schooling. In the process of explicating these two terms, we hope to articulate a distinctive model that is emerging in critical and qualitative educational studies.

A more precise description of the studies in this book depends upon placing them in the context of major theoretical shifts which have taken place within critical educational studies over the last two decades. Describing these developments will be the first task of this chapter. We shall briefly sketch the concepts of "social reproduction" and "cultural production," which gathered momentum in the 1980s. We will argue that the 1990s are witness to a broadening of horizons in the critical study of schooling. Infused by the field of cultural studies, with its focus on identities, and by practice theories, with their accounts of the production of cultural forms, critical educational studies build upon, but do not limit themselves to, an understanding of schools as one of the major sites of struggle for classes disadvantaged by advanced capitalism. Such studies have arrived at the point, in fact, where the concept of cultural production can be developed in "relative autonomy" from the problematic of class reproduction. Other forms of power and subordination, other critical concerns are now addressed, sometimes in addition to, sometimes in place of, class. Indeed, we forward the concept of a culturally variable "educated person" in order to displace structural (read class) "reproduction" as the privileged vantage point from which to view all forms of cultural production.

Our second task in providing a context for the papers is to explore the differences between schools, as sites for the production of educated persons, across cultural and social space. Much of the critical education literature has developed in and focused upon schools in privileged, Western societies—that is, in societies positioned favorably in world political and economic systems. There are, of course, differences among these Western societies. Streams of educational literature reveal different historical circumstances and different social formations of privilege, which in turn give rise to varying theoretical and practical preoccupations. In British studies, for example, issues of class, and now race and gender dynamics, have dominated theorizing about education, whereas in the United States, cultural differences based on race and ethnicity have been more salient. Yet the empowerment, displacement, or de-skilling of first-generation schoolgoers that we see in Third World countries is a different sort of process (see Rival, Levinson, Rockwell, Skinner and Holland, this volume). The citizen-building goals assigned to schools in countries such as Mexico or Nepal cannot be the same as those expected of schools in the United States or Europe. Also, patterns of class mobility, ethnicity, and gender can be quite different in developing countries (at times of rapid economic growth, schools may indeed contribute to fluid social mobility). For these reasons, it is time to more clearly expand the horizons of critical educational theory to include processes occurring in places other than the privileged societies of advanced capitalism.

From here we move on to an extensive review of the literature, along with a discussion of key concepts in critical educational discourse. Readers interested in moving on to a restatement of our argument, as well as an introduction to the case studies, can skip to the section on "Building Strengths and Charting New Directions," on page 21.

can skip to the section on "Building Strengths and Charting New Directions," on page 21.

DEVELOPMENTS IN CRITICAL EDUCATIONAL STUDIES

Social Reproduction

Our insights into schools are informed by current developments in anthropological and sociological studies of schooling. Over the past fifty years, these developments have proceeded through a series of theoretical and methodological debates. At first, guided by liberal assumptions about the role of schools in a meritocracy, where upward mobility was assumed to be an outcome of talent and effort, researchers (sociologists, for the most part) described the institution and analyzed educational outcomes. Designed to imitate the research products of the hard sciences, these pictures of schools came largely in the form of survey and experimental data (Karabel and Halsey 1977). In the mid-1970s, beginning for the most part in Europe, these studies were challenged by more critical approaches. Schools have since become the topic of an extensive critical literature, and surveys and experiments have been replaced, to some extent, by investigations of a more historical/ethnographic sort.

Without a doubt, the critical perspective has always been informed by a strong commitment to ideals of equality in education. Like so many others, including the contributors to this volume, we have actively appropriated Western discourses on equal rights and opportunities, and we have dedicated a significant part of our lives and careers to exploring whether these rights and opportunities are indeed offered by public education systems, across race, class, and gender lines. Moreover, we agree with Connell (1993:19) that this ideal of equality demands both "distributive" and "curricular" justice, that is, equality of educational access as well as curricular knowledge and representation.

It is for this reason that, like many educational scholars, we were drawn to the first wave of critical studies of schooling which emerged in the 1970s. With the breakdown of functionalist and "scientistic" hegemony in the social sciences, the "new sociology of education" brought important perspectives to the study of schooling.[2] Scholars such as Althusser (1971), Young (1971), Bernstein (1973), Baudelot and Establet (1975), Bowles and Gintis (1976), Sharp and Green (1975), Bourdieu and Passeron (1977), Apple (1979, 1982a), and Giroux (1983) elaborated a radical critique of the social effects of schooling in the so-called liberal capitalist democracies.[3] In particular, these scholars endeavored to show that schools were not "innocent" sites of cultural transmission, or places for the inculcation of consensual values. Nor could schools be understood as meritocratic springboards for upward mobility—the great leveling mechanism, according to dominant liberal ideology.[4] Rather, critical scholars argued that schools actually served to exacerbate or perpetuate social inequalities. In their view, schooling responded less to popular impulses for advancement and empowerment, and more to the requirements of discipline and conformity demanded by capitalist production and the nation-state. In Althusser's (1971) most (in)famous declaration, ideology "interpellated" subjects: Schools were among the most powerful "ideological state apparatuses" of modern capitalism, hence places where the student-as-subject would become ideologically positioned to assume his or her role in the class structure (see also Anyon 1981). By the end of the 1970s, "reproduction theory" had emerged to explain how schools served to *reproduce* rather than transform existing structural inequalities.

From Social to Cultural Reproduction: The Work of Pierre Bourdieu

While most of these early critical studies used the trope of reproduction to characterize enduring class *structures* in a capitalist economy, Bourdieu and his associates inaugurated a highly original approach to the reproduction of the *cultural* bases of privilege. According to Bourdieu, the highly skewed valuation of cultural styles and competencies was what buttressed an unequal social order. Michael Apple's (1982a) edited volume was one of the first to build on Bourdieu's work and clearly address cultural as well as "economic" reproduction in education. Dimaggio (1982) and Lareau (1989) also mined Bourdieu's insights on the cultural basis of class privilege, while Delamont (1989), Weiler (1988), and Holland and Eisenhart (1990) attempted to extend these insights to account for the cultural reproduction of gender privilege, and women's continued subordination.

Bourdieu first developed the idea of "modes of domination" through his comparative work on French schools and the Kabyle peasants of Algeria. The Kabyle, whom Bourdieu had studied ethnographically (1977b), reproduced their unequal social standings through face-to-face, often agonistic encounters. Drawing on discourses of shame and honor, prominent Kabyle (men in particular) developed stocks of "symbolic capital" which were key to their control over labor resources in the community. Symbolic contests of honor carried out face to face were thus key to the reproduction of the domination of one man over another, of one family over another, among the Kabyle. These contests not only reproduced unequal social and economic positions, but also the value of the symbolic capital of honor itself. In France, on the other hand, a highly differentiated and bureaucratized class structure evidenced a more impersonal means of cultural reproduction. In France, Bourdieu suggested, schools performed the complex work of validating and distributing the symbolic capital which enabled dominant groups to maintain their economic advantage.

Bourdieu's understanding of the role of schools in French society (Bourdieu and Saint Martin 1974; Bourdieu and Passeron 1977) differed from Althusser's structural Marxist formulation. Specifically, he developed the concept of "cultural capital" as a social resource analogous to, and complexly intertwined with, economic capital. "Cultural capital" refers to a kind of symbolic credit which one acquires through learning to embody and enact signs of social standing. This credit consists of a series of competencies and character traits, such as "taste" and "intelligence." Because of this credit, the actions of people with higher social standing automatically achieve greater currency and legitimacy. Those of lower standing, by contrast, receive no such legitimacy. For Bourdieu, "cultural capital" is convertible to economic capital through advanced academic credentials, or in the way that it helps its bearers, for example, to secure loans, find business partners, or otherwise receive the benefit of the doubt in financial decisions. Yet it is nonetheless separate from economic capital, and valued in and of itself. French schools, according to Bourdieu, give those of superior social standing an unfair advantage in reproducing their stocks of cultural capital.

How do they accomplish this? French schools allow elite groups to maintain power by only recognizing as "intelligent" their cultural capital, that is, *their* tastes for certain cultural products (art, literature, film, music), their manner of deportment, speech, style of dress, consumption patterns, and the like. In other words, only those particular tastes and skills possessed by elite classes are recognized as signs of "intelligence" by schools. Exams, rewards, and other disciplinary procedures ensure school success for those who already possess this particular "intelligence." Those who don't, of course, stand a good chance of lower achievement, and even failure. While those of lower social standing, such as the urban working class, may acquire some of these special styles and competencies, their background will always give them away. In this manner, French schools reproduce the value and content of the cultural capital of elite groups (Bourdieu 1974:42; see also 1984:387).

This process of schooling imposes a kind of "symbolic violence" on nonelite students, in which "instruments of knowledge . . . which are arbitrary" are nevertheless made to appear universal and objective (Bourdieu and Passeron 1977:115). Such symbolic violence has a stultifying effect upon its recipients. As they develop a sense of their social position, and the relatively degraded value of their own cultural-linguistic resources in given social situations, nonelite persons also tend to develop a "sense of their social limits." As these limits become permanently inscribed in a person's "*habitus*," he or she learns to self-censor and self-silence in the company of those with greater social standing. The recent work of anthropologists Helán Page (1994) on the "white public sphere," and Signithia Fordham (1993) on a Washington D.C. high school, can be seen as extending the idea of symbolic violence and cultural capital. Fordham, for example, dramatically demonstrates the results of symbolic violence in the self-silencing of African-American women in schools (see also Luttrell 1989).[5]

Bourdieu's account of cultural reproduction has thus constituted a significant addition to the "new sociology of education." Still, we would call attention to three important limiting features of this whole body of early work—Bourdieu's, as well as that we classify as social reproductionist. First, given its generally neo-Marxist orientation, early reproduction theory privileged class structures as the prime determinant of life chances.[6] It wasn't until the 1980s, under the impact of socialist-feminism and critical studies of race, that scholars began to more fruitfully explore the intersection of class, race, gender, and age structures.[7] Second, virtually all accounts of schooling and inequality in the reproduction literature focused on Euro-American societies. Few scholars attempted to apply its insights to expanding educational systems in non-Western or former colonial societies (see Foley 1977, 1991; Rockwell in press a for exceptions). Third, and perhaps most importantly, reproduction theory had come to rely on highly schematic and deterministic models of structure and culture, as well as simplistic models of the state and its supposed use of schools as instruments of control. As Connell (1983) phrased it, schools had become the "black boxes" which, perforce, reproduced the structural requirements of the capitalist economy and state.[8]

To be sure, though theories of social and cultural reproduction have suffered criticisms, they formed a basis for work we describe below, and thus continue to be useful for our understanding of schools. In particular, Bourdieu's notion of cultural capital helps us to think through the potential role of schools in establishing new forms of symbolic capital while displacing old ones. And as Bourdieu himself exemplified with his work on the Kabyle and the French, such a perspective can be helpful for exploring the effects of schooling across historical and cultural contexts.

American Anthropology and Studies of Schooling: The Cultural Difference Approach

As reproduction theory continued to be principally developed and critiqued by European and American sociologists, philosophers, and political scientists, American educational anthropologists directed their attention elsewhere. Just as social class had become the central problematic for reproduction theory, ethnic difference had become so for educational anthropologists. This was a logical outgrowth of anthropological concerns at the time. Educational anthropology in the United States had its roots in an earlier literature on socialization and cultural transmission in non-Western, nonindustrialized societies.[9] This literature, perhaps made most famous by Mead's (1961[1928]) description of Samoan childhood and adolescence, documented how such societies maintained social cohesion and continuity through the transmission of core values and knowledges from one generation to the next.

Disrupted by the social upheavals of the 1960s, this work was eclipsed by a new direction in anthropological thinking. With the rise of civil rights and anti-colonial movements at home and abroad, anthropologists increasingly turned their attention toward modern schooling systems, especially the problems of cultural and ethnic difference in the United States. In the wake of liberal and radical critiques of schooling, anthropologists began to participate actively in policy debates, using ethnographic research to elucidate the reasons for the disproportionate school failure of ethnic and racial minorities.

With a few early exceptions, anthropologists distinguished themselves by contributing finely detailed accounts of "differences," "discontinuities," "conflicts," and "mismatches" between mainstream school culture and the traditional cultures of ethnic/racial minorities. They conducted microethnographic studies of classrooms and communities, attempting to identify differences between their respective communication patterns, linguistic codes, and kinesic and cognitive styles.[10] According to this "cultural difference" approach, ethnic minorities tended to fail insofar as they did not successfully adapt themselves to the schools' dominant (usually considered white, middle-class) cultural styles or, conversely, insofar as the schools could not provide appropriate "activity settings" (Trueba 1988) to accommodate the minorities. While this approach was extremely important for offsetting racist models of genetic inferiority and "cultural deprivation," it downplayed the social and historical forces responsible for the reproduction of "cultural differences" in schools.[11] Neglecting to emphasize how communication styles, cognitive codes, and so on were the cultural practices of *variably* empowered groups, historically produced within relations of power, the cultural difference approach tended to essentialize the cultural repertoires of minority groups. As Ogbu (1981) pointed out, the absence of such a critical analysis permitted confident reformists to attempt amelioration of school-based conflicts in cultural styles through remedial programs and "culturally responsive" pedagogies.[12] The deeper, structural context of cultural production and school failure remained obscure and largely unaddressed.[13]

Thus, for different reasons, we find both "reproduction theory" and "cultural difference" theory, as understandings of educational process, largely exhausted of new insight by the mid-1980s. Yet we've also been able to identify existing strengths in these approaches, and the developments emerging from them, which we and the others in this volume put to good use. Although no longer a dominant force in critical educational research, questions raised by "reproduction" theorists, especially Bourdieu with his focus on cultural capital and symbolic violence, continue to be important. So too are the questions anthropologists have posed about understanding "cultural differences," and the basic cultural knowledge of the "educated person." Finally, we must not forget the origin of the concept of "cultural production" in the reproduction literature.

BEYOND REPRODUCTION THEORY:
ETHNOGRAPHY AND CULTURAL PRODUCTION

The concept of cultural production in educational studies developed as the reproduction literature was considerably nuanced by the introduction of ethnographic research. These ethnographic studies forced scholars to move beyond the more deterministic formulations of both structural Marxism and poststructural, "productivist" discourse analysis (Coward and Ellis 1977; Smith 1988). Beginning with Paul Willis' (1981b) watershed study of British "lads," ethnographers began opening up the "black box" embedded in the reproductionists' views of schooling.[14] As is well known, Willis' ethnographic account of the working-class lads of "Hammertown Comprehensive" forever shattered the image of the passive, malleable student implicit in reproduction theory. The lads were vital, active participants who shaped life in the school, preventing its smooth functioning, resisting its oppressive capacities, and largely constructing, through the cultural forms they produced, their own subjectivities. "Social agents," wrote Willis (1981b:175), "are not passive bearers of ideology, but active appropriators who reproduce existing structures only through struggle, contestation and a partial penetration of those structures." Through their celebration of a masculinity which strongly resisted and rejected the "middle-class" ideology of the school, the lads, in effect, did end up sealing their own fate. However, the eventual reproduction of their working-class position is only part of the lesson of Willis' case study. The important point is that the school itself did not unilaterally socialize the lads to conform to their working-class position. On the contrary, the lads were very much a part of the dynamic process.[15]

By the 1980s, numerous ethnographic studies of the dynamics of power relations in schools offered insights into the production of different educational outcomes.[16] Ethnography problematized the reproductionist formula by showing that students created cultural forms which resisted ideological interpellation, and that schools were not monolithic purveyors of dominant ideologies (Foley 1990; Ezpeleta and Rockwell 1983; McNeil 1986). Theorists who had earlier espoused a simpler reproduction model now advocated a more complex understanding of the popular and dominant forces which, historically, come to constitute the typical school environment (Apple 1982b; Apple and Weis 1983; Giroux 1983).[17] The term "contradiction," appropriated from an earlier Marxist vocabulary, now became common in critical educational studies, as scholars sought to understand how "reproduction" could be both contested and accelerated through actions by the same people, in the same educational institution.[18] As we have seen, then, in critical educational studies the concept of cultural production was originally employed as a means of challenging notions that schooling was unopposed, and thus invariably successful in its reproduction of wider structures. But beyond the importance of adding resistance to reproduction theory, the focus on cultural production considerably broadened the purview of critical educational studies. By the early 1980s scholars had begun to talk more about "cultural production" as an ongoing social process which could occur independently of, but enter into complex relations with, processes of the social and cultural reproduction of class structures. Simply put, studies of schooling and cultural production are now informed by a broader range of critical social theories. Social dynamics arising between those who control the material means of economic production and those who must sell their labor, certainly remain important. However, class relations are no longer the one and only lens privileged in the critical analysis of schools.

Criticisms of Willis' *Learning to Labor* offer a means to explicate this broadening. *Learning to Labour* was part of a more general intellectual and political project of Willis' home institution in Birmingham, England, the Centre for Contemporary Cultural Studies (CCCS). Affected by the reaction of the intellectual/political left in England to Stalin, the CCCS had from its beginnings rejected the determinism and economism of older Marxian thought. Instead, the CCCS emphasized the significance of local cultural forms, and the cultural politics of control and resistance (Hall 1986, 1991).[19] Still, a close look at Willis' book reveals why it was so vulnerable to feminist critiques such as that of McRobbie (1992), who questioned whether Willis had really moved beyond a structural Marxist position (see also Connell 1983, 1987).[20]

Yes, *Learning to Labor* moved significantly beyond social and cultural reproduction theory by paying attention to the cultural productions of the working-class lads. But was that move sufficient to escape the blinders of the older paradigm? Willis' lads embedded their critique of the school in highly sexist and dramatic displays of masculinity, which both expressed their sense of sexual and racial superiority, and their antagonism to "conformist" working-class boys. Nonetheless, Willis consigned the virulent sexism and deep-seated racism of the culture produced by the lads to the theoretical sidelines. His *theoretical* focus was on the lads as representative of the working-class, in relation to school officials viewed as the mediators of dominant-class interests. Willis did attribute great significance to gender. He argued that the aggressive quality of the lads' sexism was central to their eventual complicity in the reproduction of the class system. But he did not give either gender or race any *primary* significance.

Willis' (1981a and b) response to these criticisms was beneficial yet limited. He elaborated the terms social reproduction, cultural reproduction, and cultural production as general concepts that could be used by researchers concerned not just with working-class males, but with girls and women, racially identified minorities, and so forth. These concepts have been useful and continue to be useful, but they leave a number of questions unanswered:

1. How are gender and race to be conceptualized?
2. How are the *dynamics* of gender privilege and race privilege to be theorized?
3. How are these different social systems interrelated to one another and to class?

The answers seem to lie in a further dismantling of the rigid Marxist paradigm which the scholars at the CCCS had, from the beginning, found unsatisfactory for their project. Gilroy's (1987) book, *Ain't No Black in the Union Jack*, published a decade after *Learning to Labor*, exemplifies some of the moves in this further deconstruction. Although not focused on schools, and firmly situated within the Britain of the 1980s, *Ain't No Black in the Union Jack* draws attention to economic and social changes that have made the relations between capital and labor less central. In the context of national decline, economic restructuring in Great Britain has resulted in what, from the point of view of economic production, is a large "surplus population." Structural unemployment determines the fate of this surplus population. "How," Gilroy (p. 32) asks, "does political consciousness change when people move forever away from the possibility of waged work and accept the state as the provider of their income?" Alongside the dynamics between labor and capital, we now have significant political and social struggles between institutions of the state and civil society, and this surplus population.

In a related argument, Gilroy directs attention to what he considers the politically important struggles of the present day—those shaped by what some have called the "new social movements." Women's movements, civil rights movements, and environmental movements reflect political consciousness emerging from subordination that may be partially connected to, but certainly not determined by, the extraction of surplus value. These social movements include subjectivities and struggles constituted not around class, but rather around "gender, sexuality, generation, the consumption and distribution of state services, and ecological and regional conflicts as well as those defined by race" (p. 32).

These historical shifts point up another dimension of cultural production— the contingent and fluid identifications of the actors involved in these social dramas. The identities of participants in these new social movements cannot be taken as predefined by class position; neither can they be taken as predefined by any essential aspects of race or gender. In other words, the bases of identity are historical and they change through time and through political process. Focusing on race, though the point may be generalized to other dimensions such as gender, Gilroy writes (p. 39), "'race' is an open political category, for it is struggle that determines which definition of 'race' will prevail and the conditions under which they will endure or wither away."[21]

As the complexity of school-based cultural politics and identity-formation has become more apparent, ethnographers have, like Gilroy, drawn on increasingly diverse sources of critical theory.[22] Foley's (1990) ethnography of "North Town High" provides a good example of a cultural production approach set within a social theory formed from an integration of Habermas, Goffman, and Marx. Foley describes students' "expressive practices" as institutionally situated forms of "communicative labor." Ethnic and class differences in North Town have produced distinct "historical speech communities." Because of this, the instrumental and alienating communication styles comprising the broader capitalist culture work their way into the school, giving pride of place to those students, from locally dominant classes, best able to adapt their own speech patterns to such communicative styles. Indeed, Foley shows how students exercise agency in "learning capitalist culture," even as the contours of class and racial power structure their differential abilities and desires to master the communicative forms of this culture.

Likewise, in their recent, respective ethnographies of high schools in the northeast United States, both Wexler (1992) and Weis (1990) demonstrate the way in which the social identities constructed in schools are bound up with social movements and political-economic restructuring in the broader regional scene. Both draw, as did Gilroy, on the social movement theory of Touraine and Melucci to move beyond more static theories of class: Wexler provides a sophisticated, social psychological account of how students learn to "become somebody" within the organizational confines of three high schools rather differently positioned in relation to class and social movements, while Weis examines how young men and women at "Freeway High," a predominantly white, working-class school, form their identities in relation to the discourses and social movements attendant upon de-industrialization and the ascendant New Right politics of the 1980s. Like Foley, Wexler and Weis attempt to show how student identity-formation within schools is a kind of social practice and cultural production which both responds to, and simultaneously constitutes, movements, structures, and discourses beyond the school.

Cultural Studies and the Cultural Production of the Educated Person

Although we have concentrated on its place in the critical education literature, cultural production theory has been linked to a broader horizon from its inception. This multivalent history allows us, in this book, to bridge the educational literature with a broader anthropological and sociological literature, indeed with the interdisciplinary field of cultural studies. Established in the 1960s, the Centre for Contemporary Cultural Studies inaugurated one of the important methods for the study of cultural forms in social context. As we've already suggested, the CCCS's project was to fill out an underdeveloped part of Marx's thought—a focus on consciousness and subjectivity. Members of the Centre were affected by similar projects on the Continent, including that of Althusser, and were especially important in producing a very fruitful reading of the early Marxist theorist, Antonio Gramsci (see Hall 1986; Johnson 1986–87; Brantlinger 1990). Raymond Williams' early work on cultural production, summarized programmatically in his 1977 book, was also important at this stage of the CCCS.[23] Although analogous and complementary to Marx's project of describing the social forms through which human beings produce and reproduce their material lives, the project of cultural studies instead is the study of the "social forms through which human beings 'live,' become conscious, [and] sustain themselves subjectively" (Johnson 1986–87:45). Of great significance is the point that these "forms," which range from actions, practices, and ritualized behaviors to expressive artifacts and concrete objects, are always produced and read in the process of relating to concrete social and material circumstances.

The broader concept of cultural production we propose here is related to, though not encompassed by, these developments in cultural studies. In anthropology, for instance, cultural production has come to have a meaning broadly similar to that in educational studies. Emphasis has been placed on culture as a continual process of creating meaning in social and material contexts, replacing a conceptualization of culture as a static, unchanging body of knowledge "transmitted" between generations. The upheavals of the modern period, the expansion of multinational capitalism and global forms of media, the creation of new nationalisms and ethnic identities, and the increased recognition of cultural "border zones" (see Rosaldo 1989; Appadurai and Breckenridge 1988; Fox 1991), have all inspired anthropologists to look more closely at culture as process, as something which is continually produced, even as it may be reproduced.[24]

In other areas, such as media and communication studies, the concept of cultural production often relies on a more circumscribed definition of culture, generally denoting culture as "texts," where "text" is broadly delimited as any tangible form that symbolizes some aspect of the world. From this perspective, cultural production refers to the processes by which new texts, new cultural artifacts and commodities, such as art, music, and video, are created.[25, 26] Much of the work in the emerging interdisciplinary field of cultural studies has expanded on this conception of cultural production. Increasingly, much of cultural studies addresses how subordinate groups produce "popular culture" through their engagement with the products and texts of a dominant culture industry ("mass culture").[27] While this approach is a definite advance over purely textual analyses, most practitioners of cultural studies still perpetuate a muddy, often specious distinction between "dominant" and "popular" cultural forms.[28] Moreover, the analytic focus is still on textual forms, and less on "lived" culture. In many such studies, little attention is given to the way in which texts are appropriated into everyday lives as shaped by ongoing social relations and material circumstances. We find most compelling those analyses which have moved beyond the purely "textualist" analysis of popular cultural commodities to study lived culture, without naively celebrating the "popular."[29]

Earlier, Richard Johnson (1986–87) provided an important statement toward this end. His account of "circuits" of cultural production nicely captures the full range of actors, institutions, and forms of cultural production involved in the relation between dominant and popular forces.[30] Pioneering works in this more comprehensive approach to cultural studies include the CCCS study, *Policing the Crisis* (Hall et al. 1978b), Radway's (1984) work on romance novels, and Lutz and Collins' (1993) study of *National Geographic* magazine. In this latter study, not only do the authors examine the actual day-to-day tasks of generating the magazine, but they also carry out a content analysis of the photographs, a careful analysis of the magazine's readership, and a painstaking exploration of the meanings readers make as they engage with the photographs.

Transferring these ideas of cultural studies and cultural production to the schools, we see schools as sites for the formation of subjectivities through the production and consumption of cultural forms. This was one of Willis' important moves. He paid attention to the forms produced by informal, localized social groups interacting in the school—in this case, the lads.[31] His ethnographic exposition of their practice of "having a laff" provides an example. While he examined the microethnographic context of student-teacher relations in great detail, and showed how the immediate context of teacher authority generated an ironic resistance, Willis did not leave it at that. Instead, he convincingly argued that the lads' resistant classroom humor could be linked to the "penetrations" of the basic contractual ideology of the student-teacher relationship. The lads collectively grasped that for working-class students, the proffered exchange of respect for knowledge, knowledge for certification, and certification for a better job, was a false promise. Utter seriousness about schooling was thus a mistaken pursuit. "Having a laff," among other cultural forms, was their own creation in light of that realization. True, in generating that form they drew upon a variety of sources, including their familiarity with the shopfloor culture of their fathers, which had, in that moment of cultural production, developed in response to new, more oppressive techniques of capitalist production.[32] But "having a laff" was importantly their own creation in response to schooling as they apprehended it, and it was through the production of these forms that the lads' subjectivities, especially their sense of their own labor power, developed.[33]

In reproduction theory, subjects were imagined as being "interpellated" by ideology, and without agency. Reshaped by the more recent focus on practice and production, the larger question is now one of how historical persons are formed in practice, within and against larger societal forces and structures which instantiate themselves in schools and other institutions. Cultural production is one vision of this process. It provides a direction for understanding how human agency operates under powerful structural constraints.[34] Through the production of cultural forms, created within the structural constraints of sites such as schools, subjectivities form and agency develops. These are the processes we seek to evoke with our phrase, "the cultural production of the educated person."[35] Indeed, the very ambiguity of the phrase operates to index the dialectic of structure and agency. For while the educated person is culturally *produced* in definite sites, the educated person also culturally *produces* cultural forms.

Taking all of these developments into account, then, we are forwarding the concept of cultural production as a theoretical construct which allows us to portray and interpret the way people actively confront the ideological and material conditions presented by schooling. Despite the different meanings which the concept of "cultural production" has in the aforementioned authors' work, we use it to show how people creatively occupy the space of education and schooling. This creative practice generates understandings and strategies which may in fact move well beyond the school, transforming aspirations, household relations, local knowledges, and structures of power.[36] This new stage of analysis and research also allows us to go beyond a solely school-based angle on what we are referring to as "the cultural production of the educated person." Outside the school, in diverse spaces of street, home, and family, other kinds of "educated persons" are culturally produced as well.

In this volume, the importance of viewing schools as complex sites for the cultural production of educated persons is underscored in the case studies by Kathryn Anderson-Levitt, Douglas Foley, Wendy Luttrell, and Armando Trujillo, in part I.

In the set of historical-ethnographic case studies that follow in part II, chapters by Laura Rival, Margaret Eisenhart, and Thomas Shaw highlight the contrast between schools and other spaces or activities as competing sites for the cultural production of the educated person. The final set of chapters underscores the importance of a global perspective. We introduce those at the end of the next section, which advocates an expansion of studies of education and schooling.

THE WESTERN SCHOOLING PARADIGM IN GLOBAL CONTEXT

Having advanced the argument for a broader analytic perspective in critical educational studies, we now move on to our second major point: the need to more fully develop the comparative perspective. Reproduction and cultural production theories alike have developed largely in dialogue with studies of schooling in the United States, Great Britain, France, and Australia. There has been little effort to extend studies of the cultural production of the educated person, per se, to societies in dependent relation to advanced capitalism, and often still in the process of nation building and state formation (Foley 1991). Yet, without a doubt, the historical rise of mass public-education systems has generated powerful, and to some extent convergent or "global," constructions of the "educated person."

By now there exists a substantial literature on the origins and expansion of mass public schooling in the nineteenth century. Vigorous debates have attempted to sort out the rationale and social effects of state-organized education. For instance, Müller and co-workers (1987) argue from the European case that the development of state schooling had the effect of further excluding lower classes rather than democratizing educational access. Intersecting with the reproductionist view of schools, they, along with Archer (1979) and Green (1990), present a picture of schooling as largely an instrument of state and elite-class domination. In a similar vein, American revisionist historians (Hogan 1982; Katz 1975; Spring 1972) have emphasized the role that schools played in controlling new immigrant groups, "modernizing" their work habits, and incorporating them culturally into the nation, primarily to the end of capitalist labor control. Boli and Ramirez (1992), on the other hand, reject most of these explanatory schemes. According to them, while mass, compulsory education may have some of these effects, its true origins and functions should be understood culturally, as lying firmly in the economic and cultural individualism of the Christian West. Too, mass schooling developed hand in hand with the hegemony of the nation-state as a political form. The nation-state has utilized systematic education to "ceremonially induct" students into the twin identities of the modern state citizen: national and individual (1992:30).[37]

In their highly original study of English state formation, Corrigan and Sayer (1985) draw on both Foucault and Durkheim to characterize the *cultural* aspect of modern state formation as a process of "doubly disrupting" the recognition and expression of differences in popular culture. On the one hand, the state engages in a "totalizing" project, representing all people as members of a national community (cf. Anderson 1983; Smith 1991; Alonso 1994). On the other hand, the state also tries to "individualize" people in specific ways—as taxpayers, jurors, consumers, and yes, schoolchildren. Through both of these "disrupting" projects, "alternative modes of collective and individual identification (and comprehension) . . . are denied legitimacy" (Corrigan and Sayer 1985:5). We believe it is crucial to view modern schooling as a fundamental aspect of contemporary state formation, in which a new concept of the "educated person" challenges those which previously existed in popular cultures.

Schools, of course, existed before the modern period, but they did not always have the integrative function which Durkheim recognized as crucial in the transition to the "organic solidarity" of industrialized society. With the rise of the nation-state as a political form, schooling became a crucible of common culture. Yet industrialization accompanied the rise of the nation-state, and schools were also charged with producing and reproducing class distinctions in the service of particular economic and political agendas. In sometimes contradictory fashion, then, the imperatives of political and cultural legitimacy, in addition to economic production, have dictated the construction of public schooling systems (Fuller and Robinson 1992; Ginsburg 1991; Welch 1993). While many former colonial societies initially pursued a strongly socialist form of political economy, most of these Third World states have in fact now accommodated themselves to the hegemony of a capitalist world system. Accordingly, their educational models and systems represent complex variations of the English model Corrigan and Sayer examine. Then, too, many Third World states have retained important features of prior colonial educational systems. England, of course, was one of the principal "educational" innovators in the enterprise of colonial subjugation. In other parts of the world (Keyes 1991a; Rival, this volume), missionaries carried out the early work of colonial education.[38]

More recently, scholars such as Meyer and co-workers (1992) and Fuller (1991) have discussed the globalization and standardization of these Western forms of mass schooling. According to Fuller (1990), especially "fragile" Third World states (Fuller looks primarily at Africa) adopt models of education following the Western pattern in order to "signal" their commitment to Western-style progress and modernization through mass opportunity and meritocratic rules. Often enough, international lending institutions condition their loans to such Third World states upon acceptance of Western schooling models. Yet because these states may still lack the resources and political will to follow through on this commitment, they end up fomenting a popular demand which they cannot possibly fulfill. Education becomes a mere caricature of Western systems, serving largely symbolic and integrative purposes. Despite these limitations, Meyer and co-workers (1992:1) claim that formal Western-style schooling, and its increasingly standardized curricula, has come to eclipse virtually all other "means of the inter-generational transmission of culture."[39] This is an important point to complement the cultural studies emphasis on the effects of global commodity culture. If it is true that blue jeans, Coca-Cola, and Mickey Mouse define the cultural horizons of ever-increasing numbers of people, so too do the hegemonic forms of mass schooling and its "formal knowledge." Diversity is not only threatened by mass culture, but by models of schooling increasingly divorced from, indeed antagonistic to, a wealth of culture-specific moral discourses and styles of learning.[40]

Helpful as they are for conceptualizing the macro-structural dimension of schooling and educational change, none of these broad-scale educational theories really tells us what happens to students confronting these changes. In other words, we learn little about the cultural production of the educated person through Western-style schooling. There is already a rich, if not terribly prolific, anthropological literature on the introduction and effects of schooling in the Third World, and many of our authors build on this literature. Hansen (1979) and Levine and White (1986) admirably set out many of the issues anthropologists have addressed. Working within a Durkheimian framework, Levine and White pay special attention to the transition many non-Western peoples must make from an agrarian way of life, with its emphasis on "social ligatures" rooted in community, to a more urban-focused, formalized model of education, with its emphasis on individual "options." While Levine and White discuss how such educational changes tend to favor individual ambition at the expense of social responsibility, they scarcely explore the conflicts engendered by such a process. Earlier anthropological studies[41] examined these educational dynamics ethnographically, but paid insufficient attention to the question of power in the relation between state education and agrarian communities. More recently, the essays collected in a special issue of *Anthropology and Education Quarterly* (Falgout and Levin 1992), devoted to "Western schooling in the Pacific," have raised the question of power more centrally.[42] So too have the essays collected by Keyes, on how state schools "reshape local worlds" in Southeast Asia (Keyes 1991b; see especially Keyes 1991a and Vaddhanaphuti 1991).[43] Several authors in the present volume build on these studies and thus further fill the ethnographic gap in this important area.

Even as we consider the impact of Western schooling on non-Western societies, we must not forget that cultural minorities and subordinate groups in First World societies have often been subject to many of the same processes of nation-building and cultural incorporation. Several of our authors (Foley, Trujillo, Luttrell) address the way such groups in the United States respond to public education efforts. At least as early as 1971 (Wax, Gearing, and Diamond 1971), anthropologists had brought together work which drew important parallels between First World and Third World educational dynamics.[44] More recent studies of the relation between state schooling and local groups, such as those by Reed-Danahay for France (1987), and Rockwell and colleagues for Mexico (Ezpeleta and Rockwell 1983; Rockwell 1995, in press b), take important steps toward understanding the expansion of Western schooling as a global process linking First and Third Worlds. Yet none of these studies ignores the very important local angle, through which we see the richness of particular historical appropriations of schooling. In this volume, papers by Bradley Levinson, Aurolyn Luykx, Debra Skinner and Dorothy Holland, and Elsie Rockwell, comprising part III, link local and comparative perspectives by exploring how concepts of the "educated person" are produced and negotiated between state discourses and local practice.

Whither Schools? Anthropology and Global Educational Trends

The advent of cultural studies in anthropology has enriched critical educational research, and thus bridged differences between educational anthropology and other anthropological subfields. Yet at the same time, it has highlighted a discrepancy within anthropology concerning the significance of schools. Though contemporary studies of schooling, including the studies presented in this volume, may share the theoretical perspective of anthropologists who have become interested in the *popular media* as a site of the formation of subjectivities, there is still a basic disagreement. Some of the anthropologists carrying out ethnographic studies of media consumption suggest, at least implicitly, that the media are an even more powerful site of socialization and identity formation than schools (Abu-Lughod 1990; Appadurai 1990; Salzman 1993; Mankekar 1993; Silverstone 1990).[45] In our view this project has been undertaken prematurely, at a time when the full effects of schools as alternative or complementary sites of socialization and cultural production have not yet been fully explored.[46]

For instance, in Roger Lancaster's well-received book on the Sandinista Revolution and the culture of machismo in Nicaragua, he describes families and peer-based "street" culture as important sites for the learning of gender identities. He even evokes the impact of the global media, such as when a boy displays his aggressive masculinity by demonstrating how the Sandinistas will repel foreign invaders: in the manner of Rambo, with machine guns blazing (Lancaster 1992:191–192). Yet in an otherwise brilliant and innovative ethnography, Lancaster barely mentions the role of schools in Sandinista Nicaragua. Schools remain on the margins of Lancaster's narrative, only dimly structuring economic expectations and family practices (1992:180), or patterns of friendship and solidarity (1992:167–168). The relative absence of schools is especially glaring since the Sandinistas were known to have inaugurated massive literacy and school construction campaigns, and used schools as an important space for producing the revolutionary "new man" (Arnove 1994).

Similarly, Richard Maddox's (1993) fine historical ethnography of an Andalusian town addresses the "politics of tradition" in an increasingly mass-mediated age. Maddox's primary concern is to show how the forms and discourses of "tradition" in Aracena have varied historically in their manner of effecting domination and mediating forms of class consciousness. Ironically, new elements of mass culture, in the form of television shows, consumer commodities, and the like, have been incorporated uneasily into "traditional" social practices. While Maddox does mention the role of a new coeducational high school in displacing earlier, church-based models of social propriety, he does so only glancingly. Yet his own subsequent, more thorough study of the effects of school culture in Aracena has added immensely to his earlier ethnography, and resulted in an insightful account of the relation between schooling and forms of working class practice and identity (Maddox 1994).

Our aim here is not to censure those anthropologists who have largely ignored schools. On the contrary, the authors mentioned above are among those whose work, grounded in sophisticated and historically informed ethnographic description, we and most anthropologists greatly admire. Yet we wish to call attention to this trend, and question its significance for the field. While we believe that attention to the media is important and justified,[47] we urge anthropologists to avoid an exclusive attention to the media which leaves schools largely unstudied and obscure.

We find a number of reasons why schools may be understudied by anthropologists seeking pivotal sites of identity formation and cultural production. Some of these are practical; others, the result of unexamined assumptions and values.

Particularly problematic, no doubt, are the burdens that multisite studies put on the researcher. Despite the clear need for team research in seeking a fuller, more comprehensive account of all the important sites of cultural production and consumption, the lone ethnographer is still the prevalent model in the production of anthropological knowledge (Salzman 1994). We recognize that for individuals facing all the usual problems of carrying out field research, it may be easier to watch television in our informant's homes, or gather round the boom-box with dancing teenagers, than to enter the complexity of school relations. And, team research or no, methodologically and ethically, schools are difficult places to study. Schools generally have gatekeepers from whom permission must be obtained and, of course, maintained. Additionally, sustained observations and interviews are needed to construct a compelling interpretation of the effects of schooling. Finally, the finished product of this research may very likely involve a critique of the very people who made the research possible. A critical school ethnography cannot help but scrutinize the actions of school officials, even if they are not our primary research subjects.[48] Thus, while in practical terms schooling is difficult to study, we believe the continued significance of schools demands that we try.

Is it possible that anthropologists have also tended to take the effects of schooling for granted? In many of the societies anthropologists typically study, formal schooling has now been a part of the local social scene for some twenty or thirty years, perhaps longer. The practices and values surrounding schooling have had ample time to work their ways into the fabric of community life. The more relatively recent arrival of globalized media, on the other hand, has brought stark and (for anthropologists, anyway) intellectually stimulating incongruities to local life. While "imperialist nostalgia" may provide the driving force for popular magazine images of exotic otherness (Lutz and Collins 1993; Babcock 1990, 1993; O'Barr 1994), anthropologists have their own ethnographic imaginary, which increasingly includes photos of loinclothed watchers of "Dallas," or boomboxes on the Bolivian *altiplano*. Evidently the sight of children from these groups, dressed for school and carrying books, does not seem as exciting. While new and increasingly pervasive forms of media have captured anthropology's gaze, we wonder whether the effects of these media are really as powerful as the more socially and economically embedded presence of schools. This is a question that should not be settled by assumption.

Finally, anthropology has for some time largely ignored the likelihood that cultural knowing and identity formation are long-term, developmental processes, and has instead assumed that the study of "adult" forms will suffice (see Wulff and Amit-Talai 1995; Holland 1992). This has entailed an abandonment of fundamental insights generated during earlier periods of anthropological theorization (see Hansen 1979; Blot et al. in press). Ironically, excitement over the effects of media, fomented by the increasingly powerful presence of interdisciplinary cultural studies (Keesing 1994), may eventually upset this favoring of adult forms. Anthropologists have renewed their interest in the role of youth as cultural innovators, since they are often the most active and competent consumers of the new media. Yet the study of schools has still received short shrift.

Perhaps as a consequence of these trends in anthropology in general, the subfield of educational anthropology has tended to develop in relative isolation from broader theoretical currents in the discipline. Levinson (1992) notes that educational anthropology grew largely out of culture-and-personality studies, and thus lacked a legacy helpful for conceptualizing the effects of history, power, and social structure on educational processes.[49] In more recent years, the subfield has made great strides in conceptualizing these effects,[50] yet the broader discipline still largely perceives it as a marginal branch, too "applied," perhaps too beholden to the pragmatic interests of professional educators, to provide more general insights. Tellingly, Levinson can remember Holland advising him to leave the word "schooling" out of an initial session proposal for the meetings of the American Anthropological Association. Too many anthropologists' "eyes glaze over," said Holland, when they see "education" or "schools."

Have schools thus largely been written out of the emerging anthropological narrative on identity and social change in the late twentieth century? If it is true that the sweep of critical cultural theory has yet to make itself fully felt in the educational subfield, it is also true that cultural processes under modernity and "late capitalism"[51] have omitted schools, and so produced uneven and less than comprehensive accounts. Ironically, many of the critical frameworks which have been developed in the interdisciplinary field of "cultural studies," and subsequently taken up by anthropologists, first emerged in British and French work on schools.[52] Yet American anthropologists in particular are largely unaware of this history, and have been slow to recognize the continuing importance of schools as sites of cultural production and reproduction. This is the case even in non-Western societies which have experienced an unprecedented expansion of Western-oriented schooling in the past thirty years or so. While the presence of schools are at least mentioned in virtually every ethnographic work written, there has still been relatively little systematic attention paid to the ongoing effects of schooling in the practices of everyday life.

Building Strengths and Charting New Directions: Historical-Ethnographic Case Studies

Let us now summarize and restate the goals of this volume, before moving on to the introduction of the case studies.

In this volume, we extend theory and methodology beyond the school itself, disrupting the assumption, frequent outside of anthropology especially, that education is obtained only through schooling. We assert the need to conceptualize the logic of education in its varied cultural contexts. Our concept of the "educated person" is one which suggests that all cultures and social formations develop models of how one becomes a fully "knowledgeable" person, a person endowed with maximum "cultural capital." To be sure, "education" has increasingly come to be equated with schooling, as the groups serviced by Western-style schools come to internalize the dominant meanings purveyed in formal curricula and school discourse. Still, while we use the "educated person" as an analytic construct, we argue that an indigenous conception of the educated person is variably present in all known cultures and societies. Even *within* societies, subgroups such as those based on race or gender may develop distinct conceptions of the educated person, distinct "ways of knowing" (Luttrell 1989). That such conceptions are often challenged and even transformed in the practices of everyday life is a primary contention of our book.

Students in schools, then, may produce practices and identities consonant with local cultural notions of the "educated person," but some practices and identities may in fact challenge those notions. Similarly, unschooled people, or early school leavers, may produce practices and identities *against* the schooling enterprise and the formally "educated person" it is said to create. For these reasons, we strive not to focus too narrowly upon formally defined "educated persons" as the only potentially critical products of schools. Schools also create a space for the formation of social relations among people of different classes, genders, castes, ethnic, and age groups which would be unlikely in other sites. Such relations may come to reconfigure previous alliances, allegiances, and sympathies. They may indeed be empowering. Thus, schools provide each generation with social and symbolic sites where new relations, new representations, and new knowledges can be formed, sometimes against, sometimes tangential to, sometimes coincident with, the interests of those holding power. These paradoxical potentialities of schooling (both for dominant groups that seek to control the schools, and for students), and the way they play out under various historical circumstances, provide the central dynamic of our book.

Our approach is specifically interdisciplinary and international, and includes work both in Euro-American and non-Western settings.[53] These case studies cover a full range of educational levels and sites (primary school to university, urban to rural, formal to nonformal), and actors (students, teachers, parents, administrators, policymakers, school graduates and dropouts, employers, etc.). The authors employ a variety of narrative and theoretical tools within a broadly critical approach. Importantly, each of the studies employs a historical prism to understand the present. In all of the authors, we see a commitment to viewing contemporary schooling within a broad historical and cultural purview.

Historical and cultural breadth, yes, but the authors are also relentlessly local in their analyses. They follow the counsel of Haraway (1988), who rejects totalizing theories that are blind to local conditions and understandings, and which proceed as though the meanings people make of their lives are without significance. Haraway's advice is to pay close attention to local knowledges, yet from a critical perspective, with the aim of producing better accounts which will enable a more enlightened practice.

We have thus attempted to develop a critical language for understanding relations between the school, the cultural traditions of its constituent groups, and a broader political economy. Many might still argue that such a book does little service to the struggles for more empowering and democratic educational arrangements. The language of critique is, to be sure, a language of hope and possibility (Giroux, 1991, 1992), but does it really provide any direction to the debates over policy and reform which comprise the politics of everyday life around schools? What, after all, is the goal of a critically engaged educational anthropology? Can our conceptual toolkit and ethnographic descriptions provide insight for those students and educators most immediately involved in struggles for improving life-chances through schooling?

We argue that *local* analyses must retain a critical perspective on political economy and dominant socio-ideological formations, without losing sight of the particular contingencies and cultural dynamics which characterize local sites.[54] Accordingly, strategy for social change around schooling cannot issue from general condemnations of capitalist education, or racial oppression, or gender discrimination, for instance. As we show in this volume, schools are heterogeneous sites. Different models of the "educated person" are historically produced and contested in these sites, as both dominant and subordinate groups (and those, like teachers, who often stand "in between") carry forth distinctive modalities of cultural production. If we are to pursue the democratic ideals of distributive and curricular justice (Connell 1993; cf. Barber 1992, Gutmann 1987), then we must seek to expand educational spaces which might accommodate diverse models of the educated person. In some contexts, this may mean revalorizing mass public education in the face of neo-liberal privatization (Rockwell in press a). In other contexts, it may mean seeking flexible arrangements for apprenticeship and hands-on learning (Lave and Wenger 1991; Illich 1970), or extracurricular youth programs (Heath and McLaughlin 1993). Educational forms and structures should remain as heterogeneous as the people who enact them, and progressive educational movements should not be informed by any singular critical theory. Indeed, part of this call for "local heterogeneity" must also include greater attention to other, heretofore overlooked, sources of theoretical inspiration, such as the "Third World participatory research tradition" Anderson (1994:236–237) invokes, or the antibureaucratic writings of Ivan Illich which Morrow and Torres (1995) resuscitate in their new book.

Finally, while we recognize the wisdom of Haraway's advice about local knowledges, as critical scholars of education and culture we also note that we often live a contradiction. In our research and writing, through our own ethnographic practice, we may valorize "popular" knowledge and values. We often serve as advocates of subordinated groups, attempting to show the logic, vitality, and dignity of their cultural worlds. We serve, in other words, as vehicles of what has come to be called counter-hegemonic discourse.[55] Yet we also stand at the top of dominant educational institutions. We are the products of their knowledge-making machinery. However much we may have "resisted" this machinery, we bear the handiwork of its imprint. This inescapable fact makes itself apparent in the way we tend to reinforce disciplinary boundaries and accept existing distributions of symbolic capital, thus ignoring the contributions from other domains— such as schools of education, or Third World research centers.[56] Our contradictory formation also becomes apparent to us at odd moments of our teaching, when we find ourselves uncomfortably at the nexus of authority and knowledge we so often examine and critique in our own research. How do we react to college students—often members of precisely those subordinate groups we valorize in our research—who contest our own theories and explanations (see Lather 1991)? Do we encourage a rich welter of voices in the classroom, even when such voices may be inimical to our own "critical" project?

We offer this book in the spirit of attempting to work within, and perhaps even partially resolve, this contradiction. We do this by examining the way the notion of the "educated person" is culturally constructed within, outside, and against dominant, elite- and state-sponsored institutions. By thus showing how the definition of "education" is always negotiated, we hope to decenter our privileged, perhaps elitist conceptions of "proper" knowledge and conduct. Yet even as we de-center dominant notions of proper education, we also hope to explore and identify those features of state schooling (and its associated "educated persons") which, on balance, contribute to the democratization of socially valued knowledge, and the creation of more equitable social arrangements. Unlike many studies in the critical tradition, our authors here show that school knowledge can be empowering for subordinate groups, as long as it respects, and even draws upon, the cultural resources of those groups (cf. Vásquez et al. 1994; Vélez-Ibáñez and Greenberg 1992).

The papers which follow have been organized according to three conceptual points we have developed here in the introduction. In the first part, papers explore the nature of *schools as sites of cultural production*. As we indicated earlier, the concept of cultural production should be extended to account for the practices of a variety of actors within the site. Thus, on the one hand we see schools as sites of learning which hegemonic groups, in alliance with consolidating states and/or expanding bureaucracies, often utilize to form certain kinds of subjectivities. The historically specific models of the "educated person" encouraged in schools often represent the subjectivities which dominant groups endorse for others in society. Like all aspects of hegemony, schools must appeal to popular demands and popular consciousness, articulating them to dominant projects in novel ways. Teachers play a crucial role in enforcing such models of the educated person, though they may in practice challenge or ignore the models bequeathed them by policymakers and politicians. And just as school discourses and practices specify the properly "educated person," they may also reproduce inequalities by defining and producing the "uneducable person" (Cicourel and Kitsuse 1963; Erickson and Schultz 1982; Fine 1991; Kelly 1993; Mehan et al. 1986). Finally, students and their families exercise agency in responding to the practices and discourses of the school. They, too, engage in the cultural production of practices and discourses which accommodate, resist, or otherwise adapt to the dominant school definition of the educated person.

Kathryn Anderson-Levitt shows how discourses on "readiness," reading ability, and school intelligence, created through the expansion of bureaucratic and industrial models of rationality and time management, are adopted by American and French teachers and parents. According to Anderson-Levitt, American and French schools are designed to "batch produce" children in ways that restrict possibilities for diverse strategies of teaching and learning. Teachers and parents alike learn to interpret children's behavior and intelligence according to strict notions of age and maturity. As Anderson-Levitt puts it, mass schooling in the industrial era "has encouraged educators to produce such identities for children as 'the student who is behind in learning to read,' 'the immature child,' and 'the December birthday.' It has led us to measure children's ages and academic achievements in units of months, not years." Particularly in the French case, this construction of school performance privileges and legitimizes the position of the upper middle class, whose children, because of the cultural capital provided by their "milieu," tend to reach advanced reading stages and skip grades more easily than their counterparts. Yet Anderson-Levitt describes how teachers and parents alike, regardless of their class position and often for rather different reasons, come to endorse, and thus reproduce, the dominant construction of "reading ability." We are indebted to Anderson-Levitt for providing a rich local-comparative analysis of a pervasive global phenomenon, and for showing how even so fundamental a process as learning to read in school is subject to hegemonic models of the educated person.

Douglas Foley's study of the "silent Indian" as both discursive "subject position" and willfully subversive popular practice illustrates how the school serves as a site of cultural production. Growing out of his larger study of Mesquaki life in the American heartland, Foley shows how Mesquaki students who attend white schools in Tama, Iowa have been interpreted as "silent Indians" both through the racist discourse of town whites (including schoolteachers) and the liberal relativist discourse of educational anthropology. In response, the Mesquaki culturally produce their own version of the "silent Indian," counterposing the reflective, moral subject of Indian culture to the garrulous, rapacious whites in town. Mesquaki silence becomes a "situational speech style which is used strategically against the whiteman." Thus, the Mesquaki learn to playfully and knowingly inhabit a discursive category not at first proposed by them. In effect, they turn the tables on the dominant discourse of outsiders. As Foley portrays it, the site of the school, and the cultural production of the "silent Indian" discourse which it occasions, plays a major role in the structuring of race relations in Tama.

Wendy Luttrell provides an especially poignant account of how white and black working-class women in the United States return to adult education programs in order to "become somebody" whom the previous conditions of their lives had not allowed them to become. Through an analysis of rich life history narratives, Luttrell relies upon the psychodynamic concept of "splitting" to show how the women must struggle to empower an aspect of self long submerged in oppressive relations. Having been encouraged to stifle the development of their "autonomous selves" for the sake of their families and employers, these women now return to school in order to regain the knowledge and dignity denied them. Luttrell interprets these women's return to school as action in the public sphere, an attempt on the part of the women to confirm what they continue to doubt, that they *are* somebody. Moreover, Luttrell suggests that adult literacy education, which may not always have the "liberating" effects its promoters usually assume, can best serve these women by incorporating their narratives and memories of childhood schooling and work into the curriculum itself. Adult education for working-class women, Luttrell argues, is about establishing an identity, and the cultural capital this identity entails, as much as it is about acquiring specific skills. Thus the school should, and sometimes does, serve as a site for the cultural production of positive identities which may extend beyond the school as well.

Armando Trujillo's paper documents an important and instructive moment in the politics of U.S. education. Trujillo explores the relation between the rise of the movement for Chicano nationalism in South Texas in the 1970s and the schooling system itself. He traces the debates about models of bilingual education, and argues that a model of "maintenance" bilingualism, which attempted to preserve the integrity of Spanish-speaking Chicano culture, was a crucial component of Chicano attempts to construct an ethnic worldview through schooling. Yet ethnographically speaking, Trujillo's greatest contribution is to show how different models of Chicano schooling and bilingualism were not only contested between Chicanos and Anglos within school districts, but amongst Chicano educators themselves. Drawing on interviews with teachers and administrators in a school district where Chicanos rose to power, Trujillo shows how the contradiction between the "teaching ideology" of maintenance bilingualism, and the "teaching perspective" which emerged in many teachers' practical activities, led to an increased abandonment of the "maintenance" model. By the 1980s, most Chicano teachers in the district were espousing a "transitional" model of bilingual education, in which Spanish language instruction would be used only to facilitate students' eventual mastery of English. Thus, the dominant assimilationist ideology of state education in South Texas eventually triumphed over the efforts of the upstart popular Chicano movement. Trujillo's essay serves as an important illustration of how new cultural models of the educated person, produced in contexts of political (and in this case, ethnic) struggle, do not always survive the process of practical implementation. Moreover, such cultural models never reflect the beliefs and practices of all members of a community or social group, let alone a school.

The papers in the second part examine the cultural production of *the educated person in competing sites of cultural production.* Our authors here make a number of suggestive points regarding the relationship between schools and the "moral communities" (Shaw 1994) they serve. First and foremost, they show that the cultural production of the educated person often entails struggle over the value of knowledges and skills obtained in school versus the knowledges obtained from other sites of learning. Relatedly, these case studies illustrate how students may develop a perspective on schoolwork which depends on struggles, practices, and identities "imported" from other sites of cultural production.

Laura Rival provides an exceptionally well-documented account of this dynamic, based on her extensive fieldwork with the Huaorani, a small foraging group in the Ecuadorian Amazon. Rival situates the development of state schooling among the Huaroani historically, in the context of nearly four decades of missionary activity. Those converted Huaorani living in or near a mission settlement have tended to opt for the Spanish-language national curriculum, while the unconverted have either chosen a bilingual program promoted by some indigenous leaders (in conjunction with the state) or have avoided schooling altogether. Significantly, unconverted Huaorani develop a distinct cultural identity through the everyday activities of forest life, such as food procurement, chanting, and the fabrication of useful material objects. Rival calls this development of cultural identity a process of "enskillment" which is embedded in routine and the reproduction of social memory. Indeed, Rival examines the process by which modern schools, recently introduced into Huaorani settlements, "de-skill" Huaorani children. In its attempt to create "modern citizens" out of the Huaorani, the Ecuadorian state engenders resistance among some Huaorani, who defend their own activity-based cultural knowledge and practice against that being proposed by the schools.

In a very different setting, Margaret Eisenhart explores the production of "scientist identities" in specific organizational-cultural contexts: a university program in environmental biology, and a nonprofit "conservation corporation." In Eisenhart's account, students who enter the university program in environmental biology have typically arrived there through a stultifying confrontation with the "hegemony of hard sciences." Troubled by the absence of any moral discourse or reference to the problems of the world beyond science, these students find the discourse and practice of environmental biology well-suited to their moral and activist instincts. They thus come to construct a certain kind of scientist identity against the aseptic discourse of the hard sciences. Eisenhart then shifts her analysis to a local conservation corporation, where many of the environmental biologists are employed upon obtaining their bachelor's degrees. In the transition to the "real world," these former students must confront the pragmatic accommodations and business savvy of "conservation science," which is oriented to saving as much valuable and ecologically sensitive land as possible within the political and economic constraints governing their work. This new orientation to science troubles many of the former students, and they must negotiate the knowledge and identity they had previously constructed, *against* the hard sciences, within the newer, businesslike orientation of the conservation corporation. Eisenhart thus provides a wonderful illustration of how the knowledge and identity comprising the scientist as "educated person" is actually constructed within specific institutional contexts, and negotiated within and against such sites as natural science labs and the offices of conservation corporations.

Thomas Shaw, with his study of junior high school students in the capital city of Taipei, gives us a fascinating glimpse into educational change in modern Taiwan. According to Shaw, the "authoritarian" culture of Taiwanese public schools, which enforces conformity and rewards collective orientations, has increasingly come into conflict with the epistemological "subjectivism" and individualism of urban life. In particular, Shaw attributes this subjectivism to the rise of market capitalism, cosmopolitan urban youth culture, and the commodification of everyday life. As students have become more apt to formulate goals and evaluate experience according to "subjective" criteria, they have grown increasingly alienated from the imperatives of school culture. No longer do these students value the discipline and collective orientation enforced at school. Shaw marshals strong evidence of students' resistance to school culture. Most tellingly, he describes a student challenge to the hierarchical authority of the teacher, who, within the premises of school culture, must not "lose face" through students' abusive behavior. Shaw interprets one male students' comment, "She makes us lose face, so why shouldn't we make her lose face," as revealing of the "authority" he "attribute[s] to his own subjectivity." Thus, students bring their own values of increasingly "radical" subjectivism, fomented through popular youth culture, to bear on relations and practices within the school. City streets and the youth cultures they accommodate now compete with the school in defining the educated person.

The third and final part more directly addresses the role of the state in schooling. Cultural production is conceived as occurring at the interface of state and popular cultural forms, resulting in variable definitions of *the educated person in state discourse and local practice.* Because forms of state action tend to develop historically in response to popular forms of consciousness, state schools are usually heterogeneous sites, and even formal practices such as curriculum and administration may embody aspects of popular culture, perhaps from prior epochs. Still, the logic of state is ever the logic of power, and the reigning agenda of the state in schooling at a given historical moment, and in a given institution, cannot always accommodate the variety of popular interests and sensibilities.

Bradley Levinson, in his study of student responses to the school culture of a Mexican *secundaria* (junior high school), shows how the Mexican state has attempted to create a collective national identity through discourses on equality and the provision of a common "schooled identity." This schooled identity, appropriated and elaborated in different ways by students and their families, has the effect of blurring the recognition of class and ethnic differences in regional popular culture, and reconfiguring local perceptions of difference according to the distinction between "schooled" and "unschooled." Schooled identity, according to Levinson, builds students' allegiance to "state culture" and the hegemonic project of national identity which the state advances. Yet not all students adopt the schooled identity with equal fervor. Some develop cynical or alternative readings of the schooling enterprise, and may come to reinforce their allegiance to popular cultures "against" the school. Levinson explores in some detail the school careers of two students, Andrea and Fidel, who develop highly ambivalent relationships to the culture of the school. Each in their own way eventually rejects the exclusionary schooled identity which would create a chasm between themselves and their "intimate cultures" of home, village, and neighborhood. Each comes to revalorize certain forms of knowing and sociability which characterize their respective intimate cultures. Through witnessing their experience, we see the power which school relations have to define identity and aspiration. But in the students' creative action, we also see the limits to such power.

Aurolyn Luykx writes about the contradictions indigenous Aymara Bolivians face as they undergo the process of state-sponsored teacher training. In a highly perceptive ethnography of a rural normal school for primary schoolteachers, Luykx traces the obstacles and ironies involved as prospective indigenous teachers try to transform themselves from "*indios*" (a pejorative racial category) into "*profesionales*" (a term of respect for a professional educator). Through the use of humor and self-parody, these prospective teachers strive to maintain a distinct sense of cultural identity while negotiating the contradictions inherent in official discourses on nationalism and ethnicity, which alternately extol and denigrate indigenous contributions to the nation-state. Most importantly, the students bring their own "indigenous" practices and sensibilities into the school, and draw on these to contest the institution's attempts to transform them into obedient, subordinate Bolivian citizens. In a memorable piece of ethnographic description, Luykx recounts the various kinds of parody the Aymara students develop as oblique forms of criticism. Drawing on the "meanings and practices of their home culture, valorizing Aymara ethnicity and subverting the urban orientation of the 'national culture'," students attempt to "forge a coherent identity" in the contradictory program of teacher professionalization. Whether or not they succeed is a matter of some import in the future of Bolivian popular struggles.

Debra Skinner and Dorothy Holland demonstrate the contested nature of public education in and beyond Naudada, a Nepalese hill community. When public education was introduced in Nepal in the 1950s, it was tied to a national discourse of economic and social development, modernization, and national identity. Yet the schoolchildren of Naudada did not simply adopt this discourse of development and progress uncritically. Rather, within the "heteroglossic" site of the school, amidst numerous textual, teacher, and student voices, students constructed a sense of the "educated person" that was sometimes in conjunction with, sometimes at odds with, the dominant national discourse. Following thirty children and adolescents within the changing contexts of their lives over ten years, Skinner and Holland describe how local schools served as important arenas for the production of critical commentaries on oppressive caste and gender relations, and for the elaboration of activities aimed at transforming such relations. Importantly, boys focused on overcoming restrictive caste relations that maintained social distinctions and material inequalities, while girls focused on the privileges and rights historically denied their gender. Ironically, though, the same schools that fostered these liberating activities also promoted another invidious social distinction between "educated" and "uneducated" persons.

Elsie Rockwell's historical ethnography emphasizes the heterogeneous origins of rural schools in Tlaxcala, a region of Mexico. For Rockwell, the cultural production of the rural "educated person" envisioned by central state reformers of the postrevolutionary period had to contend with the antecedent material and social conditions in communities where schools would be located.

Different local and national groups vied for the appropriation of space and resources, and the school was constituted by popular initiatives and imperatives (such as literacy, school construction for community use, etc.) as much as by the state's attempt to impose a certain logic of control. The result of these historical dynamics can be seen in schools today. Teachers, parents, and students put into play discourses and practices which have become part of the school's legacy. Expectations and patterns of interaction reflect the ongoing historical encounter between the local peasantry and the state. Rockwell proposes the concept of "appropriation" in everyday life as a useful antidote to structuralist accounts of schooling. According to Rockwell, school subjects are always active historical agents, appropriating the spaces and resources of schooling from varied positions and interests.

Thus, the volume ends as it begins: emphasizing the creative agency of social actors within and against schooling. Such agency demonstrates again that, despite the commonalities of mass schooling, everywhere we find local struggles around the cultural production of the educated person. This is the forceful insight which animates the case studies assembled here.

NOTES

1. Critical theory is theory which "undertakes simultaneously critique of received categories, critique of theoretical practice, and critical substantive analysis of social life in terms of the possible, not just the actual" (Calhoun 1993:63).

2. Although the "newness" of the "new sociology of education" was indeed emphasized, we believe important, and often unacknowledged, precursors include Hollingshead (1949), Hoggart (1961), and Stinchcombe (1964). See Karabel and Halsey (1977) for an important early review of the new sociology of education, and Whitty (1985) for an equally important statement of the field.

3. Carnoy (1974) was one of the first to argue that the development of schooling in former colonies had some of these same dominating effects. See Puiggrós (1980) for a similar argument about Latin America. Mitchell (1988:63–94) adds to these studies with his Foucaultian analysis of the establishment of modern schools in Egypt.

4. See Barber (1992) for an eloquent statement of this still-powerful model of schooling. See also Ray and Poonwassie (1992) for a similarly optimistic statement of the effects of schooling on cultural minorities across the globe.

5. Fordham's analysis is different from Bourdieu's in that she includes the possibility, indeed the likelihood, of resistance. See Wacquant (1993:239), Harker (1990:98), and Lakomski (1984) for discussions of determinism and resistance in Bourdieu's work.

6. Bourdieu's early work could actually be read as owing as much to Weber and Durkheim as to Marx, insofar as it privileges the cultural, and not just the economic, determinants of social class.

7. See Holland and Eisenhart (1990) for a more detailed review of the feminist redirection of, and contribution to, reproduction theory. See also Morrow and Torres' (1994,

1995) and McCarthy and Apple's (1989) recent statements on the "parallelist," or "nonsynchronous," approach to race, class, and gender effects of schooling, with which we are largely in agreement.

8. See also Lakomski (1984), Apple and Weis (1983), and Apple (1982b). Shapiro (1990) and Carnoy and Levin (1985) have advanced more sophisticated accounts of state action and ideology in schooling, as have the scholars at the Departamento de Investigaciones Educativas (DIE) in Mexico (Ezpeleta and Rockwell 1983; Mercado 1985; Rockwell 1986, 1994, in press a).

9. See Middleton (1970) for a representative selection of this early literature. See also the new edited volume by Blot, Niehaus, and Schmertzing (in press), which revalorizes the more enduring insights of educational anthropology's founding scholars.

10. The edited volume by Cazden, John, and Hymes (1972) was one of the first programmatic statements of this approach. Some rather different, but representative, works are Au and Jordan (1981), Delgado-Gaitan (1987), Eddy (1967), Erickson and Mohatt (1982), Gilmore and Glatthorn (1981), Heath (1983), Philips (1983), and Tharp and Gallimore (1988).

11. With the possible exception of Heath (1983), who studies distinctive patterns of "working-class" language socialization in both white and black communities, and Leacock (1970), working a perspective similar to the sociologist Ray Rist (1970), these studies also tended to neglect class and gender. Yet even Heath has been criticized for not recognizing the specificity of racial subordination as one of the most important factors in the development of black language use (Rosen 1985).

12. To be sure, a number of these "remedial interventions" have claimed success in raising rates of school achievement (Ernst, Statzner, and Trueba 1994; Moll and Díaz 1987; Tharp and Gallimore 1988), though we remain skeptical of their broader ramifications in the absence of significant structural changes.

13. John Ogbu was an early and consistent critic of the "cultural difference" approach for its lack of attention to the historical and social-structural context of cultural practice. His own work, therefore, has to some extent dovetailed with developments in reproduction and production theory, with the important proviso that Ogbu shares many of the same liberal premises with the cultural difference approach. See Holland and Eisenhart (1990:17–18), and especially Levinson (1992), regarding the latter point. The new book by Vásquez, Pease-Alvarez, and Shannon (1994) makes a similar case against the cultural difference approach. They demonstrate that Mexican children are far more flexible in developing their own communication styles which draw on both classroom and community traditions. We would see this linguistic practice as a kind of "cultural production" occurring in the "border zone" of student peer culture, but we would also highlight the kinds of structural constraints which these authors, and perhaps even their informants, largely ignore.

14. While Willis was the first to self-consciously articulate and interrogate the terms of reproduction theory in the light of his own ethnographic research, we find important precursors in the work of Lacey (1970), Keddie (1971), Sharp and Green (1975), and others (see note 2).

15. Although in the case of the particular group that Willis studied, no sustained critique or systematically disruptive activity was created, he insisted that the potential for such is always present: "Cultural reproduction in particular, always carries with it the *possibility* of producing—indeed in a certain sense it really lives out—alternative outcomes" (Willis 1981b:172).

16. By no means an exhaustive list, we find the most significant of these "critical ethnographies" which focus on students to be those done by Anyon (1981), Everhart (1983), Fine (1991), Kelly (1993), McLaren (1986), Connell et al. (1982), Weis (1984, 1990), Valli (1986), MacLeod (1987), Canaan (1990), Aggleton (1987), Holland and Eisenhart (1990), Eckert (1989), Lesko (1988), Foley (1990), Walker (1988), Raissiguier (1994), and Solomon (1992). A related type of "critical ethnography" highlights those practices of teachers and school administrators, both formal and informal, which contribute to the reproduction of inequalities: McNeil (1986), Mehan et al. (1986), Cicourel and Kitsuse (1963). See Masemann (1982), Simon and Dippo (1986), Anderson (1989), Levinson (1992), and Quantz (1992) for discussions of the history and conceptual underpinnings of this "critical ethnography."

17. Rockwell and her colleagues in Mexico City insisted on historicizing the ethnographic project early on, and have eloquently demonstrated the reality of school heterogeneity which this historical perspective revealed. Although in slightly different terms ("appropriation," "historical construction"), they have also sought to problematize the relationship between cultural production and reproduction. See Rockwell (1986, 1995, in press a, b).

18. Weis (1984) was one of the first to explore the concept of contradiction as a tool of ethnographic interpretation. More recently, Collins (1993) has argued the importance of contradiction as a socially emergent phenomenon which challenges more deterministic theories of language, such as that of Bourdieu.

19. See Hall (1992) and Johnson (1986–87) for descriptions and commentaries on the Birmingham Centre for Contemporary Cultural Studies. Particularly apropos for this book, Lave et al. (1992) provide an excellent historical and conceptual overview of the Birmingham Centre for Contemporary Cultural Studies, where Willis and his colleagues carried out their work.

20. See Holland and Eisenhart (1990:43–45), Lave et al. (1992), and McCarthy and Crichlow (1993), for discussion and numerous references to those criticisms.

21. Others directly addressing schooling and education have likewise pushed us beyond a necessary correspondence between class location and identity. See Lave et al. (1992:268–271), Connell (1987), and Holland and Eisenhart (1990:152–60), who argue, along with Giddens (1979, 1984) and Bourdieu (1977b), that identity must be seen as continually constituted by practice itself.

22. Many recent strands of critical theory, including Foucault's illumination of the impetus to disciplinary procedures in the post-Enlightenment period (Rabinow 1984; Mitchell 1987), Weber's (1978) account of bureaucratization (see also Gerth and Mills 1958; Herzfeld 1992), the Frankfurt school's critique of culture industries (see Held 1980), structural Marxist explanations of class domination (Althusser 1971; Poulantzas

1974), critical theories of the state (Carnoy 1984), Touraine's (1981) exploration of identity and social movements, Habermas' (1984, 1987) account of the colonization of the lifeworld by the systemic order, Giddens' theory of institutions and structuration in time and space (1984), and Bourdieu's concept of symbolic violence (1989) all provide insights into the broadstroke dynamics within and against which agents can be seen as forming themselves through practice. Especially important, feminist analyses of history and patriarchy (see Collins 1991; Scott 1988; Tong 1989; Hansen and Philipson 1990) have provided a powerful lens for understanding the gendering dimensions of identity formation.

23. In an earlier formulation, Williams (1973:11) used the term "emergent culture" to denote the process by which "new meanings and values, new practices, new significances and experiences are continually being created" (quoted in Bauman 1977:48).

24. In addition to the aforementioned critical ethnographies (note 16), some representative works in cultural anthropology which have highlighted and debated processes of cultural production would include: Comaroff and Comaroff (1992), Hobsbawm and Ranger (1983), Roseberry (1989), Hannerz (1992), Kondo (1990), Fox (1985, 1990), and Williams (1991). It should be noted that despite this long list of works which emphasize culture in production, Keesing (1994) feels that most anthropological work still tends to portray social process in terms of bounded and unchanging cultural "wholes" which express "radical alterity." He feels these anthropologists need to learn from the way the emerging field of "cultural studies" has theorized social and cultural process.

25. Pierre Bourdieu's corpus bears a complex relationship to the concept of cultural production as we have presented it. His studies of cultural production, based upon a sophisticated joining of his notions of "habitus" and "field," certainly constitute one of the more theoretically elaborated understandings. Nonetheless, his work on "cultural production," named as such (see, for example, Bourdieu 1983, 1994), primarily addresses the kind of artistic, literary, and academic production sociologists of culture and knowledge study, not the production of popular cultural forms which we have emphasized above with regard to the CCCS. While his ideas are highly suggestive for the expansion of critical educational studies we suggest here, there are several barriers to easy incorporation. For instance, neither the concept of resistance, the dynamics of internal class and ethnic differentiation, nor the workings of the state have been particularly developed in his work (See also LiPuma 1993).

26. Peterson's (1976) edited volume exemplifies another approach to cultural production in the sociology of culture, which focuses on art, music, and other material forms of socially recognized "culture."

27. See, for instance, the wide range of topics and analyses in the new volume, *Cultural Studies* (Grossberg, Nelson, and Treichler 1992). For other useful introductions to the cultural studies approach, see Brantlinger (1990) and Turner (1990). Jameson (1993) provides a perceptive analysis of the essays comprising the Grossberg et al. volume.

28. Levinson thanks Janice Radway for reminding him of this important point, and driving it home through the example of her own recent work (Radway 1992, 1994). Radway, in turn, credits Stuart Hall's work (1981, 1980) for many of her insights.

29. Some authors, such as Fiske (1989), Jenkins (1992), Willis (1990), and Giroux (1994), tend to highlight the almost limitless possibilities for popular appropriation of mass culture texts and commodities. We feel less sanguine about the possibilities, though we do not agree entirely with Shaw's (1994) critique of the implicit individualism of "cultural-studies romanticism." Work by Willis, Jenkins, and others situates the production of meaning in precisely the kinds of collective, subcultural "moral communities" Shaw highlights in his own approach.

30. Carspecken and Apple (1992) have recently tried to apply this model to school ethnography.

31. Willis' ethnographic approach may sound somewhat similar to that of the symbolic interactionists, since members of the group of CCCS researchers studying youth subcultures were influenced by that school (see Lave et al. 1992). The approaches, however, were not comparable, in that symbolic interactionism never developed any critical theory of society.

32. By now, parallels between critical education studies and critical ethnography in anthropology in general, should be clear. Once the conceptual field of vision was broadened, "having a laff," which could be construed in one context as "mere" adolescent hijinks, or psychosocial "maladjustment," was actually exposed as a response, with ties to older forms of working-class resistance, to the class privilege safeguarded by the dominant institutions. Marcus (1986) cites as one of the hallmarks of Paul Willis' work his ability to situate and interpret local action within broader structural and historical parameters. This ability continues to be one of the primary strengths of "critical ethnography." See Quantz (1992:490ff.) for an excellent discussion of the importance of history as an implicit category of analysis in critical school ethnography.

For critical ethnographers, historical process by definition constitutes cultural forms and structural features of society, and must be a central aspect of any present-centered analysis. Ethnographic analyses produced by various members of the Centre for Contemporary Cultural Studies were able to achieve this kind of conceptual range (Hebdige 1979; Corrigan 1979; McRobbie 1992). In anthropology, a parallel development, signalled by Marcus and Fischer (1986), has produced a number of fine ethnographies, among them Abu-Lughod (1986), Briggs (1988), Comaroff (1985), Scheper-Hughes (1992), Domínguez (1989), Sahlins (1985), Ong (1987), and Keesing (1992). In critical ethnography, seemingly isolated or context-dependent events are typically interpreted in the light of extra-contextual referents.

33. See Foley (1990) and Canaan (1990) for likeminded analyses of cultural forms in schools. The idea of development of subjectivity through cultural forms is now common in the field of cultural studies writ large. The other emphases in Willis' book, such as his emphasis on production and interpretation as a collective process of *local groups*, have unfortunately been less appreciated in cultural studies.

34. Practice theory constitutes a metatheoretical shift that has been underway in anthropology, sociology, linguistics and other fields for several decades. Though Bourdieu (1977b, 1990) is the only one who self-consciously adopts the label, we see Giddens's structuration theory (1979, 1984) and Connell's account of practice (1983, 1987) as the principal expositions of what has come to be known as practice theory. See

Ortner (1984) for a good early review of anthropology's appropriation and development of practice theory. Cultural production can be seen as a specific form of practice theory which focuses upon cultural forms and emphasizes their importance in the development of subjectivities.

35. Although the concept of cultural production points to important features of the formation of subjectivities, conceptualization of the historical formation of persons in practice is only minimally developed (see, for example, Lave et al. 1992; Holland et al. in press). Bourdieu (1977b, 1990), most noticeably, has pioneered the way by concentrating his theoretical energies upon the formation of persons in practice, especially through his concept of "habitus," with its nuanced sense of agency and constraint, and an emphasis on pragmatics and sensitivity to social circumstances. However, he does not attend to those aspects of cultural forms we see as essential. See Bloch (1989) for a programmatic statement in this direction.

36. Educational scholars have used the concept of cultural production, for example, to describe such processes as the contestation of femininities distinguished by levels of education (Holland and Skinner in press), the "co-creation of knowledge" between teachers and learners (Skinner 1990), and the creation of cultural forms and practices among students (Levinson 1993a, 1993b; Canaan 1990; Holland and Eisenhart 1990; Walker 1988). Concepts closely related to "cultural production" are the notions of "negotiated meaning" and "social construction of reality" employed in the work of symbolic interactionists. In Britain, a rich sociological ethnography of schooling developed out of the work by interactionists such as Colin Lacey, Stephen Ball, Martyn Hammersley, and Peter Woods (see Woods 1990, 1992 for a review). While we see obvious similarities between the work of the interactionists and our own, the interactionists have unduly limited the "horizon of meaning" to the interaction context itself.

37. See similar arguments in Boli et al. (1985) and Meyer et al. (1992).

38. Mitchell (1988) has analyzed colonial educational provisions in Egypt as a kind of "disciplinary regime." See Corrigan et al. (1987) for a historical discussion of the disciplinary effects of public schooling in Canada. Donald (1992) does the same for England, providing a useful complement to Corrigan and Sayer's broader account.

39. Keyes (1991:12), writing about the "world of the state" proposed by Asian public schools, would offer an important caveat: Students still learn a considerable amount of "culture" through traditional religious schools, or through the traditional narrative forms of local culture.

40. Jean Lave has been particularly eloquent in her long-standing investigation of the contrasting styles of cognition and learning in West African schools and traditional apprenticeship relations. See her forthcoming volume. See also the new and important book by Serpell (1993), which makes a similar point about the "significance of schooling" in a Zambian society.

41. See Coletta (1976), King (1967), Grindal (1972), Modiano (1970), and Moore (1973).

42. See also books by Colson and Thudder (1980) and Flinn (1992). The recent issue of *Comparative Education Review*, dedicated to examining "Schooling and Learning in

Children's Lives" (Modell 1994), moves in this direction as well, though Modell's introductory essay tends to identify children with their "national culture" in a way which collapses ethnic and class differences.

43. It is important to point out that non-anthropologists have contributed some of the more critical and compelling studies of Western schooling in non-Western contexts. See, for instance, articles by Branson and Miller (1992), Coffyn Biraimah (1989), and Masemann (1974), as well as the new book by Marshall (1993).

44. See also the volumes edited by Spindler (1987) and Street (1993). Contributions to each of these volumes range across First and Third World contexts, though only Street's powerful collection of grounded studies in literacy elucidates the struggles involving the "educated person." Bloch's piece in the Street volume is a nice example.

45. In critical educational studies, a parallel development has occurred. In 1987, Wexler announced that the popular media had begun to surpass schools as the "key educative relation" in society. Similarly, scholars interested in critical pedagogy have turned their attention increasingly toward the popular media as a "site" for learning and identity formation (Giroux, Simon et al. 1989; Giroux 1994). Tellingly, though, Wexler (1992) went on to write an astute school ethnography, in which he argued for the continuing importance of school-based social relations (albeit with the media providing crucial symbolic resources for the elaboration of group and individual identities).

46. Sites alternative to the school include the family, church, guild, traditional age cohort, civic club, and a variety of other organizational forms.

47. Levinson (1993a, 1993c) has discussed the impact of media and cultural commodities at his own Mexican fieldwork site.

48. We thank Aurolyn Luykx for calling our attention to this point.

49. The forthcoming volume by Blot, Niehaus, and Schmertzing promises to fill in much of the detail on the development of anthropological studies of education and schooling, and show that, in fact, the bases for a more critical educational anthropology have always been present. As the contributors to their volume show, some of the earliest precursors of critical work in the field include, among others, Margaret Mead, Jules Henry, Dorothy Lee, and Hortense Powdermaker. We argue, along with Blot, Niehaus, and Schmertzing, that contemporary educational anthropology has largely forgotten these more cantankerous ancestors.

50. See, for instance, Watson-Gegeo and Welchman Gegeo (1992), Falgout and Levin (1992), Erickson (1987), Gibson and Ogbu (1991), and Fordham (1993).

51. The title of the Society for Cultural Anthropology's most recent conference was, "Cultural Production under Late Capitalism."

52. See Hall et al. (1987b); Willis (1981b); Lave et al. (1992).

53. Even as we advocate the inclusion of new research perspectives, we recognize that, with the exception of Rockwell and Luykx, all of this volume's contributors work out of U.S. or European institutions, and most of them are anthropologists. See the forthcoming volume by Anderson and Montero-Sieburth (in press) for a heartening model of collaborative research between U.S. and Latin American scholars.

54. Two recent analyses in the anthropology of education which move suggestively in this direction are Mehan et al. (1994) and Brandau and Collins (1994).

55. Aside from some of the contributions to this volume, one could think of many examples here: from Willis' pathbreaking work on the resistance potential of the lads' working-class culture (1981b), to Heath's (1983) explication and defense of lower-class (black and white) practices of language socialization.

56. We thank Gary Anderson and Elsie Rockwell for making this point clearer to us.

REFERENCES

Abu-Lughod, Lila. 1990. The Romance of Resistance: Tracing Transformations of Power through Bedouin Women. American Ethnologist 17(1):41–55.

Aggleton, Peter J. 1987. Rebels Without a Cause. London: Falmer.

Alonso, Ana María. 1994. The Politics of Space, Time and Substance: State Formation, Nationalism, and Ethnicity. Annual Reviews in Anthropology 23:379–405.

Althusser,: Louis. 1971. Ideology and Ideological State Apparatuses. *In* Lenin and Philosophy and Other Essays. New York: Monthly Review Press.

Anderson, Benedict. 1983. Imagined Communities: Reflections on the Origin and Spread of Nationalism. London: Verso.

Anderson, Gary. 1989. Critical Ethnography in Education: Origins, Current Status, and New Directions. Review of Educational Research 59:249–70.

———. 1994. The Cultural Politics of Qualitative Research in Education: Confirming and Contesting the Canon. Educational Theory 44(2):225–237.

Anderson, Gary and Martha Montero-Sieburth, eds. Forthcoming. Ethnographic Educational Research in Latin America: The Struggle for a New Paradigm. New York: Garland.

Anyon, Jean. 1981. Social Class and School Knowledge. Curriculum Inquiry 11(1):3–42.

Appadurai, Arjun. 1990. Disjuncture and Difference in the Global Cultural Economy. Public Culture 2(2):1–24.

Appadurai, Arjun and Carol Breckenridge. 1988. Why Public Culture? Public Culture 1(1):1–24.

Apple, Michael W. 1979. Ideology and Curriculum. London: Routledge and Kegan Paul.

———. 1982a. Cultural and Economic Reproduction in American Education: Essays in Class, Ideology and the State. Boston: Routledge and Kegan Paul.

———. 1982b. Education and Power. London: Routledge and Kegan Paul.

Apple, Michael and Lois Weis. 1983. Ideology and Practice in Schooling: A Political and Conceptual Introduction. *In* Ideology and Practice in Schooling. M. Apple and L. Weis, eds. Pp. 3–33. Philadelphia: Temple University Press.

38   *Levinson and Holland*

Archer, Margaret. 1979. Social Origins of Education Systems. London: Sage.

Arnove, Robert. 1994. Education as Contested Terrain: Nicaragua, 1979–1993. Boulder, CO: Westview.

Au, K. and C. Jordan. 1981. Teaching Reading to Hawaiian Children: Finding a Culturally Appropriate Solution. *In* Culture and the Bilingual Classroom. H. Trueba, G. P. Guthrie, and K. Au, eds. Pp. 139–152. Rowley, MA: Newbury House.

Babcock, Barbara. 1990. "A New Mexican Rebecca": Imaging Pueblo Women. Journal of the Southwest 32(4):400–437.

———. 1993. Bearers of Value, Vessels of Desire: The Reproduction of the Reproduction of Pueblo Culture. Museum Anthropology 17(3):43–56.

Barber, Benjamin. 1992. An Aristocracy of Everyone: The Politics of Education and the Future of America. New York: Oxford University Press.

Baudelot, Christian and Roger Establet. 1975. La Escuela Capitalista. Mexico City: Siglo Veintiuno.

Bauman, Richard, ed. 1977. Verbal Art as Performance. Prospect Heights, IL: Waveland Press.

Bernstein, Basil. 1973. Class, Codes, and Control. Vols. 1 and 2. London: Routledge and Kegan Paul.

Bloch, Maurice. 1989. "Anthropology since the Sixties" Seen from across the Atlantic. *In* Author Meets Critics: Reactions to "Theory in Anthropology since the Sixties." CSST Working Paper, Vol. 32. S. B. Ortner, ed. Pp. 1–14. Ann Arbor: University of Michigan Press.

———. 1993. The Uses of Schooling and Literacy in a Zafimaniry Village. *In* Cross-Cultural Approaches to Literacy. Brian V. Street, ed. Pp. 87–109. Cambridge: Cambridge University Press.

Blot, Richard K., Juliet Niehaus, and Richard Schmertzing, eds. in press. Foundations of Anthropology and Education: Critical Perspectives. New York: Bergin and Garvey.

Boli, John and Francisco O. Ramírez. 1992. Compulsory Schooling in the Western Cultural Context. *In* Emergent Issues in Education: Comparative Perspectives. Robert F. Arnove, Philip G. Altbach, and Gail P. Kelly, eds. Albany: SUNY Press.

Boli, John, Francisco O. Ramírez, and John W. Meyer. 1985. Explaining the Origins and Expansion of Mass Education. Comparative Education Review 29(2):145–190.

Borofsky, Robert. 1987. Making History: Pukapukan and Anthropological Constructions of Knowledge. New York: Cambridge University Press.

Bourdieu, Pierre. 1974. The School as a Conservative Force: Scholastic and Cultural Inequalities. *In* Contemporary Research in the Sociology of Education. John Eggleston, ed. Pp. 32–46. London: Methuen.

————. 1977a. The Economy of Linguistic Exchanges. Social Science Information 14(6):645–68.

————. 1977b. Outline of a Theory of Practice. Cambridge: Cambridge University Press.

————. 1984. Distinction: A Social Critique of the Judgment of Taste. Cambridge, MA: Harvard University Press.

————. 1988. Homo Academicus. Stanford: Stanford University Press.

————. 1989. Social Space and Symbolic Power. Sociological Theory 7(2):14–25.

————. 1990. The Logic of Practice. Stanford: Stanford University Press.

————. 1993. The Field of Cultural Production: Essays on Art and Literature. New York: Columbia University Press.

Bourdieu, Pierre and Jean-Claude Passeron. 1977. Reproduction: In Education, Society, and Culture. Beverly Hills: Sage.

Bourdieu, Pierre and Monique Saint Martin. 1974. Scholastic Excellence and the Values of the Educational System. *In* Contemporary Research in the Sociology of Education. John Eggleston, ed. Pp. 338–371. London: Methuen.

Bowles, Samuel and Herbert Gintis. 1976. Schooling in Capitalist America: Educational Reform and the Contradictions of Economic Life. New York: Basic Books.

Brandau, Deborah Mayne and James Collins. 1994. Texts, Social Relations, and Work-Based Skepticism about Schooling: An Ethnographic Analysis. Anthropology and Education Quarterly 25(2):118–36.

Branson, Jan and Don Miller. 1992. Schooling and the Imperial Transformation of Gender: A Post-Structuralist Approach to the Study of Schooling in Bali, Indonesia. *In* Contemporary Perspectives in Comparative Education. Robin Burns and Anthony Welch, eds. Pp. 223–264. New York: Garland.

Brantlinger, Patrick. 1990. Crusoe's Footprints: Cultural Studies in Britain and America. New York: Routledge.

Briggs, Charles. 1988. Competence in Performance: The Creativity of Tradition in Mexicano Verbal Art. Philadelphia: University of Pennsylvania Press.

Calhoun, Craig. 1993. Habitus, Field, and Capital: The Question of Historical Specificity. *In* Bourdieu: Critical Perspectives. Craig Calhoun, Edward LiPuma, and Moishe Postone, eds. Pp. 61–88. Chicago: University of Chicago Press.

Canaan, Joyce. 1990. Passing Notes and Telling Jokes: Gendered Strategies among American Middle School Teenagers. *In* Uncertain Terms: Negotiating Gender in American Culture. Faye Ginsburg and Anne Lowenhaupt Tsing, eds. Pp. 215–231. Boston: Beacon Press.

Carnoy, Martin. 1974. Education as Cultural Imperialism. New York: David McKay.

———. 1984. The State and Political Theory. Princeton: Princeton University Press.

Carnoy, Martin and Henry Levin. 1985. Schooling and Work in the Democratic State. Stanford: Stanford University Press.

Carspecken, Phil Francis and Michael Apple. 1992. Critical Qualitative Research: Theory, Methodology, and Practice. *In* The Handbook of Qualitative Research in Education. LeCompte, Margaret D., W. Millroy, and Judith Preissle Goetz, eds. Pp. 508–554. San Diego: Academic Press.

Cazden, Courtney, Vera John, and Dell Hymes, eds. 1985 [1972]. Functions of Language in the Classroom. Prospect Heights, IL: Waveland.

Cicourel, Aaron and John Kitsuse. 1963. The Educational Decision Makers. Indianapolis: Bobbs-Merrill.

Coffyn Biraimah, Karen. 1989 [1982]. Different Knowledge for Different Folks: Knowledge Distribution in a Togolese Secondary School. *In* Comparative Education. Philip Altbach, Robert Arnove, and Gail Kelly, eds. Pp. 161–175. New York: Advent Books.

Coletta, Nat J. 1976. Cross-Cultural Transactions in Ponapean Elementary Classrooms. Journal of Research and Development in Education 9(4):113–123.

Collins, James. 1993. Determination and Contradiction: An Appreciation and Critique of the Work of Pierre Bourdieu on Language and Education. *In* Bourdieu: Critical Perspectives. Craig Calhoun, Edward LiPuma, and Moishe Postone, eds. Pp. 116–138. Chicago: University of Chicago Press.

Collins, Patricia Hill. 1991. Black Feminist Thought: Knowledge, Consciousness, and the Politics of Empowerment. New York: Routledge.

Comaroff, Jean. 1985. Body of Power, Spirit of Resistance: The Culture and History of a South African People. Chicago: University of Chicago Press.

Comaroff, John and Jean Comaroff. 1992. Ethnography and the Historical Imagination. Boulder, CO: Westview Press.

Connell, R. W. 1983. Which Way Is Up? Essays on Class, Sex, and Culture. London: Allen and Unwin.

———. 1987. Gender and Power: Society, the Person, and Sexual Politics. Stanford: Stanford University Press.

———. 1993. Schools and Social Justice. Philadelphia: Temple University Press.

Connell, R. W., D. Ashenden, S. Kessler, and G. Dowsett. 1982. Making the Difference: Schools, Families, and Social Division. Sydney: George Allen and Unwin.

Corrigan, P. 1979. Schooling the Smash Street Kids. London: Verso.

Corrigan, Philip and Derek Sayer. 1985. The Great Arch: English State Formation as Cultural Revolution. London: Basil Blackwell.

Corrigan, Philip, Bruce Curtis, and Robert Lanning. 1987. The Political Space of Schooling. *In* The Political Economy of Canadian Schooling. Terry Witherspoon, ed. Toronto: Methuen.

Coward, Rosalind and Jon Ellis. 1977. Language and Materialism. London: Routledge and Kegan Paul.

Delamont, Sara. 1989. Knowledgeable Women: Structuralism and the Reproduction of Elites. London: Routledge.

Delgado-Gaitan, Concha. 1987. Traditions and Transitions in the Learning Process of Mexican Children: An Ethnographic View. *In* Interpretive Ethnography of Education: At Home and Abroad. George Spindler, ed. Pp. 333–362. Hillsdale, NJ: Lawrence Erlbaum.

DiMaggio, Paul. 1982. Cultural Capital and Social Success. American Sociological Review 47:189–201.

Domínguez, Virginia. 1989. People as Subject, People as Object: Selfhood and Peoplehood in Contemporary Israel. Madison: University of Wisconsin Press.

Donald, James. 1992. Sentimental Education: Schooling, Popular Culture, and the Regulation of Liberty. London: Verso.

Durkheim, Emile. 1956. Education and Sociology. Trans. S. D. Fox. Glencoe, IL: The Free Press.

Eckert, Penelope. 1989. Jocks and Burnouts: Social Categories and Identity in the High School. New York: Teachers College Press.

Eddy, Elizabeth. 1967. Walk the White Line: A Profile of Urban Education. Garden City, NY: Doubleday Anchor Books.

Erickson, Frederick. 1987. Transformation and School Success: The Politics and Culture of Educational Achievement. Anthropology and Education Quarterly 18(4):335–356.

Erickson, Frederick and Gerald Mohatt. 1982. Cultural Organization of Participant Structures in Two Classrooms of Indian Students. *In* Doing the Ethnography of the Classroom. G. Spindler, ed. Pp. 136–174. New York: Holt, Rinehart, and Winston.

Erickson, Frederick and Jeffrey Schultz. 1982. The Counselor as Gatekeeper: Social Interaction in Interviews. New York: Academic Press.

Ernst, Gisela, Elsa Statzner, and Henry Trueba, eds. 1994. Alternative Visions of Schooling: Success Stories in Minority Settings. Theme Issue of Anthropology and Education Quarterly 25(3).

Everhart, Robert. 1983. Reading, Writing, and Resistance: Adolescence and Labor in a Junior High School. London: Routledge and Kegan Paul.

Ezpeleta, Justa and Elsie Rockwell. 1985. Escuela y Clases Subalternas. Cuadernos Políticos 37:70–80.

Falgout, Suzanne and Paula Levin, eds. 1992. Transforming Knowledge: Western Schooling in the Pacific. Theme Issue of Anthropology and Education Quarterly 23(1).

Fine, Michelle. 1991. Framing Dropouts: Notes on the Politics of an Urban Public High School. Albany: SUNY Press.

Fiske, John. 1989. Understanding Popular Culture. London: Routledge.

Flinn, Juliana. 1992. Diplomas and Thatch Houses: Asserting Tradition in a Changing Micronesia. Ann Arbor: University of Michigan Press.

Foley, Douglas. 1977. Anthropological Studies of Schooling in Developing Countries: Some Recent Findings and Trends. Comparative Education Review 21(2/3):311–328.

———. 1990. Learning Capitalist Culture: Deep in the Heart of Tejas. Philadelphia: University of Pennsylvania Press.

———. 1991. Rethinking School Ethnographies of Colonial Settings: A Performance Perspective of Reproduction and Resistance. Comparative Education Review 35(3):532–551.

———. 1995. The Heartland Chronicles. Philadelphia: University of Pennsylvania Press.

Fordham, Signithia. 1993. "Those Loud Black Girls": (Black) Women, Silence, and Gender "Passing" in the Academy. Anthropology and Education Quarterly 24(1):3–32.

Fordham, Signithia and John Ogbu. 1986. Black Students' School Success: Coping with the "Burden of Acting White." Urban Review 18(3):176–206.

Fox, Richard. 1985. Lions of the Punjab. Berkeley: University of California Press.

Fox, Richard G., ed. 1990. Nationalist Ideologies and the Production of National Cultures. Washington, DC: American Ethnological Society Monograph Series, #2.

———. 1991. Recapturing Anthropology: Working in the Present. Santa Fe, NM: School of American Research Press.

Fuller, Bruce. 1991. Growing-Up Modern: The Western State Builds Third World Schools. London: Routledge.

Fuller, Bruce and Richard Rubinson, eds. 1992. The Political Construction of Education: The State, School Expansion, and Economic Change. New York: Praeger.

Gal, Susan. 1987. Language and Political Economy. Annual Reviews in Anthropology 18:345–367.

Gerth, H. H. and C. Wright Mills, eds. 1958. From Max Weber: Essays in Sociology. New York: Oxford University Press.

Giddens, Anthony. 1979. Central Problems in Social Theory. Berkeley: University of California Press.

————. 1984. The Constitution of Society. Berkeley: University of California Press.

Gilmore, Perry and Allan Glatthorn, eds. 1981. Children In and Out of School. Washington, DC: Center for Applied Linguistics.

Gilroy, Paul. 1987. "Ain't No Black in the Union Jack": The Cultural Politics of Race and Nation. London: Hutchinson.

Ginsburg, Mark, ed. 1991. Understanding Educational Reform in Global Context: Economy, Ideology, and the State. New York: Garland.

Giroux, Henry. 1983. Theories of Reproduction and Resistance in the New Sociology of Education: A Critical Analysis. Harvard Educational Review 53(3):257–293.

————. 1991. Postmodernism, Feminism, and Cultural Politics: Redrawing the Boundaries of Educational Criticism. Albany: SUNY Press.

————. 1992. Border Crossings: Cultural Workers and the Politics of Education. New York:. Routledge.

————. 1994. Disturbing Pleasures: Learning Popular Culture. New York: Routledge.

Giroux, Henry, Roger I. Simon, Paul Smith, and Elizabeth Ellsworth, eds. 1989. Schooling, Popular Culture, and Everyday Life. New York: Bergin and Garvey.

Green, Andrew. 1990. Education and State Formation. New York: St. Martin's Press.

Grindal, Bruce. 1972. Growing Up in Two Worlds: Education and Transition among the Sisala of Northern Ghana. New York: Holt, Rinehart and Winston.

Grossberg, Lawrence, Cary Nelson and Paula Treichler, eds. 1992. Cultural Studies. New York: Routledge.

Gutmann, Amy. 1987. Democratic Education. Princeton: Princeton University Press.

Habermas, Jurgen. 1984. The Theory of Communicative Action, vol. 1: Reason and the Rationalization of Society. Thomas McCarthy, trans. Boston: Beacon Press.

————. 1987. The Theory of Communicative Action, vol. 2: Lifeworld and System: A Critique of Functionalist Reason. Thomas McCarthy, trans. Boston: Beacon Press.

Hall, Stuart. 1981. Notes on Deconstructing the "Popular." *In* People's History and Socialist Theory. R. Samuel, ed. Pp. 227–239. London: Routledge.

————. 1986. Gramsci's Relevance for the Study of Race and Ethnicity. Journal of Communication Inquiry 10(2):5–27.

————. 1992. Cultural Studies and its Theoretical Legacies. *In* Cultural Studies. First ed. Lawrence Grossberg, Cary Nelson, and Paula Treichler, eds. Pp. 277–294. New York: Routledge.

———. 1993 [1980]. Encoding and Decoding. *In* The Cultural Studies Reader. Simon During, ed. Pp. 90–103. London: Routledge.

Hall, Stuart, Chas Critcher, Tony Jefferson, John Clarke, and Brian Roberts, eds. 1978b. Policing the Crisis: Mugging, The State, and Law and Order. London: Holmes and Meier.

Hall, Stuart, Dorothy Hobson, Andres Lowe, and Paul Willis. 1980. Culture, Media, Language. London: Hutchinson and the Centre for Contemporary Cultural Studies.

Hall, Stuart, Richard Johnson, and Paul Willis, eds. 1978a. On Ideology. London: Hutchinson and CCCS.

Hannerz, Ulf. 1992. Cultural Complexity: Studies in the Social Organization of Meaning. New York: Columbia University Press.

Hansen, Judith Friedman. 1990 [1979]. Sociocultural Perspectives on Human Learning. Prospect Heights, IL: Waveland.

Hansen, Karen V. and Ilene J. Philipson, eds. 1990. Women, Class, and the Feminist Imagination. Philadelphia: Temple University Press.

Haraway, Donna. 1988. Situated Knowledges: The Science Question in Feminism and the Privilege of the Partial Perspective. Feminist Studies 14(3):575–600.

Harker, Richard, Cheleen Mahar, and Chris Wilkes, eds. 1990. An Introduction to the Work of Pierre Bourdieu: The Practice of Theory. New York: St. Martin's Press.

Heath, Shirley Brice. 1983. Ways with Words: Language, Life, and Work in Communities and Classrooms. Cambridge: Cambridge University Press.

Heath, Shirley Brice and Milbrey W. McLaughlin, eds. 1993. Identity and Inner-City Youth: Beyond Ethnicity and Gender. New York: Teachers College Press.

Hebdige, Dick. 1979. Subculture: The Meaning of Style. London: Methuen.

Held, David. 1980. Introduction to Critical Theory. Berkeley: University of California Press.

Herzfeld, Michael. 1992. The Social Production of Indifference: Exploring the Symbolic Roots of Western Bureaucracy. Chicago: University of Chicago Press.

Hobsbawm, Eric and Terence Ranger, eds. 1983. The Invention of Tradition. Cambridge: Cambridge University Press.

Hogan, David. 1982. Education and Class Formation: The Peculiarities of the Americans. *In* Cultural and Economic Reproduction in Education. Michael Apple, ed. Pp. 32–78. London: Routledge and Kegan Paul.

Hoggart, Richard. 1961 [1957]. The Uses of Literacy. Boston: Beacon.

Holland, Dorothy. 1992. How Cultural Systems Become Desire. *In* Human Motives and Cultural Models. First ed. R. G. D'Andrade and C. Strauss, eds. Pp. 61–89. Cambridge: Cambridge University Press.

Holland, Dorothy, W. Carole Cain, William Lachicotte, René Prillaman, and Debra Skinner. in press. Emerging Selves: Identities Forming in and Against Cultural Worlds. Cambridge, MA: Harvard University Press.

Holland, Dorothy and Margaret Eisenhart. 1990. Educated in Romance: Women, Achievement, and College Culture. Chicago: University of Chicago Press.

Holland, Dorothy and Debra Skinner. 1995. Contested Ritual, Contested Femininities: (Re)forming Self and Society in a Nepali Women's Festival. American Ethnologist 22(2):279–305.

Hollingshead, A. B. 1949. Elmtown's Youth. New York: Wiley and Sons.

Illich, Ivan. 1970. Deschooling Society. New York: Harper & Row.

Jameson, Fredric. 1993. On "Cultural Studies." Social Text 17–52.

Jenkins, Henry. 1992. Textual Poachers: Television Fans and Participatory Culture. New York: Routledge.

Jenkins, R. P. 1983. Lads, Citizens, and Ordinary Kids: Youth Lifestyles in Belfast. London: Routledge and Kegan Paul.

Johnson, Richard. 1986–87. What is Cultural Studies Anyway? Social Text 6(1):38–80.

Karabel, Jerome and A. H. Halsey. 1977. Educational Research: A Review and an Interpretation. *In* Power and Ideology in Education. J. Karabel and A. H. Halsey, eds. Pp. 1–85. New York: Oxford University Press.

Katz, Michael B. 1975. Class, Bureaucracy, and Schools: The Illusion of Educational Change in America. Expanded Edition. New York: Praeger.

Keddie, Nell. 1971. Classroom Knowledge. *In* Knowledge and Control. Michael F. D. Young, ed. Pp. 133–160. London: Collier-Macmillan.

Keesing, Roger. 1992. Custom and Confrontation: The Kwaio Struggle for Cultural Autonomy. Chicago: University of Chicago Press.

———. 1994 Theories of Culture Revisited. *In* Assessing Cultural Anthropology. Robert Borofsky, ed. Pp. 301–312. New York: McGraw-Hill.

Kelly, Deirdre M. 1993. Last Chance High: How Girls and Boys Drop In and Out of Alternative Schools. New Haven, CT: Yale University Press.

Keyes, Charles. 1991a. The Proposed World of the School: Thai Villagers' Entry Into a Bureaucratic State System. *In* Reshaping Local Worlds: Formal Education and Cultural Change in Rural Southeast Asia. Charles Keyes, ed. Monograph #36. New Haven, CT: Yale Southeast Asian Studies.

Keyes, Charles, ed. 1991b. Reshaping Local Worlds: Formal Education and Cultural Change in Rural Southeast Asia. Monograph #36. New Haven, CT: Yale Southeast Asian Studies.

King, Richard. 1967. The School at Mopass: A Problem of Identity. New York: Holt, Rinehart, and Winston.

Kondo, Dorinne. 1990. Crafting Selves: Power, Gender, and Discourses of Identity in a Japanese Workplace. Chicago: University of Chicago Press.

Lacey, Colin. 1970. Hightown Grammar. Manchester: Manchester University Press.

Lakomski, Gabriele. 1984. On Agency and Structure: Pierre Bourdieu and Jean-Claude Passeron's Theory of Symbolic Violence. Curriculum Inquiry 14(2):151–163.

Lancaster, Roger. 1992. Life Is Hard: Machismo, Danger, and the Intimacy of Power in Nicaragua. Berkeley: University of California Press.

Lareau, Annette. 1989. Home Advantage: Social Class and Parental Intervention in Elementary Education. New York: Falmer.

Larkin, Ralph. 1979. Suburban Youth in Cultural Crisis. New York: Oxford University Press.

Lather, Patti. 1991. Getting Smart: Feminist Research and Pedagogy With/In the Postmodern. New York: Routledge.

Lave, Jean and Etienne Wenger. 1991. Situated Learning. New York: Cambridge University Press.

Lave, Jean, Paul Duguid, Nadine Fernandez, and Erik Axel. 1992. Coming of Age in Birmingham: Cultural Studies and Conceptions of Subjectivity. Annual Reviews in Anthropology 21:257–282.

Lave, Jean. in press. On Changing Practice: Three Moments in the Anthropology of Apprenticeship. New York: Cambridge University Press.

Leacock, Eleanor. 1970. Teaching and Learning in City Schools: A Comparative Study. New York: Basic Books.

Lesko, Nancy. 1988. The Curriculum of the Body: Lessons from a Catholic High School. *In* Becoming Feminine: The Politics of Popular Culture. Leslie Roman, Linda Christian-Smith, and Elizabeth Ellsworth, eds. London: Falmer Press.

Levine, Robert A. and Merry I. White. 1986. Human Conditions: The Cultural Basis of Educational Development. London: Routledge and Kegan Paul.

Levinson, Bradley A. 1992. Ogbu's Anthropology and the Critical Ethnography of Education: A Reciprocal Interrogation. International Journal of Qualitative Studies in Education 5(3):205–225.

———. 1993a. School Groups and the Culture of Equality at a Mexican Secundaria. Working Paper Series of the Duke-UNC Program in Latin American Studies. Paper #7.

———. 1993b. Todos Somos Iguales: Cultural Production and Social Difference at a Mexican Secondary School. Ph.D. Dissertation, Department of Anthropology, University of North Carolina–Chapel Hill.

———. 1993c. Who Needs School? Electronic Media, Cultural Commodities, and the Formation of Youth in (Post)Modernizing Mexico. Paper delivered at the Annual Meetings of the American Anthropological Association, Washington, DC.

LiPuma, Edward. 1993. Culture and the Concept of Culture in a Theory of Practice. *In* Bourdieu: Critical Perspectives. Craig Calhoun, Edward LiPuma, and Moishe Postone, eds. Pp. 14–34. Chicago: University of Chicago Press.

Luttrell, Wendy. 1989. Working-Class Women's Ways of Knowing: Effects of Gender, Race, and Class. Sociology of Education 62(January):33–46.

Lutz, Catherine A. and Jane L. Collins. 1993. Reading National Geographic. Chicago: University of Chicago Press.

MacLeod, Jay. 1987. Ain't No Makin' It: Leveled Aspirations in a Low-Income Neighborhood. Boulder, CO: Westview Press.

Maddox, Richard. 1993. El Castillo: The Politics of Tradition in an Andalusian Town. Champaign: University of Illinois Press.

———. 1994. Culture, Schooling, and the Politics of Class Identity in an Andalusian Town. Comparative Education Review 38(1):88–114.

Mankekar, Purnima. 1993. National Texts and Gendered Lives: An Ethnography of Television Viewers in a North Indian City. American Ethnologist 20(3):543–562.

Marcus, George. 1986. Contemporary Problems of Ethnography in the Modern World System. *In* Writing Culture: The Poetics and Politics of Ethnography. James Clifford and George Marcus, eds. Pp. 165–193. Berkeley: University of California Press.

Marcus, George and Michael J. Fischer. 1986. Anthropology as Cultural Critique: An Experimental Moment in the Human Sciences. Chicago: University of Chicago Press.

Marshall, Judith. 1993. Literacy, Power, and Democracy in Mozambique: The Governance of Learning from Colonization to the Present. Boulder, CO: Westview Press.

Masemann, Vandra. 1974. The Hidden Curriculum of a West African Boarding School. Canadian Journal of African Studies 8(3):479–94.

———. 1982. Critical Ethnography in the Study of Comparative Education. Comparative Education Review 26:1–15.

McCarthy, Cameron and Michael Apple. 1989. Race, Class, and Gender in American Educational Research: Toward a Nonsynchronous Parallelist Position. *In* Class, Race, and Gender in American Education. Lois Weis, ed. Pp. 9–39 Albany: SUNY Press.

McCarthy, Cameron and Warren Crichlow eds. 1993. Race, Identity, and Representation in Education. New York: Routledge.

McDermott, Ray P. 1987. Achieving School Failure: An Anthropological Approach to Illiteracy and Stratification. *In* Education and Cultural Process, 2nd ed. George Spindler, ed. Pp. 173–209. Prospect Heights, IL: Waveland Press.

McLaren, Peter. 1986. Schooling as a Ritual Performance: Towards a Political Economy of Educational Symbols and Gestures. London: Routledge and Kegan Paul.

McNeil, Linda. 1986. Contradictions of Control. London: Routledge.

McRobbie, Angela. 1992. Feminism and Youth Culture. London: Routledge.

Mead, Margaret. 1961 [1928]. Coming of Age in Samoa. New York: Morrow Quill Paperbacks.

Mehan, H., A. Hertweck, and J. L. Meihls. 1986. Handicapping the Handicapped. Stanford: Stanford University Press.

Mehan, Hugh, Lea Hubbard, and Irene Villanueva. 1994. Forming Academic Identities: Accommodation without Assimilation among Involuntary Minorities. Anthropology and Education Quarterly 25(2):91–117.

Mercado, Ruth. 1985. La Educación Primaria Gratuita: Una Lucha Popular Cotidiana. Cuadernos de Investigación #17. Mexico City: DIE.

Meyer, John W., David H. Kamens, and Aaron Benavot, with Yun-Kyung Cha and Suk-Ying Wong. 1992. School Knowledge for the Masses: World Models and National Primary Curricular Categories in the Twentieth Century. Washington, DC: Falmer Press.

Middleton, John, ed. 1970. From Child to Adult: Studies in the Anthropology of Education. Garden City, NY: Natural History Press.

Mitchell, Timothy. 1988. Colonising Egypt. First ed. New York: Cambridge University Press.

Modell, John. 1994. The Developing Schoolchild as Historical Actor. Comparative Education Review 38(1):1–9.

Modiano, Nancy. 1970. Indian Education in the Chiapas Highlands. New York: Holt, Rinehart and Winston.

Moll, Luis and Stephen Díaz. 1987. Change as the Goal of Educational Research. Anthropology and Education Quarterly 18(4):300–311.

Moore, Alexander. 1973. Life Cycles in Atchalán: The Diverse Careers of Certain Guatemalans. New York: Teachers College Press.

Morrow, Raymond A. and Carlos Alberto Torres. 1994. Education and the Reproduction of Class, Gender, and Race: Responding to the Postmodern Challenge. Educational Theory 44(1):43–61.

———. 1995. Social Theory and Education: A Critique of Theories of Social and Cultural Reproduction. Albany: SUNY Press.

Müller, Detlef K., Fritz Ringer, and Brian Simon, eds. 1987. The Rise of the Modern Educational System: Structural Change and Social Reproduction, 1870–1920. Cambridge: Cambridge University Press.

Nonini, Donald. in press. Beyond Hegemony, Beyond Resistance. American Ethnologist.

O'Barr, Willliam. 1994. Culture and the Ad: Exploring Otherness in the World of Advertising. Boulder, CO: Westview Press.

Ogbu, John. 1981. School Ethnography: A Multilevel Approach. Anthropology and Education Quarterly 12(1):3–29.

Ogbu, John and Margaret Gibson, eds. 1991. Minority Status and Schooling: A Comparative Study of Immigrant and Involuntary Minorities. New York: Garland.

Ong, Aihwa. 1987. Spirits of Resistance and Capitalist Discipline. Albany: SUNY Press.

Ortner, Sherry. 1984. Theory in Anthropology Since the Sixties. Comparative Studies in Society and History 26:126–166.

Page, Helán. 1994. White Public Space and the Construction of White Privilege in U.S. Health Care: Fresh Concepts and a New Model of Analysis. Medical Anthropology Quarterly 8(1):109–116.

Paulston, Rolland G. 1977. Educational Stratification and Cultural Hegemony in Peru. *In* Power and Ideology in Education. J. Karabel and A. H. Halsey, eds. Pp. 412–422. New York: Oxford University Press.

Peterson, Richard A. 1976. Cultural Production. Beverly Hills: Sage.

Philips, Susan U. 1983. The Invisible Culture: Communication in Classroom and Community on the Warm Springs Indian Reservation. New York: Longmann.

Poulantzas, Nicos. 1974. Political Power and Social Classes. London: New Left Books.

Puiggrós, Adriana. 1980. Imperialismo y Educación en América Latina. Mexico City: Nueva Imagen.

Quantz, Richard A. 1992. On Critical Ethnography (With Some Postmodern Considerations). *In* The Handbook of Qualitative Research in Education. Margaret D. LeCompte, Wendy Millroy, and Judith Preissle Goetz, eds. Pp. 447–506. San Diego: Academic Press.

Rabinow, Paul, ed. 1984. The Foucault Reader. New York: Pantheon.

Radway, Janice. 1984. Reading the Romance: Women, Patriarchy and Popular Literature. Chapel Hill: University of North Carolina Press.

———. 1992. Mail-Order Culture and its Critics: The Book-of-the-Month Club, Commodification and Consumption, and the Problem of Cultural Authority. *In*

Cultural Studies. Lawrence Grossberg, Cary Nelson, and Paula Treichler, eds. Pp. 512–530. New York: Routledge.

———. 1994. Reading at the Book-of-the-Month Club: On the Gender of the Middlebrow Consumer, or the Threat of the Culturally Fraudulent Female. Talk delivered at Telling Tales Summer Institute, National Endowment for the Humanities, 5 July, Madison, Wisconsin.

Raissiguier, Catherine. 1994. Becoming Women, Becoming Workers: Identity Formation in a French Vocational School. Albany: SUNY Press.

Ray, Douglas and Deo H. Poonwassie, eds. 1992. Education and Cultural Differences: New Perspectives. New York: Garland.

Reed-Danahay, Deborah. 1987. Farm Children at School: Educational Strategies in Rural France. Anthropological Quarterly 60(2):83–89.

Rist, Ray. 1970. Student Social Class and Teacher Expectation: The Self-Fulfilling Prophecy in Ghetto Education. Harvard Educational Review 400:411–451.

Rockwell, Elsie. 1987. Comó Observar la Reproducción? Revista Colombiana de Educación 17:109–125.

———. 1994. Schools of the Revolution: Enacting and Contesting State Forms in Tlaxcala, 1910–1930. *In* Everyday Forms of State Formation: Revolution and the Negotiation of Rule in Modern Mexico. Gilbert Joseph and Daniel Nugent, eds. Pp. 170–208. Durham, NC: Duke University Press.

———. 1995. La Escuela Cotidiana. Mexico City: Fondo de Cultura Económica.

———. in press a. Ethnography and the Commitment to Public Schooling: A Review of Research at the Departamento de Investigaciones Educativas (DIE). *In* Educational Ethnographic Research in Latin America: The Struggle for a New Paradigm. Gary L. Anderson and Martha Montero-Sieburth, eds. New York: Garland.

———. in press b. La Dinámica Cultural en la Escuela. *In* Cultura y Escuela: La Reflexión Actual en México. Elba Gigante, ed. Mexico City: Conacult.

Rockwell, Elsie and Ruth Mercado. 1986. La Escuela, Lugar del Trabajo Docente. Mexico City: DIE.

Rosaldo, Renato. 1989. Culture and Truth: The Remaking of Social Analysis. Boston: Beacon Press.

Roseberry, William. 1989. Anthropologies and Histories. New Brunswick, NJ: Rutgers University Press.

Rosen, Harold. 1985. The Voices of Communities and Language in Classrooms. Harvard Educational Review 55(4):448–456.

Sahlins, Marshall. 1985. Islands of History. Chicago: University of Chicago Press.

Salzman, Philip Carl. 1993. The Electronic Trojan Horse: Television in the Globalization of Paramodern Cultures. Paper delivered at 13th International Congress of Anthropological and Ethnological Sciences, Mexico City, Mexico.

———. 1994. The Lone Stranger in the Heart of Darkness. *In* Assessing Cultural Anthropology. Robert Borofsky, ed. Pp. 29–39. New York: McGraw-Hill.

Sarris, Greg. 1993. Keeping Slug Woman Alive: The Challenge of Reading in a Reservation Classroom. *In* The Ethnography of Reading. Jonathan Boyarin, ed. Pp. 238–269. Berkeley: University of California Press.

Scheper-Hughes, Nancy. 1992. Death Without Weeping: The Violence of Everyday Life in Brazil. Berkeley: University of California Press.

Scott, Joan W. 1988. Gender and the Politics of History. New York: Columbia University Press.

Scudder, Thayer and Elizabeth Colson. 1980. Secondary Education and the Formation of an Elite: The Impact of Education on Gwembe District, Zambia. New York: Academic Press.

Serpell, Robert. 1993. The Significance of Schooling: Life Journeys in African Society. New York: Cambridge University Press.

Shapiro, H. Svi. 1990. Between Capitalism and Democracy: Educational Policy and the Crisis of the Welfare State. New York: Bergin and Garvey.

Sharp, Rachel and Andrew Green. 1975. Education and Social Control. London: Routledge and Kegan Paul.

Shaw, Thomas. 1994. The Semiotic Mediation of Identity. Ethos 22(1):83–119.

Silverstone, Roger. 1990. Television and Everyday Life: Towards an Anthropology of the Television Audience. *In* Public Communication: The New Imperatives. Marjorie Ferguson, ed. Pp. 173–189. London: Sage.

Simon, Roger and Donald Dippo. 1986. On Critical Ethnographic Work. Anthropology and Education Quarterly 17(3):195–202.

Skinner, Debra. 1990. Nepalese Children's Understanding of Self and the Social World: A Study of a Hindu Mixed Caste Community. Ph.D. Dissertation, Department of Anthropology, University of North Carolina–Chapel Hill.

Smith, Anthony D. 1991. National Identity. Reno: University of Nevada Press.

Smith, Paul. 1988. Discerning the Subject. Minneapolis: University of Minnesota Press.

Solomon, R. Patrick. 1992. Black Resistance in High School: Forging a Separatist Culture. Albany: SUNY Press.

Spindler, George, ed. 1987. Interpretive Ethnography of Education: At Home and Abroad. Hillsdale, NJ: Lawrence Erlbaum.

Spring, Joel. 1972. Schooling and the Rise of the Corporate State. Boston: Beacon Press.

Stinchcombe, Arthur. 1964. Rebellion in a High School. Chicago: Quadrangle.

Street, Brian V., ed. 1993. Cross-Cultural Approaches to Literacy. Cambridge: Cambridge University Press.

Tharp, Roland and Ronald Gallimore. 1988. Rousing Minds to Life: Teaching, Learning, and Schooling in Social Context. Cambridge: Cambridge University Press.

Thompson, E. P. 1963. The Making of the English Working Class. New York: Vintage.

Tong, Rosemarie. 1989. Feminist Thought: A Complete Introduction. Boulder, CO: Westview Press.

Touraine, Alain. 1981. The Voice and the Eye: The Analysis of Social Movements. New York: Cambridge University Press.

Trueba, Henry. 1988. Culturally Based Explanations of Minority Students' Academic Achievement. Anthropology and Education Quarterly 19(3):270–287.

Turner, Graeme. 1990. British Cultural Studies. London: Routledge.

Vaddhanaphuti, Chayan. 1991. Social and Ideological Reproduction in Rural Northern Thai Schools. *In* Reshaping Local Worlds: Formal Education and Cultural Change in Rural Southeast Asia. Charles Keyes, ed. Monograph #36. New Haven, CT: Yale Southeast Asian Studies.

Valli, Linda. 1986. Becoming Clerical Workers. London: Routledge and Kegan Paul.

Vásquez, Olga, Lucinda Pease-Alvarez, and Sheila Shannon. 1994. Pushing Boundaries: Language and Culture in a Mexicano Community. Cambridge: Cambridge University Press.

Vélez-Ibáñez, Carlos G. and James B. Greenberg. 1992. Formation and Transformation of Funds of Knowledge Among U.S.-Mexican Households. Anthropology and Education Quarterly 23(4):313–35.

Wacquant, Loïc J. D. 1993. Bourdieu in America: Notes on the Transatlantic Importation of Social Theory. *In* Bourdieu: Critical Perspectives. Craig Calhoun, Edward LiPuma, and Moishe Postone, eds. Pp. 235–262. Chicago: University of Chicago Press.

Walker, J. C. 1988. Louts and Legends: Male Youth Culture in an Inner City School. Sydney: Allen and Unwin.

Watson-Gegeo, Karen Ann and David Welchman Gegeo. 1992. Schooling, Knowledge, and Power: Social Transformation in the Solomon Islands. Anthropology and Education Quarterly 23(1):10–29.

Wax, Murray L., Stanley Diamond, and Fred O. Gearing, eds. 1971. Anthropological Perspectives on Education. New York: Basic Books.

Weber, Max. 1978. Economy and Society. 2 Vols. Berkeley: University of California Press.

Weiler, Kathleen. 1988. Women Teaching for Change: Gender, Class, and Power. New York: Bergin and Garvey.

Weis, Lois. 1984. Between Two Worlds. London: Routledge and Kegan Paul.

―――. 1989. The 1980s: De-Industrialization and Change in White Working Class Male and Female Youth Cultural Forms. *In* Politics and the Processes of Schooling. Stephanie Walker and Len Barton, eds. Pp. 126–165. Milton Keynes: Open University Press.

―――. 1990. Working Class Without Work: High School Students in a De-industrializing Economy. New York: Routledge.

Welch, Anthony R. 1993. Class, Culture, and the State in Comparative Education: Problems, Perspectives and Prospects. Comparative Education 29(1):7–27.

Wexler, Philip. 1987. Social Analysis of Education: Beyond the New Sociology. London: Routledge and Kegan Paul.

―――. 1992. Becoming Somebody: Toward a Social Psychology of School. London: Falmer.

Whitty, Geoff J. 1985. Sociology and School Knowledge: Curriculum Theory, Research and Politics. London: Methuen.

Williams, Brackette. 1991. Stains on My Name, War in My Veins: Guyana and the Politics of Cultural Struggle. Durham, NC: Duke University Press.

Williams, Raymond. 1977. Marxism and Literature. New York: Oxford University Press.

Willis, Paul. 1981a. Cultural Production is Different from Cultural Reproduction is Different from Social Reproduction is Different from Reproduction. Interchange 12(2/3):48–67.

―――. 1981b [1977]. Learning to Labor: How Working Class Kids Get Working Class Jobs. New York: Columbia University Press.

―――. 1983. Cultural Production and Theories of Reproduction. *In* Race, Class, and Education. Len Barton and Stephanie Walker, eds. London: Croom Helm.

Willis, Paul, with Simon Jones, Joyce Canaan and Geoff Hurd. 1990. Common Culture: Symbolic Work and Play in the Everyday Cultures of the Young. Boulder, CO: Westview Press.

Woods, Peter. 1990. Happiest Days? How Pupils Cope With School. London: Falmer.

―――. 1992. Symbolic Interactionism: Theory and Method. *In* The Handbook of Qualitative Research. Margaret LeCompte, Wendy Millroy, and Judith Goetz, eds. Pp. 337–404. San Diego: Academic Press.

Wulff, Helene and Vered Amit-Talai, eds. 1995. Youth Culture. New York: Routledge.

Young, Michael F. D., ed. 1971. Knowledge and Control. London: Collier-Macmillan.

PART I

Schools as Sites for the Cultural Production of the Educated Person

2

KATHRYN M. ANDERSON-LEVITT

Behind Schedule: Batch-Produced Children in French and U.S. Classrooms

In the United States today, elementary teachers can be heard to say of a student, "He's a January child" (Graue 1993:183) or "He's an August birthday" (Graue 1993:193). Similarly, in France I have heard teachers comment that Julie was "old" because she was "born in January," that Albert was "only 5 years 6 months," and that Sébastien had the "level" of "5 years 3 months." In contrast, Kapsiki parents in Kenya measure childhood not in months but in chunks of time that span years. They divide childhood into only three stages (Harkness and Super 1983), as do Ifaluk parents on the other side of the world (Lutz 1985), while Marquesans do not differentiate among "kids" at all until the sexually active stage (Kirkpatrick 1985). Western Europeans themselves only gradually broke childhood into stages during the sixteenth and seventeenth centuries (Ariès 1962) and, even when they did, age grades mattered little in some rural areas until well into the twentieth century (Prost 1981).

How is it that today in France and the United States teachers and many parents describe children as "young" or "old" on the basis of age measured *in months*? And how is it that we also measure with equal precision elusive notions we call "mental age," or "maturity," or, as in Sébastien's case, "level"?

I will argue here that the contemporary industrial world's novel model of childhood, a model focused on a chronological age and a "mental age" that are both measured in units of months, is a cultural construction that grew out of the factory-like nature of schools and out of the schools' need to sort children. First, I will present evidence from my own ethnographic research in France, and from other researchers' studies in the United States, to show how first-grade teachers use concepts of age and "maturity" when evaluating their students' "progress" in learning to read. Along the way, I will point out how the evaluation process works to the advantage of "precocious" upper-middle-class children. Then I will demonstrate how the obsession with age and "maturity"—among academic psychologists as well as classroom teachers—depends on the particular way in which Western Europe and the United States have organized mass schooling for roughly a century. Three institutional arrangements of mass education—graded instruc-

57

tion, compulsory school-entry age, and batch rather than individual instruction—permitted the development of an ideology that rationalizes the re-segregation of the "precocious," "advanced" children of the elite from the children of the masses.

The French examples come from "Villefleurie," a medium-sized metropolitan area in central France where I conducted ethnographic research in 1976, 1978–79, and 1988. Like all the proper names here, it is a pseudonym.[1] This report is based on visits to thirty first-grade classrooms and eight nursery-school and kindergarten classrooms in public and private, large and small schools in the Villefleurie area. It will make particular reference to the first-grade classes taught by Madame Marie Berger, Madame Jeannette Durand, and Monsieur Paul Alain, classes I observed regularly from September through March of the 1978–79 school year.

Defining Children in Terms of Age and "Maturity"

Chronological Age

Age mattered in Villefleurie classrooms. Teachers referred to certain students as "young" or "old" and, not infrequently, I found a list of the children's birthdays posted on a cupboard or attached to a teacher's planning book.

All else being equal, the older the child the better, for teachers expected older children to be more "mature (*mûrs*)" and hence more "ready" to learn. For example, when I interviewed a group of first-grade teachers about variation among children in their classrooms, one teacher commented,

> "You have a difference between the children born in December and the children born in January. Well, it's not always the same, you could have a child born in December who's brilliant, but . . ."
>
> "So it's often a question of age?," I asked.
>
> "Yes. Maturity. Milieu," she clarified.
>
> "Yes, yes, of milieu," added another teacher. "There are some who express themselves well, who write almost as in first grade, then you have others who don't express themselves at all orally and squirm like a baby."

In other words, these teachers felt they could predict performance partly on the basis of age. Of course, the word "milieu," which refers to a child's home environment and thus, implicitly, to social class, stands out as sharply as the words "age" and "maturity" in these comments. The following section will make clear the importance of social class.

The age paradox in France. In Villefleurie, teachers made a noteworthy exception to the rule that older is better in the case of children who had skipped or repeated a grade.

By law, French children enter first grade during the calendar year in which they turn 6 years old; in other words, the "cut off" date is January 1. Thus the "normal" age range for children beginning first grade in September is from 5 years 9 months (born in December) to 6 years 9 months (born in January of that year).

However, a few parents sought official permission to place their children in first grade a year early, as young as 4 years 9 months. Today, less than 2 percent of children enter first grade early, as compared with 20 percent in 1960 (Ministère 1991b). However, the strategy was prominent in the schools I visited in 1978–79, and it was employed most often by the better-educated parents. (Perhaps they had in mind that children who graduated young from high school would have more years in which to try to pass the entrance examinations for France's highly selective postsecondary *grandes écoles*, which have an age-limit for entry [Mendras and Cole 1988:100].) Five of the twenty-three children in Madame Durand's class, two of Monsieur Alain's twenty-two students, and one of Madame Berger's twenty-seven students had entered first grade a year early, and of these children, 50 percent had professional parents or guardians and only 12 percent had working-class parents (the remaining children came from the "intermediate" classes).

Meanwhile, teachers traditionally retained—or "flunked," to use the English vernacular—first graders who did not learn to read. Thus, two children in Madame Durand's class, three in Monsieur Alain's, and three in Madame Berger's were repeating first grade. Again, there was a relation to milieu; 75 percent of the repeaters had working-class parents and none of them had professional parents.

As a result of repeating and skipping, first-graders' ages actually covered a three-year range. When school began in September, 1978, the first-graders in my three principal informants' classes ranged in age from 7 years 6 months to 4 years 10 months.

Despite the teachers' general preference for older students, those children who entered first grade a year ahead were *more likely* than the other, older children to be identified as excellent students. In the three classrooms in question, 38 percent of the grade-skippers (3 out of 8), but only 13 percent of the children "on schedule" (7 out of 56) and none of the eight repeaters were judged to be superior readers by their teachers at the end of the year. The paradox, then, was that, while teachers in France considered *older* students better than *younger*, they tended to see the *youngest* students as the best. Meanwhile, the *oldest* students, the repeaters, were already marked by failure.

The paradox is hardly surprising once social class is taken into account, for, as noted, many of the grade-skippers came from professional families: Florence's grandmother and sometime guardian was a nursery-school director, Michel's father was a professor, and Didier's and Yann's fathers were doctors. These well-educated adults knew the best strategies for long-range school success and could provide their children with the "cultural capital" to succeed from the earliest grades. Indeed, Madame Durand observed sardonically that Yann's life at home had turned him into a "word mill." Madame Corneille, a nursery-school director, cast milieu in a more positive light:

> Those who skip from the 4-year-old class of nursery school directly to first grade are gifted (*doués*), mature . . . and are often the best in first grade, too. It's a question of intelligence and milieu—their parents are doctors, professors, schoolteachers.

Her comment expressed what Bourdieu and Passeron (1977) call the "ideology of the gift"—the assumption that children of professionals manifest effortless, natural talent.

"Immaturity"

Obviously, then, teachers in Villefleurie did not assume that academic or mental "maturity" always depended on chronological age. As one teacher put it, "Some children are behind what's normal for a 6-year-old. Naturally, what's normal is relative, but one can still say they're behind others in the class." Madame Berger labeled as "the little ones" not the smallest, nor, in all cases, the youngest children in her class, but rather those whom she felt "needed her all the time," as opposed to the "more mature" students. Another teacher commented about a 6-year-old boy, "Sébastien was tested by the psychologist, who found that, as far as reading and math go, he has the age—that is, the level—of 5 years 3 months to 5 years 6 months, so he cannot learn to read." She made it dramatically clear that she predicted performance on the basis of "developmental," not chronological, age.

Beliefs of U.S. Teachers

Teachers in the United States hold similar beliefs about age and "maturity." For example, one of the kindergarten teachers interviewed by Mary Lee Smith (1989) commented on chronological age: "If you take an average group of 6-year-olds and an average group of 5-year-olds, the 6-year-olds will be able to sit and do one thing longer" (1989:137). The same teacher added an observation about "maturity," saying, "But the timeline differs so much from child to child." Similarly, another of Smith's informants said, "Some children when they come to school are ready for the school situation. . . . Other children are just not ready developmentally" (1989:136). Elizabeth Graue elicited similar beliefs in her case studies of three kindergarten teachers (1993), as did Tomchin and Impara in their survey research (1992).

FALLING BEHIND

Age and "maturity" matter because schools are built around the expectation that children move through predefined stages of learning according to a predictable schedule. In this section I examine the various ways in which academic failure gets defined as *falling behind schedule* in France and in the United States.

A Schedule of Expectations in Villefleurie

When talking about students and explaining their performance in class, teachers in Villefleurie used a rich vocabulary and wove anecdotes about individual children into sometimes rather elaborate theories (Anderson-Levitt, f.c.). However, when I asked the teachers to talk specifically about the children's performance in reading, they assessed it very specifically in terms of the *timing* of key events— events they cast as stages in learning to read:

1. From the beginning of first grade, the teachers said, most children should be able to *"read globally,"* by which they meant to recognize a few words by sight.
2. By January or February, they expected that many first-graders would *"decode,"* by which they meant to sound out words.
3. By the end of the school year, they expected many first-graders to *"read fluently,"* by which they meant to read with a smoothness that implied understanding what one read.

There was wide agreement among my informants about the order of these presumed stages and the pace at which children were supposed to move through them (Anderson-Levitt 1987).

Students whom the teachers called "average" or "good" were those identified as moving through the stages of learning to read according to this schedule. The handful of children they called "strong" students were those they described as "already decoding" at the beginning of the year or "already reading fluently" before Christmas, from 2 to 4 months "ahead of schedule." The "weak" students were the children who were "not yet decoding" by the end of the year and thus were far "behind schedule" (Anderson-Levitt, f.c.).

Of course, the teachers also described good students as "paying attention," "making an effort," "working by themselves," and "participating." However, the importance of "paying attention," or any other criterion, varied depending on whether the teacher considered the child to be "on schedule," "ahead," or "behind" in reading. For instance, there were certain students who, in Madame Durand's eyes, "acted like babies" or failed to "pay attention" or "apply themselves," but whom she *nonetheless* identified as superior students because they had persuaded her they were "decoding" ahead of schedule. Similarly, in September Madame Berger classified young Didier with "the little ones" because of his sloppy writing, but she soon recategorized him as a good student because she observed that he learned to "decode" quickly. Thus, public demonstration of "decoding" was the one conclusive indicator of academic ability.

The students' experiences. Although my research focused on the teachers' perspective, I inevitably observed students' classroom behavior, and their behavior hinted at the varying degrees to which they accepted or resisted school-generated identities of "ahead" and "behind." Despite occasional fidgeting, yawns, and whispering, many of the "strong" readers participated enthusiastically. In fact, some of them volunteered demonstrations of their skills rather than waiting passively for the teacher to recognize their capabilities. For example, very early in the year in Madame Durand's classroom, Florence proved her knowledge by volunteering to decipher a label that said "*Fromage* (cheese)." In early December, one boy in Monsieur Alain's class wrote on his slate "*la pétrole* (oil)" and "*léopare*" (his phonetic version of "leopard"). "He's understood everything, how to put together words," Monsieur Alain noted with approval.

For students who could not or would not demonstrate in a timely manner the ability to "decode," first grade was a far different experience. In the classrooms I followed, the teachers put pressure on the "weak" students—at least those not considered hopeless cases—to perform. Madame Durand, for example, once cajoled and scolded "weak" student Jacques through the reading of a long text at the board, syllable by painful syllable, before allowing a "strong" student to "reread it as it should be read." Seen through my own cultural lenses, Jacques appeared nervous, flustered, and unhappy throughout the months I observed him. However, I heard almost no discussion of the need to protect a child's "self-esteem," and in some classrooms tears were treated as a normal part of learning to read.

Many of the "weak" readers manifested what the teachers called a "will" to succeed. There were even a few children who started out on the wrong foot but at some point in March or April successfully demonstrated "decoding." Here, it is important to make clear that most instruction in Villefleurie was whole-class instruction; first-graders were not placed into "ability groups" until springtime, if at all, and even then teachers usually continued whole-class instruction for morning reading lessons. Therefore all children, whether "ahead of" or "behind" schedule in their grasp of reading, received essentially the same instruction through most or all of the year, thus easing the task of a child who tried to "catch up."

While most students cooperated, however, a few children appeared to resist the pressure to demonstrate that they could "decode." For instance, Madame Berger's student Claude turned in a blank sheet when the class did its first pen-and-paper dictation. Monsieur Alain said of his student Carole, who was already repeating first grade, "She does nothing. . . . She copies everything from her neighbors and boasts about it to her mother. . . . I admit I'm in the dark; I have no hypothesis. She has an opposition." Carole's brother Grégoire, who was in the same class, was even more puzzling because Monsieur Alain had discovered that "he reads words the others don't read," complicated word like *sauvage* (wild), but refused to do it on demand.

Repeating and Skipping Grades

French children who resisted the school's schedule by refusing to read "on time" risked having to repeat first grade. Repeating was the traditional treatment for students who did not "decode" by the end of the year. Thus students who "fell behind" by a few months during first grade could end up an additional year behind their classmates.

Note that it was not the demonstration of "decoding" per se that mattered, for almost every student in France eventually demonstrated "decoding" (although perhaps not "fluent reading"). Most of the children who were already repeating first grade in my informants' classrooms persuaded their teacher that they could "decode" reasonably well by the end of their second year in first grade. Rather, it was the *timing* of the achievements that mattered. Not having "decoded" on time and having repeated a grade, those children had a much lower chance than average of ever succeeding in the academic track.[2]

Falling Behind in U.S. Classrooms

In the United States, one way children fall behind is to get placed in the low reading group, where they will receive instruction at a slower pace. In contrast to practice in France, grouping is not only nearly universal but usually begins very early in the year in the United States (Wilkinson 1988–89:290; Barr and Dreeben 1983).[3]

To check first-hand on the pervasiveness of grouping, I visited seven classrooms (4 first grades, 2 first/seconds, 1 second grade) in the Los Angeles area in 1978 as well as one first grade in the Detroit area in 1988. In every classroom, whether the school was public or Catholic, whether the children were poor or affluent, the teachers divided the class into three or four reading groups during part of the day, and in all but one classroom the teacher grouped homogeneously.

Typically, each reading group in a classroom moves through the same series of published workbooks and readers, encountering new vocabulary and new elements of phonics as they go. (The one exception I witnessed was a separate Spanish-language group in one Los Angeles classroom.) As a result, every group is ahead of or behind every other group in the classroom, and the differences among groups can be measured in months (cf. Collins 1986:123), just as one can measure the differences among individual children in French classrooms.

The difference between two groups can also be measured by comparing the number of concepts taught. U.S. educators deliberately teach low groups less, in the belief that these children will learn better when burdened with less material (Barr and Dreeban 1983:108); another rationale is to protect a child's "self-esteem." In the fifteen carefully sampled first grades studied by Barr and Dreeben (1983), the high groups encountered an average of 288 basal vocabulary words and the low groups 93; the high groups covered an average of 54 phonics concepts and the low groups 31 (1983:112). Moreover, the amount that individual children actually learned depended mainly on how much they were taught (1983:130ff.). Thus the attempt to protect members of the low group from instruction put them further "behind schedule."

Retention and Delayed Entry in the United States

According to David Larabee (1984), educators introduced ability grouping in the United States as a strategy to reduce retention rates without abandoning emphasis on achievement and selection. Nevertheless, recently U.S. teachers have been retaining more and more children in kindergarten and the primary grades. Shepard and Smith (1989) report rates of retention in first grade ranging from 1.6 percent to 20 percent, with an average by state of 11 percent, for the 1985–86 school year.[4] These rates of retention have risen markedly since 1970 (Shepard and Smith 1989:6) and, if the figures are accurate, the first-grade retention rate in the United States now surpasses the French rate, which has declined to below 9 percent (Ministère 1991b:59).

Meanwhile, more and more U.S. children are entering first grade a year later than the legal entry age of about 6. Sometimes the delay takes the form of a belated entry into kindergarten, a practice called "red-shirting" (see Graue 1993). Sometimes it takes the form of retention for an extra year in kindergarten, sometimes of placement in a "developmental first grade" or "junior first grade" to be followed by placement in an ordinary first grade the year after. Walsh (1989) found that as many as 48 percent of kindergartners in some Virginia schools were not promoted to regular first grades in the 1988–89 school year.

Remarkably, these delays for individual children are taking place in the context of newly legislated delays of school entry for entire cohorts of children. Many U.S. districts have raised the minimum school-entry age. In the 1950s, children usually had to reach their sixth birthday by December 1 or January 1 in order to attend first grade, but today two-thirds of the states use a cut-off date of October 1 or earlier—some as early as July 1 (Graue 1993). July 1 is half a year earlier than France's January 1 cut off.

Also in contrast to the situation in France, where better-educated parents were more likely to request that their children be *accelerated*, in at least some U.S. school districts better-educated parents intervene to see that their children are *held back* a year (Graue 1993; Lareau 1992). For instance, Graue (1993) contrasts a suburban middle-class kindergarten, where almost a quarter of the parents had chosen to delay their child's entry, with a rural working-class kindergarten, where it never occurred to parents to do so. Unlike the French professional parents, who may have been anticipating age limits for entry into the top postsecondary schools, the U.S. middle-class parents' concern was to ensure that their children would be among the most accomplished members of their kindergarten and first-grade classes—and an older child was likely to be seen as more accomplished.

"Ahead" and "Behind" as the Common Idiom of Achievement

In terms of the experiences and strategies of the individual actors, French and U.S. practices differ significantly. Teachers and parents in France consider it nearly impossible, and certainly inequitable, to teach reading in small, homogeneous groups, whereas U.S. teachers say it is impossible *not* to group (Anderson-Levitt, forthcoming). Well-educated parents in France accelerate their children, while their U.S. peers hold their children back. Most importantly, children's experiences differ dramatically inside the classroom. Essentially, certain first-graders in France "fall behind schedule" and *then* teachers identify them as "weak" students. In the United States, teachers identify certain first-graders as "weak" students and *then* the children fall behind by moving very slowly through the curriculum in the low ability group. Meanwhile, the "weak" students in France get taught the same curriculum as their classmates throughout the year, albeit at the cost, in many classrooms, of scolding and shaming from the teacher. "Weak" students in the United States usually escape that kind of pressure, but neither do they have the opportunity to learn as much as their classmates.

Despite these very real differences, however, practices in both countries draw on the same underlying logic. *Learning to read is construed as a series of stages, and failure consists of "falling behind schedule" in mastering them.*

Teachers in France take that view so much for granted that the phrases "*en retard* (behind schedule)" and "*en avance* (ahead of schedule)" serve as a common idiom for talking about problematic students and superior students. What's more, teachers sometimes refer to entire schools as "ahead" (in bourgeois neighborhoods) or "behind" (in housing projects). Teachers in the United States likewise use metaphors of timing and speed for success and failure. It is no accident, I will argue, that such talk conjures the image of school as a racetrack with students as the competitors.

INSTITUTIONAL ARRANGEMENTS BEHIND THE FASCINATION WITH TIMING

Where did the idea that children can "fall behind," whether French or U.S. style, come from? How did the fascination with precise chronological and developmental age originate? This section argues that these ideas presuppose three institutional arrangements. First, instruction must be organized as a series of stages or grades. Second, children must begin moving through the stages or grades at a specified chronological age. Third, students must move through those stages or grades in groups rather than as individuals.

Stages of Instruction

Children can't "fall behind schedule" if there is no schedule, of course. Now, in Villefleurie, as one might expect to find anywhere, the teachers' implicit schedule for children's *learning*, noted above, corresponded to the stages of *instruction*. That is, most children had already been exposed to a bit of "global reading" in nursery school. (In France, virtually all children attend a 3-year-long nursery school/kindergarten, which is called *école maternelle*, from the time they are 3 years old.) First-grade teachers introduced "decoding" some 6 or 7 weeks after the beginning of the year, and they expected many children to "read fluently" by the end of June, because by that time their classes would have studied the sounds of most letters and would have practiced a great deal of oral reading (Anderson-Levitt 1987).

As the history of Western schooling reveals, these stages of instruction, and the corresponding schedule of expectations for student learning, are culturally arbitrary, not inherent in the task (if it *is* a single task!) of learning to read. By way of contrast, in seventeenth-century France, children learned to read in Latin first, then in French (Claeyssen 1980). In the eighteenth century, French children learned to read first and learned to write only as a second, optional stage (Maynes 1985), whereas today in France learning to write is part and parcel of learning to read. The "monitorial" or "Lancasterian" schools that spread through France in the early nineteenth century[5] divided the reading curriculum into *eight* stages rather than three (Vincent 1980).

By the 1880s, the one-room school rather than the monitorial school was the norm in France, and the curriculum avoided rigid stages of instruction. In 1923, however, the Ministry of Education established a systematically graded curriculum in its Official Instructions for teachers (Prost 1981; Vincent 1980). In the 1923 Instructions—and not before—one finds a timetable for learning to read that is similar to the one my informants in Villefleurie used: The ideal student would "know how to read" (that is, to "decode") after 3 months of instruction, and would "read fluently" by the end of first grade (Ministère 1934:16–18).

Meanwhile, in the United States, the standardization of stages or grades of instruction coincided with the development of large, graded, urban schools. One watershed was the appearance in 1836 of the first McGuffey Readers, graded through six levels (Goodlad and Anderson 1963:47), and another was the publication in 1862 of an influential graded curriculum for Chicago schools (Tyack 1974:45–46). In the United States, as in France, organizing instruction into stages helped coordinate the work of supervising large numbers of teachers in huge educational institutions. A graded system of instruction meant that ministries, inspectors, superintendents and principals would know exactly what teachers at each level should be doing, and exactly what students ought to be learning every few months.

Linking Stage with Age

The institutional arrangement that encourages elaboration of the concept of "immaturity" is the requirement that children begin moving through a given set of stages or grades at a specified chronological age. The age for school entry became fixed, however, only when authorities passed and enforced laws making schooling compulsory.

A school-entry age of about 6 years evolved slowly in Europe. By the seventeenth century, most children started school between ages 4 and 8 in England, France, and Germany (Maynes 1985:88). By the 1830s, most children began British National School at ages 6 to 8, and most children entered school in southern France at age 5 (Maynes 1985). Fifty years later France made primary school compulsory and legally fixed the age of school entry at 6 years.

Meanwhile, in the early nineteenth century in the United States, starting age varied from place to place (Goodlad and Anderson 1963:48). Gradually, between 1852 and 1918, one state after another passed laws that required compulsory attendance and hence established legal ages for school entry.

Holding starting age constant and comparing it to children's stages or levels inclines one to compare children in terms of achievement, and to use the metaphor of "age" to describe that achievement. Although children all start at the same age, they perform differently in class; as we saw, teachers see some 6-year-olds as "reading fluently" at the same time that they see others as simply "decoding" and some as "not yet decoding." It is an easy next step to claim that the majority of children will "reach" a certain stage by age 6. The few 6-year-olds who go "further" are more like 7-year-olds, hence they are (mentally) "old" for their age, that is, very "mature." Those who don't go that "far" are more like 5-year-olds, hence "young" for their age or "immature." Thus the concept of "mental age" or "maturity" derives not from some "natural" process of learning or development, but from the combination of two institutional arrangements: graded instruction and a fixed starting age.

Batch Production

If children begin school at the same age, why do teachers talk so much about "old" and "young" first-graders? Attention to precise chronological age makes sense only in light of a third institutional arrangement, the instruction of children in groups rather than as individuals, or what Larabee calls "large-scale batch production" (1984:69).

Even when instruction is organized according to graded stages, batch production is not a necessity. The system may move learners through the stages at an individual pace, as did the "dame schools" of seventeenth-century North America and the one-room schools of eighteenth-century Europe (Maynes 1985:29). Advancement through the strictly graded monitorial schools was also an individual affair (Vincent 1980:69).

Moving children through stages in batches was an innovation introduced in France by the Christian Brothers, La Salle's order. In schools like theirs, which served up to half the male pupils in eighteenth-century France (Maynes 1985:30; Vincent 1980:66), more or less homogeneous groups received "simultaneous" rather than individual instruction and moved together through a precisely graded curriculum.[6] However, the Christian Brothers' schools eventually disappeared and most of the public schools that spread through France a century later were small, ungraded, rural schools. As late as 1900, 65 percent of France's primaries were one-room schools (Grew and Harrigan 1991) where children were likely to move at an individual pace. Multigrade schools, which invite batch production, became the norm in France only in the 1950s (Prost 1981).

Instruction of children in graded groups rather than individually began in the United States—indeed, was promoted as a significant educational reform—with the population boom and expansion of urban schools in the mid-nineteenth century. The first school built to house a number of separate grades opened in 1848 and thenceforth served as a model for urban school architecture (Goodlad and Anderson 1963:48–49; Tyack 1974:44–45).

One common feature of batch production today is that all members of a class begin school on the same day of the year. Whereas the rural French children Wylie (1974) observed in the 1950s began their studies on the day of their birthday, and some urban school districts in the United States used to let children begin their studies in either September or January, nowadays in both countries virtually all children begin their school careers on a specified day in September. This feature of batch production means that children do not begin moving through the stages of instruction at *exactly* the same age. The legal school-entry age is actually a range of ages within a twelve-month year; for example, in France, given a January 1 cut-off, the school-entry age of 6 captures the range from 5 years 9 months to 6 years 9 months.

In the context of the four-*year* range of school-starting ages of the seventeenth century, this twelve-*month* range would have appeared negligible. Even in the context of the three-year age range of real French first-graders (including the grade-skippers and grade-repeaters), one might think this twelve-month range unremarkable. However, educators seem to focus on legal age and not the actual age range of first-graders, and, given the pretense that "almost all" children start first grade at age 6, age differences of just a few months become newly salient. As one prominent French developmental psychologist put it,

> The legal [school-entry] age is not point-like; it has a breadth of one year. . . . This 12-month range coming at the beginning of the school career . . . translates into considerable differences, as much mental as physical. . . . *The legal criterion of age, although seemingly homogenizing, is in fact a source of differences among the new schoolchildren.* (Zazzo 1978:170, my translation and my emphasis)

Imagine a seventeenth-century educator or a twentieth-century Kapsiki parent trying to make sense of this remarkable argument! Still, however astounding in a broad global and historical context, the focus on age in months makes sense in the specific context of graded instruction, a fixed school-entry age, and a fixed date for the beginning of the school year.

Mass Education and the Science of Psychology

Many teachers would argue that the concept of "maturity" or "mental age" comes not from institutional requirements of schooling, but from the science of psychology. It turns out, however, that psychologists' versions of these ideas also spring from the same roots, the development of mass education.

Alfred Binet and his collaborators were the first psychologists to use age as a yardstick of mental ability (Fancher 1985; Linden and Linden 1968). They linked stage to age by the process already described. Identifying what they considered to be the "intellectual level" of the average 6-year-old child, they then reasoned that a 7-year-old who performed at the same "level" manifested a one-year "delay."

The establishment of compulsory mass education explains the timing of Binet's insight. France had made elementary schooling mandatory in 1882, and by 1904 the Ministry of Public Instruction was grappling with the problem of mentally subnormal students—children who used to attend school few years, if at all, but now had to attend from ages 6 to 13. The ministry commissioned Binet to identify children who needed special education, and Binet and his colleague Simon hit upon age as a measure because they were the first researchers in the field of intelligence to work with children rather than adults (Fancher 1985).

Quantification led to finer and finer measures of intellectual level—and chronological age. When calculating a child's "intellectual level"—what later researchers, though never Binet, called "mental age"—Binet divided each year into decimals to reflect the number of test questions for each age. Later testers continued his practice of measuring "mental age" in fractions of years, but expressed it in months rather than decimals. In 1914, William Stern modified Binet's idea of "intellectual level" by expressing it as the *quotient* of "mental age" divided by chronological age, rather than as the *difference*—that is, the delay—between them. Terman multiplied the quotient by 100 to produce the familiar IQ scale (Fancher 1985).

Binet was hardly the only psychologist inspired by mass schooling. American psychologists developed a number of intelligence and achievement tests from 1910 to 1918 (Linden and Linden 1968), culminating in mass intelligence testing during World War I, and the eventual entrance of the concept of "mental age" into popular culture. By no coincidence, the emergence of standardized testing occurred almost simultaneously with an outcry over the number of children falling behind grade level in U.S. schools (Morgenstern 1966). During the same era, the study of child development became a field of systematic scientific inquiry, also drawing increased attention to chronological and mental age. Again by no coincidence, one of the fathers of developmental psychology, Jean Piaget, began his psychology career working in Binet's laboratory to improve Binet's intelligence test (Cleverley and Phillips 1986).

CONCLUSION AND DISCUSSION

Many of the authors in this book ask how schooling can transform identities in the course of producing "educated persons." I have argued that mass education inserted chronological age and "mental age" as new elements in the identity of schoolchildren. Specifically, in France and the United States, since about the turn of the century (at least in urban areas), mass schooling has combined graded instruction, batch production, and a legally mandated school-entry age. Instruction by stages or grades has made "falling behind" and "getting ahead" key metaphors for academic success and failure. Historically, graded instruction, in combination with a compulsory starting age, encouraged (very specifically, in the case of Binet's theorizing) the elaboration of a concept of delayed intellectual level, or "immaturity." Those two institutional arrangements, in combination with a kind of batch production that requires all children within a 12-month age span to begin school on the same day, led to a focus on precise chronological age. In short, mass schooling as our societies have organized it has encouraged educators to produce such identities for children as "the student who is behind in learning to read," "the immature child," and "the December birthday." It has led us to measure children's ages and academic achievements in units of months, not years.

Ironically, we schedule childhood according to the most precise and unforgiving timetable in just those societies that have achieved the longest human life-spans and have constructed the most protracted "adolescences." At present, less industrialized nations, where life expectancies are much shorter, do not schedule childhood so rigidly. Although 94 percent of the world's children now attend school for at least a year or two (World Bank 1994:217), compulsory school-entry ages are not so well enforced that every child begins at the same age, nor do children (or teachers) attend so regularly that the starting date significantly differentiates among them (e.g., Baker 1988; Fuller 1991; Stevenson 1982).

School as Factory, School as Racetrack

The analysis so far has implied the metaphor of school-as-factory, where children are batch produced on the "assembly line" of graded instruction, and speed is highly valued. Indeed, nineteenth-century school reformers in the United States deliberately drew on the factory metaphor, which they viewed positively, to guide their efforts to find an "efficient" way to educate the masses (Tyack 1974:41–42). Metaphors aside, industrialization explains why urban schools grew so large that they seemed to require graded instruction and batch production, and the fact that France industrialized and urbanized later than the United States probably explains why multigrade schools became the norm so much later in France.

The factory metaphor suits schooling when the entire system is viewed from the outside. However, seen from inside classrooms, a different metaphor (albeit still linear, like the image of the assembly line) is more apt. Teachers' use of "ahead" and "behind" as the idiom of achievement makes going to school sound like running a race, and the racetrack metaphor fits well. The contestants all begin from the same starting place, that is, at the same age; they all take off at the same point in time, the beginning of the school year; they all move along the same linear path, that is, through the stages or grades of the curriculum. Moreover, as Suzanne Mollo-Bouvier puts it, the race—which she refers to as an obstacle course—is "richly endowed with prizes for the winners" (1986:164).

In fact, those who "fall behind" lose prizes. French children who fail to demonstrate "on time" that they "decode" are often retained, and they then stand a smaller chance of making it to academic high school (Levasseur and Seibel 1984). In the United States, children held back because they are "immature" will probably not improve their situation by repeating a grade (Jackson 1975; Shepard and Smith 1989), while children placed in the low group because they are not "ready" fall further "behind" (Oakes 1992).

What is wrong with structuring the school as a racetrack? First, as the French-U.S. comparison has hinted, the ways in which children are sorted by the timing of their achievements contain more than an element of arbitrariness (cf. Downing 1977). Whole-class instruction in France and ability grouping in the United States would not put exactly the same group of children at risk if the children were to magically switch countries. In France, children who "fall behind" during first grade, but who continue to profit from whole-class instruction, have a chance of "catching up" by the end of the year; if they had fallen behind in the United States they would not have had that chance. On the other hand, an emotionally sensitive French child may crumble from the shame of performing poorly in front of the whole class, as Jacques seemed to do; in the United States, such a child might have found some protection in the low-ability group.

However, the deeper problem is that we sort by timing at all. In doing so we accept the premise that learning takes place in stages along a narrow linear path, as if one could learn more only by progressing further along that path instead of by wandering off the track. This is the same flawed idea that Stephen Jay Gould finds at the core of intelligence measurement (a phenomenon closely related to schooling, as we have seen). He calls it the "fallacy of ranking," that is, "our propensity for ordering complex variation as a gradual ascending scale" (1981:24). Learning to read, or learning anything, for that matter, is actually a process of "complex variation." Different children learn to read at different times and in different ways, as a number of Villefleurie teachers acknowledged. To rank those children nonetheless as "ahead" and "behind" is to reduce the "complex variation" among the children to a single linear scale. Such a ranking falsely portrays their real talents and achievements.

Deeper yet is the problem that schools sort, period. Like the ideology of the "gift," to which it is closely allied, the ideology of "immaturity," however arbitrary, serves to legitimize that sorting. The ideology rationalizes the success of children whose families have given them the "cultural capital" they call on to demonstrate "decoding" or other presumed stages of learning "ahead of schedule." It locates their success inside the children, defining them as "naturally" precocious. In France, "precocious" children tend to be the offspring of the upper class and upper-middle class (mostly professionals)—and also of elementary teachers, who are defined as merely middle class but who possess special insight about what their children have to do to get ahead in school (Levasseur and Seibel 1984). These "precocious" children make it to the finish-line first.

Tensions over Stages and Their Timing

Curiously, as convenient as the "immaturity" ideology is for people in power, the Ministry of Education and scholars who inform its policy have apparently tried to undermine the notion since the early 1970s. The Ministry's official instructions to teachers in 1972 *explicitly repudiated* the 1923 schedule for learning to read that had been in force for almost fifty years (Ministère 1973:14–15). Since then, the Ministry, and at least some of its inspectors in the Villefleurie area, have been lobbying hard *against* the idea that all children must decode by the end of first grade (Ministère 1977, 1985). Most dramatically, in 1989 the Minister of Education launched a reform requiring that reading be taught over the course of a three-year period, from kindergarten through second grade, and forbidding retention of students within that period (Ministère 1991a).

Now, not all Villefleurie teachers embraced the idea of instructional stages unreservedly. As one teacher commented uneasily about the timing of "decoding," "We impose this moment on them." Some teachers complained that they felt constrained by the Ministry of Education's program of instruction. "Do you realize all they have to learn in first grade?," exclaimed one second-grade teacher.

Nonetheless, and in spite of the Ministry's new prohibition on holding back first-graders, many teachers I observed as late as 1988 still maintained the criterion of "decoding" for promoting students to second grade. Some continued to retain two or three students every year, and others, to avoid disputes with the local inspector, created strategies such as first/second grades in which weak "second-graders" would actually repeat the first-grade program. Teachers are still using similar strategies today, at least in middle-class schools (Duhart 1994).

These cracks and contradictions between teachers and the Ministry may surprise those who imagine the "educational apparatus" in France to be a centralized, state-run monolith. However, hegemonic ideas need not be coherent (Reed-Danahay and Anderson-Levitt 1991), nor need the people who promote them speak with one voice (Hannerz 1992), not even in France. The Ministry itself is sending a mixed message. On the one hand, it is officially sanctioning the situation of schools in the poorest neighborhoods, where all children "fall behind," probably in order to mollify the angry and frustrated teachers who work in those schools (Karen Duhart, personal communication). On the other hand, although advancing the deadline for "decoding" by a year, the Ministry still retains the language of the racetrack in its reforms. Meanwhile, whatever the Ministry says, teachers remain the arbiters of academic success on the ground. Those who teach in the less impoverished neighborhoods have no reason to abandon an ideology that meshes so well with the structure of their institutions, not to mention with their own children's achievements. Besides, why shouldn't they resist promoting all first graders as long as the Ministry holds them responsible for the old second-grade curriculum as well as the new?

Contradictions in the Way "Immaturity" Gets Institutionalized

This chapter has examined teachers' talk about students, and the relationship of that talk to the institutional arrangements of schooling. But the symbolic messages built right into the institutional arrangements also invite examination.

Educators have long wavered between a model of "maturity" that emphasizes biological maturation, and one that emphasizes the acquisition of skills prerequisite to the new task at hand. Although individual teachers in the United States and France may subscribe to either view, the organization of schooling in the two countries implicitly institutionalizes different models of "immaturity." The U.S. system operates more or less as if "readiness" were a matter of the child's inner development; educators protect "immature" children from too much instruction, as if the children need more time rather than more instruction. Indeed, the new cut-off dates in many states give entire cohorts of children "the gift of time." In contrast, the French system is organized as if "immaturity" were primarily a lack of prerequisite skills; weak readers receive the same instruction as everyone else, as if they just might benefit from it. No one questions the minimum school-entry age of 5 years 9 months.

"Immaturity"—or "stupidity"? Although each country's practice takes a different slant on "maturity," both systems ultimately construct in the students they label "immature" something that resembles our notion of "stupidity" more than mere "delay."

Binet, you recall, expressed academic problems in terms of delay, that is, number of years behind grade level. His measure resembled the notion of "immaturity," strictly defined, because he did not rule out the possibility that "delayed" children might someday "catch up" with those on schedule. He would have taken terms like mental "retardation" or developmental "delay" more literally than we do today; in fact, he believed in educating "retarded" children to help them "catch up" (Binet 1909; Gould 1981). When Stern and Terman measured intellectual ability in terms of a quotient, however, they transformed Binet's concept into a notion of intelligence as we usually understand it now, that is, as a quantity remaining constant over one's lifetime. A constant intelligence quotient means that the older the child, the further "behind" they fall.

Given the way ability grouping works in the United States, and retention in both France and the United States, children who "fall behind" in either country are likely to fall further behind over time. At first, the accepted schedule for learning to read distinguishes good from poor performance in terms of only a few months' difference in the timing of "decoding" or other key achievements. However, the gap soon widens. Those children who "fall behind" by a few months soon fall behind several more months if assigned to the low reading group; they fall behind by a full year if flunked. Meanwhile, those who demonstrate that they are a few months "ahead" of schedule get the opportunity to jump several more months ahead by joining the high reading group or, albeit less often, to jump a year ahead by skipping a grade.

Because the gap widens as children get older, the phenomenon in question resembles an intelligence quotient more than it resembles "immaturity" strictly defined. Few of the "late bloomers" catch up with the "early bloomers." For all educators' talk about "immaturity," schools operate over the long run to ensure that most failing children look "stupid," not "immature." Mass education leads to a discourse about "immaturity," but actually constructs "stupidity."

NOTES

The research described here was made possible by the Council for European Studies, the National Institute of Mental Health, the National Science Foundation, the University of Michigan Rackham Fund, and University of Michigan–Dearborn grants. I am also indebted to many educators in France and the United States, and to Bradley Levinson, Douglas Foley, Deborah Reed-Danahay, Elsie Rockwell, and Daniel Moerman for their insights—those I've absorbed and those I haven't.

Since my description of school in the United States does not apply to Latin American nor even necessarily to Canadian schools, I use "U.S." as an adjective despite its awkwardness.

1. Villefleurie's schools are fairly typical of schools in provincial France, all the more so because education is centrally controlled by a national Ministry of Education. Most of what I observed in Villefleurie resembles other descriptions of urban and suburban schools in France (e.g., Henriot-van Zanten 1990; Mollo-Bouvier 1986; Sharpe 1992; Sirota 1988).

2. Levasseur and Seibel (1984) report that 93 percent of students who repeat first grade, as opposed to 54 percent of the population in general, never make it to *lycée* (academic high school).

3. Barr and Dreeben used data from the late 1960s, but more recent surveys and case studies jibe with their findings. For details on how reading groups operate in the United States, see, for example, Allington (1983), Cazden (1988), Collins (1986), Eder (1986), McDermott and Gospodinoff (1978).

4. Data were available from only thirteen states.

5. In "monitorial" schools, a single teacher supervised the instruction of hundreds of students in one large hall. Monitors listened to small groups of students recite their lessons and passed successful students on to the next level (see Maynes 1985).

6. Whereas the schools Larabee (1984) describes associated batch production with efficiency, Vincent (1980) points out that graded group instruction in Christian Brothers schools was *not* intended to "improve productivity." Rather, the brothers moved students through the minute stages of instruction at a painfully slow pace in order to keep the boys in school studying catechism as many years as possible.

REFERENCES

Allington, Richard L. 1983. The Reading Instruction Provided Readers of Differing Reading Abilities. Elementary School Journal 83(5):548–559.

Anderson-Levitt, Kathryn M. 1987. Cultural Knowledge for Teaching First Grade: An Example from France. *In* Interpretive Ethnography of Education. George D.

Spindler and Louise Spindler, eds. Pp. 171–192. Hillsdale, NJ: Lawrence Erlbaum Associates.

———. forthcoming. Teaching Cultures: Knowledge for Teaching First Grade in France and the United States. Cresskill, NJ: Hampton Press.

Ariès, Philippe. 1962. Centuries of Childhood. New York: Vintage (Random House).

Baker, Victoria J. 1988. The Blackboard in the Jungle: Formal Education in Disadvantaged Rural Areas, a Sri Lankan Case. Delft, Netherlands: Eburon.

Barr, Rebecca, and Robert Dreeben. 1983. How Schools Work. Chicago: University of Chicago Press.

Binet, Alfred. 1973 [1909]. Les Idées Modernes sur les Enfants. Paris: Flammarion.

Bourdieu, Pierre, and Jean-Claude Passeron. 1977. Reproduction in Education, Society and Culture. Beverly Hills: Sage Publications.

Cazden, Courtney B. 1988. Differential Treatment. *In* Classroom Language: The Language of Teaching and Learning. Portsmouth, NH: Heinemann.

Claeyssen, Michel. 1980. L'Enseignement de la Lecture au 18e Siècle. *In* The Making of Frenchmen: Current Directions in the History of Education in France, 1679–1979. Donald N. Baker and Patrick J. Harrigan, eds. Pp. 64–74. Waterloo, Ontario: Historical Reflections Press.

Cleverley, John, and Denis C. Phillips. 1986. Visions of Childhood: Influential Models from Locke to Spock, rev. ed. New York: Teachers College Press.

Collins, James. 1986. Differential Instruction in Reading Groups. *In* The Social Construction of Literacy. Jenny Cook-Gumperz, ed. Pp. 117–137. Cambridge: Cambridge University Press.

Downing, John. 1977. How Society Creates Reading Disability. Elementary School Journal 77(4):274–279.

Duhart, Karen. 1994. Ethnographic Study of Teachers' Thinking in France. Manuscript, Anthropology apprenticeship, University of Michigan–Dearborn.

Eder, Donna. 1986. Organizational Constraints on Reading Group Mobility. *In* The Social Construction of Literacy. Jenny Cook-Gumperz, ed. Pp. 138–155. Cambridge: Cambridge University Press.

Fancher, Raymond E. 1985. The Intelligence Men: Makers of the IQ Controversy. New York: W. W. Norton & Co.

Fuller, Bruce. 1991. Growing Up Modern: The Western State Builds Third-World Schools. New York: Routledge.

Goodlad, John I., and Robert H. Anderson. 1963. The Nongraded Elementary School, rev. ed. New York: Harcourt, Brace & World.

Gould, Stephen Jay. 1981. The Mismeasure of Man. New York: W. W. Norton.

Graue, M. Elizabeth. 1993. Ready for What? Constructing Meanings of Readiness for Kindergarten. Albany: SUNY Press.

Grew, Raymond and Patrick J. Harrigan. 1991. School, State, and Society: The Growth of Elementary Schooling in Nineteenth Century France. Ann Arbor: University of Michigan Press.

Hannerz, Ulf. 1992. Cultural Complexity: Studies in the Social Organization of Meaning. New York: Columbia University Press.

Harkness, Sara and Charles M. Super. 1983. The Cultural Construction of Child Development: A Framework for the Socialization of Affect. Ethos 11(4):221–231.

Henriot-van Zanten, Agnès. 1990. L'Ecole et l'Espace Local. Les Enjeux des Zones d'Education Prioritaires. Lyon: Presses Universitaires de Lyon.

Jackson, Gregg B. 1975. The Research Evidence on the Effects of Grade Retention. Review of Educational Research 45(4):613–635.

Kirkpatrick, John T. 1985. Some Marquesan Understandings of Action and Identity. *In* Person, Self, and Experience. Geoffrey White and John Kirkpatrick, eds. Pp. 80–120. Berkeley: University of California Press.

Larabee, David F. 1984. Setting the Standard: Alternative Policies for Student Promotion. Harvard Educational Review 54(1):67–87.

Lareau, Annette. 1992. Red-shirting and Retention: Class Difference in Parental Involvement in Schooling. Paper presented at the annual meeting of the American Educational Research Association, San Francisco.

Levasseur, Jacqueline and Claude Seibel. 1984. Réussite et Echec Scolaires. Données Sociales (Institut National de la Statistique et des Etudes Economiques) 5:483–490.

Linden, Kathryn W. and James D. Linden. 1968. Modern Mental Measurement: A Historical Perspective. Boston: Houghton Mifflin.

Lutz, Catherine. 1985. Ethnopsychology Compared to What? Explaining Behavior and Consciousness among the Ifaluk. *In* Person, Self, and Experience. Geoffrey White and John Kirkpatrick, Eds. Pp. 35–79. Berkeley: University of California.

Maynes, Mary Jo. 1985. Schooling in Western Europe: A Social History. Albany: State University of New York Press.

McDermott, Raymond P. and Kenneth Gospodinoff. 1978. Social Contexts for Ethnic Borders and School Failure. *In* Nonverbal Behavior. Aaron Wolfgang, ed. Pp. 175–195. New York: Academic Press.

Mendras, Henri with Alistair Cole. 1988. Social Change in Modern France. Cambridge and Paris: Cambridge University Press and Editions de la Maison des Sciences de l'Homme.

Ministère de l'Instruction Publique et des Beaux-Arts. 1934. Plan d'Etudes et Programmes des Ecoles Primaires Elémentaires et Instructions du 20 Juin 1923. Paris: Librairie Vuibert.

Ministère de l'Education. 1973. Instructions Relatives à l'Enseignement du Français à l'Ecole Elémentaire. (Circulaire 72-474 du 7 Décembre, 1972). Paris: Imprimerie Nationale.

———. 1977. Réforme du Système Educatif. Contenus de Formation à l'Ecole Elémentaire. Cycle Préparatoire. Paris: Centre National de Documentation Pédagogique.

———. 1985. Ecole Elémentaire. Programmes et Instructions. Paris: Centre National de Documentation Pédagogique.

Ministère de l'Education Nationale. 1991a. Les Cycles à l'Ecole Primaire. Paris: Hachette/Centre National de Documentation Pédagogique.

———. 1991b. Repères et Références Statistiques sur les Enseignements et la Formation. Paris: Imprimerie Nationale.

Mollo-Bouvier, Suzanne. 1986. La Sélection Implicite à l'Ecole. Paris: Presses Universitaires de France.

Morgenstern, Anne. 1966. Historical Survey of Grouping Practices in Elementary School. *In* Grouping in the Elementary School. Anne Morgenstern, ed. Pp. 3–13. New York: Pitman Publishing Corporation.

Oakes, Jeannie. 1992. Can Tracking Research Inform Practice? Technical, Normative, and Political Considerations. Educational Researcher 21(4):12–21.

Prost, Antoine. 1981. Histoire Générale de l'Enseignement et de l'Education en France, vol. 4. L'Ecole et la Famille dans une Société en Mutation. Paris: Nouvelle Librairie de France.

Reed-Danahay, Deborah and Kathryn M. Anderson-Levitt. 1991. Backward Countryside, Troubled City: French Teachers' Images of Rural and Working-class Families. American Ethnologist 18(3):546–564.

Sharpe, Keith. 1992. Educational Homogeneity in French Primary Education: A Double Case Study. British Journal of Sociology of Education 13(3):329–348.

Shepard, Lorrie A. and Mary Lee Smith, eds. 1989. Flunking Grades: Research and Policies on Retention. New York: Falmer.

Sirota, Régine. 1988. L'Ecole Primaire au Quotidien. Paris: Presses Universitaires de France.

Smith, Mary Lee. 1989. Teachers' Beliefs about Retention. *In* Flunking Grades: Research and Policies on Retention. Lorrie A. Shepard and Mary Lee Smith, eds. Pp. 132–150. New York: Falmer.

Stevenson, Harold W. 1982. Influences of Schooling on Cognitive Development. *In* Cultural Perspectives on Child Development. Daniel A. Wagner and Harold W. Stevenson, eds. Pp. 208–224. San Francisco: W. H. Freeman.

Tomchin, Ellen M. and James C. Impara. 1992. Unraveling Teachers' Beliefs about Grade Retention. American Educational Research Journal 29(1):199–223.

Tyack, David B. 1974. The One Best System: A History of American Urban Education. Cambridge, MA: Harvard University Press.

Vincent, Guy. 1980. L'Ecole Primaire en France. Etude sociologique. Lyon: Presses Universitaires de Lyon.

Walsh, Daniel J. 1989. Changes in Kindergarten: Why Here? Why Now? Early Childhood Research Quarterly 4:377–391.

Wilkinson, Louise Cherry. 1988–89. Grouping Children for Learning: Implications for Kindergarten Education. Review of Research in Education (Ernst Z. Rothkopf, ed.) 15:203–223.

World Bank. 1994. World Development Report 1994. Oxford: Oxford University Press.

Wylie, Laurence. 1974. Village in the Vaucluse, 3rd ed. Cambridge, MA: Harvard University Press.

Zazzo, Bianka. 1978. Un Grand Passage: De l'Ecole Maternelle à l'Ecole Elémentaire. Paris: Presses Universitaires de France.

3

DOUGLAS E. FOLEY

The Silent Indian as a Cultural Production

One of the most enduring images in the educational literature is that of the silent, underachieving Indian. After reviewing how other educational anthropologists have explained the silence of Indian youth in white classrooms, I would like to present an alternative perspective derived, in part, from field research among the Mesquakis. The Mesquakis are an Algonquin-speaking tribe of one thousand presently residing on a five-thousand-acre settlement in central Iowa. They have resided there since the Black Hawk wars of the 1840s, when they relinquished their old hunting grounds—roughly the present state of Iowa. Since the Indian Reorganization Act of 1934, the Mesquakis govern themselves through an elected tribal council. Economically, the settlement is a low-income community with many social, economic, health, and educational problems. Tribal members work in the factories, nursing homes, and schools of central Iowa. The tribe also employs approximately three hundred adults in various tribal social service programs, a convenience store, and a multi-million dollar gambling operation.

Culturally, most Mesquakis still practice their native religion and speak Mesquaki. They are generally considered one of the most traditional Midwestern tribes. Educationally, the tribe runs a K–8 Bureau of Indian Affairs–contract school for approximately 25 percent of their youth. The remainder of the youth (two hundred plus) attend the K–12 program in Tama, an adjacent town of three thousand. This loss of children to the white-run town schools is a source of great consternation to many tribal leaders, and the Mesquakis have recently obtained a 7.5 million dollar grant from the Bureau of Indian Affairs (BIA) for constructing a K–12 educational complex.

My recent year of fieldwork among the Mesquakis has special meaning for me because I went to Tama High school with many of the present-day tribal and town leaders. In addition to the usual participant-observation, informant, and interview data, I have many personal memories from which to draw. I also had access to an extraordinary set of historical materials on the Mesquaki. From 1948 to 1958, the University of Chicago ran an anthropological field school on the settlement. Professor Sol Tax and his students developed what they called an "action anthropology" project to help the Mesquaki (Gearing et al. 1970; Gearing 1970). The project initiated a successful college scholarship program and several unsuccessful economic development schemes. Further, Tax and his students

79

produced a variety of popular press materials on Mesquaki culture. They hoped that these writings would counter stereotypical and racist attitudes among whites. The fieldnotes from this project generally provide an exhaustive account of post–World War II Mesquaki society and culture. They serve as a benchmark for understanding cultural and educational change in present-day Mesquaki society.

In the full account of my fieldwork (Foley 1995), I conceptualize change among the Mesquakis since World War II as a process of ethnogenesis (Roosens 1989). This study chronicles both organized Mesquaki political activity and the tribe's broader "cultural and discursive struggle" against the ideological hegemony of mainstream American culture. Put succinctly, the civil rights era spawned a new, more assertive generation of Mesquaki political leaders. In the early 1970s, the American Indian Movement (AIM) inspired a series of racial confrontations in the local bars and schools. Since that time, the tribe has taken advantage of several federal laws to encourage self-determination and economic and educational autonomy. This new generation of leaders is building a tribal welfare state based on their social service programs and gambling enterprises.

On the cultural and ideological front, these new tribal leaders—the first Mesquaki generation with greater access to higher education—are also beginning to exert control over popular and academic representations of the tribe. A young tribal historian, a crusading journalist, a heart-stopping poet/novelist, a political cartoonist, and a host of drum groups and graphic artists are producing new representations of Mesquaki culture. These same leaders are also developing a more bilingual-bicultural tribal school program to preserve and transmit Mesquaki culture. It is within this historical process of ethnogenesis and ideological struggle that we must situate any discussion of "silent Indians" in white classrooms.

EARLIER ANTHROPOLOGICAL EXPLANATIONS OF NATIVE AMERICAN SILENCE

Before presenting a small slice of my fieldwork, I would like to sketch how educational anthropologists have typically explained the silence of Native American youths in white classrooms. A number of educational anthropologists (Wax 1969; Dumont 1972; Philips 1974; Erickson and Mohatt 1982) document how white teachers are quick to read the silence of Indians as evidence of low motivation, lack of competence in English, or, worse still, low cognitive ability. This leads white teachers to lower their expectations for Indian students and include them less in classroom activities. These anthropological findings add further confirmation to the "self-fulfilling prophecy" explanation of failure in schools (Rosenthal and Jacobson 1968; Rist 1970).

In addition, these studies produce a sociolinguistic explanation of ethnic school failure (Foley 1991). This perspective emphasizes that speech style differences lead to miscommunication and low rates of student participation. Susan Philips' (1983) study of Warm Springs Indians illustrates this explanation of school failure particularly well. She portrays the "silence" that Indian youth express in white classrooms as a widely shared, traditional speech style passed from generation to generation. She exhaustively describes how these youth learn to use less nodding and gazing, less body and facial movement, and a lower voice tone—all of which teaches the importance of stillness. Indian youth also learn to use visual channels of communication more, thus becoming keen observers who use subtle, indirect cues to get others' attention. Philips contends that Indian youth learn a very collective, democratic mode of communication which has no single adult authority. It is a speech style in which there is little competition for adults' attention, talking out of turn, and drawing attention to oneself as a speaker. In short, Indian students' tendency to be silent in white classrooms is due to their distinct, learned linguistic and cultural tradition.

Although this portrayal of the "silent Indian" has real merit, the work of another linguistic anthropologist, Keith Basso (1979), suggests a "cultural politics" dimension missing in Philips' sociolinguistic account. Basso's *Portraits of the Whiteman* describes how Apaches use such differences in speech styles to produce a cultural image of the whiteman. According to Basso, the white "other" of Apache jokes and stories is this back-slapping, garrulous, nosey, arrogant, bossy, and rude person who asks too many questions and never listens. These self-indulgent, uncontrolled white creatures are lampooned as little children and old women who talk too rapidly in loud, demanding, high-pitched voices—yet imagine themselves to be chiefs and authorities.

Basso originally portrayed what critical theorists would label a "counter-hegemonic Apache discourse" against the stigmatization of Indians as "silent" inarticulate, unfeeling dummies. Although Basso frames his book as a classic sociolinguistic study, he ends up detailing how Indians symbolically invert the negative portrayal of their "silent" speech style. In the Apache discursive construction of the silent Indian, being silent becomes positive. The "silent Indian" becomes noble, humble, wise, communal, and egalitarian, while the loud, unsilent white "other" becomes ignoble, stupid, individualistic, and inegalitarian.

What Basso has done is lay bare the politics of how ethnic groups generally construct oppositional cultural identities through their expressive cultural forms. This type of cultural analysis, often associated with the performance school of folklore (Paredes 1971; Bauman and Briggs 1990; Limón 1994; Peña 1985), zeroes in on the political and power dimensions of speech play. From this general perspective, there *may be* objective speech style differences between whites and Indians, but what interests cultural performance scholars is the way each ethnic group uses discursive forms to produce a positive group image or identity.

Studies of identity-producing cultural performances provide an alternative critical paradigm for interpreting the silence of Indian youth in white classrooms. From this perspective, the expression of silence is much more than the simple enactment of learned language patterns and speech styles. It is part of a much larger discursive or ideological struggle between whites and Indians over cultural representations. With this point in mind, I would like to present a few examples of the white discourses against which all Mesquaki adolescents must construct a group identity.

THE LOCAL IDEOLOGICAL CONTEXT FOR PRODUCING THE SILENT INDIAN

Like the educational anthropologists cited earlier, I observed many Indian adolescents sitting passively and silently in white classrooms. Like the white teachers in earlier studies, many teachers explained Mesquaki silence as shyness, backwardness, lack of English proficiency, and laziness. Lurking beneath these explanations was their view that federal welfarism had promoted the moral decay of the once noble Indian. In contrast, a few liberal white teachers stressed that Indians are racially oppressed, and have thus learned to be failures in an unforgiving, racist system. Two of these teachers recited views learned in classes on multiculturalism that sounded remarkably like Philips' perspective. In general, however, most local white educators still read Mesquaki silence as a cultural and linguistic deficit to be corrected by learning the white cultural and linguistic code.

This assimilationist perspective recurred in four basic narratives. For me these four narratives constitute a "discursive field" (Foucault 1972) which continually reproduces the hegemonic ideology of cultural assimilationism. First, white leaders have historically advocated an official policy of forcibly closing down the settlement school. They portrayed the Mesquaki-run tribal school as unprofessional and corrupt. According to them, Indian youths get a "superior" education in the academically advanced white town school. In response, the Mesquakis have always battled the Bureau of Indian Affairs and local white leaders to keep their tribal school open.

Second, whites consistently idealized *some* Indian students over others. Many white teachers extolled what Mesquakis call "town Indians" or "half-breeds." According to whites, the more traditional Indian youths sit silently because they lack the entrepreneurial drive of the semi-assimilated town Indians. Whites invariably illustrated this view with stories of exemplary Indians. In my era, it was Ben Warrior, a high school sports star, who eventually married a white woman and moved away from the settlement. In the current era, it was Len Moline, the first Mesquaki to be accepted into West Point. Len was raised on the settlement, but he eventually came under the tutelage of a prominent white lawyer. Len's denunciations of the settlement as a drunken, slothful, violent place received considerable play in Iowa newspapers. Whites were quick to celebrate him as an ideal role model for other Indian youth. Conversely, the Mesquakis saw him as either a traitor to his race or a confused pawn of whites.

Third, in contrast to these "super-Indians," whites portrayed most Mesquaki adolescents as indulging in a self-destructive cycle of drinking and dropping out. Most agreed that this cycle begins in junior high. Teachers generally attributed the high rates of substance abuse to "what goes on out there." In the white mind, the settlement was this dark, mysterious, dirty, unsafe place where Indian youths followed their alcoholic parents into despair, hopelessness, and violence. By the high school years most Mesquakis became "at risk" students, and nearly 50 percent finished their secondary diploma in Indian boarding schools or in the local GED program.

Fourth, most whites portrayed the tribe's claims allotment policy as ruinous to Indian youth. In the 1970s the tribe received seven million dollars in reparations for lands taken during the 1830s. Approximately half of this money went into the tribal operations fund, and the other half was allotted equally to every tribal member. For the present-day Mesquaki youth who turn 18, their original share, plus interest, has grown to approximately twenty-three thousand dollars. The oft-told tale of how profligate Indian youth used this money goes as follows: After receiving their claims check the Indian youth drops out of school, buys and wrecks an uninsured car, loans his friends money freely, and drinks up his/her claims money. In this scenario, the passive, "silent Indian" of the classroom becomes the loud, irresponsible, "hell-raising Indian."

As I have pointed out elsewhere (Foley 1993), this ideological construction of Indian youth contains an element of truth. Many Mesquaki youth, especially the males, do go through an unusually long cycle of rebellion, drinking, and hell-raising. Some of these youth are very self-destructive, and as many as 50 percent drop out of school. But any fair-minded observer would note that their rebellion is also laced with moments of pride and self-valorization. Moreover, adolescent rebellion is a stage in life rather than a way of life. If one follows the lives of these rebellious youth over a period of years, nearly all marry and settle down into stable, productive lives in their tribal community. Observers bent on proving the need for cultural assimilation tend to greatly exaggerate the permanent effects of Mesquaki adolescent rebellion and hell-raising.

SOME OBSERVATIONS IN CLASSROOMS

Despite a good deal of open rebellion and hell-raising, most Mesquaki adolescents become "silent Indians" in white classrooms. It is important to note, however, that most Mesquaki children were initially anything but silent and passive. As Philips' study of Warm Springs Indians indicates, Indian students actually do not become nonparticipatory and silent until about the fifth grade. Observations in the Mesquaki tribal school and the testimonies of K–3 white teachers generally corroborate her findings. Mesquaki youth in the early grades were neither passive nor particularly silent. They talked and played like most other youth. More importantly, by fifth grade, unlike in the Warm Springs setting, racial peer groups developed. This led to almost daily battles on the playground and at the local swimming pool. Beyond the gaze of the teachers, the Mesquaki kids were quick to defend themselves. In white-controlled territories like classrooms, however, the Mesquaki youth were becoming "silent Indians." By high school, no more than a handful of college-bound Mesquaki students were verbally outgoing, and most teachers agreed, the Mesquaki youth were generally silent in their classrooms.

Conversations with white students undermine the teachers' sweeping portrayal of the Mesquaki students as silent. White students, especially girls, remember sarcastic remarks and whistles from clusters of Mesquaki boys hanging out in the hallways. White athletes recall Mesquaki players talking back and making fun of them when no whites were around. Several white students exhorted me: "Don't make them out to be angels because they aren't! They like picking on whites, and they do!"

One liberal white student, who supported a 1993 Mesquaki school walkout against racism, described how she saw white teachers responding to Mesquaki silence:

> I heard there's a policy by teachers. If Native Americans don't want to answer, they can't keep asking the question. There must be a policy because they kinda act that way. Teachers let Native Americans stay in the back row and let them be. They give up and go on to others. They don't even ask them questions. If they do, the Native American kid just shrugs and says I don't know. They say that is how their culture is. They want to be left alone. The teachers need to try. It isn't fair to whites or Indians, I mean Native Americans. The deal is, lots of Mesquaki students don't really care. They don't work at school. They can't see any future in it.

This student went on to explain that many white students resent the non-partici-pation of Mesquakis. They think their teachers have a double standard for Mesquakis because they are reluctant "to push Indians as hard as they do whites." They also think that Mesquaki kids take advantage of timid white teachers, who fear being labeled racists. For them, Mesquaki kids use the "silent Indian" image very effectively to avoid schoolwork. They persuade white teachers to accept their indifference towards school as a cultural difference.

When I tried this explanation out on Mesquaki ex-students, several laughed, and one admitted that they used, as he put it, "the old silent Indian thing" to keep white teachers off their backs. During one class, I observed a particularly politi-cized Mesquaki student use a stern, stoic posture to keep a rather timid white teacher at bay. Based on thousands of hours of interacting with Mesquakis, I have little doubt that they play with the whiteman's negative image of the silent Indian. During initial conversations, many Mesquakis responded with stern-faced stoicism and feigned ignorance. As time passed, the same people invariably dropped these postures. But as we shall see, silence is much more than a commu-nicative practice that Mesquakis use strategically. Such a reading of Mesquaki silence imposes too sweeping a political reading on these speech acts. Being silent with whites means many different things to different Mesquaki students.

When I first started to explore the silent Indian image, I initially got a good dose of commonsense logic from tribal elders. I asked Lee Kingfisher, an old classmate and clan leader, why he and other Mesquakis were always so quiet in class. Lee answered my question with another question, "When you and other whites come out to the settlement, do you talk as much as you do in town?"

I sat there speechless, and Lee sensed he had an anthropologist in his muskrat trap. He said slyly, "Why not?" I had to answer, "Well, it's a strange situation. Anyone with any sense would hold back to see how you should act."

That brought a big smile to his face, and Leo said it was the same with Mesquakis. He was just trying to say that Indians are people like everybody else. If you have any sense, a strange situation calls for less talking. My grandfather, a taciturn Iowa farmer, could not have said it better.

There was a basic truth in what Leo was saying, but many other Mesquakis explained their reserve in the white schools in much the same manner that Susan Philips does. They emphasized that Indian children were brought up to listen and observe and to avoid calling attention to themselves like whites do. They described Indians as more shy and reserved than whites. Having seen such behavior in Mesquaki settings as well as in white classrooms, there may well be a cultural speech style difference between whites and Indians. Educational anthropologists' models of an "Indian speech style" may explain some of the reserve and silence of Mesquaki students.

On the other hand, this sweeping linguistic explanation becomes porous when filled with the narratives of Mesquaki students talking about their school experiences. When asked to explain why they sat silently in the back of white classrooms, Mesquakis recounted a variety of feelings and motivations. For example, youth counselor Andrew Peacemaker gave a poignant, less linguistic explanation of Indian silence in white classrooms:

> When I look back on it, most of the Indian kids chose to sit in the back and were very quiet, but that is changing a little now. I didn't talk much because I wasn't sure if I had the right answer. I felt like the whites were looking at me and might laugh if I got it wrong.

As we talked, Andrew said he knew other Mesquaki kids who also had "self-esteem problems." Then he cited cases of other youth with whom he works who were bored with school and had many personal problems. For Andrew, silence in the classroom was either a self-esteem problem, or a question of boredom and indifference. Both of these themes occurred again and again in discussions with former Mesquaki students. Oftentimes, the theme of low self-esteem was entwined with a strong strain of rebellion and anger.

One excellent example of the complex emotions which feed silence was the experience of George TallTree's children. The three spent their early years in a nearby college town while their parents pursued college degrees. They recalled how strange it was to transfer from an urban school with no Indians to South Tama County High (STCH). After getting along well with whites at previous schools, they were suddenly constructed as a minority, and it was, "Us vs. them. We were no-good Indians. The white children on the bus did not want to sit beside us because they said we stunk." The brothers, Joe and Jack, remember junior high days as marked with gang fights between Mesquakis and "the better off white kids who got all the praise and good grades." They all remembered teachers calling on these white kids more, giving them little privileges, joking with them. Both brothers and Sally remember having friends among whites who played sports or were farm kids, but "racial lines were hard to cross in the early 1980s." There was also very little interracial dating and few strong friendships.

Academically, all three eventually went to prestigious Iowa State University. Sally finished a B.A. in fine arts and is presently working on an M.A. in creative writing. Joe finished all but one semester in an engineering program, and Jack finished two years in engineering. All the TallTree children were A and B students in grade school, but finishing at STC High School was a very different matter. Sally stuck it out because she made white friends, "Eventually the farm girls in sports became friends, but white boys who dated Indians got a lot of crap about their 'squaws.' Being part white, we also got it from Mesquakis, even though we were enrolled." Meanwhile, her brother Joe sat quietly in the back of class until his junior year. His silence was a mixture of feeling angry and very bored, so he opted to drop out and do a GED.

In contrast, Jack was more openly rebellious, and he eventually got into trouble with the law. His story of quitting school and football during his senior year was told with a mixture of sadness, pride, and relief:

> When I finally quit I went to school and turned in my books. Then I went to the football game that night. I was just standing there on the sidelines in my jersey watching. Several guys came up and asked me why I wasn't suited up. I didn't say anything because I had proven what I wanted to. I got good grades when I wanted to. I started on the varsity football team. It wasn't a big a deal, so I just left.

So there was Jack making his final statement. Upon returning to Tama he had been made to feel inferior. He had gotten himself into trouble with drinking and drugs. He probably had some self-esteem problems, but he also wanted to prove that he was as good as rich white kids in academics and sports, and that "succeeding in rinky-dink STCH was no big deal." In Jack's story, he is standing silently and stoically at the whiteman's football game. Then, in one noble, heroic act he gives it all up and just walks away from his tormentors. Like many other stories that I collected, Jack's tale evokes the image of the noble, silent Apache (Basso 1979) in the face of a loud, insensitive white world. Although teachers called the TallTree brothers "drop outs," like many other Mesquaki youth, they were actually "push outs."

Too many white teachers, and even some Mesquaki educators, were quick to psychologize the silence of the TallTree brothers as a sign of low self-esteem. Indeed, the silent retreat of these youth, especially Jack, was laced with self-doubt and self-destructive behavior. In the cases of Sally and Joe, if they had self-esteem problems, it did not stop them from succeeding academically in a major university. These cases suggest that the feelings and motivations of Mesquaki youth, like all other youth, may often be complex and contradictory.

Basso's (1979) study of Apache storytelling helps underscore that the silence of many Mesquaki youth like Jack and Joe TallTree has a definite political edge. As indicated previously, these youth are part of a much larger verbal battle over cultural images that has escalated since the 1970s. Consequently, Mesquaki students' silent retreat is sometimes a very self-assured political statement. As University of Iowa graduate Len Firstley put it, "I sat there and said nothing because it was easier. I just wanted the whites to leave me alone." Len, who now runs the tribal housing program, was a quiet, self-assured kid. He dealt with what he considered loud, blustering whitemen by just sitting there quietly. Many other Mesquaki students who are now successful tribal leaders told essentially the same story.

Unfortunately, silent rebellion in the classroom does not lead most Mesquaki youth to the academic promised land. Too many Mesquaki students like Jack TallTree end up getting a GED. Others, like Debbie Rock Island, transfer to boarding schools like Flandreau "to get away from all the racial stuff." The GED and boarding school alternatives leave Mesquaki students less well prepared academically or less motivated to go to college. The price for heroic retreat into silence may be lost future educational opportunities. Although far quieter than the noisy, wise-cracking youth in other studies (Willis 1981; MacLeod 1987), many Mesquakis also end up dropping out. In their cultural milieu, it is often the honorable way of handling the garrulous, aggressive whites.

SOME REFLECTIONS ON READING AND PRODUCING CULTURAL IMAGES

So how are we to read the "silence" of most Mesquaki adolescents? As anthropologists like Philips (1983) have noted, there may be an objective, learned "Indian speech style" which uses less nodding, gazing, body and facial movements, and a lower tone of voice. Indians may also tend to talk out of turn less and rarely try to draw attention to themselves. To most white observers, both academic and nonacademic, Mesquaki students seem more reserved or taciturn. They seem to have a cultural speech style that is different from mainstream whites.

Although this linguistic perspective has general merit, Mesquaki silence or reserve can also be thought of as a strategic, situational speech style that ethnic minorities deploy during relations with whites (Foley 1990). From this perspective, a complex historical, political process of ethnic identity construction is taking place. Cultural groups in modern complex societies have no stable, essential cultural identities which are transmitted unproblematically from generation to generation. There are only "discursive moments" or "discursive skirmishes" between ethnic, gender, and class identity groups in the ceaseless production of shifting cultural images.

This perspective also assumes that the struggle over cultural representations takes place in a number of oral, written, and cinematic texts in the general sphere of popular culture, particularly in mass media and schooling institutions. Such cultural institutions may be used to systematically misrepresent non-mainstream, ethnic groups. In response, these misrepresented groups often challenge and seek to control these mass-mediated images of their culture.

In my South Texas study (Foley 1990), I emphasized class differences in expressive speech styles. Working-class Mexicano youths resisted white domination through a rude, aggressive working-class speech style that constantly challenged the polite, deferential, deceitful speech styles of middle-class youth. Conversely, rebellious middle-class Mexicano youth learned how to manage their images and deceive and manipulate the authorities much like their middle-class white counterparts.

In sharp contrast, Mesquaki youth utilized rather different discursive resources. They tapped into a long, distinguished tribal memory of place and military resistance against the whitemen. They drew heavily upon the separatist ethic that Mesquaki traditionalists have always expressed. Mesquaki elders supplied their youths with a resistance discourse on the difference between white and Indian speaking styles. Like the Apaches (Basso 1979), Mesquaki youth grew up learning a cultural construction of their "silence" that emphasizes how the silent, noble, dignified Indian often fools or tricks the loud, rude, unobservant whiteman. This trickster tale was expressed orally in much everyday joking and humor. It was also in Ray Youngbear's (1992) novel, Jonathan Buffalo's (in press) history, and Everett Kapayo's (1986) cartoons. Disgruntled Mesquaki youth tapped and used this rich cultural construction of themselves as the noble silent Indian, thus reversing the negative connotations that many white teachers placed on their silence.

Unlike many Hispanics and African-Americans, few Mesquakis have ever wanted to be integrated into white society. They simply want to be left alone in their solitude. These youth constantly recounted their anger and indifference towards teachers and school. One youth spoke for many when he said, "I sit there and say nothing because it is easier. Teachers know I want to be left alone." Silence is this political retreat into a separate cultural space and identity far from the white world.

A FINAL NOTE ON DECONSTRUCTING MODELS OF THE CULTURAL OTHER

Having made a case for reading the silence of Indian youth in classrooms as a discursively constructed and contested image, I must, however, end with a cautionary note. Several recent works on Native Americans (Clifton 1991; Clifford 1989; Bruner 1985; Berkhoffer 1979) provide insights into how anthropologists, literary figures, lawyers, and government bureaucrats have created the cultural identities of subjugated indigenous peoples. Bruner's (1986) incisive categorization of anthropological narratives as assimilationist and anti-assimilationist helps clarify that modern sociolinguists and critical theorists, like earlier social scientists, are a bit too anxious to side with down-trodden Native Americans. As a result, well-meaning liberal social scientists replace the old assimilationist narratives with anti-assimilationist narratives that glorify their heroic political resistance—hence they replace one simplistic cultural image with another.

The poststructuralist critique of knowledge production (Foucault 1972) shows us that the disciplines that produce "cultural others" must deconstruct their own constructions. In addition, we knowledge producers must open up our totalizing, rationalistic models of linguistic and cultural behavior to those caught in complex historical articulations. One antidote for totalizing "scientific models" or "master narratives" seems to be a philosophical committment to collecting many contradictory voices (Clifford 1988; Rosaldo 1989).

When I simply listened to the stories of Mesquaki youth, I heard a welter of different feelings. Despite the common cultural and political forces that made these youth rebellious (Foley 1995), they were still unique individuals. Everything in the stories of these youth was not heroic political resistance and self-constitution. Many expressed anger and rebelliousness against white rules and stereotypes. Yet some of these same students expressed a nagging self-consciousness about speaking in front of whites. Some admitted that they were afraid of sounding stupid, others that their English was poor, others that they were ignorant and lacked information. Still others were indifferent and distracted, rather than politically motivated.

In retrospect, it would seem that sweeping sociolinguistic explanations of Indian silence as a learned speech style are susceptible to glorifying the survival of traditional culture. Conversely, sweeping cultural production interpretations of Mesquaki adolescent rebellion are susceptible to glorifying cultural resistance and rebellious speech acts. Any interpretive model that overemphasizes rational, intentional linguistic acts of cultural preservation may miss the paradoxically self-destructive/self-valorizing quality of the silence of many rebellious Mesquaki youth. A comprehensive ethnographic account of how the silent Indian image is produced must include how local actors "articulate" (Hall 1980; Gilroy 1987) their own history. If we leave out the subjects of history, we may be left with the sound of our own discourses in the academic forest.

REFERENCES

Basso, Keith. 1979. Portraits of the Whiteman. Cambridge: Cambridge University Press.

Bauman, Richard and Charles L. Briggs. 1990. Poetics and Performance as Critical Perspectives on Language and Social Life. Annual Review of Anthropology 19:59–88.

Berkhoffer, Robert F. Jr. 1978. The Whiteman's Indian: Images of the American Indian from Columbus to the Present. New York: Vintage.

Bruner, Edward. 1986. Ethnography as Narrative. *In* The Anthropology of Experience. Victor W. Turner and Edward Bruner, eds. Pp. 139–155. Urbana: University of Illinois Press.

Buffalo, Jonathan. in press. A History of the Mesquaki People. Iowa City: University of Iowa Press.

Clifford, James. 1988. The Predicament of Culture: Twentieth-Century Ethnography, Literature, and Art. Cambridge, MA: Harvard University Press.

Clifton, James, ed. 1991. The Invented Indian. New Brunswick, NJ: Transaction Press.

Dumont, R. V. 1972. Learning English and How to Be Silent: Studies in Sioux and Cherokee Classrooms. *In* Functions of Language in the Classroom. C. Cazden, V. John, and D. Hymes, eds. Pp. 42–61. New York: Teachers College Press.

Erickson, Fred and Gerald Mohatt. 1982. Cultural Organization of Participant Structures in Two Classrooms of Indian Students. *In* Doing the Ethnography of Schooling: Educational Anthropology in Action. George Spindler, ed. Pp. 132–174. New York: Holt Rinehart and Winston.

Foley, Douglas E. 1990. Learning Capitalist Culture: Deep in the Heart of Tejas. Philadelphia: University of Pennsylvania Press.

———. 1991. Reconsidering Anthropological Explanations of Ethnic School Failure. Anthropology and Education Quarterly 22(1):60–85.

———. 1993. Mesquaki Sports as an Adolescent Rite of Passage. Journal of Ritual Studies 7(1):28–44.

———. 1995. The Heartland Chronicles. Philadelphia: University of Pennsylvania Press.

Foucault, Michel. 1972. Power/Knowledge: Selected Interviews and Other Writings, 1972–77. New York: Pantheon Books, 1977.

Gearing, Fred. 1970. Face of the Fox. New York: Aldine.

Gearing, Fred, Robert McNetting, and Lisa R. Peattie. 1960. A Documentary History of the Fox Project, 1948–1959. Chicago: University of Chicago Press.

Gilroy, Paul. 1987. There Ain't No Black in the Union Jack: Cultural Politics of Race and Nation. Chicago: University of Chicago.

Hall, Stuart. 1980. Race, Articulation, Societies Structured in Dominance. *In* Sociological Theories: Race and Colonialism. Pp. 306–324. Paris: Unesco.

Kapayo, Everett. 1986. The Larry Andy People Fun Book. Tama: Mikona Publishing.

Limon, Jose. 1994. Dancing with the Devil: Society and Cultural Poetics in Mexican-American South Texas. Madison: University of Wisconsin Press.

MacLeod, Jan. 1987. Ain't No Makin' It: Leveled Aspirations in a Low-Income Neighborhood. Boulder, CO: Westview.

Paredes, Americo. 1971. With His Pistol in His Hand: A Border Ballad and Its Hero. Austin: University of Texas Press.

Peña, Manuel. 1985. The Texas-Mexican Conjunto: History of a Working Class Music. Austin: University of Texas Press.

Philips, Susan. 1983. The Invisible Culture: Communication in Classroom and Community in the Warm Springs Reservation. New York: Longman.

Rist, Ray. 1970. Student Social Class and Teacher Expectations: The Self-fulfilling Prophecy in Ghetto Schools. Harvard Educational Review 40:411–450.

Rosenthal, Robert and Lenore Jacobson. 1968. Pygmalion in the Classroom: Teacher Expectation and Pupils' Intellectual Development. New York: Holt.

Roosens, Eugene E. 1989. Creating Ethnicity: The Process of Ethnogenesis. Newbury Park: Sage.

Rosaldo, Renato. 1989. Culture and Truth: The Remaking of Social Analysis. Boston: Beacon Press.

Willis, Paul. 1981. Learning to Labor: How Working-Class Kids Get Working-Class Jobs. New York: Columbia University Press.

Youngbear, Ray. 1992. Black Eagle Child: The Facepaint Narratives. Iowa City: University of Iowa Press.

4

WENDY LUTTRELL

Becoming Somebody in and against School: Toward a Psychocultural Theory of Gender and Self-Making

INTRODUCTION

I don't think the world ends if you didn't finish high school. I didn't finish and I'm not a bum. But I always wanted to finish, just so I could feel like I was somebody.

If you know how to read, write, do your figures—if you have that diploma, then you feel like you're somebody, you know.

Despite very different backgrounds, these two women agree that receiving a high school diploma is self-making—it allows you to "feel like you're somebody." Based on in-depth interviews and participant observation with white and black, rural and urban, working-class women about why they were returning to school as adults, I aim to shed new light on the self-making process.[1] Their views about "bettering themselves" through adult education, as well as their coded stories about becoming somebody (or not), reveal common insights about and disillusions with how selves are formed within and against school.

This paper is part of a larger comparative ethnographic study of women literacy learners in two adult basic education programs: the first, a community-based program in Philadelphia and the second, a workplace literacy program at a state university in North Carolina. My research included classroom observations in both programs, semistructured interviews with 200 women, and in-depth interviews with fifteen women from each program.[2] In this paper I draw most heavily on in-depth interviews that were conducted in the women's homes on three different occasions, each lasting from one and one-half to three hours. The excerpts I have selected and analyzed about childhood aspirations were part of the women's response to my opening question, "Tell me what you remember about being in school." In the course of telling me their school memories, all but two women provided unsolicited accounts of childhood aspirations. Elsewhere I have written about the women's contrasting aspirational stories as illustrations of the variable meaning and salience of gender, race, and class in the formation of aspirations, and how these aspirations link what society offers and what individuals choose in complicated and unpredictable ways (Luttrell 1994). In this paper

I analyze these same stories as "accounts" which explain why they failed to become somebody.[3] These accounts tell us much about the complex formation of selves. My aim is to complicate the picture further by highlighting how institutional, cultural, and psychodynamic forces join up in ways that make "becoming somebody" a daunting, if not threatening, project for these women in school.

SCHOOLS AND SELF FORMATION

Schools are sites of cultural production, places where certain styles of selves and knowledge are authorized amidst race, class, and gender inequalities.[4] Studies have documented the dynamics of how different identities get played out in schools, both as challenges to and accommodations of dominant social norms and expectations. Moreover, different school contexts and historical periods produce their own versions of gender identity, knowledge and power (Luttrell 1993; Connell et al. 1982; Hansot and Tyack 1988). Despite considerable research, however, the complexities of how schools produce multiple and sometimes conflicting subjectivities are underplayed and under theorized. This paper attempts to expand current thinking about self formation in the hopes of finding new ways for students and teachers (in this case adult literacy learners and instructors) to make use of the "paradoxical potentialities" of schooling as a vehicle for social change (Levinson and Holland, this volume).

Central to my thinking about how selves are formed in relation to schools is the work of sociologist Philip Wexler (1992). In his detailed and provocative ethnography of three "all-American city" high schools, he shows how each school (defined as "working-class," "professional middle-class," and urban "underclass") produces its own set of student understandings about the self. He analyzes how each school is organized in distinct, if unintended, institutional and pedagogical ways to "attack" the self. In response, students strive to "create a visible, differentiated and reputable self" as their primary activity in school (132):

> In their own words, students are trying to "become somebody." They want to be somebody, a real and presentable self, anchored in the verifying eyes of friends whom they come to school to meet. . . . [T]heir central and defining activity in school is to establish at least the image of an identity. "Becoming somebody" is action in the public sphere, and this is what life in high school is about. (155)

I agree with Wexler that (1) students' attempts to assert a self (or at least an image of a self) and to have this self (image) be recognized and valued by others is what life is all about in high school (and I would add at every level of schooling); and (2) that this important dimension of schooling has been missing or underestimated in current educational literature. But while Wexler emphasizes how schools produce what he calls a "defensive" self (a self that must defend against different forms of institutional "lacks" and "attacks"), my emphasis is different.

Institutionally and pedagogically speaking, I am concerned with how schools encourage some aspects of the self more than others. Psychodynamically speaking, my emphasis is on the doubleness and paradox of psychic life—the built-in tension between self assertion and recognition such that "in the very moment of realizing our own independence, we are dependent upon another to recognize it. At the very moment we come to understand the meaning of I, myself, we are forced to see the limitations of that self" (Benjamin 1993:134). I am especially interested in how this tension breaks down into relations of domination, particularly in the school setting. This breakdown, or splitting, happens when the subject/self gives up the tension (between self and other or between different aspects of the self) in favor of an opposition where one side is devalued and the other is idealized (Benjamin 1988, 1993). I aim to apply this concept of splitting not only in its technical sense (as both a psychic defense and organizational feature of psychic life), but also as a paradigm for understanding how cultural and institutional forces and resources become implicated in the self-making process.

I want to stress that I do not view the self or one's "inner world" as fixed (unchanging), unitary, or experienced as whole.[5] I am aware that the concept of a self, as well as the meanings and structures of subjectivity, is hotly disputed, especially in postmodern and feminist texts.[6] My sympathies, however, lie somewhere between symbolic interactionist and (feminist) psychoanalytic accounts which stress how the self is known through others and through patterns of internalized object relations.[7] I aim to ground these abstract theories about self formation in the women's everyday experiences and spheres of activity, emphasizing their creative use of and response to certain institutional, cultural, and psychic dynamics.

Particularly relevant for understanding the women's selves in relation to school is the work of psychoanalytic and political theorist Jane Flax (1987:98). She describes the self-making and gender-making process (for both men and women) as growing out of and depending upon the repression of women's desire and ambition. Flax says that women in American culture tend to repress autonomous and aggressive aspects of the self. Her model of women's selves stresses the conflicts between:

> a mostly false (but predominant) "social self," an autonomous (and highly underdeveloped) self, and a "sexual" self (also underdeveloped, but not as forbidden or constricted as the autonomous self).

Flax offers this model as an alternative to one that casts Western women's selves as "relational" in contrast to men's selves as "autonomous."[8] Flax warns against simplifying and essentializing gender differences in this way and emphasizes that the forces of psychodynamic and cultural-political repression make it appear as if women's selves are relational in contrast to men's. Moreover, Flax says that what is repressed in Western women's selves is not the existence or demands of the social self, but rather its costs. She asks us to scrutinize the conditions under which women's social selves are constituted.

Such scrutiny is central to my analysis of the women's self understandings in relation to school. That the desire for intellectual, creative or interpersonal mastery and autonomy jeopardizes a woman's "social" self and "connection to others" is a cultural assumption impeding women's development. This assumption implies that certain aspects of the self can threaten or endanger both the subject/self and others, and that one way to assuage this threat is to split off (and deny, disavow, or repudiate) those needs and desires which are least acceptable (and most threatening) to ourselves and others. Such "split" depictions of the self or others are said to enable people to protect themselves from or defend themselves against their own vulnerabilities, conflicts, or contradictions—or at least give them the illusion of coherence or unity in the face of tension.[9] This breakdown of one's subjectivity, in which unwanted parts of self are split off and projected elsewhere, organizes both psychic and social-cultural understandings about gender. As we shall see through the women's narratives, this splitting also organizes psychic and cultural understandings about who is and is not a "somebody."

My interest in the formation of the women's selves is undertaken in a spirit akin to the sociologist Susan Krieger's (1991:44):

> I emphasize a view of the self that acknowledges inner experiences of individuality both because I think these experiences are important sources of knowledge, sources traditionally minimized in social science, and because I think a sense of individual uniqueness is often hard won. Such a sense is frequently a difficult achievement that is felt as precarious by the individual and that is experienced as a struggle: a struggle against being like everyone else, a struggle to hold together or hold up, or a struggle simply to feel that one has a self.

This sense of narrative urgency about "how it is/was for me"—expressed by the women as a hard-won sense of uniqueness, and as a desire to be seen as a "somebody"—is my subject.

Yet I was not prepared for the task of recognizing the unique presence and inner experiences of the selves I encountered in my research. I did not anticipate the intensely charged emotional forms that the women's "memory work" took during the interviews.[10] Nor did I realize how recollections of childhood aspirations might be told in ways that defy simple explanation or conceptual clarity.[11] At the same time, I was also unprepared to encounter my own self as part of or as insight into my field research.[12] That the women's stories and struggles at times resonated, at times conflicted, with my own is indeed part of the dialogue that took place.[13] This dimension of my research deserves attention, but is beyond the scope of this paper.

Self Accounts, Ambitions, and the Figured World of Success

> My parents then sit down and tell us, you going to be a school teacher. You know how they think. They told us what they wanted us to do, you know, so

we wouldn't have to work as hard as them. But we knowed we weren't going to be. 'Cause we didn't have too many school teachers no way. The two schools we went to weren't but one school teacher.

So is that what you wanted to do—to be a school teacher?

I don't know, I guess a school teacher. That's the only thing we knowed. We didn't think about anything else.

—Ola, North Carolina interviewee

When I was in grade school they asked us what we wanted to be when we grew up. I wrote that I wanted to be a judge. The nuns got very upset with this and asked me if I had copied it from somewhere. I mean, what little kid from the neighborhood ever thought about being a judge?

—Joanne, Philadelphia interviewee

Both statements, told by women with different backgrounds and biographies, typify how all the women talked about their childhood aspirations. Sometimes told as cautionary tales about the risks inherent in childhood longings and sometimes told with a sense of irony about the gap between dreams and reality, the women's stories highlighted formative experiences through which they came to understand and defend their selves in American society, where some people count and others don't. In this section I examine two related phenomena: first, how the women drew upon a shared cultural understanding of success and how success works to form (or at least to create a fantasy image of) a valued and legitimate self; and, second, how the ideal construct of a "somebody" is created by the psychodynamics of splitting. Split images of who is and is not a somebody are symbolic, unconscious parts of American understandings of gender, self, and success.

Most striking is how the accounts evoke social divisions and antagonisms, described in detailed ways and with narrative urgency about life in the past. These social divisions unfold as part of a drama about who succeeds, who fails, and why. Common patterns with familiar and prototypical events, actors, motives, and outcomes emerge across these dramas—patterns that Holland and Quinn (1987) would call a cultural model of success. According to the women I interviewed, there are those who we expect will "become somebody" and those who won't; there are people who do the right thing (finish school, get married, etc.) and those who don't (or can't), which explains who gets ahead and why; there are those with brains, ambition and drive who can make it in school or on the job, while others are deficient and thus cannot expect to succeed. The women explained themselves and their failed ambitions in part as a critique of, and in part as an acceptance of, this shared conceptualization of success and how success works.

The women's accounts feature both fantasies and real perceptions of the meaning of and struggle for success. For instance, success meant escaping a particular kind of work for which they felt destined. Lilly recalled that as a child she had dreamed of becoming a nurse, explaining that "mostly I knew I didn't want to farm":

But I really liked going to school and I said a million times I wished that I could have stayed in school like other kids did 'cause I wanted to be a nurse but that didn't work out. Mostly I knew I didn't want to farm. Because we got tired of farming. Whenever we farmed on half we always wind up with nothing. We farmed one year and ended up with one hundred dollars apiece and I bought our first refrigerator and record player. But mostly we ended up with nothing. It was hard work—my sister and I, we was just working with children, the man wouldn't hire nobody else. We had to go out in the field and prime tobacco; we had to get up on the barn and get on those tills and hang it. We had to set up at night, you know, so the tobacco could dry out in the barn. We had to do all that stuff and, well, we had a hard time then. I knew I didn't want to do that all the time.

Helen wanted to avoid factory work and described her fantasy of becoming a secretary in the following way:

I knew I wanted to be a secretary—which I am [now] and I wish I weren't. I didn't know how crummy some secretarial jobs could be. But my sister was a secretary. I used to see her in the morning to work and she was all dressed up— she looked real nice. It was either that—and then I had another sister who worked in a factory. She always look like she was overtired, looked like a bum. I didn't want to do what that one did, I'd rather do what the other one did.

It was common for the women to account for their selves and ambitions by invoking familiar work scenes, stressing the exigencies of life and daily social encounters in factories, offices, or on the farm. Set within historically specific contexts and conditions (note the women's persistent emphasis upon the past tense, "when I grew up"), dreams of becoming somebody were set against certain realities:

The time I was coming along you could do housework, you could babysit, work jobs in the back of a kitchen, you know, or you could clean up outside, if you were a man.

When I got grown up you couldn't find no job nowhere but tending to some-body's babies or cleanin' somebody's house. If you were lucky you could end up like well, out there like where I'm working [at a university as a house-keeper].

In the neighborhood there were four choices: you could either be a secretary, nurse, mother, or nun (if you were Catholic).

When I grew up the choices were clear—either a nurse, nun, secretary, or mother. We didn't think about other things, we didn't know anything different.

If and when notions of "anything different" were to arise, they were met by some form of resistance or opposition. Typically, resistance came from more powerful others and was cast in symbolic terms based on race, class, and gender antagonisms. Consider Joanne's story which casts the nuns as enforcers of the social divisions between middle-class judges and working-class kids from the neighborhood, and Ola's story about the narrow field of opportunity that was open to rural, Southern black girls in the segregated South. In Lilly's story, race- and class-based antagonisms between the (white) man employer and his (black) child employees left her and her sister "nothing" after a year's worth of work. Similarly, Helen's story about becoming a secretary was told as part of the symbolic class- and gender-based struggle between manual and mental work where one sister "looked like a bum" and the other looked "real nice," and it was up to Helen to decide which side she was on.

The women account for their selves and their pasts by formulating answers about and defenses against why certain aspirations were "unthinkable." They narrate these defenses according to opposing or split voices and images. Their stories are told "in the voice" and "in the image" of those with whom the women identified (family members and peers), and also in the voice and image of those who the women viewed as opposite or distinct (and in many cases dominating), such as school or workplace authorities or idealized peers or co-workers. The phrases "in the voice" and "in the image" come from Dorothy Holland's work on American understandings of attractiveness (1988; Holland et al. in press). She notes that cognitive presentations of who is and is not attractive are evaluated in reference to particular social practices or activities (i.e., "dating") and particular groups (i.e., "jerks," "jocks," "bitches") that comprise what she calls the "figured world of romance." For Holland's interviewees, critical self-appraisals were narrated in the voices of their peers—one interviewee "seemed to (re)experience the comparison of herself to the ideal through the questions and criticism of her peers" (1988:2). I found a similar pattern among the women I interviewed in that their ideas about who is and is not a "somebody" refer to specific spheres of activity (school and work) and particular groups (teachers' pets, "good" and "bad" girls). Moreover, as I will elaborate in the following section, the women seemed to (re)experience the comparison of themselves to the ideal (or fantasy) image of a "somebody" as they narrated the past actions of others (peers, family members, more powerful others).

These observations about how different groups of women narrate (and evaluate) their selves can be explained, in part, by the psychodynamics of splitting. What is notable about these images and voices is how they are split and cast in either/or terms. Elsewhere I have discussed how the women's stories about school featured "good" and "bad" teachers and "good" and "bad" students (described in terms of who was and who wasn't a teacher's pet) as antagonists in the struggle for success in school (Luttrell 1993a, 1993b). In the case of the women's aspirational stories, split images of femininity were featured—good and bad, attractive and unattractive, clean and dirty, black and white women were pitted against each other as symbolic antagonists in the struggle for success. All the women drew upon these split images to define, evaluate, or fantasize about themselves as a somebody (or not). For example, one of the most important marks of success was the ability to "get dressed up to go to work," or as Gloria put it, to have a job where "you get to go to work looking like you're somebody." Consider Helen's "choice" between the sister who worked in the factory and "looked like a bum," and the other sister who went to her secretarial job "all dressed up—she looked real nice."

As I explained earlier, these split images ease psychic or inner tensions between unwanted or thwarted parts of the self (such as the tensions among women's social, sexual, and autonomous selves). Cast in either-or terms, these split images are projected outwards where one side (or antagonist) is devalued and the other is idealized, as in the "good" or valued sister who looks nice and the "bad" or devalued sister who looks like a bum. In this way splitting works at a cultural level to ease social tensions and inequalities. Furthermore, these split images promote women's continued participation in the institutions of femininity (such as the institutions of motherhood, marriage, and compulsory heterosexuality).[14] Politically, these idealized and split images divide women from each other, directing attention away from the economic, political, and psychological subordination women share (Palmer 1983; Matthews 1984). The images vary over time, within specific institutional contexts, and have different consequences for different groups of women.[15] This last point is central to my analysis of the women's self formation.

In the following section I examine these split images and voices more closely to show that each group of women drew upon distinct events or scenes to account for their selves. Whereas the North Carolina women's accounts featured work scenes characterized by social encounters between self (as devalued black employees) and other (as idealized and dominant white employers), the Philadelphia women's accounts featured school scenes characterized by social encounters between self (as distinct and oppositional) and other (as an idealized person who is "college-material" or already a professional).

THE NORTH CAROLINA WOMEN'S ACCOUNTS

I was wanting to be a nurse, but then we stopped school to help mama out. When she got straightened out I didn't want to go back [to school]. I felt like all the kids that we went to school with had moved on. And then when we went back we went back with a younger group. I was ashamed to be so big so I started to work in my first job that I had, in a restaurant. And the blacks had to be in the back, had to work in the back. Nobody could see you in the front unless they run short, unless the lunch hour would get busy and they couldn't keep up. Then they would pull somebody black from the back. I started as a dishwasher and helped the lady cook who was in the back. And then one day at lunch time when they couldn't keep up they would pull me out of the kitchen to make hotdogs. I still didn't get out on the floor to clean up, nothing like that. I had to stay behind the counter making hotdogs. All the white peoples was in the front and all the black was in the back. And you didn't see the blacks out until it was time for us to leave or if they needed some help. But I really liked going to school and I wished that I could have stayed in school 'cause I wanted to be a nurse.

Lilly's story is typical of how the North Carolina women narrated their childhood aspirations. Louise's account begins and ends with her thwarted desire to become a nurse. In between she charts a sequence of events that appear in all the North Carolina women's stories: school attendance is limited because of family and farmwork demands, and it becomes necessary to leave school before graduating; entrance into a racially segregated labor market is riddled with difficulties and disappointments, and as a result, dreams of a different future are deferred, if not abandoned. Implicit notions of success and failure weave these events together. Success (becoming a nurse) depends on finishing school. School, however, is not a neutral place: some kids move past others who feel (or are made to feel) shame for their failure. Success in the work world (defined as being visible and valued) is a white privilege; blacks are unable to "get ahead" even though business is dependent upon their labor. Lilly characterizes the world of work as split between those (devalued) positions in the "back" and those (idealized) positions in "front" which served not only to diminish the worth of black employees, but to disavow their presence altogether. As Lilly describes it, the world of work was organized so that "you didn't see the blacks."

It is within (and against) this world of work that Lilly formed her ambitions and critical self appraisal. Her account reveals a pattern of blame that was common to the women interviewed. Notice how she at once externalized and internalized the blame for her school failure (emphasizing her mothers' illness as the reason she fell behind in school and the shame she felt for having grown bigger than the other children). This pattern of blame (both self- and (m)other-blame) emerged as a partial explanation for why the women had failed in school. Despite the North Carolina women's recurrent references to structural or institutional forces and their negative effects (economic disadvantages, racial discrimination, familial constraints, especially as older siblings responsible for the care of younger siblings, and inadequate school resources and facilities), ultimately, they referenced their own (and others') character flaws and traits to explain why they hadn't "become somebody."[16]

Examples of being viewed as "behind," unworthy, or undeserving emerged across all the North Carolina women's accounts. Ella's story begins with her desire to escape the farm through marriage and migration north:

He came down here from New York, nice and sweet, and I was getting out of the country. I didn't have to work on no farm, I was getting out of the country. So I left and got a good job in New York, to me it was good.

She describes her industrial job, but says that due to inadequate childcare for her baby, she felt forced to return home to work as a domestic. Ella concludes with an anecdote about being treated without respect by her white employer, followed by the statement "some of the people were nice and some of them were not":

> We would say if we did any kind of work it wasn't going to be nothing but babysitting, that's right, we would say that too. Haven't you heard me tell you how I worked for this lady? I worked for this lady and she fixed dinner for me. Her husband was in a wheel chair and she sat her dog and her husband up at the table and sat me off at a little table back (*laughing*). I'll tell you something, that hasn't been too long ago. I babysat for another lady. Some of the people were nice and some of them were not.

Ella's account draws on the voices and images of her peers—what other rural, black girls in the segregated South "would say" about what they could anticipate for themselves. Her story also draws on the image of her white employer who sought to deny her legitimacy and worth. Both sets of voices and images are heard and seen internally as a struggle not only between two opposing social groups, but also as a breakdown of recognition between self and other.

Linda's account opens with her dreams of owning a small business. She explains that she loves children and would consider running a daycare center more than "just a job." She traces her desire to instill "positive self-esteem in each and every child I care for" to her experience of domestic service work. She recalls an incident where the "white lady" she worked for began spraying her with Lysol before she started her domestic chores:

> We was in the kitchen when she came at me with a can of spray. I wasn't going to let nobody spray me. I could feel my hand on the knife behind me on the counter. I might have killed that woman, I could feel the knife in my hand. But I got out of there before any damage could be done. Not all the white peoples I worked for were that bad, some of them was nice people, but then I could never forget. Black people were treated as dirt back long and then.

Examples of being treated "as dirt" evoked strong feelings as each woman seemed to (re)experience the comparison of herself to an idealized and more valued other.[17] Betty's account further illustrates the pervasive and deep effects of racial inequities and violence in the self-making process as she remembers her struggle to defend personal dignity without endangering one's self or others (and her regrets about her particular defensive strategies):

> You can't imagine what people got beat out of in those days, how they had to answer to white people. It could make you ashamed to see them take it. But as my mother always say that kindness don't hurt anybody. You can get more by being easy and kind than you can by being harsh and ugly. She would say you can get right next to a person being nice, but you can't by being ugly. As ugly as that person talks to you, the nicer you be, that really does something to them. But I didn't see it like that. I wanted my mother to talk ugly to the teachers or to the man whose land we farmed. But see, she didn't do it. She took whatever it was and went on. And that's what I got mad with her. And I regret it. I reckon

I'll regret it till I die. But I wanted to do it so—so much so that I wanted to talk for everyone, you know take up everybody's battle. I didn't want nobody thinking I was a coward. But I seen a lot of people being made to be cowards and some of them is cowards and some of them are just afraid they might say the wrong things. They're afraid they will say something that will hurt their own self or get someone else hurt. So that's why I wanted to be a social worker. I wanted to be somebody, that's why I always tried in school and was interested in learning.

Betty's account stresses the conditions under which she strove to create a visible, differentiated, and worthy self in the face of racial discrimination. These conditions further assisted the splitting off (and disavowal) of those parts of the self (most especially ambition and aggression) which were dangerous to self and other. Moreover, these either-or terms of existence, where one could either "be nice" or "talk ugly," left costly scars, including Betty's wish to become a social worker. Such an aspiration served to sustain, if not resolve, the tension between recognition and self-assertion, a tension that in her experience had often found expression in relations of domination. Yet the gap between her fantasies and her realities was still irresolvable.

The North Carolina women's formative experiences, rooted in a past when "there was a lot to worry about long and then," highlight the challenges of self-formation within specific historical and social contexts. By viewing their past feelings and actions as results of structural circumstances considered to be no longer in effect, the women could perhaps pursue new options, including a return to school. Yet the following examples illustrate that few believed schooling alone would enable them to attain their deferred childhood dreams.

All but two of the North Carolina women told of people they knew who had gotten a "good education," only to find themselves working in laundries, banks, motels, or schools as "housekeepers":

I know a lot of educated ones doing work no better than I'm doing now. Then a job is a job. It's nothin' against the job but when you got a little education I think you most likely will try to find somethin' better than cleanin'.

My niece, she has herself a master's, I was there at her graduation. But she's working at a laundry, she's been there some five years. She kept going to one interview after another and she never would get a job. Maybe it was somethin' she said, but you would think that she could be workin' in a place better than a laundry with a master['s] degree.

Discussions about the futility of education punctuate each North Carolina woman's account. Most often these examples are part of a defense of their jobs as housekeepers. One woman explained that her work, while probably not valued by anyone else, was important (if not critical) to the scientific advancements made by the professor whose lab and office she cleaned. In one sense, these examples represent "disclaimers" about their educational decisions (Hewitt and Stokes 1978). In another sense, they serve as "folk theories" about "making it" that do not valorize academic pursuit over other means (Ogbu 1988). Or, as Dorothy Smith (1987) might argue, these examples express critical insights that the North Carolina women had about the racial and patriarchal organization of work (Smith 1987). In any case, the women did not fully embrace school as a ticket for upward mobility in the figured world of success. Nor did they regard school as the primary context or sphere of activity within (and against) which they justified or defended their selves. Rather, it was within (and against) the sphere of work, characterized by conflicts between self and other, black and white, devalued and idealized antagonists, that the North Carolina women accounted for their ambitions.

THE PHILADELPHIA WOMEN'S ACCOUNTS

Whereas the North Carolina women had serious doubts about school as a pathway to social mobility, the Philadelphia women believed in the college ticket, but gave reasons why they had rejected the ride. All the Philadelphia women narrated their childhood aspirations by remembering (and justifying) their school decisions and actions, particularly why they had not pursued a college education. Doris's account is typical:

> I always wanted to be a secretary. No let me backtrack. I guess I always preferred to go to college, but the idea that there was no money to go made it that you were going to be a secretary. You knew there just wasn't an option to pick something else. There was one thing definite. I wasn't going to work in the factory.

In recalling their pasts, the Philadelphia women stressed that they thought about going to college, but that limited finances made college an impossibility:

> It wasn't that I never thought about college—it was just that nobody around me ever went. We all knew that college was for kids whose parents had the money to send them. So we just didn't even discuss it.

> I remember thinking about college in eleventh grade, but it wasn't feasible. You could sit around and think about it, but it just wasn't feasible.

Moreover, three-quarters of the Philadelphia women said that they would not have felt "comfortable" with college students whom they perceived as "different," and for this reason, they had not pursued a college education. They did not identify with students whom they saw as "college material," and as one woman explained:

> I really wanted to go to college, but I would have been with students who were completely different from me. After sixteen years of feeling uncomfortable in school, I needed a rest. Even today I can't walk on a college campus without feeling a pit in my stomach and a lump in my throat.

College represented the unknown, an unfamiliar and potentially unfriendly territory that was foreign to people they knew and with whom they could identify. As Pam remembered:

> Even though I was in the advanced track, the academic track, I really didn't think about being anything except a secretary. I wanted to stick to something *I knew* I could do.
> *And what was that?*
> I knew I could do all the things a secretary does—I had seen my older sister do it. She was great at it and I knew I'd be good at it too. I wasn't sure whether I was college material, I guess mostly because I didn't know anyone else who was.

Still other Philadelphia women, like Peggy, explained how school "tracked" working-class students into working-class jobs:[18]

> In high school I had signed up for commercial, but I got sent to kitchen practice.
> *What was kitchen practice?*
> Being a waitress, cook, chef. That was the worst course in school. There was really the low life in that course.
> *How did people get placed into kitchen practice?*
> I think they just went down and said, well this is a poor one and she's not going to do good; she probably doesn't have the mentality. Look at the income, look where she lives, she's not going to amount to anything so stick her in there. Once you got into ninth grade you ran into a lot of problems. It didn't matter how smart you were anymore, they didn't take that into consideration. It was where you lived and how much money you had backing you. There were academic courses where I went to high school, you know English and history and all. Only some of us were put into academic—I wasn't one of them.
> *Even though you were this really good student in junior high?* [She had made the honor roll every semester.]
> That's right. You know at the time I just didn't think anything of it. I accepted it. Then afterwards I thought about it, why did that happen? I could have been put into academic. If only I had pushed harder. I remember that I had wanted to become something professional, like a lawyer maybe. I did, I wanted to be somebody when I was younger.

But most often the Philadelphia women accounted for their failed ambitions by stressing a set of (alternative) values about what "really matters" in life. Anne makes this point as she tells about her childhood aspirations:

> I wasn't interested in the academic track. I didn't know why I needed to study history and all. I was interested in learning what I needed for a job like typing, bookkeeping, and the commercial courses. I couldn't wait to get out of school where I could be on my own, where I could be myself and do what I wanted to do. Some of it was to have my own money so I could buy what I wanted for myself, but we all, all the girls I hung with, all of us were in commercial and

we knew what we wanted. We knew what we needed to do to, you know, about life, we knew about life even if we didn't know what they were teaching us about in school.

Anne's account draws on the images and voices of people she valued to justify her school decision. She grounds her actions in the standpoint of "the girls I hung with," who, as part of the "commercial" track, actively opposed the dominant school culture. Sounding much like the girls in Michelle Fine's (1991) ethnographic study of an urban high school, the Philadelphia women recalled feeling trapped by dominant school values and traditions that did not fit their own experiences or desires. (In contrast, the North Carolina women spoke of school as a luxury, an escape from farmwork and family demands.) The Philadelphia women emphasized the split or opposition between "commonsense" or "streetwise" and "schoolwise" knowledge to account for why they had left school.[19] Their self appraisals were remembered in the voice and image of peers, who were not considered the ideal version of a "somebody," but nevertheless were viewed as legitimate.

Joanne's account provides another case in point. Recall that she began her aspirational account with her dream of becoming a judge, for which she had been reprimanded in school. Joanne describes her troubled school career in terms of her "bad attitude" toward school authorities and impatience with petty rules and regulations. Her education is put on hold when, as the oldest daughter, she leaves school to support her younger siblings through school. At this point Joanne's account shifts to her uncharacteristic work history and travel abroad. After years of "scrimping and saving," she takes a trip to Europe, shedding both her clerical and familial duties. Upon her return, Joanne lands a good job as a receptionist in a doctor's office, followed by an even better job in a law firm. Joanne concludes:

> You know I think a lot of working-class people put professional people with educations on a pedestal. It is like with blacks—if all you see of blacks is that they are trash men, then you think they must all be like that. But I met a lot of professional people—people with more knowledge than me, and maybe more ambition, but they weren't really any better than me. They weren't really any different, even if they were somebody. You know, the thing is, with all the people I met I still married the boy on the corner. I just always felt most comfortable with him. Maybe I had a strong homing instinct, but that's just who I am.

Joanne draws on the image and voice of those "working-class" people with whom she is "comfortable," and the image and voice of "professionals" (on pedestals) who may have more status, knowledge, and ambition, but are no "better" than she is.

This account is typical of how the women's stories reveal, even as they disguise, the deeply ingrained, yet implicit value of upward mobility within American culture. This value is best captured by Lillian Rubin's (1976:8–9) observation that we judge people by how well they "move up or down, not just through" the class structure. Perhaps with this judgment in mind Joanne defends her choice not to "marry up," which she casts as a struggle for recognition, an "instinct" to return home to enjoy the company of those with whom she feels "comfortable."[20]

Summary

Whether they discussed their ambitions and self-understandings in light of work or school, both groups of women felt compelled to account for their lack of social mobility.[21] The women's accounts also reveal the self-making process as a tension and most often a breakdown (cast in race and class terms) between self assertion and recognition. Given the North Carolina women's doubts about school as an avenue of social mobility and the Philadelphia women's resistant view of school, most unresolved is the question of why both groups of women decided to eventually continue their schooling as a way to "better" themselves. Now we are ready to address that question.

THE PUSH AND PULL OF SCHOOL

All the women's accounts illustrate the importance of developing other selves outside the world of success—selves that are worthwhile regardless of schooling or job; selves that enjoy, depend upon, and are affiliated with others. In both sets of accounts, the women stress their "social selves," that part of the self that strives to satisfy the expectations and needs of others, is capable of empathy, and seeks interaction. This part of the self is what women are usually praised for; it is what women learn makes them appealing. Thus, it should be no surprise that the women's accounts stress this aspect.

Beyond the obvious gender typecasting of their typical aspirations (e.g., nurses, teachers, secretaries, models, social workers), the best illustration of the women's emphasis on their social selves is how consistently they described their current educational pursuits and their desires to "better themselves" in terms of their children's needs, not their own.[22] Joanne's comment is typical of the hundreds I heard:

> My mother thinks I am crazy for coming back to school; she doesn't see the point and thinks I should be home with my kids. I try to explain that my going to school is good for my kids; I'm being a role model for them and I feel good about that.

As noted earlier, this relational propensity has been cited by some as an essential (albeit devalued) feature of female development and socialization (Gilligan 1982; Chodorow 1978). Others, like Flax and Benjamin, insist that while women's relational needs may be more developed, they are by no means the only ones. Much less developed, if not repressed, are women's needs to assert and be recognized for their intellectual or creative mastery, otherwise referred to by Flax as the autonomous self. This need/desire (characterized by the culture as unfeminine) is threatening to women's selves (and to others), and as such, gets split off (and disavowed).[23]

This, in my view, is the deeper meaning and the more radical ramification of the women's desires to return to school to "better themselves." In one sense, by claiming that they are returning to school to benefit their children, the women split off (in part disavowing and in part protecting themselves from) other aspects of their selves, such as intellectual or creative mastery. This psychic defense in favor of the social over the autonomous self also has the weight of the culture behind it, as women (particularly as mothers) are encouraged to put their needs second to others.'

Even if they shortchange girls, as current research documents (AAUW Report 1992), schools outpace other institutions in encouraging the expression of their ambitions and desires to "become somebody." American schools are, without a doubt, one of the major public spaces where girls get recruited into (and put out of) the world of success. With all its requisite and paradoxical cultural and psychic tensions, schools offer girls an opportunity to express, if not fully develop, autonomy. Ironically, the same cultural and psychic forces which pushed the women out of school, pull them back as adults: the desire for mutual recognition between themselves (as students and as mothers) and others (their teachers and their children). I suggest that the women's return to school asserts that part of the self most forbidden or constricted for women, and as such should not be minimized or viewed as simple accommodation to dominant ideologies of success and upward mobility.

CONCLUSION

We need a more sophisticated cultural and psychodynamic understanding of how selves are made within specific contexts, under certain conditions, and with different risks and costs attached.[24] My hope is that feminist and adult literacy educators will seize upon the cultural and psychic meanings and struggle to "become somebody" as the crux of adult literacy education. I would encourage literacy educators to be more attuned to how adult learners seek to establish at least the image of a valued and legitimate self as part of classroom exchanges or tutoring sessions. Moreover, I would caution adult literacy educators against programs and curriculum, such as current family or intergenerational literacy initiatives, which unwittingly deny or suppress women's autonomous wishes for intellectual mastery (independent of the needs of children, for whom they are primarily responsible).[25] My research suggests that, at the very least, collecting and examining childhood memories of school and ambitions are worthwhile learning opportunities for both teachers and students. Perhaps in an effort to collect and reconstruct women's schooling memories and childhood desires as differentiated yet collective experience, adult education programs and curriculum can tap into powerful (if not paradoxical) impulses toward mutual recognition between student and teacher, and among students, which can in turn lead to political action.

NOTES

1. I would like to thank the editors for all their helpful comments on this paper. I am especially indebted to co-editor Dorothy Holland for her long-standing interest in my work and the feedback she provided; Naomi Quinn for her insightful, detailed, and timely feedback and her keen sense and support of my intellectual project; and Mary Rogers for constant validation and help making my prose more reader-friendly.

2. I refer to the two groups of women in terms of locality, as the Philadelphia and North Carolina women. In the past I have identified the women by race and class (Luttrell 1989). However, these labels can serve to fix the women's identities and make it difficult for the reader to focus on how selves are formed and reformed, which is the subject of this paper. The Philadelphia women were white and had been raised in the same neighborhood, which, when the study began, was in flux and disarray because of industrial relocation and massive social service cutbacks. They had all attended neighborhood schools during the late 1940s, the 1950s, and the early 1960s; only 20 percent had finished high school. They had moved in and out of the work force as clerical workers, factory hands, waitresses, hospital or teachers' aides. Two women were displaced homemakers when the study began. All the North Carolina women referred to themselves as black and had grown up in southern, rural communities where they had experience doing farmwork; most had picked cotton or tended tobacco during their youth. They had attended segregated rural schools, but because of the demands of farm life, lack of transportation, and racial discrimination, their school attendance had been sporadic. Only two of the North Carolina women had graduated from high school, one of whom had completed one year at a local black college. All were employed at the university and shared similar work histories, which included domestic work in white people's homes.

3. For analytical purposes I treat the women's stories and the explanations they give about their past and present actions as "vocabularies of motive." People are said to seek vocabularies of motive that will appeal to both themselves and their audiences. Vocabularies of motive are "accounts" when they are used to explain what might be perceived by others as unexpected or inappropriate behavior. "Indeed, the giving and taking of accounts in everyday life represents one of the most fundamental characteristics of the social order" (Weinstein 1980:591). From this symbolic interactionist perspective, the women's aspirational stories serve dual purposes. In the first instance, they serve to defeat in advance any negative judgments that I, as a white, middle-class, college-educated professional might have of them (Hewitt and Stokes 1978). Secondly, the women's accounts could be said to provide them a means whereby they can reconcile past experiences, feelings, and selves in school with current ambitions. It is understood that these accounts are partial, yet they provide important insight into the conditions under which, and contexts within which the women's selves were made. See Burke (1969, 1954), Mills (1940), Foote (1951), Scott and Lyman (1968), Weinstein (1980), and Hewitt and Stokes (1978) for discussions about accounts and accounting strategies, and McLaren (1982) for an application of this concept to adult women's educational ambitions and pursuits.

4. See Bourdieu 1977; Bernstein 1975; Canann 1990; Carby 1982; Connell et al. 1982; Fine 1991; Foley 1990; Fuller 1980; Holland and Eisenhart 1990; Lesko 1988; McRobbie 1978, 1991; Thorne 1993; Walkerdine 1990; Weis 1990; Wexler 1983; Willis 1977.

5. I also do not mean to suggest that notions of the self are universal or that there is only one way to know the self. See Taylor (1989) for his description of the key feature of the modern Western concept of the self, and Marcus and Fisher (1986) for their discussion of the cultural variability in ideas about self.

6. While I am sympathetic to the feminist and postmodernist project of deconstructing notions of the self as artifacts of white, male, and Western culture (Foucault 1977; Irigaray 1985), I reject the notion of a "de-centered" self as either fiction or the cause of celebration. See Flax (1990) for an excellent critique of postmodern notions of the self/subjectivity. My understanding of the self and the process of self formation is both intersubjective and intrapsychic, a helpful distinction made by Jessica Benjamin (1988).

7. See symbolic interactionists Cooley (1983); Mead (1962); Goffman (1959, 1963); and object-relations theorists Benjamin (1988); Chodorow (1978, 1989); Fairbairn (1952); Greenberg and Mitchell (1983); Hughes (1989); Klein (1975); Jacobson (1965); Mahler (1975); Stern (1985). Also of interest is the recent rediscovery and augmentation of relational theory: Kohut (1978), Sullivan (1970, 1964), and Winnicott (1971, 1965, 1975).

8. Gilligan (1982) and Ruddick (1989) are examples of the models that Flax rejects.

9. Anthropologist Katherine Ewing (1990) says that in all cultures people can be observed to project multiple and shifting self-representations, often being unaware of these shifts and inconsistencies. Despite this fact, people experience their self as whole and continuous.

10. During the interviewing process, more than half of the women took the opportunity to reflect upon a painful experience from the past. In some instances, the women shared buried or abandoned memories about which they developed new understandings (and which also prompted me to recover bits of my buried past as well). In most cases, memories unfolded through emotional displays (crying, halted speech, requests for me to turn off the tape recorder as they expressed their feelings). In one case, the interviewee became angry with me, crying, "I haven't thought about this for years, why did you make me talk about this?" When I asked her if we should stop the session, she said no, she needed to talk about the incident. I am drawn to the term "memory work" from Frigga Haug et al. (1987) to describe both the social scientific method I used and my own experience conducting research, which was filled with both perils and possibilities. I am also drawn to the term because of its correspondence to Arlie Hochschild's (1983) notion of "emotion work" which women are more prone to perform in our society than men. And as Flax (1987) asserts, memory (and the psychic force of repression) is different for women than for men in our culture. This claim deserves empirical investigation.

11. For a brief discussion of my coding procedure for identifying inter- and intragroup patterns in the structure and meaning of the interviews I collected, see Luttrell 1993.

12. Krieger (1991) notes that in traditional social science research the self of the researcher is treated as a variable which must be minimized, countered, balanced, or neutralized. I am intrigued by her assertion that in social science, "we write to protect as much as we write to express the self and to describe the world. Although we speak of protecting others—usually the people our studies are about—the main object of our protective strategies is always our selves" (32). See Thorne (1993), Behar (1993), Briggs

(1986), Paget (1990), Williams (1988), and Foley (1990) for discussions about the presence of the self as a source of knowledge for the researcher.

13. See Hunt (1989) for a discussion of transference and counter transference in the interviewing process.

14. See Snitow, Stansell, and Thompson (1983) and Ginsberg and Tsing (1990) for excellent collections of essays that explore this issue; see Patricia Hill Collins (1990) and Evelyn Brooks Higginbotham (1992) for how split images about African-American women also serve this purpose.

15. Milis (1940:908) writes about how motives "have careers that are woven through changing institutional fabrics." The motives accompanying the institutions of femininity vary from one historical period to another, across classes, regions, and nations. Research with women literacy learners growing up in the 1970s would shed further light on these women's vocabularies of motive, as would comparative international research on women's pursuits of literacy.

16. See Luttrell (1993a, 1993b) for a discussion of the difference between the North Carolina and Philadelphia women's perceptions of their "problems" in school. While the women explained their problems as due to character flaws, I explain their problems as being rooted in and responses to each school context (rural-community and urban-bureaucratic) and to the psychodynamics of splitting and maternal omnipotence.

17. See Judith Rollins (1985) for her discussion of the social-psychological dimensions of domestic work.

18. See Bowles and Gintis (1976) for the classic text on how schools "track" different groups of students, preparing them to take on jobs for which they are destined, and Willis (1977) for how students creatively (and sometimes oppositionally) respond to and internalize these school values and expectations.

19. See Luttrell (1989, 1993a) for a discussion of how each group of women distinguished "commonsense" from "schoolwise" intelligence, and how these different perspectives on knowledge influenced their schooling.

20. References to their need to feel "comfortable" with others (particularly in school) were found in every Philadelphia woman's account.

21. The reasons why each group of women identified a different institutional context are complicated and cannot be answered fully, based on my research. I suspect this is related, in part, to the difference in school context. The North Carolina women's view of and experience in the rural-community school was more integral to their family, farmwork, and community life, whereas the Philadelphia women's experiences of school were set apart from family and community (Luttrell 1993a). However, further comparative research with Southern, rural white women and northeastern, urban black women is necessary to fully explain these differences.

22. More than 80 percent of the 200 women surveyed mentioned their roles or responsibilities as mothers and the need to be "better mothers" as a reason for returning to school.

23. See Walkerdine (1990) for an excellent discussion of these issues as they relate to girls' (mis)education.

24. See Rockhill (1987) for her analysis of the risks attached to literacy acquisition for the group of Hispanic women she interviewed.

25. See Luttrell (forthcoming a, b) for a critique of literacy programs and practices which undermine women's autonomous selves.

REFERENCES

American Association of University Women Report. 1992. How Schools Shortchange Girls: A Study of Major Findings on Girls and Education. Researched by the Wellesley College Center for Research on Women.

Behar, Ruth. 1993. Translated Woman: Crossing the Border with Esperanza's Story. Boston: Beacon Press.

Benjamin, Jessica. 1988. The Bonds of Love: Psychoanalysis, Feminism and the Problem of Domination. New York: Pantheon.

————. 1993. The Omnipotent Mother: A Psychoanalytic Study of Fantasy and Reality. *In* Representations of Motherhood. D. Bassin, M. Honey, and M. M. Kaplan, eds. New Haven and London: Yale University Press.

Bernstein, Basil. 1975. Class, Codes and Control, vol. 3. London: Routledge and Kegan Paul.

Bourdieu, Pierre. 1977. Outline of a Theory of Practice. Cambridge: Cambridge University Press.

Bowles, Samuel and Herbert Gintis. 1976. Schooling in Capitalist America. New York: Basic Books.

Briggs, Jean. 1986. Kapluna Daughter. *In* Women in the Field: Anthropological Experiences. Peggy Golde, ed. Pp. 19–44. Berkeley: University of California Press.

Burke, Kenneth. 1954. Permanence and Change: An Anatomy of Purpose. Los Altos, CA: Hermes Publication.

————. 1969. A Grammar of Motives. Berkeley. University of California Press.

Canaan, Joyce. 1990. Passing Notes and Telling Jokes: Gendered Strategies among American Middle School Teenagers. *In* Uncertain Terms: Negotiating Gender in American Culture. Faye Ginsberg and Anna Tsing, eds. Pp. 215–231. Boston: Beacon Press.

Carby, Hazel. 1982. Schooling in Babylon. *In* The Empire Strikes Back, Centre for Contemporary Cultural Studies, ed. Pp. 183–211. London: Hutchinson.

Chodorow, Nancy. 1978. The Reproduction of Mothering: Psychoanalysis and the Sociology of Gender. Berkeley: University of California Press.

————. 1989. Feminism and Psychoanalytic Theory. New Haven and London: Yale University Press.

Clifford, James and George Marcus. 1986. Writing Culture: The Poetics and Politics of Ethnography. Berkeley: University of California Press.

Collins, Patricia Hill. 1990. Black Feminist Thought: Knowledge, Consciousness and the Politics of Empowerment. London: HarperCollins Academic.

Connell, R. W., D. J. Ashenden, S. Kessler, and G. W. Dowsett. 1982. Making the Difference: Schools, Families and Social Division. Sydney: George Allen and Unwin.

Cooley, Charles H. 1983. Human Nature and the Social Order. New Brunswick, NJ: Transaction.

Ewing, Katherine. 1990. The Illusion of Wholeness: Culture, Self and the Experience of Inconsistency. Ethos 18(3):251–278.

Fairbairn, W. R. D. 1952. An Object Relations Theory of the Personality. New York: Basic Books.

Fine, Michelle. 1991. Framing Dropouts: Notes on the Politics of an Urban Public High School. Albany: SUNY Press.

Flax, Jane. 1987. Re-membering the Selves: Is the Repressed Gendered? Michigan Quarterly 26(1).

————. 1990. Thinking Fragments: Psychoanalysis, Feminism, and Postmodernism in the Contemporary West. Berkeley: University of California Press.

Foley, Douglas. 1990. Learning Capitalist Culture. Philadelphia: University of Pennsylvania Press.

Foote, N. 1951. Identification as the Basis for a Theory of Motivation. American Sociological Review 16:14–21.

Foucault, Michel. 1977. Language, Counter-memory, Practice. Donald F. Bouchard, ed. Ithaca: Cornell University Press.

Fuller, Margaret. 1980. Black Girls in a London Comprehensive School. *In* Schooling for Women's Work. R. Deem, ed. London: Routledge and Kegan Paul.

Gilligan, Carol. 1982. In a Different Voice: Psychological Theory and Women's Development. Cambridge, MA: Harvard University Press.

Ginsberg, Faye and Anna Tsing, eds. 1990. Uncertain Terms: Negotiating Gender in American Culture. Boston: Beacon Press.

Goffman, Erving. 1959. The Presentation of Self in Everyday Life. New York: Doubleday Anchor.

————. 1963. Stigma: Notes on the Management of Spoiled Identity. Englewood Cliffs, NJ: Prentice Hall.

Greenberg, Jay and Stephen Mitchell. 1983. Object Relations in Psychoanalytic Theory. Cambridge, MA: Harvard University Press.

Hansot, Elizabeth and David Tyack. 1988. Gender in American Public Schools: Thinking Institutionally. Signs: Journal of Women in Culture and Society 13(4):741–760.

Haug, Frigga and Others. 1987. Female Sexualization: A Collective Work of Memory. Erica Carter, trans. London: Verso.

Hewitt, J. P. and R. Stokes. 1978. Disclaimers. *In* Symbolic Interaction: A Reader in Social Psychology. J. Manis and B. Meltzer, eds. Pp. 308–318. Boston: Allyn and Bacon, Inc.

Higginbotham, Evelyn Brooks. 1992. African-American Women's History and the Meta-language of Race. Signs: Journal of Women in Culture and Society 17(2):251–274.

Hochschild, Arlie. 1983. The Managed Heart: Commercialization of Human Feeling. Berkeley: University of California Press.

Holland, Dorothy. 1988. In the Voice of, In the Image Of: Socially Situated Presentations of Attractiveness. IPA Papers in Pragmatics 2(1/2):106–135.

Holland, Dorothy, Carole Cain, William Lachicotte, Deborah Skinner, and Reneé Prillamann. In press. Emerging Selves: Identities Forming in and against Cultural Worlds. Cambridge: Harvard University Press.

Holland, Dorothy and Margaret Eisenhart. 1990. Educated in Romance: Achievement and College Culture. Chicago: University of Chicago Press.

Holland, Dorothy and Naomi Quinn, eds. 1987. Cultural Models in Language and Thought. Cambridge: Cambridge University Press.

Hughes, Judith. 1989. Reshaping the Psychoanalytic Domain: The Work of Melanie Klein, W. R. D. Fairbairn and D. W. Winnicott. Berkeley: University of California Press.

Hunt, Jennifer. 1989. Psychoanalytic Aspects of Fieldwork. Newbury Park, CA: Sage Publications.

Irigaray, Luce. 1985. Speculum of the Other Woman. Gillian C. Gill, trans. Ithaca, NY: Cornell University Press.

Jacobson, Edith. 1965. The Self and the Object World. London: Hogarth.

Klein, Melanie. 1975. Love, Guilt and Reparation, and Other Works, 1921–1945. London: Hogarth.

Kohut, Heinz. 1978. The Search for the Self: Selected Writings of Heinz Kohut, 1950–1978. New York: International Universities Press.

Krieger, Susan. 1991. Social Science and the Self: Personal Essays on an Art Form. New Brunswick, NJ: Rutgers University Press.

Lesko, Nancy. 1988. Symbolizing Society: Stories, Rites and Structure in a Catholic High School. New York: Falmer Press.

Luttrell, Wendy. 1989. Working-Class Women's Ways of Knowing: Effects of Gender, Race, and Class. Sociology of Education 62 (January):33–46.

———. 1993a. The Teachers They All Had Their Pets: Concepts of Gender, Knowledge and Power. Signs: Journal of Women in Culture and Society 18(3):505–546.

———. 1993b. Women's Narratives of School: The Quest for Maternal Love and Schoolwise Knowledge. Paper presented at the 1993 American Sociological Association Annual Meeting.

———. 1994. "Becoming Somebody": Aspirations, Opportunities, and Womanhood. *In* Gender, Class and Country. Gay Young and Bette Dickerson, eds. London: Zed Press.

———. forthcoming a. Taking Care of Literacy: A Feminist Critique. Educational Policy.

———. forthcoming b. School Smart and Mother Wise: Women's Selves, Voices and Values. New York: Routledge.

McRobbie, A. 1978. Working Class Girls and the Culture of Femininity. *In* Women Take Issue: Aspects of Women's Subordination. Women Studies Group CCCS, ed. Pp. 96–108. London: Hutchinson.

———. 1991. Feminism and Youth Culture: from "Jackie" to "Just Seventeen." Boston: Unwin Hyman.

McLaren, Arlene. 1982. Ambition and Accounts: A Study of Working-Class Women in Adult Education. Psychiatry 45:235–246.

Mahler, Margaret, Fred Pine, and Anni Bergman. 1975. The Psychological Birth of the Human Infant: Symbiosis and Individuation. New York: Basic Books.

Marcus, George and Michael M. J. Fisher. 1986. Anthropology as Cultural Critique: An Experimental Moment in the Human Sciences. Chicago: University of Chicago Press.

Matthews, Jill Julius. 1984. Good and Mad Women: The Historical Construction of Femininity in Twentieth Century Australia. Sydney: George Allen and Unwin.

Meade, George H. 1962. Mind, Self, and Society. Chicago: University of Chicago Press.

Mills, C. W. 1940. Situated Actions and Vocabularies of Motive. American Sociological Review 5:905–913.

Ogbu, John U. 1988. Class Stratification, Racial Stratification, and Schooling. In Class, Race and Gender in American Education, Lois Weis, ed. Pp. 163–182. Albany: SUNY Press.

Paget, Marianne. 1990. Life Mirrors Work Mirrors Text Mirrors Life . . . Social Problems 37(2):137–148.

Palmer, Phyllis Marynick. 1983. White Women/Black Women: The Dualism of Female Identity and Experience in the United States. Feminist Studies 9(1):151–170.

Rockhill, Kathleen. 1987. Literacy As Threat/Desire: Longing to Be Somebody. *In* Women and Education: A Canadian Perspective. Jane Gaskell and Arlene McLaren, eds. Pp. 315–333. Calgary: Detselig Enterprises.

Rollins, Judith. 1985. Between Women: Domestics and Their Employers. Philadelphia: Temple University Press.

Rubin, Lillian. 1976. Worlds of Pain: Life in the Working-Class Family. New York: Basic Books.

Ruddick, Sara. 1989. Maternal Thinking: Toward a Politics of Peace. Boston: Beacon Press.

Scott, M. B. and Scott Lyman. 1968. Accounts. American Sociological Review 33 (February):46–62.

Smith, D. 1987. The Everyday World as Problematic: A Feminist Sociology. Boston: Northeastern University Press.

Snitow, Ann, Christine Stansell and Sharon Thompson, eds. 1983. Powers of Desire: The Politics of Sexuality. New York: Monthly Review Press.

Stern, Daniel. 1985. The Interpersonal World of the Infant: A View from Psychoanalysis and Developmental Psychology. New York: Basic Books.

Sullivan, Harry Stack. 1964. The Fusion of Psychiatry and Social Sciences. New York: Norton.

———. 1970. The Psychiatric Interview. New York: Norton.

Taylor, Charles. 1989. Sources of the Self: The Making of Modern Identity. Cambridge, MA: Harvard University Press.

Thorne, Barrie. 1993. Gender Play: Girls and Boys in School. New Brunswick, NJ: Rutgers University Press.

Walkerdine, Valerie. 1990. Schoolgirl Fictions. New York: Verso.

Weinstein, R. M. 1980. Vocabularies of Motive for Illicit Drug Use: An Application of the Accounts Framework. Sociological Quarterly 21:577–593.

Weis, Lois. 1990. Working Class Without Work: High School Students in a De-industrializing Economy. New York: Routledge.

Wexler, Philip. 1983. Movement, Class and Education. *In* Race, Class and Education. L. Barton and S. Walker, eds. Totowa, NJ: Croom Helm.

———. 1992. Becoming Somebody: Toward a Social Psychology of School. London: Falmer Press.

Williams, Patricia. 1988. On Being the Object of Property. Signs: Journal of Women in Culture and Society 14(4):5–24.

Willis, Paul. 1977. Learning to Labour: How Working-Class Kids Get Working-Class Jobs. Westmead, UK: Saxon House, Teakfield.

Winnicott, D. W. 1965. The Maturational Processes and the Facilitating Environment. New York: International Universities Press.

———. 1971. Playing and Reality. New York: Basic Books.

———. 1975. Through Pediatrics to Psycho-analysis. New York: Basic Books.

5

ARMANDO L. TRUJILLO

In Search of Aztlán: Movimiento Ideology and the Creation of a Chicano Worldview through Schooling*

On 9 December 1969 Chicano students in Aztlán City, Texas staged a three-week walkout of the public schools in protest against the discriminatory policies practiced by the Anglo school staff and administration (Hardgrave and Hinojosa 1975; Gutiérrez 1976).[1] The students, with the support of their parents, had presented the third of a series of petitions to the school board calling for relevant and equal-quality education. The petition listed a number of demands, among them a call for bilingual/bicultural education, the creation of a Mexican-American history course for credit, and the recognition of Diez y Seis de Septiembre (16 September) as a Mexican-American holiday.[2] The local struggle for relevant, equal-quality education had been a long one, and was brought to regional and national attention by the massive student walkout. While the walkout strategy was successful and the students and parents won some initial concessions from the Anglo administration (Smith and Foley 1975), the walkout achieved only modest change in the structure of ethnic power relations in the schooling domain. It nonetheless constituted a moral victory for Chicanos, for it was a statement of contemporary ethnic identity that gave the confrontation historical significance (Smith and Foley 1975). More than anything, this moral victory signaled the end of the era of local Anglo domination, and ultimately led to Chicano control over schooling.

A Chicano intellectual, José Angel Gutiérrez, and the Mexican-American Youth Organization (MAYO) helped the students and parents in their struggle for equal educational opportunity and treatment. Utilizing community support from the school walkout, an alternative political party, La Raza Unida, was organized and became the vehicle for Chicano political education and mobilization to overturn the political and socioeconomic domination imposed by the Anglo minority

---

* The concept of Aztlán represents a collective symbol through which an historically oppressed Mexican American ethnic minority can recognize their identity in the group's history and cultural heritage. *Movimiento* is the Spanish term for the Chicano Civil Rights Movement. For an expanded discussion on the concept of Aztlán, see the numerous essays in Anaya and Lomeli (1989).

since the turn of the century.[3] In the local elections of 1970, the Chicano community gained political control of both the school board and city council. After this important political victory, Aztlán City and the Raza Unida Party (RUP) became a major icon for the Chicano Civil Rights Movement in Texas and throughout the Southwest.[4]

After gaining local political control in Aztlán City, the RUP initiated a variety of reform programs designed to empower the Chicano community; among them were a variety of housing, mental health, health care, economic, and education programs. The institution of schooling was particularly recognized for the role it plays in processes of socialization, cultural and linguistic maintenance, and social change. José Angel Gutiérrez, the school board president of the Aztlán City School District from 1970 to 1972 and founder of the RUP in Zavala County, expressed his view and, by extension, the RUP's view of education when he stated:

> Education in this kind of society is mandatory if not a prerequisite for survival. [It] is also the fountain of socialization where our values get distorted and cultural imposition takes place. Not only do we want to reject that, but we want to substitute that with our own values which are just as dear and important. Education, finally, is important for us because from that kind of leadership that will emerge from those schools we will have the leaders for tomorrow to build a greater Aztlán (Reskin and Williams 1974).

Gutiérrez' statement captures the emergent cultural nationalist philosophy of the RUP in the early 1970s. It reflects, as well, the ideological position of the role schools were to play in the cultural production of a Chicano/a "educated person."

The concept of cultural production is akin to the notion of "emergent culture" as used by Raymond Williams (1973). Bauman (1977:48) refers to emergent culture as that process of continuous creation of new meanings and values, new practices, new significances and experiences. In studies of education, the concept of cultural production has been used to portray the way people "actively confront the ideological and material conditions presented by schooling" (Levinson and Holland this volume). The RUP's philosophy of cultural nationalism, when channeled through the institution of schooling, was tantamount to the cultural production of an emergent Chicano/a "educated person." When placed within the historical context and discourse of Aztlán and cultural nationalism, educational leaders in Aztlán City were striving to create not only Chicanos and Chicanas who would be able to survive in the mainstream society, but more than that, they were hoping to create the future leaders who would carry forth the struggle of building a greater Aztlán (Gutiérrez 1976). Through a comprehensive philosophy of bilingual/bicultural education, Chicano leaders in the school district sought to reverse the effects of acculturative and assimilative schooling under Anglo control, and to cultivate a "new" Chicano worldview (Smith and Foley 1975). In other words, they sought to create a "subject-position" for a

Chicano/a "educated person," specifically a bilingual, culturally proud, communally oriented individual. In essence, leaders sought to create politicized subjectivities in line with the distinct cultural and political-economic interests of the RUP. However, because of the nature of relations of power in the region, community and school, the model of a Chicano/a educated person quickly became contested and modified.

In this chapter, I analyze this struggle by looking at the changes in the structure of school politics in Aztlán City over twenty years, 1969–1989. The school walkout served as a watershed moment for cultural production and the divergent formation of identities—some for, some against the new ideology of Aztlán and the proposed Chicano/a educated person. Within this historical and cultural context, the actors who have played a prominent role in this development have been Chicanos and Anglos initially, and ironically Chicano educators themselves. In order to explore the relationship between the cultural production of the discourse of Aztlán and cultural nationalism, and the conceptualization of a Chicano/a "educated person," I first discuss Chicano nationalist ideology, national bilingual education policy, and the process of decolonization. Second, I explore the emergence of a new teaching ideology at the school district level, the ideological framework guiding the cultural production of a Chicano/a educated person. Third, I discuss the difference between teaching ideology, teaching perspective, and practical ideologies, and the Mexican-American educator's understanding of this difference. In deciphering these differences, I will rely on interviews conducted among educators in the school district. Finally, I present a synthesis of how educators' perspective on the school district's teaching ideology has changed from the decade of the 1970s to the decade of the 1980s, and the role that practical ideologies have played in this change. In pursuing this line of analysis, I will show that schools, as Levinson and Holland suggest in their introduction, are heterogeneous sites, and the target of a variety of efforts to construct knowledges and identities. As a result, Chicano educators have had access to a variety of "voices" and practices which have influenced their perspective on rejecting the new Chicano teaching ideology of maintenance bilingual/bicultural education; in turn, they have adopted a transitional bilingual education program model which is more acceptable to the dominant socio-ideological formation of the nation-state.

CHICANO NATIONALISM, BILINGUAL EDUCATION, AND DECOLONIZATION

Previous studies have shown a strong correlation between the struggle for equal educational opportunity by the Mexican-American community and the passage of the Bilingual Education Act (BEA) of 1968 (Mackey and Ornstein 1977; Trujillo 1993). Given the context of the Civil Rights Movement, with its political mobilization efforts emanating from different ethnic/racial communities, Chicanos were not alone in pressuring for governmental action in the area of educational equity and cultural recognition. It is not surprising, therefore, that one of the ways the government sought to address the provision of equal educational opportunity for non–English-dominant students was through the BEA. Bilingual education programs funded through the BEA, however, range with respect to the varied communities the programs serve. Because of this variety there have been various definitions and applications of the concept. Nonetheless, the Department of Education has provided the official definition:

> Bilingual education is the use of two languages, one of which is English, as mediums of instruction for the same pupil population in a well-organized program which encompasses part or all of the curriculum and includes the study of history and culture associated with the mother tongue. A complete program develops and maintains the children's self-esteem and a legitimate pride in both cultures. (Paulston 1980:8)

While this definition provides the guidelines for the development and implementation of bilingual education programs at the community level, the structure and program content have varied considerably. Furthermore, national bilingual education policy has undergone marked changes in its twenty-seven year history. Yet despite the changing character of bilingual education, the basic assumptions and overall goals of this innovative program have remained virtually intact. Paulston (1978) has identified five assumptions that have guided the implementation, practice and evaluation of Title VII bilingual education in the United States. The foremost assumption is that of "'equal opportunity' and the belief that bilingual education helps equalize such shortcomings of opportunity" (p. 411). The other four assumptions are concerned with the issue of "cultural diversity" and its related implications for improving the teaching-learning environment. In other words, it was assumed that inclusion of opportunities to study the history and culture of the ethnic group, as well as the provision of instruction in the group's native language, would result in the improved self-image of ethnic group members. In turn, through an improved self-image, ethnic group members would be better prepared to achieve positive schooling success. Supporters of bilingual education expected that the learning facility afforded through native language instruction, coupled with improved self-image, would in turn greatly facilitate participation and acceptance of ethnic-group members within the larger society. In short, based on these assumptions, Paulston emphasizes that the long-range goals of bilingual education programs have always been those of harmonious integration, by either economically incorporating or culturally assimilating the ethnolinguistic group into the larger society through the process of equalizing opportunity.

Kjolseth (1982) notes that many ethnic and nonethnic education leaders further assumed that bilingual education programs would facilitate the goal of cultural bilingualism and pluralism. In this respect, Chicano leaders within the movement came to regard bilingual education in general as an innovative policy with the potential for facilitating not only educational equity but the maintenance of community, as well (cf. Barrera 1988). By including native language instruction as well as the study of history and culture associated with that language, bilingual education programs had the potential to address the educational problems facing Chicano students, contributing to the maintenance of community and cultivating positive ethnic group relations.

For the first five years of its history, the BEA encouraged school districts to develop and implement bilingual programs which sought to address the issues of educational equity and cultural diversity through programs both innovative and experimental (Padilla 1984). The relative openness of the legislation allowed school districts wide latitude in developing the type of program that met both local needs and federal program guidelines. However, research on the implementation and structure of most bilingual education programs reveals that few programs in practice actually promoted bilingualism and cultural pluralism (Kjolseth 1982). The type of educational model operative within schools oftentimes reflected who held political control of the educational system. If the ethnic group had made significant inroads into the decision-making structure, then there would be a higher likelihood that the resultant structure of the bilingual program would follow a pluralistic model of education. While there are few documented cases where Chicanos had gained community control of schools, the discourse of the early 1970s among different Chicano political organizations struggling for political control at the regional and community level was one often centered on improving educational equity through institutional change and community empowerment.[5]

Bilingual/Bicultural Education as Pluralistic Education

The distinction between a pluralistic and assimilation model of education has been elaborated by Kjolseth (1982). The two models differ in their long range goals of promoting or discouraging the maintenance of the ethnic language and culture, and in the manner in which they conceive the implementation of the bilingual education program. Kjolseth (1982) stresses that a bilingual program under the pluralistic model is initiated by a group of ethnic and nonethnic community leaders, and often becomes a social issue around which the ethnic community becomes politically mobilized. Great effort is placed on hiring teachers and aides in the program that are of local, ethnic origin. Special training is arranged for them in order to develop their communicative competence in using the local and regional ethnic varieties of language and culture. In addition, because teachers live in the community and are active in the local activities, they contribute to the development of stable biculturalism and bilingualism. Ideally, a pluralistic bilingual education program includes members of both the ethnic and nonethnic groups learning the ethnic language and English. Thus, the long-term goals of such a program are to develop bilingualism and literacy in both languages.

The assimilation model of education is the polar opposite of the pluralistic one. Kjolseth (1982:14) stresses that the model is "originated from 'above' by elites and administered . . . by non-ethnic and supra-ethnic interests and forces." Teachers tend to be from the nonethnic community and exemplify a "superior" brand of ethnic culture and language. In such cases, teachers give more value to the high linguistic and cultural varieties than they do to the lower varieties (cf. McCollum 1993). The long-term goals of such a program are primarily to use the ethnic language to the extent necessary to facilitate instruction and learning of the second language (English), not the attainment of bilingualism and biliteracy. As such, it encourages the loss of the ethnic mother tongue. In this respect, the program does very little to restructure the vertical articulation of power and hegemony enjoyed by the nonethnic group (Kjolseth 1982).

Bilingual Schooling and Pluralism in Aztlán City

Smith and Foley (1975), in their historical study of the schools in Aztlán City, state that the schooling process operative there from 1930 to 1969 was controlled by Anglos and dedicated to "Americanizing" the Mexicans. In other words, the education model operative under Anglo control was one of cultural assimilation. The language of instruction was English as the use of Spanish was forbidden by the state. This practice illustrates the hegemonic model of the "educated person" operative at the time. When the Chicano community gained control, following the school board elections of 1970, Spanish was finally recognized as a viable language for instruction and literacy development. As a result of this shift in power, the model of education that had been extant during the era of Anglo schooling started to change to one that was more pluralistic.

Shockley's (1974) analysis of this transition illuminates the strategies and political alignments between the newly elected Chicano RUP school trustees and a Mexicano member of the board who had been appointed in 1965 by the Anglo contingent. The Mexicano member of the school board aligned himself with the RUP. In this manner, the RUP obtained majority rule and moved to select José Angel Gutiérrez, one of the three RUP members elected, as the new school board president. Under his strong leadership, schooling reforms were introduced which promoted the development of a Chicano worldview in the public schools. Consequently, the structure of the education program changed, especially in its curricular design and in the ethnic composition of the faculty and administration.

Shockley adds that the major changes instituted in the district during the transition year, 1970–1971, were not easily accepted by the Anglo teaching staff nor the Anglo minority in the community. As a result, the Chicano-controlled school board had to fight several battles in its push to restructure schooling. Despite the battles and opposition from the Anglos and anti-RUP Mexicanos in the community, the RUP-supported school administration proceeded to introduce changes. Thus, within the first year of RUP rule there was a considerable percentage increase of Mexican-American faculty and administrators within the school system (Shockley 1974). With the hiring of more Mexican-American teachers and administrators, as well as supportive Anglo teachers, the content of the curriculum began to change. For example, there was a conscious attempt by some teachers to introduce material written by Chicanos or reflecting Chicano themes. In addition, initial steps were taken to introduce bilingual/bicultural education in the early grades, and courses in Mexican-American history and culture in the upper grades.

In extracurricular activities in the upper grades, such as the cheerleading squad, the Chicano student body was able to select majority representation. However, the changes which seem to have caused the most conflict in the schooling domain were the ones involving the changes in the high school band. According to Shockley (1974), the new Chicano band director had introduced a number of changes, including the adoption of a new fight song, "Jalisco," and the inclusion of the formation "RAZA" on the football field.[6] The band director also began translating his English announcements into Spanish during the half-time ceremonies. Many Anglos became indignant and charged racism. When the practice continued, most Anglo student members quit the band. Shockley adds that most Anglos felt that the schools were being transformed into agents of "Chicanismo."[7] In a strong reaction to the changes in the schools, many Anglo parents withdrew their children and enrolled them in a newly organized private school, or in the schools of nearby communities. In addition, several Anglo teachers resigned their posts because they did not support the new board policies. An Anglo teacher who resigned her post in protest reflected on changes within the schools by saying: "The Raza Unida changed the schools to the point that our children could not learn. They wanted to teach them in Spanish."

In general, Anglos and anti-RUP Mexicanos saw the transformation of the schools as undermining authority in the schools which, prior to the Chicano takeover, had always been under Anglo control. The values and acculturation patterns which had been part of schooling during the era of Anglo control were being discarded, and new values were being emphasized. These new values gave emphasis to a revitalized ethnic identity involving, among other things, pride in being Chicano. School curricular changes recognized the ethnic group's history and cultural heritage, and validated Spanish by incorporating it as a legitimate language of instruction. In addition, many Chicano symbols of the Movimiento were introduced into the school setting.

Bilingual Schooling and Decolonization in Aztlán City

Among other things, the school restructuring effort facilitated a changed attitude among the predominantly Chicano student body, and the development of a new school ethos. In short, it was a challenge to the dominant, conservative ideology which Anglos had historically perpetuated through the schools in the region. This ideology functioned to maintain the Anglo minority in power. Within the school culture, teachers and administrators assured that Anglo students were always elected to the status positions such as school cheerleaders, student council, and so on. Trillen (1971) observed that this ideology was so entrenched that it was regarded as part of the natural order of things, and above all nonracist. Other researchers note that individuals who have enjoyed the privileges of a colonized situation are often unconsciously aware of asymmetrical patterns of power (Fanon 1963; Freire 1974, 1981, 1985). However, when there is an inversion of power relations through a process of struggle, privileged individuals consciously become aware of such patterns. The process of decolonization is essentially the inversion of the colonial situation on its head. Fanon (1963) stresses that decolonization means that those on top will be on the bottom, and those on the bottom will be on top. Thus, the decolonization of asymmetrical relationships involves a process of critical reflection through such concepts as exploitation, colonialism, discrimination, and self-determination, as well as aspects of struggle, adaptation, and creativity at all levels of social organization (Arvizu 1978).

In Aztlán City, the Chicano leadership pushed for decolonization by inverting the power relationships in the school district and municipal government. This inversion of power in turn contributed to the development of a Chicano worldview, and raised it to the forefront in a very short time. When this happened the offended parties reacted in unexpected ways. In the schools, Anglo parents and some anti-RUP Mexicano parents withdrew their children, and Anglo teachers and a few Mexican-American teachers left to teach elsewhere.[8] With the departure of this opposition, the Chicano leadership seemed well on its way to restructuring the schools and its curriculum to produce a Chicano/a "educated person" supportive of RUP educational policy.

The structure of the bilingual/bicultural education program, as I show elsewhere (see Trujillo 1993), provides evidence that the program as it was developed and implemented in Aztlán City during the decade of the 1970s followed the pluralistic model of education. However, by the early 1980s the program structure and goals had changed to one that largely resembled the assimilation model of education in its long-term goals. Why did the structure of schooling change, given that the Chicano community remained in control of the schools? The reasons for this shift are explored below through an analysis of key school-district policy documents and interviews collected among the school district leadership.

TEACHING IDEOLOGY AT THE SCHOOL DISTRICT LEVEL

In placing bilingual/bicultural education philosophy at the center of the restructuring schooling effort in the early 1970s, the new Chicano administration essentially set in motion the process of giving structure to what some scholars have called a teaching ideology.[9] Sharp and Green (1975:68) define the concept of teaching ideology to be "a connected set of systematically related beliefs and ideas about what are felt to be the essential features of teaching." They stress that the concept is broad and encompasses both cognitive and evaluative aspects, including general ideas and assumptions about the nature of knowledge, human nature, society, the role and functions of education, the tasks teachers have to perform, and the criteria to assess adequate performance of students, teachers, and staff. In other words, the teaching ideology involves the task of educating and a set of prescriptions for performing it; however, the cognitive and evaluative aspects of teaching remain at a high level of abstraction. They note, however, that the teaching ideology is embedded in a broader network of social and political worldviews that influence the socialization experiences of each individual actor.

The history of Aztlán City reveals that the network of social and political worldviews operative there in the 1960s and early 1970s was very conflictual. It was a time of heightened political tension and political realignment among the Anglo and Mexicano ethnic groups. The studies of this situation conducted by Shockley (1974), Navarro (1974), Smith and Foley (1975), and Gutiérrez (1976) stress that when the power base changed hands from the Anglo minority to the Mexicano majority, fundamental reforms were introduced which gave prominence to a Chicano worldview in various public spheres within the community. This emergent Chicano worldview was shaped by a long history of political subordination and economic exploitation, and the struggles for civil rights locally and within the broader Chicano movement. Consequently, leaders within the movement sought to decolonize those institutions contributing to the reproduction of subordination and exploitation of the ethnic group.

In particular, these leaders were concerned with the lack of equality in the schools and the destructive effects of acculturation on Chicano culture. Hence, they sought ways to unite the different historical and cultural experiences of Mexican-Americans in the United States by emphasizing a common Raza heritage. This common heritage is embodied in the concepts Aztlán and Chicanismo. During the decades of the 1960s and 1970s, the concept of Aztlán gained special cultural and political significance within Chicano intellectual and political circles. Through the Chicano Civil Rights movement or the *Movimiento*, as it is referred to in Spanish, Aztlán became a collective symbol by which an historically oppressed ethnic minority could recognize its identity in its cultural roots and history. According to Anaya and Lomelí (1989), the concept symbolizes a unifying cohesion through which the Chicano intellectual community has been able to define the foundations of the group's ethnic identity. In this manner the concept has provided a framework through which a dispersed Mexican-American population has been able to understand its history and cultural heritage. Chicanismo, on the other hand, involves an historical and cultural identification with the ethnic group, and it advocates the concept of a bilingual and bicultural reality. Ríos (1978) states that "Chicanismo is an ideological method of reaffirming in the minds of our Raza, that we do have history and culture" (p. 63, n. 1).

In the schooling sphere, elements of this emergent Chicano worldview made their initial public appearance in the form of demands presented in the student petitions to the school board in 1969. In particular, the demands calling for: (1) implementation of bilingual/bicultural education, (2) courses on Mexican-American history and culture, (3) elimination of unacceptable teacher behavior, and (4) more Chicano teacher aides from the community, could be said to have embodied the spirit of Chicanismo (see Trujillo 1993, appendix B for full list of demands). Consequently, once the Chicano community gained majority control of the school board in 1970, it quickly moved to incorporate many of the demands on the student petitions into the restructuring effort. However, not all demands were easily accommodated, especially those pertaining to student rights. Smith and Foley (1975) note that student demands such as a free speech area on the high school campus were soon thwarted by the new Chicano administration. Nonetheless, the broader social and political context of the Movimiento and the success of the RUP locally contributed to heightened feelings of Chicanismo. While Chicanismo at times represented a very abstract, political, and subjective concept, the more concrete cultural modalities of ethnic group behavior, such as language and expressive culture (ballet *folklórico*, music, and Chicano *teatro*), came to occupy a featured place in the new teaching ideology and curriculum.

Content of the School District Teaching Ideology

During the fall of 1970, the new Chicano school administration initiated a bilingual/bicultural education program in the first and second grades.[10] By 1973, the program had been expanded to the high school level, and the district had adopted a policy document known as the *22 Bilingual Recommendation[s]*. This policy document, in essence, served as the embodiment of the new teaching ideology which guided the process of creating new meanings and values, practices, and experiences. The content of this policy document was based on the research literature in bilingual education at the time. However, as is usually the case with much research, it did not necessarily translate into "usable" day-to-day form for teachers. While the overall goal of the policy document was to articulate a step-by-step outline that would enable the district to develop and implement a bilingual/bicultural education program which would assist each student in becoming proficient in both Spanish and English, the twenty-two recommendations remained at the abstract conceptual level. For example, the following statements, taken from the policy document, offer specific guidelines on how to handle reading in the native and second language:

1. Bilingual children will be taught to read in their dominant language (stronger language). Only those children whose mastery of both languages is *so strong* that they can fully comprehend the beginning reading materials can receive instruction in either language, or both.
2. In either case reading will be introduced in only one language. Reading in the second language will be *delayed* until the child becomes fully literate in his first language. We will not confuse the problems of learning a new language.
3. Children will not be introduced to reading in English before they have learned to *read well* in their mother tongue; to do so would only mean that they would be almost as confused as if they were taught to read in English from the start. (pp. 11–12)

I have focused on these three statements specifically because in my interviews several teachers and principals identified dual language reading instruction as being one of the primary reasons why students had difficulty mastering their reading skills. The confusion caused by dual language reading instruction was also a reason given by some teachers and administrators for eventually abandoning their commitment to a maintenance bilingual/bicultural education program. In the section that follows, I will discuss the concepts of "teaching perspective" and "practical ideology" in order to explain the difficulty educators had in implementing the guidelines of the teaching ideology found in the *22 Bilingual Recommendation[s]* policy document.

Contrasting Teaching Perspectives and Practical Ideologies of Mexicano Educators

In order to gain a working knowledge of the complexity of teachers' ideologies, I use the concept of "teaching perspective" as elaborated by Sharp and Green (1975). They use the concept to distinguish between the ideas of an actor which exist at a higher level of generality, the teaching ideology, and those sets of beliefs and practices which emerge from practical teaching situations. In other words, the context of teaching in a public school setting gives rise to a body of knowledge and actions which teachers use in helping themselves confront the day-to-day problems of their situation. The dialectic between the intellectual beliefs of educators (which comprise their teaching ideology) and their everyday actions in the classroom gives rise to practical ideologies (Everhart 1988; Sharp 1980). Practical ideology in education, as Everhart (1988) notes, is the end result of educators interacting with others relative to their involvement in the educational productive process. For Chicano educators in Aztlán City, the experience of the Movimiento, intra-ethnic relations in the community, and national and state bilingual policy change provide the context within which the teaching ideology, teaching perspective, and practical ideology can be understood. In what follows I will compare and contrast educators' teaching perspective and practical ideology as they were revealed in interviews.[11]

It should be kept in mind that any discussion of educators' teaching perspectives and practical ideologies must be situated within the broader sociohistorical context of the Movimiento, the south Texas region, and Aztlán City politics specifically. This broader sociohistorical context includes class relations between Mexicanos and Anglos, and the increasing class differentiation among the Mexicanos in Aztlán City. In order to reveal the nature of the social imagery and the conscious and unconscious messages transmitted to Mexicanos while they were students in Aztlán City schools, as well as in institutions of higher learning, I will discuss various aspects of the collective memory of key Mexicano informants. In discussing their life experiences, key elements of their teaching perspective will become apparent as it has been shaped by theoretical (teaching ideology) and practical ideologies. Sharp and Green (1975) stress that in order to reveal the content of an ideology one must take into account a complex of interrelated factors, of which the most important are: (1) the image of teaching that teachers have formed while they were students, (2) the ideological orientation they have received in the course of their professional training, and (3) the network of experiences they have encountered in the day-to-day practical task of teaching. The following profile of educators in the Aztlán City school district is an attempt at deciphering the content of their ideological orientation and teaching perspective.

Educators' Image of Teaching

The majority of educators that I interviewed came from working class migrant families. Most of them had attended public schools in Aztlán City. A few of those who had married natives of the community or moved there to work, had attended school in nearby communities within the region. More often than not, these educators were among the first members in their family to have graduated from college. The factors and experiences which played a part in their image of teaching were various, but chief amongst them were family background and generation, and schooling experience in Aztlán City and south Texas. A small percentage of Mexicano educators, the older generation, had become teachers prior to the 1969 school walkout. They had been fortunate enough to graduate from Aztlán City schools, go to college, and get hired under the Anglo administration. After the Chicano takeover of the schools, most of them continued to teach under the new Chicano leadership. Given that there had been a high turnover rate among Anglo educators after the takeover, and the fact that they were among the few local Mexicanos with professional degrees, some of them were offered administrative positions in the school district. Due to this experience, this small group of Chicano educators had a different vantage point on the educational changes that had transpired, and were able to reflexively compare and contrast the two school administrations and their respective educational philosophies. The following sketch of educators with this type of experience will give insight into the factors and experiences that have influenced their image of teaching.

One of the more influential factors that has affected Chicano educators as a group has been their experience growing up in Aztlán City and attending a school system that was controlled by the Anglo minority. Several educators recall attending schools that were segregated, and which catered to the Anglo students. To illustrate this experience, I offer the following sketch of Mr. Segovia, the newly appointed superintendent in early August of 1988.

Mr. Segovia is a native of Aztlán City. He recalls starting school at *cero bola* (zero point), the entry level for most Mexicano students at the time. *Cero bola* is the term most Mexicanos, who attended school during the Anglo era, use to refer to the beginning entry level. *Cero bola* classrooms grouped those Mexicano students who spoke no English or very little English. Mr. Segovia notes that after *cero bola* the sequence of class levels for those who spoke some English or had some schooling was "*primero altito* and *primero alto*" (first and high first). He adds that when he entered school, Mexicanos and Anglos went to separate schools: "You had campuses that were totally Chicano or Mexicano and then you had campuses that were totally Anglo. If I remember correctly, I was in the second grade when I was allowed to go to an Anglo campus. And that was the first time that I ever interacted with an Anglo at any level."

Mr. Segovia's family, like many other Mexicano families in Aztlán City, was a migrant family; they travelled to the northern states to work the seasonal crops from April to November. When the family returned to the community, the children would normally be enrolled in school. Most of the migrant students were enrolled in the "Mexican" school. There were a few students, however, who enrolled in the "Anglo" school because of the insistence of their parents. These parents had greater familiarity with the system, or they had taken special steps to assure that their children "qualified" for enrollment. The majority of Mexicano parents, especially migrant parents, however, experienced hassles with the school authorities in getting their children enrolled. Consequently, some of them made a conscious choice of forgoing the annual trek to the northern states in order to provide more stability to their children's education. Mr. Segovia comments on this:

> My dad was a crew leader here with the different seasonal crops that we had [in the Winter Garden region]. And we [the family] used to leave around April and come back late October or early November. My parents made the decision to stop migrating when I was, I'm going to say, in third grade or fourth grade, somewhere in there. I don't recall going back to Ohio, Indiana, or all of those places that we used to go. . . . I didn't go back until 1962 when I graduated from high school, just to see what it was like. And then I went back in '68, and I haven't been back since.

The conscious choice by parents to "settle out" of the migrant stream is an illustration of practical ideology. In other words, it is the end result of the interaction of the migrant farmworker lifestyle and the family's experience of enrolling its children in school upon their return from the north. The act of staying in the community throughout the year afforded more stability to the children's education and transmitted the message that schools were not only important institutions, but that schooling was an essential process in preparing students for the world of work beyond that of the parents' job experience. The Segovia's family decision to settle out was probably greatly facilitated by the fact that the parents also owned a neighborhood grocery in the barrio. The grocery store, located in the barrio which natives in Aztlán City call México Grande (Big Mexico), gave the family stability as well as status within the community.

Another indicator of the value given to schooling and education within the Mexicano community was the existence of "barrio schools." Several of the educators I spoke with reflected on their early school experiences. They recall that in Aztlán City barrio schools were run in the two Mexican barrios—México Grande and México Chico (Little Mexico). These schools were run by Mexican women, usually in their homes, who conducted classes for both preschoolers and older students. The older students were usually from returning migrant families. Mr. Segovia recalls that at times his parents had trouble getting him enrolled in public school upon their return: "I think that was one of the main things that they considered, upon arriving in Aztlán City in early November. A lot of times we were held back from enrolling. The principal would make the decision that it was too late and that I should wait, or we should wait until the following year. And this is where the barrio schools came into play. That's when we went with Señora González." He adds that the instruction was given in both Spanish and English:

> She did have Spanish instruction, but instruction was in English the majority of the time [for us older students]. We had the ABCs in both languages and the pledge of allegiance and things like this. She would read to us and explain the words and it was interesting. And you had to stand up in front of the class and do your oral reading. We had math class. You had to go to the board and do your math and show how you arrived at the answer.[12]

One of the practical concerns of Mexican parents in the 1940s and 1950s was exposing their children to English. Mr. Segovia reflects that barrio schools served this purpose as well:

> We learned the ABCs in English and Spanish, you know, the sounds and this and that. I would say yes, that was an introduction to bilingual education. Of course, the majority of us, I think, were hurting in the fact that we did not have the exposure to the English language. Living in the México Grande barrio, the only possible Anglos that we would see through there would be the ranchers that might come by to pick up a worker, or a farmer that might come through there to call on a group [crew] leader. Or maybe a salesman of some kind visiting the neighborhood store and that was it. You had to walk into the downtown area and talk to them. So that [barrio school instruction] was our introduction to the English language also.

Mr. Segovia attributes his success with schooling to the barrio school experience, the backing from his parents, and his own initiative. However, he gives special recognition to Mrs. Susie González who ran the barrio school in México Grande. "I have very positive thoughts about everything that happened in that setting with Mrs. González. I remember her well. I think I would thank her for where I am right now."

Mexican students who were successful in adapting to schooling under the Anglo administration were eventually integrated with the Anglo student body in the upper grades. By the time they started middle school, they were attending school with Anglo students, even though, as several Chicano educators recall, the Mexicano students were concentrated in the lower academic tracks. Mr. Segovia recalls that as he progressed through the grades, especially in middle school and high school, he came to interact more with Anglo students and develop positive relationships. "We had a very close relationship amongst ourselves. I was in the band since the fifth grade, so I remember very positive relationships with the members of the band. . . . We had good components mixing together [Anglo and Mexicano]. I know that we felt very proud of the band, and it's reflected in the pictures that you see at the band hall." Not all of Mr. Segovia's recollections of attending school with Anglo students were positive though.

> The other parts, or the other things that we were faced with, of course, was that we had the grade level situation at the junior high school, especially where Anglos were never placed beyond a track like let's say we [Mexicanos] had. . . . Anglos were not placed in the fourth, fifth, or sixth track. They were kept within the one through three. We, of course, never really understood why that was because we thought that there were definitely some Anglos in the group that functioned at a lower level than one, two, or three.

Mr. Segovia's experience, and that of the few other Mexicano students who had been fortunate enough to be integrated into classrooms with Anglo students early in their schooling career, illustrates the positive outcomes of this type of socialization. Not only did he have positive interaction with his peers, he recalls being influenced greatly by certain teachers:

> I remember some of those teachers that really came out of their way to help you. Some of them visited our home, some of them never did and wouldn't have. But some, I'm sure, made every effort to go out and encourage our parents to not take us out as early as they did and not come back as late as we did, for those of us that continued in the migrant track. And there were . . . some very positive things that developed with me, and how I chose social studies as a field of study. I had good social studies teachers throughout, and as a result I went into this area.

Other factors that played a role in encouraging students to excel in school were parents and the individual initiative to compete: "Our parents, of course, were the other driving force behind us. Then there was the individual desire to climb up and do what we needed to do to stay in school and struggle with that. But there was definitely a combination of factors."

Mr. Segovia graduated from high school and went on to college, where he received his bachelor's degree. He was hired by the school district as a social science teacher in the mid-1960s. When he came back to teach with the school district, he found that, structurally, the schools were still practicing the old pattern of steering the Mexicano students into the lower tracks and Anglo students into the upper tracks. Since he was teaching social science in the middle school, he had a mixed classroom of Anglo and Mexicano students. Thus, he didn't have to directly deal with the segregated tracks. However, the practice of segregated academic tracks was challenged when the Mexicano students walked out in December 1969. Mr. Segovia was sympathetic to the student's cause, given that he understood the problem, but he tried to remain politically neutral.

We [Chicano educators] understood what was happening. We have feelings for what was happening. Some of us were assisting, some of us were not. We were saying [to students], "You know, that's entirely up to you and your parents, that's a decision you have to make." But word came out, the school board came out with some specific things that they were going to do with people that walked out and so on. The majority of the students, I think, had the parent's or family's backing, and they moved it. Some of us were cautioning, some of us were saying, "Do your parents want you to do that?" And I know some of the teachers were given specific instructions, don't let anybody out of your room. How do you control a crowd that's been mobilized to walk out?

Ideological Orientation Received

The majority of educators in the Aztlán City Independent School District are products of the institutions of higher education in south Texas. The four-year institutions that have played a key role in training teachers in the school district are Texas A & I University at Kingsville and Laredo State University at Laredo. The Winter Garden region has a junior college affiliated with Southwest Texas State University, and a satellite graduate program through Sul Ross State University; both of these are located in a community thirty miles from Aztlán City. This network of second-tier universities and colleges has been utilized by the majority of educators I interviewed. Most completed their first two years at a junior college and then transferred to Texas A & I or Laredo State University to finish their degree program.

In the early 1970s, the need for teacher preparation programs was exacerbated by the high teacher turnover rate at the end of the first year of the new Chicano administration. Amancio Cantú, the school superintendent in 1974, notes the critical position the district was in with respect to implementing the new teaching ideology:

When we [the Chicano administration] first got here in the fall of 1970, we had 140 staff members in our school district. At that time it was about 70 percent Anglo and 30 percent Chicano. The average age of that faculty was 59. At the end of the first year that we were here, we had a tremendous rate of teacher turnover. Eighty percent of the faculty left us. So we had roughly about 95 teachers coming in, brand new, out of college most of them. And they didn't know very much about bilingual education or the education of Chicanos. So we had to bring in programs, as many programs as possible, to help train these teachers. (Reskin and Williams 1974)

The RUP, through their cadre of grant writers, was able to obtain funding for various programs which provided opportunities for both undergraduate and graduate training. The undergraduate programs made use of the existing network of universities and colleges in the region. Programs such as the Career Opportunities Program (COP) provided opportunities for Chicanas and Chicanos to get their B.A. degrees and teaching certificates.[13] The graduate programs, on the other hand, were facilitated through foundation and federal funding, and special arrangements with San Diego State University and Chicago State University (Lizcano, Meléndrez, and Solís 1974).

The interviews I collected among educators during my fieldwork ranged the spectrum from top administrators to mid-management to teachers. Even though I was not seeking to determine ideological orientation at the time of the interviews, I did ask them questions regarding their university training. After analyzing my interviews with a focus on identifying ideological orientation, I discovered two broad patterns: (1) educators who had received their university training prior to the walkout, and (2) educators who received their university training after the walkout and/or had enhanced their skills through RUP-sponsored programs. These broad patterns are useful in determining ideological orientation. Mexican-American educators who had attended college prior to the 1969 school walkout revealed different ideological orientations than those who received their degrees after the walkout. The school walkout was a watershed moment for cultural production. It served as the key event of a specific historical and ideological juncture of the local Movimiento, where the discourse of the newly proposed conception of the Chicano/a "educated person" started to take form. The following sketches will show how Chicano educators differ in their views regarding the schooling reforms introduced by the RUP, and more specifically their views on the cultural production of a Chicano/a "educated person."

Perspectives from Educators Not Supportive of RUP-Sponsored Changes

Mr. Segovia, the educator we met above, falls within the first broad pattern of postsecondary schooling. He graduated from high school with the class of 1962. José Angel Gutiérrez and other Chicano students who later played prominent leadership roles in the community in the seventies were members of his graduating class. As we have seen, Mr. Segovia went to college and majored in social studies. He was hired under the Anglo administration as a social studies teacher. He remained with the school district following the Chicano takeover and was soon placed in a role of greater responsibility. When the school restructuring efforts unfolded, he was promoted to an administrative position following the first year of the walkout. He recalls being promoted to the high school principalship in the early seventies: "We had an outside principal for a year right after the walkout, and then I became the high school principal and without any experience or anything (*laughs*). And I still remember being called from the auditorium floor, 'the next high school principal will be so and so.' From that point on I began to look forward to administration and working in that capacity. I enjoyed it." The following year he served as principal of the junior high school. Mr. Segovia's reflections give insight into the lack of training he had received in his university program when he was thrust into an administrative position. His lack of training, along with the rapid pace of educational change being introduced in the schools, were important factors that played a role in his growing disagreement with the new Chicano school administration. The following excerpt gives Mr. Segovia's reflexive view of the school restructuring efforts, changes that he generally regarded as positive but which he saw as moving too fast.

> I was supportive, I think, to the point that I felt good about some of the changes that were taking place. . . . I think some of the cautions that I kept looking at and pointing out was that we were moving in a very positive way to make some corrections, but we were moving too fast without adequate preparation in place. . . . I kept arguing with administration. Are we not considering slowing down? . . . Let's look at the results. Let's look at the end product. Are we really getting any benefit from this situation? And, we were driven by proposal writing. I think everybody was involved in here comes another proposal, and drop everything, we need to get this out tonight.

Mr. Segovia's concerns about too rapid change without adequate evaluation were informed by the practical ideology rooted in his training as a classroom teacher. In particular, he was concerned that people were being pulled from classrooms to serve as directors or coordinators of newly funded programs, "without any thought being given to . . . How about those kids that you are leaving behind? Those were situations that I was very much against." He was also opposed to the manning of leadership posts by people from outside the community, and the lack of consideration given to locals because "they were considered too traditional, or they didn't join us in the walkout."

Mr. Segovia did not share the same vision of education as the new school board president at the time, José Angel Gutiérrez. Not only did Gutiérrez and the new school administration view education as the process by which students would gain biliteracy skills, education also had an explicit political role in preparing future leaders to build a greater Aztlán. Mr. Segovia, on the other hand, saw himself as primarily an educator and not a politician. He never became a member of Ciudadanos Unidos (United Citizens)[14] or the RUP, even though he had close friends and compadres who were members. The following reflects his outlook:

> I was invited to join the group, Ciudadanos Unidos, that was heading the Partido [RUP]. As far as myself, I've never been involved directly in politics and *movimientos*. I've been an educator, and I'm trying to maintain that status among the students that I've worked with. During the walkout students would ask me directly, "Who's side are you on?" Your side. I'm for you and for the improvement of whatever you feel we need here in this classroom. And that's been my main course. I've never really been identified *que te haces para acá o te haces para allá* [that you join this group or you join that group]. I think, my vote is my own, and I move in that direction that I feel like.

As a result of the increasing conflict between his role as an educator and the explicit political goals that education had taken under the RUP, Mr. Segovia distanced himself from what was happening in the school restructuring effort: "I had a feeling of disenchantment with what we had created with ourselves, let's put it in that frame. We were moving too fast. . . . We were thinking way up there into the future and really not considering what I, as a classroom teacher, saw in my kids and whether this would work for us. You know, . . . I didn't see that I should continue." In 1973, after two years of working under the new Chicano administration, he left the district and took a position as an assistant high school principal elsewhere.

When placed within the context of the *Movimiento*, and the discourse of Aztlán and Chicanismo, Mr. Segovia's ideological orientation did not coincide with the Chicano worldview that the RUP was striving to create through schooling. His ideology was much more individualistic than collective, and infused with the concerns and actions of practical ideologies. Everhart (1988:32) stresses that "ideology can also be seen as a practice of representation, a practice that produces certain meanings and which necessitates certain subjects as its support." Practical ideologies are made as people live out their lives in the real world. In this framework, ideology is the practice through which individuals are produced and in turn produce their orientations to the social structure they inhabit (Everhart 1988). Practical ideologies, therefore, are linked to the process of production. Sharp (1980) identifies two aspects of practical ideology and the productive process; the first aspect is concerned with the reproduction of the agents of production, and the second with the reproduction of places within the productive process. The Chicano worldview, espoused by José Angel Gutiérrez, encompassed both aspects of ideology. Schools would prepare students for slots in the labor force by transmitting the necessary skills (especially skills in English) so that they could function in the mainstream society. Yet, within the discourse of Aztlán and Chicanismo, the schools were concerned with the second aspect by helping to create new opportunities for individuals with different skills (communally oriented individuals with bilingual and biliterate skills advocated by the new teaching ideology). Mr. Segovia's ideological orientation is primarily concerned with the first aspect of practical ideology. His model of an educated person can partly be explained by his family/personal history, university training, and experience in the classroom and with administration.

The views held by Mr. Segovia are not singular; they were expressed by several of the educators working with the district in the 1980s. To amplify on the views held by Mr. Segovia, I will discuss the case of Mr. Delfino, a federal programs administrator with the school district. Mr. Delfino was a classmate of Mr. Segovia's and graduated with the class of 1962. As such, he follows the pattern for educators receiving their degree prior to the school walkout. He attended Southwest Texas Junior College and then transferred to Texas A & I University, where he received his bachelor's degree. He returned to the community and worked as a teacher for five years under the Anglo administration. After the school walkout he remained with the school district and worked both as a teacher and administrator under the new Chicano leadership. This experience enabled him to compare and contrast the two philosophies of education, one Anglo and the other Chicano.

His reflective view of teaching and schooling under the Anglo administration was very positive even though he saw the system as being very structured and catering to the Anglo-American student:

> It was a good experience in the sense that they [Anglos] were very well organized, as far as curriculum, as far as what they wanted to do. They were more systematic. . . . Their education was oriented more towards the Anglo-American with their ideas of American education defined by the Anglo administration. But you do have to give them credit, because they worked at it for years. . . . They had years to get organized, so they refined the system. If you [the Mexicano student] were able to fit into the system and you were able to function, you would be a very good product. Of course, if you didn't fit into the system, you'd probably drop out.

In contrast, he notes that after the Chicanos took control of schooling the Anglo administrators and teachers that stayed had a difficult time adapting due to the difference in philosophy and the loose structure:

> I don't think they could function under the new system. It was too loose. The system was too loose for them to adapt. When you stop to think about it, this is why there was a backlash against the Raza Unida Party. The more orientation there was towards streamlining the system, the more disagreement there was between those people who were from Aztlán City and those people who were from outside Aztlán City.

He adds that the people of Aztlán City eventually resisted many of the educational changes being introduced. In his eyes the changes were too fast and too radical politically for three reasons:

> One is that the people of Aztlán City didn't want to go that fast in education. They wanted a slow, moderate, conservative, approach to changing the educational system. Second, they wanted to use what the Anglo had that was good and change all those things that needed to change to give the Mexican American a better chance of getting a quality education. Thirdly, most of La Raza are not liberals; they are conservatives. But politicians are liberal and there's a difference between politicians running the school board and people being more conservative towards what they want [in education], and it created a great rift. So those three things would eventually come to a dead end.

Mr. Delfino is essentially arguing that the educational philosophy that came in with the RUP did not have the support from most Mexicano educators who had been successful students under the Anglo administration and had received their college degrees prior to the walkout. The educational restructuring that was being proposed was too different from what they had experienced as students and teachers under the Anglo system. He stresses that the new Chicano administration pushed the philosophy of bilingual/bicultural education as part of the political ideology and failed to build on the previous structure under the Anglo administration:

> I don't think the administration really knew what the bilingual program stood for, not everybody. If you know about bilingual programs, you would have known that if you would have gone slow, you would be successful. Incremental steps, a phase-in program. It was not a phase-in program. It happened overnight. It's too quick. It doesn't work. . . . This is the way that I felt the bilingual program began.

Mr. Delfino's case illustrates the challenge to the ideological orientation that educators like him had received. Not only was their ideological orientation being challenged, but the new Chicano administration was asking some of them to teach classes in Spanish, which some didn't feel comfortable doing. Mr. Delfino amplifies on this situation when he was teaching history and government at the high school:

> It got to the point that this bilingual deal got out of hand, even when I was teaching government. They wanted me to teach government in Spanish and teach history in Spanish which is all right, but you don't have the materials. You didn't even have the dictionaries. Most people who were teaching those subjects didn't qualify to do it in Spanish either, you know, correctly. You could use slang words and whatever and get the message across, but that was only tried a few months. It didn't materialize. They [the administration] knew that after a while, you just said, hey this is not going to work. After a while, I said, forget it.

Mr. Delfino's argument makes a strong case for the lack of support for the bilingual/bicultural program among educators of his outlook and worldview. Like Mr. Segovia, his ideological orientation is primarily concerned with the first aspect of practical ideology. As such, Mr. Delfino's model of an educated person emerges from his family/personal history, and teaching experience.

Perspectives from Educators Supportive of RUP-Sponsored Changes

Educators who obtained their college degrees after the walkout, in general, had a very different perspective on the *Movimiento* and the ideology of cultural nationalism, the philosophical foundation of the new teaching ideology in the school district. Those educators who were students at the time of the walkout underwent a dramatic change in perspective and outlook. Many students felt a sense of empowerment, and vindication from a discriminatory system. This new development contributed to both individual and group introspection, as well as positive and hopeful views of the future. Mr. Manríquez, a high school student at the time of the walkout, and presently a middle school teacher, expressed this feeling succinctly:

When I was a student in the junior high, my dream was to be the janitor of the junior high. This was the job that I aspired to get. It was the highest type of job that I expected. It was the type of job where I thought that I could contribute the most in this world, as a person. I didn't think that I could have any other type of job because those jobs were part of the world of the Anglo-American. It's not that God intended for them to have those jobs, it's just that they were destined to have the better-paying jobs. One could not go to college. We didn't have the money, and aside from that, college for me was a type of work, you know. Why use it? It's something out of my reach, you know. Why should I be thinking of something which is out of my reach? I didn't have the means, and I didn't even have the basic knowledge of how I could do it. . . . It's not until the last years of my high school, during the walkout, that I started to think in terms of what I could do with my life. If they [Anglos] can do it, why can't I do it?

This new outlook and sense of empowerment on the part of many Chicano students was the incentive that motivated many to pursue postsecondary education. Mrs. Moncivais, an elementary school teacher, recalls how she was influenced by the *Movimiento* and given the opportunity to get a college degree:

I was greatly influenced by a person that came from somewhere else during the time that Raza Unida was very active here. I had just retired from the beauty shop business, and I was hired as the city manager's secretary. He was a very intellectual man and encouraged me to apply to the Career Opportunities Program. I was fortunate enough to get selected. That's how I received my education, through this program and through the efforts of the Raza Unida. You know, the takeover benefited everyone in one way or another, or at least I did. Of course, I had made up my mind that I would stay here and help out, and I'm still here, no intentions of ever leaving Aztlán City.

Mrs. Moncivais expands on the benefits that the Career Opportunities Program (COP) brought the community: "A lot of us had given up the idea of even going to college. . . . I know several other married women, it gave the married women a chance to go and get educated. The program had a good set-up. We would go to classes at night and work during the day. During the summer, we would leave and attend Texas A & I and Laredo State." Mrs. Moncivais' experience and others like her who benefited from COP illustrates the ideological context affecting their worldview.

Post-walkout educators demonstrated a very different attitude than the pre-walkout educators. The sociohistorical context of the *Movimiento* had a big impact in attitude and outlook among many of the Chicano students who became educators. This attitude of empowerment, along with the opportunities for post-secondary education, benefited the community as a whole and helped to foment a different ideological orientation among the new teaching staff. Mrs. Moncivais captures this attitude in the following:

Everyone started to want to get an education. Those that critique what happened, don't want to remember the benefits that the [movement] gave us. Before Angel and the Raza Unida, a few Mexicanos did get an education, right, but very few ever got their doctorate. At most, they would get their master's, if they were lucky. He [Angel] brought us the strength, the attitude that I can be more. I want to be more educated. I can be, you know, something higher than I am. The biggest difference is that people started to change their attitude as far as education is concerned. We also had that Carnegie program where administrators, some of the principals that are here, received their education. That's how they were able to get their superintendent certification.

The experiences relayed by both Mr. Manríquez and Mrs. Monciváis express a very different ideological orientation toward the cultural production of a Chicano/a "educated person" than that of Mr. Segovia and Mr. Delfino. The differences in their orientation and support for the new teaching ideology (maintenance bilingual/bicultural education) rests on their experiences with the Movimiento, their theoretical beliefs and practical ideologies.

DISCUSSION AND CONCLUSION

In this section, I offer a synopsis of the different perspectives voiced by educators to illustrate the contrasting factors that have had a direct bearing on why the bilingual/bicultural education program structure changed. Given the changed ideological orientation within the community, especially since the demise of the RUP in 1979 and the ouster of José Angel Gutiérrez from the community in 1981, support for maintenance bilingual/bicultural education and a Chicano/a educated person has weakened substantially. As is apparent in the discussion of the teaching perspectives and practical ideologies of educators, there exist two factions with differing viewpoints regarding the role that bilingual education should play in the school district. The faction supporting transitional bilingual education has been the predominant one since the early 1980s. Members of this faction support native language instruction to the point that such instruction facilitates the transition to the all-English curricular track. The goal of biliteracy in Spanish and English is not a primary concern, as the transitional bilingual education program cannot address it. A second faction, which in the 1980s lost vocal support and membership, is made up of supporters of maintenance bilingual/bicultural education. This group of educators and community people continue to support the merit of developing literacy skills in both English and Spanish, but given the changed politics at the local, state, and national level, they have been left with few alternatives. At best they point out the shortcomings of transitional bilingual education for its inability to cultivate biliteracy skills. As they see it, the short- and long-term effects of this type of bilingual education is that the students, the community, and the region as a whole will lose out in intellectual ability, economic potential, and cultural development.

In order to illustrate these contrasting perspectives, I draw on my interview data among educators. An example from the first faction is provided by Mr. Segovia's family experience and his outlook regarding his children's bilingual competence. His oldest child, who participated in the bilingual program starting in 1978, is now in high school. According to Mr. Segovia, he has taken Spanish in high school and done well. Consequently, Mr. Segovia regards his son as being biliterate in both Spanish and English. He regards this as a big advantage: "If my kid can read and write Spanish and read and write English, I think we've come a long way." However, his younger children, who have received English-only instruction, have not had the opportunity to pick up dual literacy skills. He does not see this as a disadvantage though, and is hopeful that they may pick up literate skills in Spanish as they go through their schooling: "My younger ones are more dominant in English. They don't know the writing phase of it in Spanish. But, you know, I think expression and all of that comes on with time and the writing thing will be reinforced as they go through the junior high school and on in the high school."

Like other parents in Aztlán City, Mr. Segovia is primarily concerned with issues of practical ideology, especially as they interface with what Sharp (1980) calls the reproduction of the "agents of production." That is, parents and educators holding his perspective are concerned with having their children master English. In their view, English competence will facilitate their entry into the economic structure of the United States more than being biliterate in Spanish and English. The goal of biliteracy that was such a central component of the teaching ideology of the school district in the 1970s has in the 1980s been removed from the formal curriculum. The bilingual/bicultural education program was restructured into a pre-kindergarten through first grade transitional bilingual program in 1985 (Trujillo 1993). In the transitional program Spanish is used for instruction in order to facilitate mastery of English. Once the student achieves a certain level of English proficiency, she/he is placed in the English-only instructional track. While being biliterate is still important among some members of this group, as is indicated by Mr. Segovia, the school, through the transitional bilingual program, lacks the necessary structure and support to develop them. Consequently, opportunities to develop literacy skills in Spanish and English through schooling has, for all intents and purposes, been reduced to essentially an individual initiative on the part of the student and his/her family.

A different perspective is provided by those educators and parents within the second faction who regard the changes in the bilingual/bicultural program as having long term repercussions for students and the Mexican-American community. Some educators see the restructuring of the bilingual/bicultural education program as a setback to the goals of bilingual education and the cultural production of a Chicano/a educated person. Their concerns are also linked to issues of practical ideology. For example, a school district educator put forth the argument regarding the obligation that educators have to educate parents about the merits of being bilingual and biliterate:

You see, that's where I think we, as educators and as a school district, have . . . such a tremendous obligation to the Spanish-speaking community. We need to be able to tell parents that we want the kids to do well in the English language, but we also need to tell parents not to forget the maintaining of the home language in a correct manner—because the system out there still kicks us in the teeth . . . over [such matters as] applying for a job. Where you have an Anglo that has taken three or four years of advanced Spanish and [is able to] use it formally, we on the other hand, speak it incorrectly because we never learned it well. We, . . . those of us who have made it, so to speak, . . . have an obligation to tell the parents . . . the importance of . . . learning English . . . because it is a language in which you are going to compete. But there is also nothing wrong, in fact, it is a plus to have the first language developed and developed well . . . so we can be that much better trained and . . . much better prepared.

This educator feels that the school district is doing the community a disservice in failing to support the development of the biliteracy skills of students through maintenance bilingual/bicultural education. Her argument is also concerned with practical ideologies as they relate to processes of production (Everhart 1988). In other words, she acknowledges the need to master English skills but not at the expense of Spanish literacy, because to do so places Chicano students at a disadvantage in the labor market (as "agents of production").

In a broader sense, educators with this outlook are also concerned with that aspect of practical ideology which Sharp (1980) calls the "reproduction of places within the productive process." This concern takes into consideration an increasingly interdependent world economy. For example, persons in this faction hold the perspective that the cultivation of literacy skills in both English and Spanish would enhance economic opportunities for graduates of the district, as well as strengthen the economic viability of the region, especially in the present context of the North American Free Trade Agreement (NAFTA). The former bilingual education director for the school district made a similar point during an interview in 1988. Her argument does not directly refer to NAFTA, but it does recognize that as closer links are cultivated between the United States, Mexico, and the rest of Latin America, opportunities will develop for U.S. citizens with literacy skills in Spanish and English.

With the passage of time, I guess, the community has to see [the value of bilingualism] just like they see the value of English. . . . Maybe with time [Spanish will be just as important]. In time and . . . with the proximity of our Latin American countries and the fact that they are boiling pots in terms of what is going to happen in those areas politically [and economically] . . . we will be negotiating and doing as much work with our Latin American countries, that are right across the border, than we've had to do for the last twenty years, . . . negotiating peace agreements, with Russia. . . . In time, we'll see the growth of more business over there [in Latin America] and . . . a greater need for [the necessary] . . . skills of working there.

In short, this perspective holds that as the world economy becomes more interdependent and new trade pacts are formalized, there is a need for bilingual agents of production, as well as new opportunities or places within the productive process. The latter aspect of practical ideology (the reproduction of places, within the productive process) is more complex and oftentimes overlooked by educators. Schooling is concerned with this aspect of social reproduction only to the extent that the transformation of the labor process creates new places which require workers with new skills to fill them. Thus, educators in this faction are perhaps ahead of their time in their vision of new economic opportunities opening up for students with literacy skills in Spanish and English, based on new trade relationships between the United States, Mexico, and the rest of Latin America. Under such circumstances, students with biliterate competency would be much more competitive in the labor market.

In conclusion, this case study has presented an analysis of the historically specific cultural production of a Chicano "educated person," which was part and parcel of a Chicano nationalism. Within the discourse of Aztlán and Chicanismo, educators in Aztlán City sought to create a subject-position for a Chicano/a "educated person," specifically as a bilingual, culturally proud, communally oriented individual. The cultural production of this discourse went hand-in-hand with a Chicano Movement that developed at a specific historical and ideological juncture, with specific political-economic determinations and goals. The school walkout served as a watershed moment for cultural production and the divergent formation of identities—some for and some against the newly proposed Chicano/a educated person. Those that opposed this conception hold different models of the educated person, models which emerge out of family/personal history and teaching experience. As such, this study confirms that schools are heterogeneous sites where educators and students get exposed to a variety of "voices" and practices which affect the construction of knowledge and identities.

NOTES

1. Following anthropological convention, I use a pseudonym for the actual name of the community in order to maintain confidentiality. The name, Aztlán City, has been chosen because it has been used in previous anthropological studies to refer to this community (see, for example, Foley Post, Mota, and Lozano 1989). More importantly, however, the name symbolizes the broader concept of Aztlán, the reappropriated mythical homeland for the Chicano population in the United States, and serves as an appropriate metaphor for a discussion of the cultural production of a Chicano worldview through schooling. Furthermore, in order to assure the confidentiality of my informants, I also make use of pseudonyms in the text when referring to the actual people I interviewed. With respect to the use of ethnic labels, I use the terms Chicano, Mexicano, Mexican-American, and Anglo-American. Chicano is a self-reference term used by ethnically and politically conscious Mexican-Americans, and put forth as an alternative to terms such as Spanish-American, Latin, Spanish-surnamed, or Hispanic, which have been used by the dominant society/culture to refer to members of this ethnic group. I will

use this term interchangeably with Mexican-American. Mexicano is the preferred self-identity term used by many Mexican-Americans in south Texas, especially members of the older generation. In this paper the term will at times be used interchangeably with Chicano and Mexican-American, especially when emphasis is placed on the historical and cultural links of ethnicity. Anglo-American is a term used to refer to members of the white mainstream population.

2. A previous petition with seven demands, among them a call for establishing bilingual/bicultural education, had been signed by 350 students and presented to the superintendent at the end of April 1969. The demand over equal representation of Anglo and Chicana cheerleaders had been met by the superintendent, who promised to institute a quota system of three Anglos and three Chicanas. The other demands, however, were stalled with the promise that they would be taken into consideration (Shockley 1974; see also *Zavala County Sentinel* 58(18), 1 May 1969).

3. For a recent treatise on the rise and fall of the Raza Unida Party, see García (1989).

4. Aztlán City became a major icon for the Chicano Movement because it was one of the first communities where Chicanos took control of the governing institutions from the Anglo-American minority. Shockley (1974) covers changes in ethnic relations in the community since 1963, when a slate of five Mexicanos, referred to as Los Cinco, won the city council elections, defeating the Anglo administration. In 1965, however, the Anglo minority formed a coalition with more acculturated Mexican Americans to regain political power. It was not until the city and school district elections of 1970 that Mexicanos regained political control under the leadership of native son José Angel Gutiérrez and the RUP. As a result of this outcome, Aztlán City came to represent the epitome of self-determination, and consequently, numerous Chicanos, engaged in political mobilization, looked at the success of this community as a model to emulate.

5. Early studies that capture the discourse for institutional change range from the university level to the elementary school. See La Causa 1970; Macías, Macías, De La Torre, and Vásquez 1975.

6. "Jalisco" is a traditional Mexican folk song with strong appeals to ethnoterritory; it is usually sung with a Mariachi ensemble. "Raza" is the term used by Chicanos and other Latinos to refer to ethnic membership.

7. The term Chicanismo refers to those meanings, values, practices, and experiences which members of the Chicano community use to designate their politicized struggle and communal identity.

8. Anti-RUP Mexicanos had aligned themselves with the Anglo minority as a result of Anglo sponsorship. In other words, Mexicanos who supported the Anglo minority status quo in the community were often sponsored by Anglos to political positions of influence. This practice was seen as nonexclusionary, yet perpetuated the hegemonic power structure. See Shockley 1974, and Smith and Foley 1975 for further discussion of this practice.

9. The policy document which captures the emergent educational ideology of the school district is the *Aztlán City Independent School District 22 Bilingual Recommendation[s]*. This document contains the goals, priorities, and recommendations adopted by the Aztlán City Board of Trustees on 1 February 1973 to assist the school staff in the design and implementation of a bilingual/bicultural education program. The policy document also provided guidelines for the selection and development of educational materials. See Trujillo 1993, Appendix A for complete copy of the document.

10. A bilingual education program was begun in the first and second grades with local funds during the fall of 1970. The district submitted a preliminary proposal for regular Title VII funding in November 1970, but was unable to get any funding until the 1971–72 school year when a formal proposal had been prepared. Nonetheless, as Hardgrave and Hinojosa (1975) report, the district in cooperation with the Edgewood Independent School District in San Antonio, which had been funded through Title VII for the 1969–70 project year, and with the approval of the Texas Education Agency was able to obtain a $32,000 grant from the U.S. Office of Education of the Department of Health, Education and Welfare to begin a "satellite component" of the San Antonio program in Aztlán City. During the 1971–72 school year the district expanded the bilingual program to include kindergarten through third grade as part of its newly funded five-year Title VII bilingual program (*Cristal*, September 1971).

11. Interviews with educators were conducted at the schools or at the school district administration buildings. In a few instances interviews were also conducted in their homes. The language used for the interviews was either Spanish or English, depending on the language preference of the person being interviewed. At times, informants spoke in a mixed code of Spanish and English, in keeping with the language-use patterns of many bilingual speakers in south Texas. Once the interviews began, I followed the language-use preference of the interviewees. In presenting excerpts of oral text from my interviews with educators, I have not followed this practice however. At the request of the editors of this volume, I have translated all Spanish language text into English. While this practice makes for easier readability among non-Spanish readers, the reader loses out on the flavor of the language-use patterns among speakers in the community and region. Nonetheless, in presenting excepts of oral text, I follow the presentational format employed by Bauman (1986) when representing a record of language in spoken, not written, mode. No words were added except in those cases where the addition of a word or words help the flow of the message being conveyed (additions are enclosed in square brackets). No words were deleted except for repetitions, hesitations, or pauses (ellipses indicate these deletions).

12. Mr. Segovia, like many bilingual speakers in south Texas, uses a mixture of English and Spanish. I have taken the liberty of translating the segments of his responses in Spanish into English in order to facilitate the accessibility of the interview material to non–Spanish-speaking readers.

13. For further amplification on the nature of these programs, see Trujillo (1993).

14. Ciudadanos Unidos, founded as a community organization in 1969, was initially an all-male organization. There was a woman's affiliate as well. However, in December

1970, at one of the regular Ciudadanos Unidos' meetings, the women confronted the men with a petition demanding full membership, the right to vote, and the right to hold office. The men accepted and the women became part of the organization, playing an exceedingly important part in the success the organization had in its push for community political mobilization (Lizcano, Meléndrez, and Solís 1974).

REFERENCES

Arvizu, Steve. 1978. Critical Reflections and Consciousness. Grito Del Sol: A Chicano Quarterly 3(1):119–123.

Anaya, Rudolfo A. and Francisco Lomelí. 1989. Aztlán: Essays on the Chicano Homeland. Albuquerque, NM: El Norte Publications/Academia.

Barrera, Mario. 1988. Beyond Aztlán: Ethnic Autonomy in Comparative Perspective. New York: Praeger.

Bauman, Richard, editor. 1977. Verbal Art as Performance. Prospect Heights, IL: Waveland Press.

Bauman, Richard. 1986. Story, Performance, and Event: Contextual Studies of Oral Narrative. Cambridge: Cambridge University Press.

Cristal. 1971. Partido Newspaper [Special Issue]. September. Aztlán City, TX: La Raza Unida Party.

Everhart, Robert B. 1988. Practical Ideology and Symbolic Community: An Ethnography of Schools of Choice. New York: The Falmer Press.

Fanon, Frantz. 1963. The Wretched of the Earth. New York: Grove Press.

Foley, Douglas E., C. Mota, D. E. Post, and I. Lozano. 1988. From Peones to Políticos: Ethnic Relations in a South Texas Town, 1900 to 1987. Revised edition. Austin: Center for Mexican-American Studies, University of Texas Press.

Freire, Paulo. 1974. Pedagogy of the Oppressed. New York: Seabury Press.

———. 1981. Education for Critical Consciousness. New York: Continuum Publishing.

———. 1985. The Politics of Education: Culture, Power and Liberation. South Hadley, MA: Bergin & Garvey.

García, Ignacio M. 1989. United We Win: The Rise and Fall of La Raza Unida Party. Tucson: Mexican-American Studies and Research Center, University of Arizona.

Gutiérrez, José Angel. 1976. Toward a Theory of Community Organization in a Mexican-American Community in South Texas. Ph.D. dissertation, University of Texas, Austin.

Hardgrave, Robert L. and Santiago Hinojosa. 1975. The Politics of Bilingual Education: A Study of Four Southwest Texas Communities. Manchaca, TX: Sterling Swift Publishing.

Kjolseth, Roth. 1982. Bilingual Education Programs in the U. S.: For Assimilation or Pluralism? *In* Bilingualism in the Southwest. Second edition. P. R. Turner, ed. Pp. 3–28. Tucson: University of Arizona Press.

La Causa Publishers. 1970. El Plan de Santa Bárbara: A Chicano Plan for Higher Education. Santa Barbara, CA: La Causa.

Lizcano, Jeanette, Ambrosio Meléndez, and Eliseo Solís. 1974. Cristal. Aztlán City, TX: Aztlán City Independent School District.

Macías, R. F., C. W. de Macías, W. De La Torre, and M. Vásquez. 1975. Educación Alternativa: On the Development of Chicano Bilingual Schools. Hayward, CA: Bayview/Regal Printing.

Mackey, William F. and Jacob Ornstein. 1977. The Revolt of the Ethnics. *In* The Bilingual Education Movement: Essays on Its Progress. W. F. Mackey and J. Ornstein, eds. El Paso: Texas Western Press.

McCollum, Pam. 1993. Learning to Value English: Cultural Capital in a Two-Way Bilingual Program. Paper presented at the Annual Meeting of the American Educational Research Association, Atlanta, GA.

Navarro, Armando. 1974. El Partido de La Raza Unida in Crystal City: A Peaceful Revolution. Ph.D. dissertation, University of California, Riverside.

Padilla, Ray. 1984. Federal Policy Shifts and the Implementation of Bilingual Education Programs. *In* The Chicano Struggle: Analyses of Past and Present Efforts. F. T. Córdova and J. R. García, eds. Pp. 90–110. Binghamton, NY: Bilingual Press/ Editorial Bilingüe.

Paulston, Christina B. 1978. Rationales for Bilingual Educational Reforms: A Comparative Assessment. Comparative Education Review 22(3):402–419.

———. 1980. Bilingual Education: Theories and Issues. Rowley, MA: Newbury House.

Reskin, Henry S. (Producer and Director) and Roger Williams (Director). 1974. The Schools of Cristal: An Experiment in Change [film]. Stanford, CA: Stanford Center for Research and Development in Teaching, Stanford University.

Ríos, Sam. 1978. An Approach to Action Anthropology: The Community Project, C.S.U.S. Grito Del Sol: A Chicano Quarterly 3(1):51–65.

Sharp, Rachel. 1980. Knowledge, Ideology and the Politics of Schooling: Towards a Marxist Analysis of Education. London: Routledge & Kegan Paul.

Sharp, Rachel and Anthony Green. 1975. Education and Social Control: A Study in Progressive Primary Education. London: Routledge & Kegan Paul.

Shockley, John Staples. 1974. Chicano Revolt in a Texas Town. Notre Dame: University of Notre Dame Press.

Smith, Walter Elwood, Jr. and Douglas E. Foley. 1975. The Transition of Multiethnic Schooling in Model Town, Texas: 1930–1969. Final Report, NIE Project No. R020825 and No. 3-4003. Washington, DC: Office of Education, U.S. Department of Health, Education and Welfare.

Trillen, Calvin. 1971. U.S. Journal: Crystal City. The New Yorker (17 April):102.

Trujillo, Armando L. 1993. Community Empowerment and Bilingual/Bicultural Education: A Study of the Movimiento in a South Texas Community. Ph.D. Dissertation, Department of Anthropology, University of Texas, Austin.

Williams, Raymond. 1973. Base and Superstructure in Marxist Cultural Theory. New Left Review 82:3–16.

PART II

The Educated Person in
Competing Sites of Cultural Production

6

LAURA RIVAL

Formal Schooling and the Production of Modern Citizens in the Ecuadorian Amazon

To look at formal schooling in non-Western contexts is a necessary part of arguing, as this book does, that cultural transmission, far from being a straightforward process, involves resistance, and that schools, aimed at producing homogeneity, may give rise to heterogeneity. State education in less-developed countries has often been presented as the main mechanism to bring about "economic growth" and achieve "modernization" (Anderson and Bawman 1965; Harbinson and Myers 1964; Rogers and Shoemaker 1971). In the 1950s and 1960s, it was believed that national education systems in the Third World were to provide skilled laborers and modern citizens free of divisive ethnic allegiances, ignorance, and backward religious beliefs. If these ideas have come under strong criticism, along with the unfounded and Eurocentric contentions of modernization theory, the effects of state schooling in the non-West have yet to be properly researched and analyzed.

This chapter deals with the introduction of formal schooling among the Huaorani,[1] a small group of Amazonian hunters-and-gatherers.[2] It shows that state schools, sought for their promotion of social cohesion and their promise of free access to manufactured goods, do not come without a whole range of constraints and obligations which, even when actively resisted, have an impact on Huaorani society and culture. By contrasting models of socialization, cultural settings, and processes of cultural acquisition in forest settlements and school villages, this chapter attempts to elucidate the unforeseen and contested institutional effects of formal schooling, and explore the ways in which such effects hinder the reproduction of Huaorani cultural practices. It ends with a discussion of how formal schooling, a major site of cultural production in contemporary societies, creates the conditions for dominant identities to undermine the continuity of minority identities. These conditions are resisted to a certain extent by local actors, but once the school institution has transformed local social relations, pre-school identities can no longer exist.

FROM "GOD WEALTH" TO SCHOOL RICHES

The Huaorani inhabit the heart of the Ecuadorian Amazon, between the Napo and Curaray rivers. Before their "pacification" by an evangelical mission, the

153

Summer Institute of Linguistics (SIL), in the early 1960s, they lived in highly dispersed and transient collective dwellings located on hilltops away from rivers. Traditional longhouses of approximately 10 to 35 members were typically composed of an older couple (often a man married to one, two, or three sisters), their daughters (with, when married, their husbands and children), and their unmarried sons. Each of these self-sufficient and dispersed residential units formed strong alliances with two or three other ones, while avoiding contact with all others. Allied houses formed in this way regional groups within which most marriages took place.

The SIL "pacification" campaign—arguably one of the most infamous missionary stories in Amazonia—followed the death of five North American missionaries in 1956 (Rival 1992; Stoll 1982; Wallis 1971). The SIL missionaries who, from the mid-1960s to the mid-1970s, prompted the Huaorani to relocate on their mission-base, have progressively introduced new garden crops, shotguns, dogs, and Western medicine, as well as the intensive use of air transport and radio contacts. They have strongly advocated monogamy, sexual modesty, and praying, while vehemently discouraging feasts, chants, and dancing. Relocated sometimes hundreds of kilometers away from their traditional lands, long-feuding bands have had no choice but to coexist and intermarry. If the "mixing" of traditionally antagonistic groups and the high number of monogamous marriages between former enemies has put an end to warfare, it has also severely undermined the long-established boundaries between endogamous groups. Yet the SIL did more than trigger changes in traditional alliances, subsistence activities, and residence patterns. It habituated converted Huaorani to a sedentary existence in communities under the guidance of powerful outsiders who, through their ability to "attract" large flows of free manufactured goods, were able to secure social unity and stability.

The advance of oil prospecting and the SIL missionary work have resulted in the concentration of 80 percent of the population on less than 10 percent of the traditional Huaorani territory—formerly called the Protectorate.[3] The Huaorani number 1,250 today—they were no more than 600 twelve years ago—and 55 percent of the present-day population are under 16. The creation of primary schools in the Huaorani territory has furthered the concentration of people in a few villages, adding to the dramatic character of their demographic growth.

The Huaorani have not endured the exploitation suffered by many other Amazonian Indian groups: their native language has never been suppressed (nor was Spanish forced on them), and they were exempted from the alienation of religious boarding schools. All this is due in large part to the fact that all the SIL has wanted is to translate the Bible into their language, and to design a literacy program (aimed at *both* adults and children) in order to give them the opportunity to read "God's words"[4] for themselves. However, a number of state schools have been established in their territory over the last decade, and teachers now act as "powerful outsiders." The Ecuadorian Ministry of Education appoints and pays the teachers, but most other costs (school buildings, radios, uniforms, textbooks, teaching aids, and so forth) are privately financed by oil companies and the North American evangelical missions which have replaced the SIL. According to my 1990 census, eight communities—out of seventeen—had a school. In 1990, approximately 500 school age children—that is, children between the ages of 6 and 15—were enrolled. The first elementary school was created in December 1973 on the northern edge of the Protectorate. Only in this village are there today parents who were themselves schooled and who thus can share the experience of formal education with their children. All the teachers are trained and qualified, but only three of them have some competence in speaking Huaorani.

Until recently, successive Ecuadorian governments have promoted state education in order to enhance economic growth, give unity to the young Ecuadorian nation-state, and modernize its citizens' views and ways. But today, with the slow recognition that the national society is multilingual and pluricultural, there is more political will to adopt a national project of official bilingualism in the country. Moreover, bilingual education has been actively promoted by the Ecuadorian Indianist movement. Given the current situation of intense interethnic contact, most Indian leaders think that the Indian cultural heritage will not resist the influences of the dominant culture if kept in its oral forms. They firmly believe that Amerindian cultural identities depend on the continuous use of the native languages in writing and at school, and that state education can play a major role in the maintenance of Indian cultural identities (see Luykx this volume for similar developments in Bolivia).

The Huaorani's responses to these developments have been mixed and varied. Huaorani settlements are very isolated and transient—often only accessible by helicopter. Among the Huaorani 95 percent are monolingual in their own language, and not one is fully fluent in Spanish. Some communities refuse state education altogether. Others have received a teacher, only to decide within a few months against the schooling of their children—a decision at times resulting in a community split. Villages which have accepted a school are further divided between those who, allied with the evangelical missions, have opted for the Spanish national curriculum, and those who, aligned with the CONFENIAE (Confederation of the Indian Nationalities of Amazonian Ecuador), have chosen a program of bilingual education. These choices, however, reflect more intratribal dynamics, enduring enmities between regional factions, and patterns of political alliances with powerful outsiders, than real convictions.

Three main reasons seem to have pushed local groups to accept state schools and a sedentary existence. First of all, and as I hinted earlier, the "mixed" communities created by the SIL cannot be maintained without the centripetal force exercised by outsiders such as teachers, who alone can lower tensions and smooth animosities between old factions. Secondly, outside leaders are sources of "natural abundance," that is, of goods and foodstuffs created outside the living community. Thirdly, it is realized that the centuries-long isolation can no longer be maintained. Willing or unwilling, the Huaorani are now part of the national society, and some are eager to become modern citizens. The school provides the public and secure arena they need to rehearse modern demeanors.

LEARNING TO BE MODERN CITIZENS

It is the quest for a modern identity that informs learning activities in school villages. My aim here is to explain the local meaning of "learning to be modern." I also show that schools introduce a new type of spatiotemporal organization, de-skill children in relation to their indigenous knowledge, alter the forest environment, and modify traditional social relationships.

The schools found in Huaorani land, like any other school in rural Latin America, or, indeed, in any part of the world,[5] are conceived as models of modern culture. With their concrete floors, plank walls, and corrugated iron roofs, they are the only "modern" buildings in the village, and house all that is "modern" and "foreign." The school village, clustered around the schoolhouse and the airstrip, is linked to the provincial capital by modern systems of communication and transport—contact-radios and airplanes. The schoolhouse is usually flanked, on one side, by an experimental plantation in which children—and their parents— learn to cultivate new tropical plants and cash crops (such as coffee, sugar cane, and coconut trees). On the other side, a school canteen is equipped with the modern cooking and serving implements necessary for the preparation of "proper" meals and modern eating. The rural development projects (for instance, the introduction of water mains, showers, and toilets), promoted by teachers as part of their professional duties, are inspired by the same ideology of modernism. Finally, teachers promote the deforestation of vast areas around the school village, both for pragmatic and cultural reasons. On the pragmatic side, they argue that large open areas facilitate aircraft landings and take-offs. On the cultural side, they regard deforestation as necessary for their ideal of a modern built environment clearly marked off from the forest, the domain of savagery.

People are also, if not primarily, the targets of modernization. This is why the Ecuadorian government, despite its limited budget, regards the education of a "deprived" and "backward" population such as the Huaorani as a priority. Convinced by the teachers that Huaorani children do not do well in school because of their deprivation from proper food, hygiene, and medical attention, government officials have ordered the allocation—through special aid programs of medicine, clothes, soap, toothbrushes, toothpaste, and food considered nutritious (rice, powdered milk, porridge, and sugar) to all school villages. In addition to these free goods, villagers can usually buy from teachers the consumer goods they need to become "educated and modern citizens."

There exists a striking consensus between the teachers and the Huaorani communities on one point: to be educated is to be modern, and to be modern means to consume imported, manufactured goods. For the teachers, the very low rates of proficient literacy and numeracy among the Huaorani, even after the completion of six years of primary education, are not caused by curriculum deficiencies, but due to a lack of modern socialization. Formal education, however good the program, they argue, will not be effective if Huaorani children have not acquired the discipline and concentration that mental work demands, that is, if they have not become "modern" and "civilized." To teach Huaorani children the general cognitive skills of reading, writing, and counting requires not only their disembedding from the context of daily life—as is the case in all forms of schooling—but, more specifically, from the context of the forest and the longhouse. As there is no routine context for literacy or math activity in Huaorani social life, what the cognitive development of Huaorani students calls for is not the de-contextualization of reading, writing, or counting for general application, but the *creation of a new context*, of a new social and cultural environment. This is why the teachers feel obliged to attend to the children's deficient *habitus* first, and dedicate a large part of the teaching time to reforming their diet, hygiene, and general behavior. This they achieve primarily through promoting the consumption of the right food (such as powdered milk and oat flakes), of the right medicine and toiletry (for example, antibiotics and toothpaste), and of the right gear (a school uniform, sportwear, notebooks, pens, and so forth).

Schoolchildren, therefore, learn to be modern by memorizing textbook lessons on hygiene, executing school commands such as, "Brush your teeth before entering the classroom!," and, above all, by *imitating* the teachers. Much informal teaching—and active learning—goes on in the school compound before, during, and after normal school hours. It is when off-duty (when getting ready in the mornings or when relaxing in the evenings) that teachers become involuntary masters, eagerly modelled by unwanted apprentices—youths, schoolchildren, or passing villagers. The teachers' ways of waking up and dressing, washing, cooking and eating, playing the guitar, conversing, reading, and listening to the radio, are scrutinized and endlessly commented upon (as are the activities and behaviors of tourists who, incidentally, when in need of shelter, are invariably lodged in the schoolhouse).

For Huaorani parents and children, in sum, competent literacy and numeracy are correlated with the acquisition of a new lifestyle, inscribed in the way one dresses, eats, and behaves. To learn new skills is to learn a new identity so one becomes at once educated, modern, and "civilized." Parents believe that children having access to school uniforms, bookcases, school dinners, and toothpaste will eventually learn how to write, read, and count. After having completed their primary education, youths still hang around the school, showing off (perhaps with a hint of nostalgia?) their decisive way of crossing the airstrip while looking straight ahead and holding a pen and a notebook—the characteristic manner of literates. Villagers of all ages (except perhaps the oldest ones, for whom clothing is an unbearable nuisance, and the waiststring the only proper decorum) carefully avoid the schoolhouse if not wearing bright and clean clothes, even if this implies long detours. And no one approaches the school compound without first combing one's hair and washing off the mud from one's legs and feet. These are just some of the behavioral changes observed in the public sphere that the school creates. Other aspects, such as restrained bodily postures, verbal exchanges across age-sets and genders, and socializing through sports could also be analyzed at length to show that to opt for "modernism" and "civilization" is to choose the develop-ment of a public life around the school compound. These behavioral changes would show further that if the change of collective identity is primarily effectu-ated through performance (not through the adoption of a new worldview), then the performance of modern identity also calls for the use of specific consumer goods.

I have discussed elsewhere the way in which the school, the modern center of the village, creates a new type of community (Rival 1992). Here I simply summarize the main points of my analysis in order to show how time and space are restructured, social relations modified, and Huaorani social habits relegated to the intimacy of family homes. We have seen that Huaorani settlements are imper-manent locales that barely disturb the forest cover. Over time, they leave an imprint on the landscape, not in the form of buildings, but of enduring palm groves, the materialization of the feasting activities of past generations and of the continuity of endogamous groups (Rival 1993). Given the substantial amount of capital and labor represented by schoolhouses, villages, by contrast, are con-ceived as permanent sites of human occupation. As people invest an increasing amount of time and energy in equipping and maintaining them, they feel less inclined to simply abandon them, even when forest resources have become depleted and soils infertile.

As I have tried to show, the most direct consequences following from infra-structural deployment are sedentarization and higher population density. At the infrastructural level, a school cannot function unless there are enough children to attend classes regularly. The government will create the first teaching position in a school village only when there are at least 24 schoolage children. It will not open a second post for less than 56 schoolage children. In other words, a minimum of 150–70 villagers (i.e., a population equivalent to eight longhouses) are required for a school to function.

Not only does the school, a state institution, promote the continuous growth of the Huaorani villages, but it also increases their integration within the nation-state. As soon as the state grants a school to a village, it appears on the map of Ecuador, and the Huaorani villagers, now formally recognized as Ecuadorian citi-zens, especially in their parental capacity, are faced with new obligations and administrative formalities. They must vote, get birth and marriage certificates, and own identity cards.

Another direct consequence of schooling is the remaking of the social space, with the creation of a public sphere, and the introduction of a new division of labor based on the redefinition of production. These developments bring two new social categories into being: "children" and "parents." "Children" are those who go to school and become dependent consumers. "Parents" are those who produce food and do not go to school. To the deep resentment of villagers, far from being a "natural" source of free and abundant manufactured goods making sharing possible on a larger scale, the school imposes and constrains more than it enables. One has to live, socialize, and work with "others"—that is, former enemies—for, given the fast rate of decay and jungle growth, school buildings, lavatories, airstrips, and sports fields need constant maintenance and repair. Worse, teachers and schoolchildren must be fed every day. This implies giving up hunting and gathering, taking up agriculture, and running into debt by purchasing imported foodstuff from the teachers' stores.

Wealth, in Huaorani thought, must be created outside the living community.[6] Villagers, aware of the fact that schooling and the removal of children from subsistence activities lead to the creation of social divisions, are constantly searching for new sources of "free food," and resist the intensification of agriculture. They have no difficulty in accepting new sources of wealth, as long as no additional labor is involved. But in the end, parents become responsible for the village's agricultural production,[7] and children ("those who work mentally") become dependent consumers. This new social division of labor, explicitly presented as rational and progressive, is reinforced in the teachings dedicated to changing the conceptions of work, production, and gender. Children are taught, for example, that agriculture, the creation of abundance and welfare through hard labor, represents an evolutionary stage superior to that of hunting and that if their parents intensify horticultural production, food will be more nutritious and varied.

Schools, with their strong pro-agriculture advocacy, remove children from their natural environment and *de-skill* them with regard to forest knowledge. School children spend considerably less time in the forest than their nonsedentary counterparts, and when they go, it is during school holidays with their parents and other adults. In school most days, they tend to stay indoors when back home, helping with the washing or cooking. As the village environment (with its large grassy spaces, its compounds, and its dispersed plantations) differs substantially from the forest environment, and as the children have little exposure to the latter, their knowledge of the primary rainforest and its resources is undermined. From the survey I conducted with fifth- and sixth-graders in two school villages, it appeared that only 40 percent of the children knew how to climb trees (the majority of nonclimbers being girls); 80 percent of the boys had hunted with a blowpipe[8] (and only one girl), and none had prepared curare poison; 35 percent had hunted with a shotgun (and no girls); 5 percent of the girls had made a hammock on their own, but none had ever made a clay pot. Only two children had seen stone axes, and no one seemed to know that armbands were woven on simple looms in the past. These figures clearly indicate a high degree of de-skillment for traditional productive activities. I conducted another survey in the oldest school village to test the children's relative knowledge of plant and animal classification. The results suggest that both schooled and nonschooled children can name the same amount of species, but that only nonschooled children successfully associate names and wild specimens collected from the forest. Although too tentative to be taken as a firm indication, this test signals a loss of cultural knowledge affecting practical skills more than categories.

In the built environment of school villages, the forest has become marginal in people's practical activities, and in their *imaginary* as well. It is very rare to hear someone chant in a school village. Of course, youths who own "ghetto blasters" record and listen to the chants of elders, particularly of those who do not live in their communities. But they do not chant themselves, except—occasionally—during drinking ceremonies. Schoolchildren, despite the school lessons they have sometimes received in Huaorani cultural knowledge, do not chant either.

In conclusion, the school introduces new ways of interacting with the environment, new habits and new experiences.[9] It is through the reform of ordinary practices, particularly those centered around the body and the domestic space, that social practices are reorganized and social identities reshaped. It is also through routine activities such as wearing a school uniform, brushing one's teeth before entering the classroom, or eating with a knife and a fork that new values and beliefs are acquired as normal and commonsensical ideas.

BECOMING A HUAORANI IN THE FOREST AND IN THE LONGHOUSE

My aim in this section is to show that Huaorani people consider learning[10] an integral part of growing. Children, who progressively become full members of the longhouse through their increased participation in ongoing social activities, learn to be Huaorani *experientially* by getting forest food and sharing it, by helping out in the making of blowguns, pots, or hammocks, and by chanting with longhouse co-residents.

Toddlers are encouraged to like being on their own, detached from the caregiver's body and exploring their surroundings. The basis of Huaorani pedagogy (and, more generally, of Huaorani social life) is that action should result from the exact correspondence between feeling (*huë*) and desire or will (*â*). This is why adults never order children around; they do not command, coerce, or exercise any kind of physical or moral pressure, but simply suggest and ask, without getting annoyed when the answer is, "No, I won't do it, I don't feel like doing it now" (*ba amopa*). The belief that harmonious social life should be based on the full respect of personal expression and free choice to act corresponds to the fear that actions performed under constraint result in social harm. This is why children, who grow in uxorilocal longhouses where bodily attitudes are extremely relaxed and the needs of individuals fully respected, are, by any standard, very independent and self-sufficient. As adults do not have a sense of hierarchical superiority, and are not overprotective (see Rival 1992, chapters 5–6), relations between what a non-Huaorani would call "adults" and "children" are totally devoid of authority.

Walking, talking, and eating meat are seen as three simultaneous acquisitions which mark the beginning of personal autonomy and which can be stimulated by the application of certain plants (for a full description, see Rival 1993:639–641). Only when they can walk on their own, do toddlers start wearing the distinctive Huaorani cotton string around the waist. From field observations, I formed the impression that grownups attach far more importance to the first steps walked than to the first words uttered. Moreover, whereas I witnessed real excitement at a child's first attempts to sing, I never noticed any special reaction in response to a child's first efforts to speak. Older children, however, spend a lot of time with toddlers, making them repeat words and name body parts or objects. In any case, the child's activity that really arouses the pride of grown-ups is food sharing, the real measure of independence. Nothing is more cheering for a Huaorani parent than a three-year-old's decision to join a food gathering expedition. The young child, whose steps on the path are carefully guided away from thorns and crawling insects, is praised for carrying his/her own *oto* (a basket made of a single palm leaf hurriedly woven on the way), and bringing it back to the longhouse filled with forest food to "give away," that is, to share with co-residents. Food procurement is an essential area of learning for children who are "old enough to go on their own" (*piquèna bate opate gocamba*). Parents do not *teach* but encourage children to grow, mature and participate in productive activities. And it is by participating more fully in the social relations of sharing that children learn subsistence skills, while increasing their knowledge of plants and animals.

If food procurement is the part of the process of culture-learning that takes children to the forest and makes them know about the natural world, the skilled practices of craft-making and chanting—two inseparable activities—are important means of entering the social world of the longhouse. Although Huaorani material culture is minimal, there are a few elaborate artifacts, such as the blowpipe. These objects are difficult to make, and like almost everywhere else in the world, their manufacture involves learning by observing masters and by doing. In other words, it involves apprenticeship in the sense defined by Lave (1977, 1990, 1993) and Lave and Wenger (1991). From a very young age, Huaorani children are given raw materials to hold, feel, and touch, while people around them weave, carve, or make pots. If they seek more participation, they are entrusted with the simplest phases of the productive process. For example, a boy[11] willing to help in the making of a blowpipe starts by sanding the surface of a nearly completed one. While he learns to make more difficult parts, he receives a small blowpipe for hunting practice. In this fashion, he acquires simultaneously the art of making and the art of using the full-size blowpipe, a gradual process through which he not only reaches technical competence, but also achieves personal style (Huaorani craftsmen "sign" their works with individual decorative designs). He also, and perhaps more fundamentally, becomes a grown man, ready for marriage and fatherhood.

People usually chant—several hours a day when at home, either resting in their hammocks or busy with some home-based activity. Chanting while making tools and artifacts can therefore be seen as the combination of "vocal artistry" and "technical artistry" (Ingold 1993:463), that is, the concurrent performance of mental and manual activities through which skilled practices and symbolic knowledge are simultaneously learned. In the combined action of chanting and making objects, of knowing and practicing, individuals not only communicate their feelings to co-residents, but also share with them their personal interpretations of Huaorani symbolism. It is within the communal life of the longhouse, and amidst practical activities, that children acquire the knowledge of myths, histories of warfare, and family sagas, while also learning the poetic imagery depicting significant aspects of their environment. This leads me to suggest that chanting and craft-making are two inseparable aspects of the same social activity, embedded in the social relations that characterize the longhouse. As acquired by children through participation, this cultural knowledge combines technical enskillment and many idiosyncratic versions of the ways in which Huaorani come to experience the world. By gradually becoming performers of practical skills, and learning the associated chants, attitudes, and values, children simultaneously acquire and reproduce Huaorani culture.

Their identity, therefore, is entirely bound to their learning experiences, which are in turn influenced by the structuring features of the social environment. They learn and acquire their identity in the longhouse and in the forest through performance, in much the same way as children who live in school villages acquire their modern identity through their participation—that is, their active engagement—in the process of decontextualized knowing. Hunting, gathering, chanting, and making artifacts are cultural and context-specific activities. They are sustained through specific practices, the use of particular objects, the consumption of special food, and the mastery of certain bodily techniques. Moreover, these activities produce and reproduce particular dispositions and cultural norms, most of which have to do with the concepts of personal autonomy and the collective sharing of natural abundance.

We have seen that the modern identity acquired through state schooling is entirely antithetical to such dispositions and cultural norms. Are these dispositions and norms used, then, to resist the undermining effects of school education? An example will illustrate how school modernity is enthusiastically adopted, but in a way that subverts its cultural dichotomies (that is, modern versus traditional, school versus home).

Villagers are actively defending their free and equal access to large quantities of manufactured goods. They want these goods which enable them to act modern. But they do not want to pay or work for them, nor do they want to economize, save, or make scarce commodities last. In the teachers' words, "they do not want to learn the value of things." In Ecuadorian cities, each school has its own uniform.[12] School uniforms are a sign of progress, development, and national pride. However, not many rural schools have one. Clothes wear out too quickly in the humid tropical lowlands, and Indian families are generally too poor. But

Huaorani children do have a school uniform, offered by a North American evangelical mission, in exchange for reciting biblical verses twice a year. Teachers attach great importance to the proper use of these uniforms, and stress that they must be handled with care. Children are constantly reminded that they must not wear their uniform outside of school time. Those who come to school without their uniform on, or with a dirty one, are sent back home for the day. However, far from being deterred by these warnings, many children wear their uniforms all the time, and even sleep in them. In some villages, the population was astute enough to get school uniforms supplied in sufficient quantity for each villager to receive his or her own. In a village I visited while the school was closed for the holidays, virtually every one, old and young, male and female, parents and children, was wearing a school uniform. Through field observations and informal conversations, I soon realized that children refused to confine their modern identity to school time, and that parents wished to feel modern, even if they had passed the age of schooling.

Huaorani villagers, who wish to be modern *on their own terms*, seek a collective identity which does not fragment them into differentiated sociocultural categories. By wearing school uniforms *uniformly*, they are in fact perverting the system of differences built into formal education. Their prime concern is to defend their egalitarian social relations in whatever cultural context. This may hardly qualify as resistance, but it is a way of producing cultured persons, while rejecting the hierarchy of knowledge and sociability that comes with becoming school educated. Their way of wearing school uniforms is not determined by their decision to challenge school culture. Rather, it is a form of local appropriation, a semiconscious attempt to control the terms of modern behavior in practice. But the day-to-day wearing of school uniforms in villages (they are never worn in the forest) nevertheless recreates the conditions of its establishment. A school village is a very different environment from a longhouse in the forest.

THE POWER TO DE-SKILL

This chapter has discussed the introduction of formal schooling among a population of Amazonian hunter-gatherers. It has been argued that state schools are modernizing institutions which have the power to transform indigenous lifeways—whatever the adopted curriculum. The school institution creates a community around itself which calls for the restructuration of Huaorani social relations, subsistence activities and, more generally, mode of existence and identity. It is not so much that social life is now determined by new—modernist—cultural trends, but that new activities, through which a different type of knowledge gets distributed across minds, bodies and cultural settings, impede the practice and the development of typically Huaorani activities.

The impact of state education on Huaorani social life is, as we have seen, largely due to the infrastructural requirements of the school institution. Fixed standards corresponding to a model of what the school institution should offer, and to what an ideal learning situation is, determine the ways in which primary schools operate in Huaorani land. Like all institutions, formal schooling is the historical product of specific social relations and cultural norms. It is therefore possible to find, embedded in the apparently neutral infrastructure, a cultural model of what knowledge is, and how it should be acquired. Knowledge, which can only be acquired in isolation from everyday activities, demands discipline, obedience, and respect for the teachers' authority. Formal schooling, moreover, requires particular family relations. The social roles of parents and children must exist—or must be created—for schooling to occur. In addition, and the case under discussion fully illustrates this point, literacy and numeracy, the basics of school knowledge, are not dissociable from wider modes of cultural expression—here, from "modernization." Moreover, children learn more than literacy and numeracy skills; they learn to be members of a modern community, the school village and, beyond it, the national society. For the Huaorani, then, the educated person is above all a modern person, the product of a distinctive form of sociability, the end-result of particular acts of performance and consumption.

By comparing two sites of cultural (re)production, the school village and the longhouse in the forest, I have tried to show that culture is not primarily acquired through the internalization of norms and values, or the transmission of factual information and abstract skills, but through interactive learning. In the two learning settings I have examined, learning activities and the sociocultural order are dialectically constituted. The disparity between what schoolchildren in villages and children raised in longhouses in the forest know about their culture is best explained as resulting from the differences between the two social environments in which learning activities take place. As Lave (1988:14) so rightly states, "knowledge-in-practice, constituted in the settings of practice, is the locus of the most powerful knowledgeability of people in the lived-in world." Both in her work on craft apprenticeship among Vai and Gola tailors in Liberia (1977, 1982, 1990) and her investigation of everyday arithmetic practices (1984, 1988), Lave has demonstrated that culture is the acquisition of particular skills through active learning and repeated practice, as well as the reproduction of *ways of being in the world.*

Lave (1988:188–90) argues that knowledge is not isolated from experience and context, that social life is formed of continuing practices, and that, consequently, continuity results from social habits and routines. As she says so well "Everyday practice is a more powerful source of socialization than intentional pedagogy" (Lave 1988:14). This implies that cultural continuity requires the continuity of community practices. In the case under study, the two "communities of practice" (Lave and Wenger 1991) are the school village and the longhouse in the forest, where continuity, the product of routinization (rather than of the internalization of transmitted facts, norms or values), is more likely than structural change.[13] However, as I have tried to demonstrate, these two communities of practice are incompatible. In school villages, Huaorani people can be seen to engage practically, actively and consciously in new social processes, which, given the relational nature of the self, the (partly) physical nature of cognitive processes, and the social construction of bodily experiences, undermine their Huaoraniness.

NOTES

Fieldwork among the Huaorani was generously supported by the Wenner Gren Foundation for Anthropological Research, with additional funding from the Linnean Society of London. The work on which this article is based was originally presented at the Conference on Hunter-Gatherer Societies (CHAGS 7) in Moscow, Russia, in August 1993. It has subsequently been read in various departmental seminars. I would like to thank the participants for their suggestions, especially Harvey Feit, Megan Biesele, and Jean Briggs. I am very grateful to Maurice Bloch, Dorothy Holland, and Aurolyn Luykx, who commented on an early draft, and to Bradley Levinson and Doug Foley for their helpful editorial comments.

1. I spent eighteen months working with schooled and nonschooled children. I lived both in school villages and in settlements with no school. The following observations and analyses are based on the data I recorded between January 1989 and June 1990.

2. I have argued elsewhere (Rival 1993) that Huaorani gardening is exceptional. Manioc and plantain are cultivated incipiently and sporadically for the preparation of ceremonial drinks, while daily subsistence is traditionally secured through hunting and gathering.

3. Two percent of the population is still uncontacted and lives in hiding.

4. By 1981, 20 percent of the population in the Protectorate could read the SIL translation of the Gospel according to St Mark (Rival 1992:15). That the SIL has not created a new dialect of Huaorani remains to be proven. I suspect that their linguistic analyses, which are shaped by the priorities and constraints of biblical translations, do not pay enough attention to everyday speech. Rather, they prioritize and formalize narrative styles, and standardize linguistic expressions which do not arise from the Huaorani cultural environment, but from the needs of Bible translation. For instance, a large number of figurative phrases and metaphors have been created in order to fill the semantic and cultural gaps between Huaorani and the biblical texts in Huaorani. Moreover, for the SIL, vernacular literacy is a definite sign of *salvation*, a notion which includes not only the idea of Christianization, but also of progress and modernization, and which, thus, comes close to meaning *civilization*. In any case, this is how the Huaorani themselves express it, when they say that the SIL has "civilized" them. See Rival (1992:323–348) for a fuller account.

5. The constraints which govern schools and limit learning have concerned educationalists for many years. Illich's (1973) *Deschooling Society* remains one of the most radical, provocative, and insightful essays on this subject, particularly for the Latin American context.

6. Forest resources represent the bounty created by the everyday activities linked to consumption of past generations. I have argued elsewhere (Rival 1992, chapter 4) that

Huaorani social relations are based on consumption rather than production, and that their sharing economy relates to a fundamental belief in "natural abundance," that is, the exogenous creation of wealth. In the same way as the trees associated with their forefathers continuously provide for the living and secure their subsistence (Rival 1993), foreign organizations such as the SIL, the oil companies prospecting on Huaorani land, and now schools, are expected to behave like giving agencies and meet people's modern needs, *without asking anything in return*. The Huaorani have adjusted to demographic growth and increased population density by tapping new sources of food. Former enemies in mixed communities are willing to share with each other as long as sharing neither creates obligations, nor requires the management of scarce resources.

7. Parents are classified as *agricultores* (farmers) on school social category for registers. "Hunter-gatherers" is an unacceptable social category for people who send their children to school.

8. One should not be too impressed by the high rate of boys having used blowpipes. They use them as toys around the house (monkeys and birds are rare in the vicinity of sedentary villages), which, while giving them good practice, does not amount to the same skill as actual hunting.

9. It also creates new political discourses and competing ideologies about cultural identity and modernity. The evangelical missionaries now working with the Huaorani are highly critical of the SIL's attempt to translate the Bible in Huaorani. They are totally opposed to bilingual education, which they equate to "communism." They support financially state schools which implement the national curriculum in Spanish and teach religion—in Spanish as well.

10. To my knowledge, there is no Huaorani term to translate the idea of learning. In answer to my questions about children engaged in the making of a pot, a fishing net, or darts, my informants would simply say: "he is busy making darts, she is busy weaving a net . . ." Interestingly, SIL missionaries have used the word *iñe* (to listen) to translate the Western concept of learning. This term is indeed appropriate for the learning of the Bible, which takes place in the Church, when Christians assemble to listen to *Huegongui apene*, God's stories or teachings.

11. The same can be said of girls, who traditionally made clay pots. Clay pots, which have been replaced two decades ago by traded metallic pots, are no longer made. Today, girls and women are almost exclusively responsible for the making of hammocks, an activity which was not gender-specific in the past.

12. In addition to their normal school uniform, children have a second uniform for official ceremonies, parades, and the raising of the flag, which takes place every Monday.

13. A conclusion also reached by Giddens (1979:216), for whom routinization is an essential part of the concept of structuration.

REFERENCES

Anderson, Charles A. and M. J. Bawman. 1965. Education and Economic Development. London: Frank Cass.

Giddens, Anthony. 1979. Central Problems in Social Theory. London: Mcmillan.

Harbinson, Frank and C. Myers. 1964. Education, Manpower and Economic Growth. New York: McGraw-Hill.

Illich, Ivan. 1973 [1971]. Deschooling Society. UK: Harmondsworth, Penguin.

Ingold, Tim. 1993. Epilogue. *In* Tools, Language and Cognition in Human Evolution. K. R. Gibson and T. Ingold, eds. Pp. 449–472. Cambridge: Cambridge University Press.

Lave, Jean. 1977. Cognitive Consequences of Traditional Apprenticeship Training in West Africa. Anthropology and Education Quarterly 8(3):177–80.

———. 1982. A Comparative Approach to Educational Reforms and Learning Processes. Anthropology and Education Quarterly 13(2):181–187.

———. 1988. Cognition in Practice. Cambridge: Cambridge University Press.

———. 1990. The Culture of Acquisition and the Practice of Understanding. *In* Cultural Psychology: Essays on Comparative Human Development. J. W. Stigler, R. Shweder, and G. Herdt, eds. Cambridge: Cambridge University Press.

———. 1993. The Practice of Learning. *In* Understanding Practice: Perspectives on Activity and Context. S. Chaiklin and J. Lave, eds. Pp. 3–32. Cambridge: Cambridge University Press.

Lave, Jean, M. Murtaugh, and O. de la Rocha. 1984. The Dialectic of Arithmetic in Grocery Shopping. *In* Everyday Cognition: Its Development in Social Context. B. Rogoff and J. Lave, eds. Cambridge, MA: Harvard University Press.

Lave, Jean and E. Wenger. 1991. Situated Learning: Legitimate Peripheral Participation. Cambridge: Cambridge University Press.

Rival, Laura. 1992. Social Transformations and the Impact of Schooling on the Huaorani of Amazonian Ecuador. Ph.D. dissertation. University of London.

———. 1993. The Growth of Family Trees: Understanding Huaorani Perceptions of the Forest. Man 28(4):635–52.

Rogers, Edwin and F. Shoemaker. 1971. Communication of Innovations: A Cross-Cultural Approach. New York: Free Press.

Stoll, David. 1982. Fishers of Men or Founders of Empire? The Wycliffe Bible Translators in Latin America. London: Zed Press.

Wallis, Elizabeth. 1971. Aucas Down River. New York: Harper & Row.

7

Margaret Eisenhart _____

The Production of Biologists at School and Work: Making Scientists, Conservationists, or Flowery Bone-Heads?

Scientists are produced in contexts. In this chapter, I explore and compare the production of "scientists" in a U.S. university biology program and an American workplace that employs biologists. In particular, I describe how the organizational and cultural contexts of the university and the workplace produce different kinds of scientist identities. These identities, and the knowledge associated with them, are formed both within and against the hegemony of the hard sciences and schooling.

Scientists as Cultural Productions

It is commonplace for Americans to act as if scientists are born, not made. For example, we hear ourselves and others say that the public is not "capable" of understanding scientific theories. We behave as if girls are not psychologically inclined toward scientific interests or reasoning. We portray scientists as individuals who are "naturally" intelligent, esoteric, and nerdy. But, ethnographic studies of science and scientists suggest that the situation is far more complex: the meanings assigned to the identity of scientist vary in context. A biologist at the U.S. Forest Service does not do the same work, worry about the same things, or evoke the same image as a biologist at Stanford. A man who has "made it" in chemistry is unlikely to think of his accomplishment in the same way a female chemist does. A student who has been "weeded out" of physics will probably not have the same view of the discipline as a physics major. In these ways and many others, the meanings of being a scientist are made in context.

In the literature on science or engineering education and work, the concept of "cultural production" has been used to capture the process by which identities are given meaning in context. This use of the concept focuses on how local structures, for example, a curriculum, degree program, or organizational setting, create the conditions for some identities to be made central or hegemonic while others are marginalized. For example, in Jan Nespor's study of the physics degree program at a large comprehensive university (1990), he demonstrates how the meaning of being a physicist was constituted by the physics curriculum. The

169

curricular structure forced students to behave and to think about their work, themselves, and their relations with others as theoretical problem-solvers who work in cooperative groups with other physicists. In this sense, the curriculum "produced" a way of being a physicist, which students took up, or "consumed," as they progressed through the program. Other possible student identities, such as loner, party-er, or jock, were discouraged and thereby marginalized within the physics curriculum. Gary Downey and his colleagues, in their study of an engineering program (Downey, Hegg, and Lucena 1993) point out that some programs with a "weed-out" philosophy, such as engineering, physics, and biology, don't just produce a single identity. They also produce students who have been "weeded out" of the progam or who are "not the real engineer [scientist] type" (see also Seymour and Hewitt 1994). Downey and co-workers show, in students' encounters with "weed out" courses and talk about them, that women and minorities are "produced" as categories of people who can't succeed in a rigorous program like engineering. Although this literature demonstrates the locally specific ways in which scientists are defined through structure, it does not, for the most part, examine the forms of cultural production that Paul Willis and many other school ethnographers have been so interested in: how individuals creatively occupy these structures, respond to them, and sometimes transform them (see Levinson and Holland, this volume).

Willis defined "cultural productions" as the emergent outcomes of societal subgroups using "discourses, meanings, materials, practices, and group processes to explore, understand, and creatively occupy particular positions in sets of general material possibilities" (Willis 1981:59). In Willis' study of working-class boys (the "lads") in a British secondary school (1977), the lads actively produced social practices and a meaning system (cultural forms) that opposed the school culture. This counterculture was organized around working-class models of adult masculine identity, which the lads appropriated to challenge the school's ideology. In the lads' case, their opposition to school eventually led them to working-class jobs, that is, to the social reproduction of their position in society. However, because of the dynamic, active role of groups, like the lads, in defining what was important (or not) to them about the structures they encountered, Willis argued that social reproduction is not inevitable. Groups *might* produce counter-hegemonic practices, ideologies, and identities that could disrupt the status quo.

Other anthropologists have recently demonstrated how the cultural productions of individuals or groups can lead to significant change. For example, Holland and Skinner (1995) demonstrate how Nepali women's songs, produced by individuals for the Tij festival, serve as vehicles of individual identity, collective protest, and change in their patriarchal society. The songs tend to be structured and presented in familiar ways, yet they can have novel elements, stemming from the individual writer's creative modification of existing cultural forms, her unique personal experiences, or changing social/historical conditions. When the women produce and publicly perform their songs, they add to personal and collective ways of thinking and acting in the world, some of which are new and radical. In my own recent work, I have suggested that some U.S. working women, who are trying to manage careers and families within patriarchal institutions, are similarly producing radical "songs" (representations) of identity that challenge existing ways of thinking and acting around work and motherhood (Eisenhart 1994, 1995).

Because people must act within structural constraints and by mobilizing resources, a comprehensive approach to studies of how scientists or other identities are made seems to require both of the perspectives described above (see also Levinson and Holland, this volume). In this chapter, I sketch out such an approach in a comparison of the cultural production of scientists in a university biology program and a nonprofit conservation corporation that employs biologists. I begin by examining how the structure of the university program constitutes the meaning of being a scientist; then I consider how students seem to respond to this cultural form. Next, I turn to an examination of a corporation that employs graduates of the university program but where a different meaning of scientist is constituted. I describe new employees' responses to this situation and their implications for change.

SITES AND METHODS

The university program I studied is one of two biology departments on the campus of a large, publicly supported research institution in the middle of the United States. The department's emphasis is environmental biology; thus, I refer to it as "EB." It confers undergraduate, master's, and doctoral degrees. Data about the program come primarily from catalogues and degree program descriptions. These data are supplemented by other ethnographic studies of university science and engineering programs on this and similar U.S. campuses.

The workplace is the state office of a nonprofit conservation corporation, which I call "CC." It is devoted to preserving biodiversity by protecting land where species, habitats, or ecological processes are threatened. CC's work is organized into two areas: the science area which includes biologists, botanists, and ecologists; and the business area, which includes fund-raisers, administrators, and a few lawyers. Generally, the scientists are expected to use methods of scientific inquiry to identify land worth protecting, and state-of-the-art models of ecological processes to build a case for protection and how it will be accomplished. Then the business people take over to negotiate the land deals and raise the financial and community support necessary for the protection project. During my study of CC, approximately twenty-two people, mostly scientists and fund-raisers, worked there at a given time.

Data about CC come from an eighteen-month ethnographic study that I conducted there from October 1992 until March 1994. During that time, I spent an average of four days/per month participating in and observing CC's ongoing activities. I participated as a volunteer who worked on reseeding projects, seed collection, and monitoring at preserves; stuffed envelopes in the office; distributed materials at fund-raising activities; contributed to conversations; and became friends with many staff members. I observed at field trips, public activities to raise support, and biweekly staff meetings. After approximately nine months, I conducted formal interviews with most of the staff and began to follow closely the experiences and learning trajectories of five new scientists who joined the organization at that time. All of them were making the transition from full-time school to full-time work.

THE PRODUCTION OF BIOLOGICAL SCIENTISTS IN THE UNIVERSITY PROGRAM

Structural Productions

Jan Nespor's ethnographic study of undergraduate degree programs at another university (1990) demonstrates that the curricular structures of degree programs constitute identities in distinctly different ways. Some programs, such as those for physics and management, were tightly structured in ways that produced graduates with shared ideologies and strategies for acquiring and using knowledge. In contrast, loosely structured programs (such as in sociology) exerted little in the way of *curricular* pressure toward collective knowledge or academic identities.

Nespor proposed that curricular structures be analyzed along three dimensions: density (the proportion of hours or courses required in the major field); tightness (the proportion of named courses that must be taken, that is, that are completely determine by the curriculum); and interlocking (the number of courses linked by prerequisites into strings). He found that the physics degree program was dense, tightly organized, and highly interlocked. Management was also tightly organized but had low density and less interlocking. The differences in the two structures had implications for how the students spent their time (e.g., with whom, doing what) and what they learned (e.g., the extent to which useful knowledge was delimited by the boundaries of the discipline). Yet, the two programs' similar tightness created shared academic orientations as well as career identities within each cohort. Nespor's comparison of course requirements in physics and management is reproduced in table 1.

In both programs, curricular pressure produced conditions wherein students came to embody the socio-academic relations of the discipline. However, the relations encouraged by physics were considerably more "within" schooling than those of management. The physics program worked to organize students' academic world so that physics knowledge and career success came to be understood as a function of group effort to solve academic problems. Academically oriented peer groups became the means by which physics students achieved and came to understand themselves and others as physicists. "What the physics curriculum did, then, was to create a structural pressure for the development of friendships, or 'strong ties' . . . oriented around the performance of academic tasks"

TABLE 1
Course Requirements

	Physics*	Management*	Environmental Biology
Total Hours for B.S.	126	120	120
Hours in Major	40	21	38
Completely Determined Hours	66-69	53	46–48
Longest String of Interlocked Hours	52	15	20

* Taken from Nespor (1990:219).

(1990:221). The management program, in contrast, produced a sharp division between schooling (academic work) and knowledge or success in business. The low density and limited interlocking of the management curriculum pressured students to rely on the nonacademic world of the university (e.g., sororities, fraternities, informal peer groups), and on business associations or clubs, for academic information (e.g., about which courses or professors were best to take) and social relationships that contributed to success in business. Especially through their contacts with business associations, students learned that good grades were often seen by recruiters as a detraction, indicating that students did not spend enough time developing social contacts and networking skills. One business student told Nespor that for jobs in marketing, advertising, or management, a high GPA would: "go against me. . . . I would have to prove myself. I would have to show them that I didn't spend the last four years of my life locked up in a room with a book" (p. 230). The nonacademic part of the management curriculum created connections between students and the business world that virtually bypassed the school and rejected its model of success. In place of school, connections to business associations engaged the students in tasks that directed them away from academic identities and toward distinct identities and status within the business world.

At the end of his article, Nespor suggests that physics and management deserve special attention because "they involve the production of the people who will inherit the positions and institutional apparatuses of disciplines that control or influence important domains of everyday life. . . . [From] the evidence presented here one could speculate that fields preparing students for positions of power and status are structured so as to produce cohorts of graduates with shared outlooks, ambitions, definitions of reality and strategies for acquiring and using knowledge . . . [thereby] suppressing difference and 'deviation' and insuring social and cultural 'reproduction' in spheres of power" (pp. 231-232).

In comparison to Nespor's programs, EB is similar to physics in its high density, and similar to management in its tightness (somewhat less than physics) and relatively low number of interlocking courses (see table 1). Yet, EB is not preparing students for positions of power and status, at least not in the same sense as physics or management. The structure of physics encourages its students to develop identities as academic problem-solvers headed for success in laboratory and university research settings. The management program encourages students to develop identities in extracurricular social networks valued for success in corporate businesses. EB, in contrast, is preparing students to become conservationists, ecologists, wildlife managers, and forest rangers.

What distinguishes EB's curriculum is the content of its upper-division undergraduate courses which stress applications of biological science. EB describes itself as follows:

> The established disciplinary strengths of the department include behavior, ecology, genetics, morphology, endocrinology, physiology, and systematics. Approximately half of the Department focuses on the adaptation and functioning of organisms in the context of environment, while the other half studies higher levels of organization, including populations, communities, and ecosystems. Research programs have relevance for global change, conservation biology, and revealing fundamental mechanisms underlying the structural and functional adaptations of organisms.

As in physics, EB's course work encourages students to work in groups to solve problems. However, unlike in physics, where the problems are theoretical and abstract, EB's problems involve applying scientific principles to conservation policy, forest management, and other current environmental issues. Excerpts from two upper-division course announcements reveal this focus:

> Microbial approaches and solutions to environmental problem areas in which microorganisms play favorable or unfavorable roles: in . . . soil, water and waste management, current pollution problems, resource recovery, energy production, ecological control of pests, and biotechnology.

> Demanding, problems-oriented methods course . . . emphasizing techniques appropriate to realistic biological problems.

Like management, the EB program encourages extra-academic contacts and network-building. But EB network-building occurs in class assignments to solve "realistic" environmental problems and in internships and field placements with local environmental agencies, not in fraternities, sororities, or other social clubs.

However, unlike in management, which makes almost no attempt to integrate students' academic work with their social activities, EB's curriculum seems to produce a practitioner identity that is considerably more "within" school. EB selects and requires outside-of-school contacts that align students' academic and social relationships in specific ways. In EB's case, the program encourages students to develop identities as scientists who spend their time working with others on contemporary environmental problems. The density and tightness of EB's curriculum, coupled with the time demands of internships and field placements, suggest that EB exerts powerful pressures on students to develop strong commitments to applied biology and environmental activism.

On the other hand, the meaning of "scientist" produced within EB is pointedly "against" the one produced by programs like physics. The EB view of a scientist is a kind of challenge to the hegemony of the theoretical, laboratory, or research scientist who is widely celebrated in the physical sciences (see, for example, Traweek 1988) and touted as the best model for elementary and secondary school science (American Association for the Advancement of Science 1989). The hegemonic model of "science" that appears, for example, in undergraduate physics textbooks and courses suggests that "science is . . . independent of all social or political contexts; [and] that all knowledge is dependent on or derivative from physics" (Traweek 1988:78). In the textbook materials Traweek studied, she found that they reflected a public image of scientists as rational, dispassionate, and open minded investigators (taken from Brush 1974 and Merton 1957 in Traweek 1988:80). In Traweek's case, as well as Brush's, this image was used explicitly to inspire students to pursue a career in physics.

In EB's insistence that biological science be applied to "real-world" environmental problems, this degree program is an institutional dare to the hegemony of laboratory science. Where the "hard sciences," such as physics, define controlled, cumulative, abstract problem-solving and knowledge production as the *sine qua non* of "real scientists," EB defines a "good scientist" as someone who contributes to species and habitat protection. Where the hard sciences portray science as separate from political or social issues, EB places itself in the midst of such issues. Thus, the curriculum structure of EB produces a scientist identity that is at least in some ways counter-hegemonic to the one produced in physics.

Student Responses

In one sense, EB's challenge to the hegemony of the laboratory scientist is minor. It does not oppose laboratory science per se, only how and where its principles are used. The power, politics, and privileges of laboratory science and university hard science are not directly confronted in the program.

On the other hand, many of the students majoring in EB are "drop outs" from physics, chemistry, engineering, and medicine. They have chosen EB as a major after leaving the harder sciences. Thus, the EB program may offer a "space" for some students to articulate and further develop a critique of the hard sciences.

My own investigation of EB did not include observations or interviews with students. However, a comparative study, conducted by Nancy Hewitt and Elaine Seymour (1991; see also Seymour and Hewitt 1994), of college students who did and did not switch out of science, mathematics, or engineering (SME) programs provides some clues to student responses. Hewitt and Seymour interviewed 149 students (61 switchers; 88 nonswitchers) on four college campuses, including the one where EB is located, about the factors that influenced their decisions to stay in or switch majors. Hewitt and Seymour's major finding was that switchers and nonswitchers differed very little in their statements about SME programs. Both groups had various and similar complaints about SME. Hewitt and Seymour concluded that nonswitchers learned to live with their discontents, while switchers did not. Judging from excerpts of interviews included in Hewitt and Seymour's report, students who experience the hard sciences, mathematics, or engineering—both switchers and nonswitchers—have fairly similar, radical critiques of it. Some illustative comments, taken from Hewitt and Seymour's report (1991:79–83), are provided below. Many students view SME course work as "irrelevant" and "uninteresting":

> It's very easy to burn out on the subject. When you start feeling the frustration, and realize there are just so many things in math that are irrelevant to anything else. [White female mathematics switcher]

> [T]hey get into engineering and they find that there's no stimulation any more. It's just numbers, numbers, numbers. And you think, "Well, all I have to do is to make it through the weedout classes, and then it'll get interesting." But you're completely wrong, because you've no room for humanities. You find out you'll just be taking six aerospace courses a semester. . . . You'd have to be some kind of drug addict to do it. [Asian male engineering switcher]

Others found it degrading of other disciplines:

> I only wish I could switch over to political science and not feel guilty about it. . . . All the input you're getting from everybody in engineering is that arts and sciences are for flowery bone-heads. [Asian male engineering nonswitcher]

The term "flowery bone-head" is used on the EB campus to refer derisively to a person who does not give priority to "facts" and "knowledge" defined by numbers and hypothesis-testing with experimental controls. Interestingly, I also heard it used in my study of CC to refer pejoratively to environmentalists who are more passionate than they are "scientifically grounded."

Many students complained about how rigidly and narrowly the programs defined good and bad practice.

> [T]hey see [science] as a religion. I mean, these people are devoted to it: "This is the way that you do things," and if you do it another way, it's "Get out of here." [White male science nonswitcher]

> Some of us are saying, "Hey, we'd really like to broaden our scope." But with seventeen hours of required credits per semester, there's not much room for going anywhere else. You have to stay exactly on line in the program. [White male science nonswitcher]

> It's really important to learn how to think critically in any field that you're in— to be able to read something, and say, "Well, do I believe that?" So you can go out into the world and make decisions. I've had some really good classics classes that helped me with that. [White female science nonswitcher]

> It seems like you would want to encourage a person to be well-rounded— someone that's an engineer, but who can play the piano or speak French. And

it doesn't seem like that's cultivated or encouraged in the least. [Black female engineering nonswitcher]

Given these students' concerns for more relevance, greater interest, and increased breadth, it seems reasonable to assume that some students find a place and means of expressing their discontent with the hard sciences in EB. Like Willis' lads when frustrated by the school, students disillusioned with the hard sciences probably look elsewhere for discourses and practices in which they can more fully participate and excel. Although the EB program does not fully address the students' concerns, and contains its own set of limitations (as did the working-class culture appropriated by the lads), it is a setting that would seem to provide an alternative for students who object to the practices and identities of the hard sciences produced in the university.

Because of my limited data on EB, I could not directly investigate student responses to EB or the scientist identities produced in the university. Because Hewitt and Seymour did not identify students who switched from one science discipline to another (e.g., from biology to EB) and did not follow individual students, I could not tell what students actually did with their critiques of hard science. Nor could I tell whether the students came to revise their understandings of the softer sciences and the "flowery bone-heads" who occupied them and the humanities.

In CC, I was able to see some of these things more clearly. I turn now to the scientist identities produced there.

THE CULTURAL PRODUCTION OF SCIENTIST IN CC

Most ethnographic studies of scientists in the workplace have been done in laboratories (see, for example, Latour and Woolgar 1979, Traweek 1988). These studies have revealed some of the social and cultural processes through which hard science and scientists are produced. CC also produces scientists, but they look different ftom those produced in laboratories or EB.

The Structural Production of "Scientist" in CC

Through the organization of its work activities, CC encourages its staff to engage in "serious" conservation science. The meaning of "good conservation science" within CC has three components: The work must be "science-driven"; it must be applied to important conservation issues; and it must make good business sense. A management plan for one year of one of CC's twenty-one conservation sites (statewide) suggests the breadth of CC's work:

> Map the distribution of the two highly-ranked plant associations; identify and map other plant communities; initiate inventory of vascular plants; initiate inventories of butterflies and moths, reptiles, and amphibians; inventory. . . for spotted owls; locate and map raptor nests; initiate breeding bird atlas program; continue mammal inventory. . . . [Determine] how much public visitation can

be conducted without affecting wildlife. [Determine] how much grazing (if any) should be allowed. [Determine whether] controlled burns [are] a good idea. (Canyon Management Plan, pp. 9–10)

An even more extensive and ambitious management plan identifies the work necessary to conserve riparian forest, shrubland, and wetland communities in areas encompassing a third of the state. This plan, prepared by CC staffers with the assistance of a few outside experts (such as a water attorney), includes scientific analyses, protection recommendations, and specific CC tasks regarding river hydrology; geomorphology; forest regeneration; wetland restoration; water quality; endangered species protection; migratory bird corridors; threats from dams, reservoirs, agriculture, mining, tourism, highways, and residences; nonnative species introductions, and changing plant, animal, and water dynamics (River Strategic Plan, pp. 3–24).

A fundamental principle of all CC's conservation work is that it be "science-driven": "[CC's] work, and most land protected by [it], meet certain strict criteria established by our scientists" (Strategic Plan, 2/1/93, p. 2). But, business considerations are never far from view:

[CC's] conservation science must also be used in ways that make good business sense. Our efforts are based on pragmatic, scientific methods. We work to achieve tangible conservation results. We seek solutions that are ecologically and economically compatible. (Strategic Plan, p. 3)

And our success comes from the fact that we talk business, not confrontation. We work in cooperation with farmers, corporations, government and private land owners. And we do not single out an "enemy" and launch an orchestrated attack. (CC promotional literature)

Because CC is a nonprofit, the organization must raise all of its own operating expenses, as well as a considerable portion of the money to purchase land for protection. CC also negotiates land deals directly with private property owners. These are the primary responsibilities of staff members in the business areas.

Although work responsibilities are clearly divided between the two areas, everyone is involved in some way in both. The organizational context of CC work creates a kind of "tightness," that is, wherein a large portion of the work to be done is required of everyone, and which is similar to the tightness of the curricular programs discussed above. For a small staff to accomplish the myriad and pressing demands of CC work, everyone puts in long hours and considerable evening or weekend work. Further, CC's three-part construal of "good conservation science" exerts pressure on all staff members to develop expertise beyond the field in which they received their academic training. The following excerpt suggests the kind and range of issues of which CC scientists must have command. The speaker is a CC oldtimer. She is talking about her efforts to close a deal on a property containing a threatened wetland area.

It's a very high-quality ephemeral wetlands site, probably the best in the Valley. In general, in the Valley the wetlands have been drastically altered. What were once shallow wetlands have been drained for agricultural uses, and there's been a lot of deep water added (by Fish & Wildlife) to make duck habitat. This has disturbed the shallow playa lakes that serve as habitat for many shorebirds, such as sandhill cranes.

We knew from the beginning that the Bureau of Land Reclamation's pumping project was right next door. And, there are a lot of water issues in the Valley—arguments between farmers and developers—that have been ongoing for a long time. In a sense "water" is THE issue in the Valley. And especially around the ephemeral wetlands which hardly exist at all there any more.

Then the serious water questions came up. There were questions about whether the deep and shallow aquifers were connected, what the effects of the Bureau's project would be; these were complicated hydrologic questions. We had hired a hydrologist to do a literature study—examine the existing data— and interviews with various people and agencies in the Valley. Her report was due in January. I had talked to the landowners in December; I wanted to be honest. I said here are our concerns and we're getting a hydrologist to do a study. Let me get back to you in January when the report is done.

They said fine, but it wasn't quite that simple. They didn't have other buyers, so that was not a problem. But there was the threat that I was gonna make them mad, that I would lose their confidence.

Then, the report was inconclusive, and I think we probably knew that it would be before it was in. I was honest with them; I'm not the kind of person who can work by hiding things from landowners. The report wasn't going to tell us definitively whether we should buy the land. CC would have to estimate the risks. . . and then just make a decision. I couldn't keep them waiting forever. Finally we decided just to go with it. They had been so understanding; they expected us to buy.

This way of talking about science evokes a very different image than that of the dispassionate, laboratory scientist, free of political or social concerns. The excerpt reveals an attempt to accommodate scientific rigor, environmental applications, public interests, and business practice that is daily enacted at CC. The organization of work in CC produces a way of talking and thinking that deeply entangles political, economic, and personal concerns with science. The highest status identities in CC belong to those who know how to apply up-to-date science in ways that contribute to the business side of CC's work. This entails, fundamentally, the ability to "speak" effectively to the public about CC's priorities. Whether in oral or written form, "good scientists" at CC must be able to present the organization's goals and needs to an array of potential supporters, including individual donors, foundation representatives, conservationists in other agencies, environmental groups, public officials, schoolchildren, and unsympathetic landowners.

CC's orientation to science is in some ways like that of EB. CC's applied practices oppose those of laboratory science, but CC does not challenge the value or importance of "real science." Also like EB, CC is committed to using science to address contemporary and complex environmental problems. For these reasons, CC seems to be a workplace extension of the counter-hard-science tendencies of the EB program. It seems to create a space that graduates of programs like EB's would find comfortable.

In fact, in one way at least, CC employees expect that students from programs such as EB will make a smooth transition from school to work at CC. CC expects its newcomers to already possess credentials in science acquired at school. In its job announcements, CC makes clear that a bachelor's or master's degree in a field of science is expected. In interviews with prospective employees, CC oldtimers tell newcomers that they will be expected to build upon their academic science as they develop proficiency in CC.

On the other hand, CC oldtimers also make clear to newcomers that even "good" school programs such as EB do not fully prepare students for CC work. Three of the four science program directors independently described the lack of preparedness to me and other newcomers. One said, "We use science, we apply it. [But] we have to train people in what's really needed [here]. For example, natural history is no longer taught at the university so we need to train the experts [we need]." This CC scientist was concerned that recent graduates did not possess the knowledge of regional natural and cultural history necessary to make decisions that could be accepted and supported by environmentalists, and which affected local residents. Another CC scientist said, "[Recent graduates] come to us knowing statistical procedures for ecological modeling; they have to be willing to learn how to join what they already know about science and statistics with the kinds of things we deal with." What CC deals with are such things as: landowners reluctant to allow biologists in search of threatened species or habitats onto their property; oil companies who question CC's motives; ranchers who object to removing land from production; community pressure on elderly farmers not to sell or bequeath land to CC; and inconsistent scientific findings. Although EB may try to produce conservation scientists who are prepared to handle these kinds of "real-world" issues, CC oldtimers do not think that schooling prepares students for this kind of work.

The CC newcomers who were making the transition ftom school to work had a different view of what they were unprepared for. For them, it was CC's savvy business practices that complicated the transition.

Newcomer Responses

Certainly, adding savvy business practices to science is another way in which CC opposes the model of the hard sciences, but doing so poses a serious challenge to the image of the model scientist produced in programs such as EB. CC's positions and activities that make good business sense function to constrain the application of biological principles. Especially to recent college graduates who join CC, its business concerns seem to challenge EB's core conviction: that environmental scientists must conscientiously and consistently apply state-of-the art science to environmental matters if serious environmental problems are to be averted or lessened. All five of the newcomers that I followed during my study were troubled by the way in which CC's business considerations sometimes interfered with conservation science.

Newcomers decide to work at CC in part because it is a setting with a reputation for doing serious and publicly responsive conservation work, yet they regularly oppose CC actions that they perceive as too business-oriented. The following two fieldnote excerpts reveal their opposition. In the first, Marty expresses her discomfort about finding a place for her environmental commitments at CC:

> CC's . . . not an advocacy organization and that affects how I talk about things now that I'm a staff member. I'm not quite comfortable with that yet. Take for example the [proposed] airport [near Creek Reserve]. Bill talks about this a lot. We [CC] have a concern because the airport might pollute the ground water, but otherwise we don't care [that there are a lot of other environmental problems associated with the airport]. And then there's peat: I wouldn't buy [local] peat because it's such a rare resource [peat was mined at Creek Reserve before the land was protected], but that's not the CC position. Some people will give money to CC for Creek Reserve so they can mine peat somewhere else [in the state]. That's a problem for me, but not for the organization . . . . I'm trying to come to terms with this: my personal stance versus my stance as a CC employee.

In the second excerpt, Bill, an oldtimer, and Ted, a newcomer, are discussing which of two pieces of land is the better choice to serve as the center piece of CC's next major protection effort.

> Bill threw out the question, "In our new budget, we've designated $1.4 million as the target for our next capital campaign, but we haven't got a site yet; what should it be?" Ted said he liked Border site. He named the rare species there and said the habitat was in good shape, and the land was beautiful. Bill said there were a lot of problems with Border: It is completely surrounded by private land; it's a long ways from a population center; it's a three-day trip to get down there, do something, and come back; it would be hard to manage. Bill said the fund-raising director would have a fit because Border was so far away, and it would be so costly to go down there; . . . they would have to spend the night, provide food; and so few people [members of the public] were close enough to visit. Ted persisted, saying he really thought Border was important to protect, that its biodiversity ranking [a scientific calculation based on number of rare species and quality of their habitat] was very high.

Both Marty and Ted seemed committed to ways of thinking about how they should apply scientific knowledge. Based on my knowledge of the EB program, it seems likely that they had practiced these orientations in the college programs they recently left. Both expressed frustration that CC did not share or was unable to accommodate their positions, which they considered to be more environmentally sound than CC's. Both Marty and Ted, as well as the other newcomers, attributed CC's position to its need to engage in good business practices.

Interestingly, although both Marty and Ted enjoyed their work at CC and wanted very much to stay with the organization, they did not give up their efforts to bring CC's positions more in line with their own. In Ted's case, he continued for over a year to push Border. Marty has continued to be outspoken about what she believes are weaknesses in CC's environmental positions. Her persistence has produced new discussions within CC about its political stands. Although the obvious effects of their challenges are small or nonexistent, the organization has not squelched the challenges which Marty and Ted seem to bring from their previous experiences, probably in school.

DISCUSSION AND CONCLUSION

This look at both structural and individual cultural productions in context adds to the emerging body of anthropological literature that demonstrates how structures are locally disorganized into diverse spaces for the expression and negotiation of identity, and how individuals actively occupy and sometimes change these spaces. The identities of scientist actually constructed in EB and CC are produced in specific institutional contexts, and they are contested and negotiated by individuals there. Yet, these identities are not unrelated to each other; they are formed within and against each other and those of related sites.

EB's applied scientist identity is produced *within* and *against* the image of the laboratory scientist that is hegemonic in the university and in U.S. society. The EB identity is constituted *within* hegemonic science in the sense that "serious science" is expected. Yet the EB identity is *against* hegemonic science in that "real-world" applications, rather than controlled and abstract problem-solving, are considered the context for scientific work. Clearly, this institutional challenge to the hegemony of laboratory science is minor: the power, politics, and privileges of laboratory science are not directly confronted by or in the program. Nonetheless, EB offers an alternative setting and discourse for students who have experienced "minor liberations" (Willis 1981) from hegemonic science in the university. In college or earlier, many students drop out of hard-science courses and degree programs, and apparently they develop some fairly radical critiques of it. EB seems to be a space for the articulation and development of at least parts of their critique.

The scientist identities produced in CC also differ in important ways from those produced in universities and research laboratories. CC scientist identities also are produced *within* and *against* science and schooling. CC expects its scientists to come to the organization already possessing knowledge and credentials in science acquired in school (usually a bachelor's or master's degree). CC further expects that newcomers will build upon their academic science as they develop proficiency within CC. It is important to CC's reputation that its scientists are academically credible. As in EB, CC expects its scientists to apply scientific principles to important, current environmental problems, and as such to have already rejected the laboratory science model of scientific work. However, unlike in EB, state-of-the-art applications of scientific principles cannot necessarily be made. CC's business activities often require modifications to applications, and limitations on their widespread use. Good business practice also may lead CC to make environmentally consequential decisions without conclusive scientific information. Further, CC oldtimers make clear that not even "good" academic programs such as EB adequately prepare students for CC work. Even good programs do not teach the regional natural, economic, or cultural history considered necessary to CC's environmental decision-making. Nor do they teach how to situate environmental concerns in political or corporate arenas.

These different contexts offer structural alternatives for expressing the meaning of being a scientist. These stuctural alternatives are more locally specific, heterogeneous, and relational than the social reproduction literature often recognizes. Degree programs and workplaces are varied sites for the varied production of knowledge and identities. Institutional identities take form in relation to others both inside and outside the institution, thereby creating situations that contain both hegemonic and counter-hegemonic possibilities.

In the particular cases examined here, the counter-hegemonic science orientation that is produced within EB is itself countered within CC. The effect is not a return to hegemonic science; in fact, EB and CC share a counter-hegemonic orientation toward the hard sciences. The effect is to create a break in what might be powerful linkages between applied university and non-university-based science and scientists. Linkages between the university and non-profit corporations that might produce well-grounded environmental activists and powerful coalitions are partially dismantled as individuals struggle with the different demands of identity in the two sites. The meaning of being a good environmental biologist within EB rejects the acontextual orientation of the hard sciences but simplifies the political and business demands of CC's work. Conversely, the meaning of being a good CC scientist depends on fitting science with business, and thus it seems to compromise the identity of the environmental biologist. In these ways, within-group differences create possibilities that both enable and fracture counter-hegemonic coalitions.

Individuals respond to these structural alternatives, and as they do, they actively negotiate and sometimes contest the identities produced for them. Their responses also are both within and against schooling. Many students, for example, are turned off by the meaning of being a scientist that is produced in schooling in the hard sciences. Some apparently find the identity of EB, another school program but with a different meaning of "scientist," more appealing. Individuals, who obtain degrees in programs such as EB and take jobs such as with CC, face another identity challenge in the workplace. CC's pragmatic busi-ness-oriented approach comes as something of a shock to newcomers who are recent graduates from programs such as EB. Newcomers resent the need to mollify business interests, and they find that these efforts compromise the commitments they have earlier acquired, very likely in the process of rejecting the hard sciences and accepting programs such as EB. The opposition of CC newcomers is resilient and at least potentially consequential for the organization. Although newcomers want very much to fit in and continue to work at CC, the organization does not completely neutralize their critiques.

The processes by which EB and CC attract and shape into a collectivity indi-viduals who oppose certain forms of domination (here, in some measure, the hegemony of research science) may be informative for thinking about other forms of domination. Although EB and CC's counter-hegemony may be minor, these sites provide alternatives that beckon students and workers produced out of the hard sciences. These alternatives may be appropriated by students and workers discontented with the hegemony of the hard sciences. Some of the discontented have more radical critiques of the hard sciences than either EB or CC. To the extent that EB or CC can attract the discontented, they channel and in some ways neutralize the critique. The critique, however, is not entirely neutral-ized and, as such, it contains the seeds of organizational and individual change.

NOTE

I would like to express special thanks to Joe Harding for his careful reading of an earlier draft of this chapter and to the employees of "CC," my field site, who welcomed me into their lives and helped me with this work.

REFERENCES

American Association for the Advancement of Science. 1989. Science for All Americans: A Project 2061 Report on Literacy Goals in Science, Mathematics and Technology. Washington, DC: The American Association for the Advancement of Science.

Downey, Gary, Shannon Hegg and Juan Lucena. 1993. Weeded Out: Critical Reflection in Engineering Education. Paper presented at the meeting of the American Anthropological Association. Washington, DC.

Eisenhart, Margaret. 1994. Women Scientists and the Norm of Gender Neutrality at Work. Journal of Women and Minorities in Science and Engineering 1(3):193–207.

———. 1995. The Fax, the Jazz Player, and the Self Story Teller: How *Do* People Organize Culture? Anthropology and Education Quarterly 26(1):3–26.

Hewitt, Nancy and Elaine Seymour. 1991. Factors Contributing to High Attrition Rates Among Science, Mathematics, and Engineering Undergraduate Majors. Report to the Alfred P. Sloan Foundation. Boulder, CO: University of Colorado, Bureau of Sociological Research.

Holland, Dorothy and Debra Skinner. 1995. Contested Ritual; Contested Femininities: (Re)forming Self and Society in a Nepali Women's Festival. American Ethnologist 22(2):279–305.

Latour, Bruno and Steve Woolgar. 1979. Laboratory Life: The Social Construction of Scientific Facts. Beverly Hills, CA: Sage.

Nespor, Jan. 1990. Curriculum and Conversions of Capital in the Acquisition of Disciplinary Knowledge. Journal of Curriculum Studies 22(3):217–232.

Seymour, Elaine and Nancy Hewitt. 1994. Talking about Leaving: Factors Contributing to High Attrition Rates Among Science, Mathematics, and Engineering Undergraduate Majors. Final Report to the Alfted P. Sloan Foundation. Boulder, CO: University of Colorado, Bureau of Sociological Research.

Traweek, Sharon. 1988. Beamtimes and Lifetimes: The World of High Energy Physics. Cambridge, MA: Harvard University Press.

Willis, Paul. 1977. Learning to Labor: How Working-Class Kids Get Working Class Jobs. New York: Columbia University Press.

―――. 1981. Cultural Production is Different from Cultural Reproduction is Different from Social Reproduction is Different from Reproduction. Interchange 12(2–3): 48–67.

8

THOMAS A. SHAW

Taiwanese Schools against Themselves: School Culture Versus the Subjectivity of Youth

> You dare not injure your body, limbs, hair or skin, which you receive from your father and mother.
>
> *Xiao Jing*, or
> *The Classic of Filial Piety*

INTRODUCTION

In China's imperial past, the value of an academic degree was reflected in the prestige and status which members of a degree-holder's family and village shared as a result. For the person who acquired the degree, his self-esteem (degree-holders were exclusively male) came from being responsible for the pride of so many others, especially those who belonged to the primary groups that made up his "natural" social world. The degree-holder's sense of self had little to do with evidence of his own individual talent or excellence, but it had much to do with his ability to attract attention and praise to kin and community.

Although an individual might be recognized as having vast inner resources or "talents," these were only as valuable as the community that nurtured them, or was nurtured by them. Chinese culture has always sustained a creative tension between individual interest and collective interest (Pye 1991; Saari 1990).[1] Moreover, how much personal initiative or conformity was expected of an individual depended in part on that person's gender and social position. Women for most of their lives were expected to play supporting roles in a male drama of lineage glorification and patriline development. Of course, they were not in practice always supportive of male authority and male institutions, and sometimes sought to influence decisions by generating a critical mass of opinion through "uterine" networks of village women (Wolf 1968).

Social class also influenced who felt they possessed a certain "entitlement" to freedom of expression. As Metzger (1977, 1981) has argued, the educated elite of China were accustomed, and in fact felt it was their duty, to exercise a degree of autonomy in their thinking and moralizing. Ko (1994) describes elite intellec-

187

tual women of the seventeenth century who, in exploring inner feelings and desires through their poetry, legitimately escaped or transcended their traditional filial obligations. In any event, however much an intellectual in China might have felt antipathy toward social pressures to conform, he or she usually cast their moral commitments in terms of the well-being of others, and utilized the privilege of personal autonomy to reflect on new ways to serve or improve society (de Bary 1970).

Thus, although intellectual initiative and personal autonomy have always existed in China, rarely were they in conflict with social and moral goals and values, particularly those of the family and the state. Individual initiative and autonomy were seen as legitimate means to the fulfillment of socially sanctioned goals rather than as ends in themselves, at least until the most recent period, as described below for urban Taiwanese youth. My argument here is that Taiwanese middle school culture, by failing to support and cater to students' increasing desires for personal and intellectual autonomy—desires that are as derivative of traditional intellectual culture as they are modern cosmopolitan influences— forces young people to develop a form of psychocultural individualism that is radically subjective and solipsistic, and that therefore undermines the creative tension between personal initiative and societal interests in a way that traditional expressions of individualism did not. The school's authoritarian culture, I argue, demands subordinaton of individual subjectivity and desire to the "needs" of the school and society, and consequently produces a not so hidden transcript of resistance that celebrates personal sensation and pleasure. This paper aims to describe how sensation and pleasure then become alternative sources of self for many young people. That is, they become criteria for knowing and judging what actions and goals are worthwhile and "good."[2]

Students in middle schools in Taiwan are under much pressure to perceive their own desires and self-interests as impediments to the greater good of their classroom, school, family, and nation. The response of some (although not all) students is to pursue interests in drugs, music, and "fun," that confirm their own constructions of themselves as persons who are, first and foremost, authors and arbiters of their own experience. Self-realization seems to have become, for a small but growing proportion of young people, a radically subjective process, rather than one primarily mediated by social values or the pursuit and realization of collective goals.

Taiwanese middle school culture, I argue, is instrumental in producing a gap between perceptions of one's personal goals and understandings of one's social commitments. This gap increasingly resembles the vast chasm between individuals' needs for self-direction and communities' needs for commitment and social responsibility in the United States. Popular films, for example, about adolescence and schooling in the United States depict teenage heroes and heroines as feeling "superior to those who are caught up in the everyday world—including the world of the school—that is fashioned so as to warrant the rejection, mockery, or mere indifference it elicits" from students (Farber and Holm 1994:36). The research described here suggests that the cost of grossly suppressing youth's moral and intellectual autonomy in Taiwanese schools may also be *their* mockery and indifference toward public institutions, which they may learn to retreat from rather than engage, as they pursue a radical subjectivity that is devoid of connection or concern with the larger community or society.

In the first part of this paper I briefly chart changes in China's political culture during the twentieth century in the wake of widening differences in rural and urban lifestyles. I will argue that as an agrarian and deeply Confucian moral order slowly opened to alternative, nontraditional moral careers and pathways of mobility, traditional conceptions of "good" were nevertheless preserved. My purpose is to point to social changes that have gradually, over the last one hundred or more years, established a broad cultural foundation for individual intellectual and moral autonomy without significantly altering, at least until the last decade or so, Chinese cultural conceptions of goals worth pursuing. I also wish to show that an emphasis on individual autonomy and creativity has not suddenly sprung out of the vapors of "modernity," but has been nurtured and groomed by an array of social and cultural changes in China throughout the twentieth century. I then draw on data I collected in the course of my own ethnographic field research in 1984–86 among various youth groups in Taipei to illustrate the (arguably) unprecedented emergence of radically individualistic epistemologies as they are enacted in a popular youth culture in the urban setting.

THE FAMILY REVOLUTION

None dispute that the greatest impetus for social and cultural change in China in the late nineteenth century was the threat (and reality) of military aggression and exploitation by Western nations, as well as Japan. Influenced by this threat, combined with a complex array of forces that can be glossed as "dynastic decline," Chinese society spawned a "family revolution" as the sons, but also a handful of daughters of elite families found new sources of inspiration and moral authority beyond the social boundaries of their family and local village.[3]

In 1905 a "modern" curriculum replaced the traditional curriculum, which had been driven by the centuries-old national civil service examination system. Students with secondary degrees and higher soon found that they had little use for their progressive knowledge in the conservative countryside, and that their knowledge was just as little appreciated by village residents. Consequently, they began to set themselves apart from their rural relatives, whose traditional lifestyles had become sources of embarrassment, rather than, as in the past, bases for collective pride. As socially and symbolically the gap between rural and urban widened, the sons and daughters of rural families who'd lived for some time in urban centers manifested a clear reversal of traditional sentiment: rather than being motivated to return to their villages to soak in the limelight of community esteem, they now recognized the potential for disgracing both their families and themselves because the urban culture that they'd acquired was so "foreign" to the traditional Chinese sense of moral aesthetics (Fei 1939).

Many used their new cosmopolitan lifestyles as symbolic capital to attain, if not sometimes even define, positions of power and influence in the new municipal governments or emergent political parties. In the urban centers, a middle class developed that was oriented to Western culture, and to the accumulation of capital, while graduates of "modern" schools in China's cities acquired a new cultural identity which legitimized a tendency to seek solutions to problems in terms that were not dictated by patriarchal family interests or canonical Confucian values.[4] A middle class thus organized itself to look after its own urban-centered interests, and a new conception of the life course developed which conformed less to traditional sociocentric goals than to individualistic interpretations of the needs of self and society.

At the same time, it is important to note that citydwellers were not a uniform lot. For the urban unskilled, regional and other "native place" ties remained in force, as well as paternalistic and often highly exploitative relations with employers. These demanded compliance and obedience in new contexts of loyalty and obligation. Within the urban working class, many young people never experienced a "new" autonomy, in spite of their fond dreams and anxious anticipation of the freedoms of city life (see Honig 1986).

Ultimately in Taiwan, as on the mainland, alternatives to agriculture (which grew substantially during the Japanese occupation in Taiwan, from 1895 to 1945) played a large part in undermining parental authority. Since parents knew they had to depend on children to support them in old age, "the existence of alternatives to farming was alone sufficient to force many to concede some measure of self-determination to their adult children" (Wolf and Huang 1980:48). According to Wolf and Huang, indications of a "family revolution" in Taiwan by 1920 include: (1) the observation that sons began at this time to reject the "little daughter-in-law" marriages arranged by their parents, and (2) the fact that illegitimacy rates began to drop significantly. This suggested that daughters acquired an unprecedented authority to resist parental pressure to work as prostitutes in order to support the family, a relatively common practice in Taiwan at the time. Nonagricultural opportunities far from the family home thus eroded the ability of parents to command respect, much less behavioral conformity, from their children.

In Taiwan, during the occupation by the Japanese for fifty years from 1895 to 1945, Japanese language skills and cultural styles were mandated sources of symbolic capital without which no Taiwanese could expect to go very far (Tsurumi 1977). Many older Taiwanese citizens today are quick to demonstrate their knowledge of Japanese culture and language. And, as Wolf and Huang (1980) have pointed out, a Japanese education gave young men a valued form of symbolic capital with which to leverage parental authority and distance themselves from the waning legitimacy of a traditional, agrarian way of life. As individuals left the countryside to enter the professions of teaching and medicine, which were among the few channels of mobility open to Taiwanese during this period, categories of "modern knowledge" emerged as important markers of status. Thus, both for Taiwan under the Japanese, and for mainland China, an important, if often understated context for the increasing independence of youth from their families was the emergence of a middle class in the early part of the twentieth century, which supported a distinctively urban, cosmopolitan lifestyle.

At the same time, the moral authority of "modern" teachers and other school personnel was derived from the presumed superiority of their Western scientific and political knowledge (in the case of Taiwan, it was not immediately Western, but rather Japanese scientific, industrial, and military knowhow). While traditionally a schoolteacher's authority was a form of extended parental authority, teachers' authority in the twentieth century derived more from extrafamilial sources, notably the prestige and apparent efficacy of scientific and military-industrial knowledge, on which the "modern" curriculum was built. Not only were these sources of moral authority situated outside the circle of local kin and community, they were transnational and not even Chinese. Clearly they played an important role in weakening family and other "local" forms of authority, which were in many ways in competition with "foreign" sources for the hearts and minds of young people. At the same time the individual, rather than the "household" or community, became the effective unit of "progressive" state-building and self construction in the cities.

School Culture and "Guidance"

In the Imperial period of China's history, academic training was famously strict in its demands for conformity to canonical ways of thinking. What the civil service exams in China actually measured is still debated, but heightened subjectivity and innovation were not what the examiners sought:

> At its best the examination system, with its curricula centering on classics, literature, history, and administrative problems, produced men of sound common sense and judgment, even statesmen. At its worst it produced parrot-like scholar-officials without imagination and originality and fostered ideological conformity. (Ho 1961:259)

The normative culture of Chinese education continues to produce a hierarchical, authoritarian, and highly ritualized atmosphere. However, urban cosmopolitan influences, including nuclear family patterns in Taipei (Marsh and Hsu 1994), tend to promote a movement toward interpersonal equality and individual "choice," and away from obligatory, or ritualistic relationships (and presentations of self). Moreover, "modern" schools in Taipei now operate in an urban context that is highly international, and multicultural: foreign (Japanese, American, Middle Eastern, etc.) cultural influences are pervasive in the realms of art, business, politics, and religion.

Following a decade of explosive economic growth driven by market capitalism, Taiwanese culture is also becoming increasingly commodified. This is evident in everything from popular religion (Gates 1987; Weller 1994), which over time has shifted towards serving individuals rather than communities, to local politics, which now depends to a high degree on the purchase of votes. At the same time, survey data in Taiwan show that many young people, rather than feeling obligated to comply with social norms (especially those that encourage active efforts to care for family members), now instead *"choose"* them (Yang 1986, 1991; Zhuang and Yang 1989).

This underscores the fact that independence of thought and individual initiative are not necessarily inconsistent or incompatible with feeling a part of a significant social universe. Yet, in fieldwork with Taiwanese young people in 1985, and in subsequent contacts with different groups of youth in 1992, I have been most struck by an apparently growing tendency for young people, when thinking about goals worth pursuing, to reflect on themselves, and especially on personal and highly subjective experience, as the basic condition of "knowing" what is worthwhile and good. Thus in the rest of this paper I describe how a near total absence of recognition and support for the independent thought of youth, as is reflected in the culture of the school, is liable to erode any sense students may have of the value of reflecting on social values and commitments, if and when they are given the opportunity.

None of my informants were self-conscious of their "epistemological individualism" as a distinct ideology for orienting self and determining goals worth pursuing. That is, none were heard articulating their point of view with pithy phrases like "if it feels good, do it." And yet something akin to this served as the prevailing ethos for a small but growing proportion of young people in Taipei in 1985. I interpret this epistemological shift toward a radical subjectivity in the youth culture as a reaction, in part, to a school culture that consistently *de*legitimized the subjective sensibilities and personal perspectives of students, and at the same time alienated them from the school's aims and ideologies.

The data from my own research are primarily ethnographic, supplemented by surveys and, seven years after the original fieldwork, focus group "interviews." The ethnography was conducted over a period of eighteen months, from 1984 to 1986, and included six months of participant-observation in a junior middle school in Taipei City. The focus group data were gathered in the summer of 1992. In 1985, the young people who participated in the practices and styles of the new youth subculture—that is, those who frequented discotheques and Western fast-food establishments, followed the latest fashion in clothes and music, and spent a great deal of time with their same-age peers—constituted a clear minority in the youth population. In a survey of more than one thousand students in their eighth and final year of the junior high school, only around 15 percent indicated that they "followed the fashions" and spent most of their after-school hours with friends. Nonetheless, the adherents of this lifestyle were so distinctive among their peers that they described themselves, and were described by others, as a "new wave" (*xin chao*). However, by 1992 in Taipei, stylish dress, orientation to Western culture, and peer involvement (to the exclusion of family involvement) were rapidly becoming the rule rather than the exception.

The school's attempts to enforce a culture of compliance and conformity thus became increasingly awkward as the greater cosmopolitan culture of Taipei itself mixed "modern" cultural knowledge with traditional understandings in an expanding "marketplace" of ideas. At the same time, the criteria to be used to select the "best" values out of the market basket remained undefined, thus leaving personal "experience" as the only possible way to make a selection.

In the rest of this paper, I describe in more detail how the culture of one junior middle school served to de-emphasize the "inner" worlds of students, submerging individual talents as well as students' personal needs. What the school rewarded was students' capacity to "imitate" (same as the word for "study" in Mandarin) and learn from their teachers, and conform to group standards of achievement. At the same time, these standards of learning and achievement were not uniformly applied. As described below, they applied only to young people considered "good students," and not to students in the "nonacademic" tracks of the school (almost half of the school). Ironically, students in the "nonacademic" tracks were more or less allowed to express their own (albeit problematic) desires and subjectivities. That is, they were treated more as individuals with distinctive personalities. But these students remained in the shadows of the school in every respect, while the "good students" modelled those aspects of school culture that officials canonized and made public and visible to the surrounding community.[5]

This bifurcation of school culture into a "front" and "backstage" had interesting repercussions. Teachers in the school were credited for the successes of students, but "poor" students, with all their problematic subjectivity were blamed for their own academic failure. Student achievement worked to promote the status and prestige of the class as a whole, rather than the individual as agent of "personal success." That is, the school invariably rewarded the teacher, not the individual student, as the agency behind students' academic achievements (Shaw 1991). The assumption seemed to be that each teacher would initially earn the respect and obedience of students in the class, and would then have the moral authority to get them to want to succeed on his or her behalf (Chance 1987; see also Shaw 1991). In fact, most Chinese students are more likely than their American counterparts to attribute school success to effort, which others may be instrumental in supporting, rather than to ability, which is more person-centered in its attribution of influences (Stevenson and Lee 1990; see also Anderson-Levitt, this volume).

Classroom protocol is perhaps the most obvious extension of the authoritarian, collectivistic culture of the school. For example, when teachers in the academically tracked classes asked questions during a lesson, they addressed their questions most of the time to the class as a whole, and expected an answer, in unison, from all students in the class:

English teacher: What is the tense needed here?

Students all together: PAST TENSE.

English teacher: And here?

Students all together: PRESENT PERFECT TENSE.

English teacher: Do you have enough work to do at home tonight?

Students all together: ENOUGH.

School "guidance" at the junior (as well as senior secondary) levels also consistently emphasized strict discipline, conformity to classroom and school rules, the subordination of individual to group goals, and academic effort on behalf of the "class teacher," or *dao shi,* who "heads" one class for all three years. In the classroom culture, but only in the classrooms of the academic track, success was understood to be a normal rather than an exceptional achievement. Moreover, "good students' were encouraged to succeed in order to preserve the "face" of their teachers, and the reputation of the school.

This system of school guidance, based on the goal of strengthening students' feelings of obligation and obedience to the collective (known as *xun dao,* or "training and guidance"), has come under increasing pressure in Taiwan over the last fifteen years as critics in the universities have argued for placing greater emphasis on individual talents, competencies and thought processes, rather than on obedience, deference, and dependence. Asserting what they, too, see as a need to value the subjective worlds of students, rather than simply their outward demonstrations of conformity, these critics sound a common refrain: "It is not what is *on* the head that matters, but what is *in* the head" (Luo 1982; China Evening Times 1994; China Times 1994).

The training and guidance office was nevertheless powerful and influential in the school I observed in 1985. Staff consistently emphasized the collective behavior of the class over the actions of individuals. For example, a "disciplinary group" *(jiu fa chu)* of students in each class was appointed by staff to evaluate and then report on class order each week. Awards were then given, based on the reports, to the most "orderly" class.

Staff from "training and guidance" opened the school day with a flag-raising ceremony in the morning, and closed with a flag-lowering ceremony in the afternoon. Military style, commands were barked from a megaphone atop a platform on the athletic field: "ATTENTION." "AT EASE." "ATTENTION." "SALUTE." Standing together in clusters defined by classroom assignment, students gathered twice each day on the playing field. One day at the close of a morning flag-raising ritual, students began to march back to their classrooms as members of the school's band beat their drums. Suddenly the voice of the guidance office director boomed out: "Class Number Twenty-One, return to your position! Because some of you talked rather than quietly following your classmates back to the school building, you all must now run one lap around the track." The director of the training and guidance office later explained to me that such tactics were necessary to sustain group order, and that this is the responsibility of his office, lest such activities as flag-raising turn out to be more like "an afternoon in the park." "The government," he said approvingly "feels that people have too many ideas about freedom and that most are superficial. Students' attention should be turned toward the nation, rather than to other individuals, or oneself."

At a flag-lowering ceremony at the end of another day, the director's lecture to the entire school (over three thousand students) invoked a common theme: "Each individual's behavior reflects on the group. In the school, the individual's behavior reflects on the class. In interschool competition, individual behavior reflects on the school."

Punishment, as well as moral exhortation (which at least presumes some reflection), was also used to enforce group conformity. Behavior problems in the school were almost invariably referred to the "training and guidance" office. For example, teachers one day caught some boys playing a coin-toss game and promptly sent them to the office, where staff asked them to write "essays of repentance," and later called their homes. Students who showed up a few minutes late for school in the morning greeted "training and guidance" staff at the entrance to the school, where they often received a light paddling. Students who showed up without their school textbooks sometimes received the same. The director, brandishing a pair of scissors in front of a group of girl students one morning, admonished them to keep their hair better trimmed. The office kept "morality" report cards (behavioral records) for students from year to year, and these records followed students to their next school. Thus, an exclusive emphasis on behavior rather than motivation revealed an abiding concern with conformity, and a neglect of the subjective powers of individuals.

The same office oversees the keeping of daily reports which were taken home by students and signed every evening by the "family head" (usually the father). The report should include important classroom or school events of the day, as well as important school rules, dates of coming exams, and daily personal items like whether or not breakfast was eaten at home, what time the student arrived at school, what time she arrived home, and what time she went to bed. Opportunities for students to engage in comments or personal reflection are conspicuous, at least to a Western observer, by their absence.

Recently school guidance has taken a somewhat more person-centered turn as students' "life problems," as they were euphemistically called (for reasons pointed out below), increasingly were dealt with on a case by case, individual basis. However, in 1985 only twenty-two students out of over three thousand in the eighth grade had files containing information about home life and family circumstances, to which staff could refer. These students were identified as having the most severe behavioral problems. At the same time, although this version of school guidance is called "counseling" (*fu dao*) by staff who have a separate office from "training and guidance," most observers are apt to point out that *fu dao* is distinguishable from its more traditional cousin, *xun dao*, in name only.[6]

Pressures on students to conform to schoolwide standards, and to measure their own achievements by their ability to fulfill "normal" expectations, are maintained by an infrastructure that holds students "accountable" through regular record keeping and reporting on behavior. These pressures are actively maintained by the *xun dao* office through staff contact with the parents of students. If the coordination of this pressure (so that it emanates from *both* home *and* school) is the job of "training and guidance," the job of explaining and dealing with student resistance to this pressure seems to be delegated to "counseling."

What passes for "life counseling" is really just more "clothes management," some researchers and university-based educators have pointed out, noting that the new "counselors" simply enforce traditional behavioral expectations that insure group conformity. On the more conservative side, some have argued that counseling would not succeed as a person-centered enterprise anyway since most students are not prepared to reflect on their lives or to arrive at decisions for themselves, and prefer to see counselors as persons who can magically take over their problems, and make them happy (Luo 1982).

In the school I observed, for example, a student was encouraged to resolve his repeated tardiness as follows: He was told, that although he "did not want to study," he "*did* want to graduate." He therefore had no choice but to make a concerted effort. Here a student's subjectivity is arguably appropriated by the school for its purposes. It is not clear how much this interpretation was the product of the student's subjectivity or the counselor's (of course the lines are never entirely clear). The possibility always exists, as long as the interpretation of a student's psychological condition is the responsibility of a staff person in the school, that students' subjective worlds will be constructed in such a way as to squeeze more conformity out of them.

Most of the time school counselors failed to live up to their mandate of giving individual students a "voice," and of understanding their needs in terms of the particularities of their personal life histories. Staff in the counseling office (*fu dao*) at times resorted to exactly the same tactics used by their *xun dao* associates. In one case I was familiar with, counseling staff ordered students to copy the political inscription from the statue of Sun Yat-sen on the school campus as a form of punishment. The counseling office in the school also organized classes that were designed to teach students about national laws and social customs. The function of these classes was to impress upon students the objective, "natural" character of rules and norms, and thereby underscore the importance of subordinating personal wants and predilections to these norms.

As one counseling staff member explained to me, "We are intermediary between students and teachers, and we try to help each side adjust to the other." One day staff intervened in a problem between a student and his teacher. Employing a thinly veiled technique to make the student feel shame for having misbehaved, the staff person asked the student: "How do you feel about the fact that the teacher loses face as a result of your abusive behavior?" The student's quick-witted response in an instant revealed the legitimacy he ascribed to his own subjectivity. At the same time it illuminated the friction that existed, latently or otherwise, between the moral culture of the "new wave" of youth, which adheres to a rule of respect between individuals of equal status, and the authoritarian culture of the school: "She makes us lose face, so why shouldn't we make her lose face."[7]

THE "B" TRACK

The culture of the nonacademically tracked classroom stands in marked distinction to that described above.[8] Importantly for the purposes of this article, students in these classes are allowed subjectivity, for students' inner worlds have everything to do with the explanation for why they fail to live up to "normal" good student standards. Failure was invariably attributed to personal motivational factors or other subjective characteristics of students: he/she does not *like* to study, is too *interested* in having fun, *wants* to make trouble, cannot *take his mind* off girls, and so forth.

Even though no one would admit that the standards applied in the "B" section classes were any different from standards being applied to "good students," in actuality the difference was obvious. Teachers sometimes did not even show up to teach "B" section students, or came late. Students wandered in and out of the classrooms as they pleased (it was expected, if not accepted, that they would indeed be "pleased" to be able to do so). When teachers showed up to teach a lesson, they often lectured above the din of distracted conversation in the room (some of it directed to me, unfortunately, when I was observing in the classroom). A teacher might engage in a brief discussion with a student about his "problem" paying attention, or her preoccupation with being popular, and this, ironically, legitimized the student's inner world in a backhanded way which was purposely avoided in "good students'" classrooms.

In one class, a teacher gave a lecture on the body's circulatory system. One student sat in the back of class conspicuously reading a newspaper. Talk all around me between students made it hard to hear what the teacher was saying. Some, however, sat silently, playing with various objects on their desks. At one point the teacher asked those who didn't want to listen to leave class. Nobody left. Some sat at their desks, apparently sleeping, while facing the front of the room. As the teacher began talking about the health effects of eating ice cream, a student called out: "A scoop of ice cream is like a girl's breast." His comment, which brought sputters of laughter from other students, was completely ignored by the teacher.

Academic failure and animated subjectivity are thematically linked in that both represent deviations from the "normal." For school authorities, therefore, they are assumed to be correlated. Thus the discourses of psychology and individual subjectivity, which many critics outside the school felt should be used more frequently in student "guidance," turn out to be relevant only for "problem" students whose difficulties cannot apparently be remedied by normative pressure and conformity. This too has been a focus for criticism by those who would like to see school counseling made relevant to the personal experiences of all students, including the academically successful ones (Cheng 1983). Ironically, students who are poor in academics are thus inadvertently dignified by school authorities who attribute personal idiosyncrasies, subjective faculties, and biographical reality to them, even though they evaluate these negatively.

POPULAR YOUTH CULTURE

Outside the schools, luxurious multistoried department stores, movie theaters, discos, soft-porn dance halls and tea houses, and the seemingly ubiquitous "recreation centers" (*yu le chang*) cater to the pleasures of the body, and to "experience" as an end in itself. The sensuousness of cola ads has become a symbol of multinational corporate power, and has entered the cosmopolitan "common" culture of Taipei. So has the excitement and sex appeal of Madonna music videos, and computer simulations of violence and "white knuckle" high-speed racing. The ever-sensuous MTV is available in Taipei as public entertainment in coffee shops, and numerous "video arcades" are scattered throughout the urban landscape.

In 1985, when I gathered most of the ethnographic data on which these conclusions are based, a small proportion—maybe 15 to 20 percent—of youth in their early teenage years (ages 12–18) seemed preoccupied exclusively with one thing: experience for its own sake. Young people expressed their values and presuppositions in the pattern of their activities. An important precondition was their ability to choose how to spend their time after school and on vacations, time that traditionally, and especially for girls, belonged to the family, and nowadays even more so to the school (vis-à-vis school-sponsored trips and other events).

Ethnographic fieldwork was conducted in a wide range of settings outside the school, most of which were sites for the self-chosen leisure pursuits of youth who ranged in age from 14 to 20, and who lived throughout the greater metropolitan area. These sites included coffee shops, temples, tea houses, billiard halls, discotheques, public parks, and young peoples' residences, where in some cases they lived with their families, and in other cases with friends.

Action, the primary aim of which was the accentuation of experience itself, through drugs, music, dance or motorcycle riding, occupied the nonschool hours of participants in what I have elsewhere described as a subculture of "fun" (Shaw 1994). Taking upward-mobility through education for granted, most of the participants in this subculture performed well enough in school (although this was more true for males than for females). Survey data indicated that their distribution across the three levels of tracking was very similar to that of the "good students" in the junior middle school. If anything, they were slightly more likely to be found in the classrooms that made up the academic track, where the pressures to conform were greatest and individual subjectivity most suppressed. Yet, as it was put to me many times, "School is second to fun."

At the same time, the young people who participated actively in this subculture were disproportionately from relatively affluent families whose parents worked in professional or semiprofessional jobs in modern bureacratic environments (i.e., banks, insurance companies, trading firms). For these children of the urban middle class, schooling, followed by employment in a white-collar job in the modern sector of the economy, could be taken for granted and therefore ignored. That failing to take school seriously might diminish its potential to leverage life chances didn't seem to enter students' minds. For example, a twelve-year-old, a sixth-grader from a nearby public elementary school in an affluent neighborhood, was skipping class the morning I met him at a local discotheque. "I skip two or three times a week to come here to the disco," he said to me. After spinning a few napkins on his finger with obvious nonchalance, he told me he was still planning to go to junior high school next year, and later high school. "Why do you skip class then?" I asked him. "Because school is no fun."

Self-conscious of themselves as a "status group" whose lifestyles and interests distinguished them from other youth, participants in this subculture referred to themselves, and were labelled by other youth, as *kah-a*. This is a native Taiwanese term with no Mandarin translation. Its origins are unclear, but its function was clearly to organize the interests of this group of young people, and to distinguish them from other youth (see Shaw 1988 for a fuller discussion). It may not be a coincidence that its closest Mandarin equivalent is a word that roughly translates as "playboy."

Drug use was a small, but symbolically significant part of this lifestyle—a way to act without obligating oneself to meet any socially legitimized standards of expression or interpersonal engagement. A seventeen-year-old I met who was unusual (for this group) because he had dropped out of school, professed, "I don't like to study. I don't like to fight either. I have a soft heart. I live with my girlfriend in an apartment, just the two of us. She's in Japan now, just for fun." "What do you like to do for fun?" I asked him. "Smoke glue and take sedatives. If you first take a sedative, and then smoke glue, you get so numb you can't feel a cigarette burning your skin. Some people do this just to experience the numbness. Some do it to swear brother/sisterhood. And some do it because they're depressed, if their boyfriend leaves them or whatever." He then proceeded to make it clear to me that his aim was the fun of it, the lack of sensation, the numbness. It seemed as though young people who smoked glue and took sedatives almost parodied the absurdity of making "experience" the exclusive object of action by seeing how much, or how little, they could experience pain. A fifteen-year-old girl told me that she and her (male) friends often smoke glue. "It gets dark and smoky in the room," she says, "so sometimes we go to the roof. But most of the time we just turn on the music, enjoy the dizziness, and go to sleep."

Participants in this youth subculture used drugs to transcend the social world and to replace it with experience, sensation, and pleasure. Of course, experience is not by definition an end in itself. If, for example, burning one's skin were used to demonstrate one's "toughness" to others, the "experience" could be conceptualized as part of an action sequence intended to meet intersubjective goals, and thereby strengthen the group. If that were the case, taking a cigarette burn without showing pain might win a person status in the subculture of his/her peers by demonstrating an important aspect of the group's collective identity. However, young people seemed indifferent toward any socially constituted goals or person attributes. The primary goals of this action (i.e., dizziness, numbness) lay outside the scope of social ratification and regulation to the extent that the criteria for fulfillment were entirely subjective. Some might describe such action as outside the moral domain altogether (Miller and Bersoff 1992), insofar as there were no intersubjective criteria of "good" by which such actions, or experiences, could possibly be judged by others. The emphasis instead was on the experience itself or, in the case of burning one's skin, the relative absence of experience.[9]

Although technically illegal, "underground" discotheques in Taiwan were actively patronized, and served as important venues in 1985 for meeting youth's increasing demand for activities that expanded the moment and accentuated the sensuous. Kids between the ages of approximately twelve and twenty danced to pulsating rhythms from the fashionable world of Western rock music, including the latest hits of Michael Jackson and Madonna. Strobe lights illuminated sweating faces and bodies amidst clouds of cigarette smoke. Although young people no doubt had multiple agendas, including possibly meeting members of the opposite sex, most just danced for hours as if to transcend objectives in the external world (and even to transcend themselves as *objects* of their own self-interest). Reminiscent of the "cult of experience" as described by writers like Lasch (1979), activities such as these may seem quite unremarkable to Americans or Europeans, but juxtaposed against the school's extremely "collectivistic" moral order (and Confucian moral tradition), which served goals of group harmony and group identity, they were radically unorthodox in their emphasis on individualistic, subjective criteria of value. A particularly poignant expression, perhaps, of youth's pleasure in highlighting subjective self-awareness was their somewhat quixotic practice of dancing alone at discotheques in front of wall-length mirrors, making themselves both subject and object of their own gaze.

Another way to highlight experience was to pursue the pleasure (experienced mainly by males) of riding motorcycles. Of course, motorcycles are efficient tools for getting around the traffic-congested city, and as such they are widely used by young and old.[10] However, it was *how* they used motorcycles and how they rode them, rather than simply *that* they rode, which again underscores their commitment to a radical subjectivity that made experiences of sensuality and pleasure the primary aim of the activity, and the main criteria of value. This also differentiated these young people from most other people, who treated motorcycles for their purely utilitarian value.

They rode fast (males only here), and loved to leave the city to be able to race down the more "open" roads in the countryside (although city streets could do in a pinch). The excitement that riding provided—the sense of abandonment to the moment and to the action, and the feeling of leaving behind the routines and tedious social pressures of everyday life, as described by young motorcycle riders in Japan through the sociologist Sato (1990)—was a purely subjective pleasure, and thus transcended the power of social forces to regulate and control them (Fiske 1989). The pleasurableness of the experience could no more be contested or controlled by others, even if it was often enhanced by the presence of others, than could the experience of sniffing glue or disco dancing.

Parental acceptance of their teenagers' activities depended, it seemed, on whether or not their kids demonstrated an orientation to legitimate developmental goals. Subcultural activities like breakdancing could be tolerated if they somehow could be construed as means to some legitimate developmental ends such as "fitness" or "dexterity." But enhancing subjective self-awareness as an end in itself was not a legitimate goal in most parents' minds, at least it wasn't in 1985 in Taiwan where, as in many societies, turning inward is encouraged only to promote greater attunement of self to external demands and conventions. "Absent is the notion that one should 'know oneself' on basic principle or that one can even know oneself outside of the moral and social constraints that sometimes make introspection necessary" (Lutz 1985:46). Few of the activities of the youth subculture in Taipei led to socially approved goals, and none were seen to foster the personal qualities that most socially approved goals require (responsibility or academic discipline, for example). Instead they were all oriented towards the pleasure of the individual, and celebrated experience for experience's sake.

CONCLUSION

School is one of the most important settings in which young people in Taiwan (and elsewhere) construct their identities and acquire the frameworks that define and identify "goods" worth pursuing in life (Taylor 1989). However, school is not the only environment in which youth actively construct themselves as persons in Taipei, and in many of their activities outside of school, individual autonomy and personal experience are both legitimate ends. By denying the legitimacy of their subjective lives, which were valued only to the extent that they could be molded to external, institutional goals, schools alienate young people and, ironically, help foster more radical expressions of individuality than they might otherwise. The result is a quest for "experience" that is indifferent, if not hostile to most of the collective goals that schools support.

For Taiwanese students, who are highly unlikely to invoke cultural traditions that romanticize the self or personal independence, a movement toward radical subjectivity must be understood as being "motivated" by other forces, one of which is no doubt frustration with the school environment. Although the authoritarian school culture cannot be viewed as solely responsible for this radical subjectivity, an environment more compatible with the popular consumer culture and commercial ethos of city life might enable emergent forms of psychocultural individualism to find less radical, and probably more socially useful channels of expression.

What is "radical" about radical subjectivity? Most radical is its epistemology, which is a way of knowing that makes direct experience the final arbiter of "good." Such experience must remain unknowable, unverifiable and unregulable by others. For many Taiwanese students, like the American students described in the Coleman report (Coleman 1961), academic goals are at risk of becoming secondary to the more immediate goals that provide heightened subjective experience in the here and now. And like the American teens Tallman, Marotz-Baden, and Pindas (1983) describe, Taiwanese teens may be shrinking the boundaries of their subjective worlds so that "personal satisfaction" is slowly separating out from considerations of even their own future security, status, or social well-being.

At the same time, as vocational and individual counseling become more popular, the belief will grow that an individual's "talents and abilities" can be objectively identified and measured by scientific psychology. In the future, claims about the "goodness" of one's chosen activities may come to rest more and more on the moral authority of an allegedly "scientific" system of knowledge which tends to essentialize and objectify personal dispositions and other features of intrapsychic reality.

Related to this is what Dore (1976) has referred to as a "diploma disease" in developing countries, which is driven in part by labor markets that assume a direct correlation between educational credentials and individual merit and skill. Taiwan is no exception to this, in spite of the continued importance of practices that emphasize social "connections" (*guanxi*) for access to life chances. Some young people (the less radically subjective ones, or "new wave" youth when they are not being radically subjective) speak of making choices based on their ability or talent, yet they don't really quite know how to identify what their abilities or talents are, nor do they receive any support for understanding how their own talents might articulate with the needs of the social body. All they know is how certain activities make them feel:[11]

> I . . . I feel that it's up to your interests. You must do something often. Sometimes when you are at home, if you have KTV, you could sing songs along with it. After you do it for some time, you realize that it's your interest.

> My interests are those relatively quiet kinds, such as playing a musical instrument and drawing pictures sometimes. . . . I like to engage in these leisure activities because they can be taken as a kind of work for me in the future . . . it's what I like to do.

The potential social costs of an increase in psychocultural individualism, in its more radical forms especially, have been pointed out by quite a few writers (Bellah et al. 1985; Berger, Berger, and Kellner 1973; Wood and Zurcher 1988; Giddens 1991). Most of these critiques presuppose a link between individualistic orientations and alienation from social values, but this link is not a given. Opportunities to determine goals, as Giddens puts it, that are "reflexively understood by the person in terms of his or her biography" (1991:53), potentially give people leeway to decide how to exploit existing hierarchies in ways that can benefit not only themselves, but also their families and communities.

In many locations worldwide, and especially in cosmopolitan (urban) culture, the "big traditions" of historical import are open to doubt and question (Giddens 1991; Taylor 1989). The possibility for doubt and question is, typically, not lost on students, whose increasingly personal criteria for defining goals worth pursuing lead them to question the usefulness of traditional values. This questioning is valuable, and could easily lead young people to reformulate tradition so that it is more consistent with the "historical moment" (Erikson 1961). However, if not supported by the main institutions responsible for youth's transition to adulthood, this questioning may lead to a total abandonment of tradition and its replacement by an expanded present, and by "experience" as an end in itself. The historical moment may itself be reduced to a personal point of view, or worse, an individual's pleasure, which can quickly become epistemological grounds for any action, as long as it feels good.

NOTES

1. In this light, recent arguments that oppose the "collectivistic East" to the "individualistic West" can be seen as overly reductionist (see Markus and Kitayama 1991). For a critique of these arguments, see Oxfeld (1992).

2. The production of personal, psychological "space" by individuals to escape exploitation and control by schools and other "corporate" institutions has been highlighted by youth culture researchers like Paul Willis (1977), and by others as well (see Eckert 1989 and Eckert and Wenger 1994).

3. These changes in family relations are described in vivid detail in Ba Jin's literary classic, *The Family*. For a more sociological description and analysis, see Levy (1968) and Lang (1946).

4. Urban residents in many cases were landlords, who squeezed higher and higher rents from peasants in order to pay for their newly acquired "modern needs," including a western-style education and cultivation of aesthetic tastes and talents (Chesneaux 1972).

5. I am thankful to Kathryn Anderson-Levitt for helping me realize this point.

6. Today in Taiwan, various government and quasi-government youth-serving programs, like the Save the Nation Corps (Qiu Guo Tuan) and Teacher Zhang (Zhang Laoshi), are established to serve the social-psychological needs of youth. Through their visibility in the media, they play an important role in reinforcing the legitimacy of

individual psychic (subjective) reality in public consciousness, and recognizing that it is worthy of attention and consideration in its own right.

7. In a fascinating book about giving and receiving criticism in Chinese culture, Martin Schoenhals argues that the criticism of superiors by inferiors has sometimes been justified "with errant rulers or parents," or with leaders who take such criticism as a sign of subjects' loyalty (1993:58–65). Based on an ethnography of a middle school in China, Schoenhals' book argues that on epistemological grounds, sometimes inferiors (students) were granted the moral authority to "know better" than their superiors (teachers). Yet these were exceptional cases, although they became less exceptional during China's Cultural Revolution, when almost all status inferiors were granted carte blanche the power to "know better" than just about every category of status "superior" (including parents) what was right for the country. (See Schoenhals, 1993).

8. Students who were tracked into the nonacademic classes attended commercial or technical high schools, or pursued no further education after graduation from junior high. Expectations of conformity for this group were greatly relaxed.

9. It is worth pointing out that not all narcotic substances rivet the user's attention primarily on physical sensation. Some drugs stimulate individuals mentally and emotionally to demonstrate their mastery of attributes that provide status within their social worlds. However, the drugs popular among members of the new youth culture in Taiwan tended to highlight the sensation and experience of the user, while simultaneously dulling any desire to act in a socially competent way.

10. The simple fact that many of these young people were even interested in getting around the city, rather than staying, as "good students" are expected to do, in the vicinity of their home, school, or neighborhood, is something else that differentiated them from most of their peers (see Shaw 1988).

11. These comments were made by young people who participated in a series of focus group interviews I conducted in Taipei in 1992.

REFERENCES

Bellah, Robert N., Richard Madsen, William M. Sullivan, Ann Swidler, and Steven Tipton. 1985. Habits of the Heart. New York: Harper & Row.

Berger, Peter, Brigitte Berger, and Hansfried Kellner. 1973. The Homeless Mind: Modernization and Consciousness. New York: Vintage Books.

Chance, Norman A. 1987. Chinese Education in a Village Setting. *In* Interpretive Ethnography of Education. G. Spindler and L. Spindler, eds. Pp. 221–246. Hillsdale, NJ: Lawrence Earlbaum Associates.

Cheng, Cheng Po. 1983. Fu dao mian lin xiu ji. Zhang Lao Shi (Teacher Zhang) 16(4): 248–249.

Chesneaux, Jean, ed. 1972. Popular Movements and Secret Societies in China, 1840–1950. Stanford: Stanford University Press.

Coleman, James S. 1961. The Adolescent Society. New York: Free Press.

de Bary, Wm. Theodore. 1970. Self and Society in Ming Thought. New York: Columbia University Press.

Dore, Ronald. 1976. The Diploma Disease. Berkeley: University of California Press.

Eckert, Penelope. 1989. Jocks and Burnouts: Social Categories and Identity in the High School. New York: Teachers College Press.

Eckert, Penelope and Etienne Wenger. 1994. School to Work Transition: An Apprenticeship in Institutional Identity. Palo Alto, CA.: Working Papers on Learning and Identity. No. 1. Institute for Research on Learning.

Erikson, Erik H. 1961. Youth: Fidelity and Diversity. *In* Youth: Change and Challenge. E. H. Erikson, ed. Pp. 1–23. New York: Basic Books.

Farber, Paul and Gunilla Holm. 1994. Adolescent Freedom and the Cinematic High School. *In* Schooling in the Light of Popular Culture. Paul Farber, Eugene F. Provenzo, and Gunilla Holm, eds. Pp. 21–39. Albany, NY: SUNY Press.

Fei, Hsiao-t'ung. 1939. Peasant Life in China: A Field Study of Country Life in the Yangtze Valley. London: Kegan Paul.

Fiske, John. 1989. Understanding Popular Culture. Boston: Unwin Hyman.

Gates, Hill. 1987. Money for the Gods. Modern China 13:259–277.

Giddens, Anthony. 1991. Modernity and Self-Identity: Self and Society in the Late Modern Age. Stanford: Stanford University Press.

Ho, Ping-ti. 1961. The Ladder of Success in Imperial China: Aspects of Social Mobility, 1368–1911. New York: Columbia University Press.

Honig, Emily. 1986. Sisters and Strangers. Women in the Shanhai Cotton Mills, 1919–1941. Stanford: Stanford University Press.

Ko, Dorothy. 1994. Teachers of the Inner Chambers: Women and Culture in Seventeenth-Century China. Stanford: Stanford University Press.

Lang, Olga. 1946. Chinese Family and Society. New Haven: Yale University Press.

Lasch, Christopher. 1979. The Culture of Narcissism. New York: Warner Books.

Levy, Marion. 1968. The Family Revolution in Modern China. New York: Atheneum Press.

Luo, Xu Guang. 1982. Jiang xin li fu dao yuan yu xiu tong xing (A Discussion of the Counseling Staff). Zhang Lao Shi (Teacher Zhang) 10(6): 420–423.

Lutz, Catherine. 1985. Ethnopsychology Compared to What? Explaining Behavior and Consciousness among the Ifaluk. *In* Person, Self, and Experience: Exploring Pacific Ethnopsychologies. Geoffrey M. White and John Kirkpatrick, eds. Pp. 35–79. Berkeley: University of California Press.

Marsh, Robert M. and Cheng-kuang Hsu. 1994. Modernization and Changes in Extended Kinship in Taipei, Taiwan: 1963–1991. *In* Marriage and the Family in Chinese Societies. Phylis Lan Lin, Ko-wang Mei and Huai-chen Peng, eds. Pp. 53–78. Indianapolis: University of Indianapolis Press.

Markus, Hazel Rose and Shinobu Kitayama. 1991. Culture and the Self: Implications for Cognition, Emotion, and Motivation. Psychological Review 98(2):222–253.

Metzger, Thomas A. 1981. Selfhood and Authority in Neo-Confucian Political Culture. *In* Normal and Abnormal Behavior in Chinese Culture. Arthur Kleinman and Tsung-yi Lin, eds. Dordrecht, Holland: Reidel Publishing Co.

———. 1977. Escape from Predicament: Neo-Confucianism and China's Evolving Political Culture. New York: Columbia University Press.

Miller, Joan G. and David M. Bersoff. 1992. Culture and Moral Judgment: How Are Conflicts Between Justice and Interpersonal Responsibilities Resolved? Journal of Personality and Social Psychology 62(4):541–554.

Oxfeld, Ellen. 1992. Individualism, Holism, and the Market Mentality: Notes on the Recollections of a Chinese Entrepreneur. Cultural Anthropology 7(3):297–300.

Pye, Lucian W. 1991. The State and the Individual: An Overview Interpretation. The China Quarterly 127:443–459.

Saari, Jon L. 1990. Legacies of Childhood. Cambridge, MA: Council on East Asian Studies, Harvard University.

Sato, Ikuya. 1990. Kamikaze Biker: Parody and Anomy in Affluent Japan. Chicago: University of Chicago Press.

Schoenhals, Martin. 1993. The Paradox of Power in a People's Republic of China Middle School. Armonk, NY: M. E. Sharpe.

Shaw, Thomas A. 1988. Emerging Persons: Youth Subculture, Social Identity, and Social Mobility in an Urban Chinese Setting. Ph.D. dissertation, Department of Anthropology, Columbia University.

———. 1991. Schooling for Success in a non-Western Culture: A Case from Taiwan. International Journal of Qualitative Studies in Education 4(2):109–120.

———. 1994. "We Like to Have Fun": Leisure and the Discovery of the Self in Taiwan's "New" Middle Class. Modern China 20(4):416–445.

Stevenson, Harold W. and Shin-ying Lee. 1990. Contexts of Achievement. Monographs of the Society for Research in Child Development 55 (1–2, Serial no. 221):1–119.

Tallman, Irving, Ramona Marotz-Baden, and Pablo Pindas. 1983. Adolescent Socialization in Cross-Cultural Perspective: Planning for Social Change. New York: Academic Press.

Taylor, Charles. 1989. Sources of the Self: The Making of Modern Identity. Cambridge, MA: Harvard University Press.

Tsurumi, Patricia E. 1977. Japanese Colonial Education in Taiwan, 1895–1945. Cambridge: Harvard University Press.

Weller, Robert P. 1994. Capitalism, Community, and the Rise of Amoral Cults in Taiwan. *In* Asian Visions of Authority: Religion and the Modern States of East and Southeast Asia. C. F. Keyes, L. Kendall, and H. Hardacre, eds. Pp. 141–164. Honolulu: University of Hawaii Press.

Willis, Paul E. 1977. Learning to Labour. Westmead, UK: Saxon House.

Wolf, Margery. 1968. The House of Lim. Englewood Cliffs, NJ: Prentice Hall.

Wolf, Arthur P. and Chieh-shan Huang. 1980. Marriage and Adoption in China, 1845–1945. Stanford: Stanford University Press.

Wood, Michael R. and Louis A. Zurcher, Jr. 1988. The Development of a Postmodern Self. New York: Greenwood Press.

Yang, Kuo-shu. 1991. The Moral Principle of Self-Control Emphasized in the New Filial Piety. *In* Chinese People's New Concepts of Filial Piety (in Chinese). De-hui Yu and Li-yun Lin, eds. Pp. 92–95. Taipei: Teacher Zhang Press.

———. 1986. Chinese Personality and Its Change. *In* The Psychology of the Chinese People. M. H. Bond, ed. Pp. 106–170. Hong Kong: Oxford University Press.

Zhong Guo Shi Bao (China Times). 1994. Lao shi, xun dao gong zuo bie guan: *pi mao xiao shi* (The Different Spheres of Control between Teachers and Guidance Staff: The "Superficial Knowledge" Incident). 30 March.

Zhong Guo Wan Bao (China's Evening News). 1994. Li yu fa. (Hair and the Law). 11 March.

Zhuang Yao-chia, and Yang Kuo-shu. 1989. Traditional Filial Piety: The Course of Change. A Perspective from Social Psychology (In Chinese). *In* The Psychology and Behavior of the Chinese (In Chinese), a collection of papers from the First Disciplinary Conference of the Psychological Research Institute and Department of Psychology at National Taiwan University, sponsored by the Education Ministry of Taiwan. Pp. 182–222.

PART III

The Educated Person in State Discourse and Local Practice

9

Bradley A. Levinson

Social Difference and Schooled Identity
at a Mexican *Secundaria*

> Some of my friends in the neighbor-
> hood stopped talking to me because
> one day my mother shouted at me
> that I got together with good-for-
> nothings (*burros*), that I was hanging
> out with nothing but dropouts and
> that I was in another class (*categoría*),
> that I do study. That's when everyone
> stopped talking to me. . . . But I still
> speak with a few, they don't study
> either but I talk to them behind my
> mom's back because I like to get along
> with everybody.

Andrea, the author of this quote, was a daughter of itinerant artisans and petty
merchants. She tended her parents' market stall in the afternoons and on weekends, and often watched over her two younger siblings in their modest home.
Most mornings, she attended classes at Escuela Secundaria Federal (ESF), a
federal Mexican secondary school (*secundaria*) in the west-central Mexican city
of San Pablo.[1] Escuela Secundaria Federal presented Andrea with a panorama of
local and regional social life: students came from virtually all local classes and
groups, including those of nearby rural villages. Yet by her third and final year,
while most of her fellow students, regardless of their backgrounds, had more
actively cultivated the social distinctions which a secondary education encouraged, Andrea clearly hesitated. She was not willing to reject her relatively
unschooled neighborhood friends on the basis of her own "schooled" status.
Positioning herself against her mother and older sister, Andrea attempted to navigate the rocky waters of social and personal identity. Ultimately, her solidarity
with local agemates precluded Andrea's wholehearted adoption of what I call a

schooled identity. Andrea dropped out shortly before finishing her secondary studies. In 1993, she was living with relatives, taking sporadic evening classes, and considering joining her parents, who had recently emigrated illegally to Oregon, USA.

Students developed a schooled identity at ESF by appropriating discourses of equality which constructed the space of the school and the *grupo escolar* (school group, or cohort) as a microcosm of the nation. Drawing on Lomnitz-Adler (1992), Corrigan and Sayer (1985), and others, I will argue that "official" school discourses, which exhorted students to dissolve their differences in the common cause of *grupo* (e.g., national) solidarity, served to articulate regional idioms and sensibilities to the hegemonic "culture" of the Mexican state. In secondary education, this had the (perhaps unanticipated) effect of reorienting the axis of local class and ethnic distinctions around levels of education. While class and ethnic differences *within* the school might be ignored or downplayed, then, educational differences *beyond* the school became more salient. As I will show, students appropriated "official" school discourses on equality, and developed their own distinctive and strategic uses. Among these uses was the wielding of a discourse of essential sameness ("*todos somos iguales*," "we are all equal") to demarcate schooled from unschooled. Thus, while students learned to become "equal" as Mexicans within the common space of the school, they also learned that this equality could and should not be extended to many of those they encountered beyond the school.

While most students thus came to identify with the dominant definition of schooled identity at ESF, Andrea is one example of a student who, by her third and final year, was still struggling with it. Like the prospective teachers Luykx (this volume) describes, Andrea was negotiating a field of highly contradictory discourses. While her parents and sister pulled her in one direction, she was able to draw on other discourses in popular culture to criticize the hypocrisy which schooled identity at ESF represented for her. Andrea had internalized aspects of a schooled identity, yet she was unwilling to make that break with her "intimate" culture (Lomnitz-Adler 1992) which the adoption of a schooled identity appeared to require. In my research, I found other students or former students in San Pablo who had more wholeheartedly rejected or embraced this schooled identity, thus coming to define themselves within or against what they perceived as the schooling enterprise.

In this chapter, then, I explore a process which has become one of the staples of the educational literature: Schooling, in addition to providing specific knowledges and skills, may also contribute to a new social identity (see, especially, Rival, Luykx, Skinner and Holland, and Luttrell, this volume). I define social identity as the self-understandings, acquired from social discourses and often symbolically charged through emotional attachment, which an individual has of him/herself (cf. Holland et al. in press). There is nothing particularly novel in my assertion that school knowledge builds new social identities. Yet here I propose to examine more closely the struggles which occur as students come to acquire or reject a schooled identity. More specifically, I will examine these struggles in the light of critical theories of popular culture, hegemony, and the state, and explore the degree to which the reconfiguration of social difference through schooling leads to new bases of solidarity and exclusion in popular culture.

SAN PABLO AND THE ESCUELA SECUNDARIA FEDERAL

Though most residents still call San Pablo a "town," it is now a significant regional market city in its own right. The city dates back to the colonial epoch as an important religious, commercial, and administrative center for an extensive peasant and artisanal region. Located in a region where one of Mexico's largest indigenous groups is still concentrated, San Pablo has always served a nodal function in regional culture and economy. In the area around San Pablo, the indigenous group, as well as their "mestizoized" peasant counterparts, continue to engage largely in farming, fishing, and crafts production. While this economic activity was once oriented to regional circuits of barter and trade, it has become increasingly geared toward a tourist market within a fully capitalist economy (García Canclini 1981, 1990; Novelo 1976; Dinerman 1978). Moreover, subsistence agriculture and petty commodity production have for some time been supplemented, in some cases supplanted, by both interstate and international wage labor migration.

San Pablo has always been a study in contrasts. Today, an increasingly small, landed elite traces its ancestry to the earliest colonial families, owns orchards and ranches nearby, and continues to live in the old, centrally located colonial houses. This elite shares power with an emergent upper class which has developed political connections and accumulated wealth through timely involvement in lucrative enterprises such as hotels, timber operations, or soft-drink distributorships. A small professional "middle class" (lawyers, doctors, architects, engineers) and "lower middle class" (schoolteachers, shopowners, federal and state bureaucrats, and skilled tradesmen) are in many cases interspersed geographically with the poorest classes in San Pablo, which consist of small-scale vendors, day laborers, housecleaners, construction workers, artisans, and the unemployed. The absence of large-scale capitalist operations, whether in agriculture or industry, appears to have prevented the rise of a well-defined working class.[2]

Students from among the wealthiest and poorest families alike clamored to enroll at ESF. The morning shift of ESF[3] included children from San Pablo's monied, professional, skilled, and unskilled working classes, as well as some 13 percent who lived in outlying towns and villages and travelled daily to attend school.[4] Most of those living in the outlying villages were peasants, artisans, and/or rural proletarians, and many considered themselves ethnically indigenous. In addition, the morning shift had a higher proportion of girls to boys than any of the other public secundarias in San Pablo.[5]

While numerous studies of primary education exist, few have studied the secundaria in Mexico.[6] The *secundaria*—or the level of schooling called "*educación básica media*" in Mexico—expanded exponentially in the 1960s and 1970s, incorporating new social groups which had been previously excluded. Yet there has always been a high desertion rate between the first and third years of secundaria,[7] and in recent years overall enrollment has been declining in some areas, including the one where I did the study. Secundaria is also the last point in the Mexican "basic education" cycle. After secundaria, students must choose between several very different options, including college preparatories, technical vocational schools, "business" courses, and secretarial or cosmetological schools.

Of all the students in the school, I focused especially on the third graders, in their last year of secundaria. By their third year, students were likely to have gained a high degree of social competence in, and a high level of implicit and explicit knowledge about, the rules and meanings of secondary schooling. They were already becoming "experts" at interpreting and managing the social differences presented to them in the secundaria. Moreover, students were facing the imminence of rather difficult and determining decisions. Because they had to soon decide whether to continue studying and, if so, at what type of school, the third year was pivotal for these students (cf. Mir 1979:107). I expected the politics of identity to have a strong impact on the formation of educational and occupational aspirations.[8]

Race, Class, and Intimate Cultures

Without question, racial or ethnic identities informed the practice of many students who attended Escuela Secundaria Federal. Notions of race and ethnicity in Mexico have been constructed through both dominant and popular cultural discourses which often equate Indianness with rural or agricultural life. Since the colonial period, urbanity in the dominant imagination has conversely signified "civilization," "reason," and "whiteness."[9] At ESF, in 1990, urban students tended to perceive certain bio-cultural features—language (accent), style of dress, skin color, and hair, to name just a few—along with other signs of rural life as indices of "Indianness." In other words, most students at ESF conflated the social difference of "race" with that of poor, rural lifeways.

Yet not all of San Pablo's surrounding peasant region maintains a strong indigenous identity. Indeed, most of the towns and villages closest to the city have undergone a process of steady "mestización" (Lomnitz-Adler 1992) in this century, in which political-economic forces have undermined indigenous practices of solidarity and identity. It is not uncommon for present-day residents of these communities to represent the first generation to have ceased using the indigenous language or indigenous forms of dress on an everyday basis, even within their communities.[10] Nevertheless, students who arrived at ESF from outlying communities had to contend with the dominant, city-based construction of them as rural dwellers, or as "Indians." This construction occurred largely independently of whether these students actually came from communities which still engaged in agriculture, or still retained a strong sense of Indian identity.

As I have noted, approximately 13 percent of the students in the morning shift at ESF came from the *"pueblitos"* surrounding San Pablo. Given that these rural communities were themselves socioeconomically stratified, some of the students from them were undoubtedly better off than even the poorer city residents. In other words, though the standard of living in rural communities was generally much lower than the city, some rural families had achieved a good deal of material success through the tourist trade, the acquisition of more land, or large remittances from migratory stints. They constituted a kind of emerging elite in these communities (see Reichert 1982; Wiest 1973), and they tended to send their children to ESF. Yet for the most part, students arriving from the rural communities were even materially poorer than some of the poorest city residents.

What about the perception of social class in San Pablo proper? Within the city, poorer residents described a group of *ricos* (rich), *pudientes* (wealthy), or *adinerados* (monied), while wealthy or "middle-class" residents lamented the plight of the *pobres* (poor) or *gente humilde* (humble people—an artist friend of mine, himself of rather modest means, called them the *jodidos*, or the "screwed"). Indeed, even ethnically indigenous peoples recently migrated to the city tended to be identified as "poor" rather than "Indian." Yet despite my own observations of increased economic polarization between 1985 and 1991, most San Pabloans did not highlight these trends. Indeed, students at ESF typically considered themselves "middle class" in the local terminology, despite the wide range of family occupations and income levels, and despite their placement in what Lomnitz-Adler (1992) would call rather different "intimate cultures."

Lomnitz-Adler (1992:28) conceives of "intimate culture" as a concept which replaces an abstract, insufficiently regionalized, notion of "class culture." Intimate cultures are the "real, regionally differentiated manifestations of class culture," the local configurations of people who share common social positions and practical ideologies. This concept allows us to appreciate the diversity and complexity of cultural sensibilities which exist within regions, while not losing sight of common class- and race-based identities shared across these same regions. Thus, while it makes sense to analyze the shared predicament, and the shared cultural forms of, say, "working-class San Pabloans," it makes equal sense to analytically distinguish the intimate cultures of recently proletarianized, village-resident Indians, from upwardly mobile, urban mestizos within the "San Pablo working class." Recognizing this "diversity within unity" then makes it possible to explore the symbols and discourses which allow for communication across the various intimate cultures of a region. Lomnitz-Adler calls these symbols and discourses which facilitate interaction between intimate cultures the "idiom" of a regional "culture of social relations" (29). I will argue below that the discourses comprising "schooled identity" form a major part of the local San Pablo "idiom."

Escuela Secundaria Federal in Regional and Historical Perspective

The area of west-central Mexico where San Pablo is located has a rich agrarian-based regional culture, and a long history of struggle over the land. It is a region with a deeply rooted popular Catholicism, and this religious practice often informs communities' relationship to the land. West-central Mexico has also, historically, posed a problem of control for the federal Mexican state. Regional and community traditions have often provided the resources with which to rebel against attempts at national imposition from above.

In postrevolutionary times (after 1920), the region posed a puzzle to the newly emerging secular state. The region, in other words, presented its "otherness"—Indian, agrarian, devoutly Catholic—as a challenge to incorporation. The regime responded with an aggressive agrarian reform and an all-out attack on what it called religious "fanaticism." Importantly, the new state also appropriated and resignified traditional "Indian" culture as a crucial part of national identity. The school, of course, was perhaps the most indispensable tool of state action in this zone. Indeed, in the years following the Revolution, the area constituted a kind of "laboratory" for educational developments.

Loyal followers of revolutionary President Lázaro Cárdenas, for instance, introduced rural primary schools into communities in an effort to displace the power of the church. Indeed, church buildings themselves often provided the first community classrooms. Federal teachers, moreover, fancied themselves taking over the "priestly" function of community organizing (cf. Rockwell, this volume). They attempted to "dispel the intensity of Catholicism" by co-opting traditional, often ethnic, cultural symbols, much as the church itself had previously done (Becker 1989:223). Part of this process involved the reinvention of the local Indian in school-based discourse. Traditional Indian dances and songs were alternated with propaganda for the Revolution, in an effort to associate the goals of the Revolution with the deepest aspects of local indigenous culture.

The struggles of the Cardenista period in this part of Mexico left an indelible impression both on the regional landscape and in the popular historical memory. In 1990, the local countryside was dotted with primary and secondary schools bearing the names of Cárdenas and his most illustrious apostles, while schoolchildren and townspeople alike faithfully commemorated the anniversary of Cárdenas' death. As if through a kind of ideological magic, the image of Cárdenas himself, and the state power he represented, had emerged triumphant from the endemic struggles between state and community in this region. Indeed, one of Cárdenas' enduring legacies was the creation of a cultural frame of reference, promoted through schools, which drew heavily on age-old themes of equality and solidarity to articulate a sense of inclusion across the variety of intimate cultures.

THE CONSTRUCTION OF SCHOOLED IDENTITY

Escuela Secundaria Federal was established in 1941, shortly after this intense period of cultural conflict in nearby rural zones. Unlike primary education, the introduction of secondary education at this time responded to the largely urban need for vocational and professional training. Educators presumed that primary schools would perform the necessary function of unifying the nation culturally and inculcating "modern" habits and desires (Vaughn 1982). Yet clearly, as time went by and the primary school graduation rate increased, the secundaria increasingly took on the cultural-nationalist functions of the primaria. And although ESF principally attended to the needs of San Pablo-based schoolchildren, a number of children graduating from nearby rural primary schools attended as well. This trend has continued to the present day. While the percentage of peasant and indigenous students at the two other, newer secundarias in town is greater, ESF still boasts the broadest and most even mix of social classes.

Students at ESF most often said they were in school in order to "become somebody in life" (*"ser alguien en la vida"*). Alongside the desire to "become somebody," of course, were the desires to be with friends, please parents, escape household chores, flirt with a classmate, and so on. Yet clearly, students identified further schooling with having a definite social worth—a worth increasingly unavailable or unattractive to them within the spheres of their home-based intimate cultures. In their minds, it was virtually impossible to "become somebody" without schooling. This meant at least a secondary diploma, and probably more.

Teachers, parents, and other relatives clearly played a prominent role in convincing students of the importance of secondary schooling in earning a better place in society. Teachers often threatened and cajoled students to stay in school. They suggested that students who dropped out would invariably fail in attaining important life goals. Alongside the "common-sense" notion that schooling led to economic advancement, however, there coexisted a discourse on prestige and status. Teachers forwarded a definition of "culture" as a body of knowledge which would permit students to both have a greater appreciation of the world around them, and to "defend" themselves socially. This notion of "defense" included a range of knowledges and abilities: math skills to avoid being cheated and be able to run an effcient household economy; speaking skills to make a timely point or convey a good impression to potential employers; science skills to understand and utilize technological innovations more effectively; and, especially in the case of young women, employable skills to survive possible future divorce or abandonment by a husband. According to teachers, then, school served both as a springboard for economic mobility and a means of obtaining *un mayor grado de cultura* ("A greater degree of culture").

In social spaces outside the school, students often heard the same messages about school and social success. Parents, older siblings, relatives, and adult friends alike haunted them with the prospect of educational and social failure. Typically, these messages made a sharp distinction between mental and manual labor. Among the lower social classes at ESF, schooling was seen primarily as the opportunity to break the family cycle of hard physical labor; among professional and merchant classes, schooling was seen as an important means of maintaining or advancing a status prerogative through the acquisition of more knowledge and *cultura*. In either case, there was an active construction of difference through schooling. Those students who finished school, at least through the *secundaria*, were said to possess the knowledge and skills for a productive, respected position in society. Others did not.

One day, I chatted with Franco's father at the modest tortilla shop he ran with his family. Franco, a languid third-year student with some problems in school, was working the press machine nearby. When I asked the father why he bothered to keep his son in school, he replied:

> Because one needs knowledge, he needs to be prepared in order to do well, so he'll be in a better [economic] situation than mine. And only through studying can one do this, you know? I've told him many times that you have to work hard with your head, right? It's better to work with your head than with your hands. I often tell my son that on those occasions when I'm really lazy, and I don't like to work, that's when I invent things, I cook things up all over the place in order not to exert myself too much. So it's better to use your head than your hands, right?

Throughout our interview, but at this moment, particularly, Franco's father was looking over at his son, as if to emphasize the point (he even winked at me to acknowledge this). On another occasion, later in the year, I listened as Franco's father berated his son for not having purchased a copy of his class photograph. He urged his son to get the photo and write down the names of all his classmates, especially the boys. As he explained to both of us, with such a photo Franco could more easily draw on his past social connections to get a job or a favor in the future. This concern revealed Franco's father's awareness that schooling imparts a social status and a set of social connections which count for as much as specific knowledges, skills, or credentials.

Indeed, by my final year of fieldwork—and after eight years of economic crisis—the traditional emphasis on the economic benefits of schooling was increasingly challenged by the reality of restricted labor markets. Adults, especially, were apt to point out that an entrepeneurial taco vendor in the town market could, with little education, make more money than an engineer or doctor. The latter, after all, had few job prospects, and even fewer possibilities to practice their true professions. Moreover, strategies of legal and illegal migration to the United States had already taken deep root in many local intimate cultures. Parents and schoolteachers alike might spend varying amounts of time as illegal migrant workers. For these reasons, the return on educational investment had long ceased to make "rational" economic sense. While schooling was still acknowledged to provide a kind of cultural capital, hence a hedge against social marginalization, it no longer promised a secure route to economic capital per se.

Many wondered if school was even still worth the effort and expense. For example, Fidel was a boy who travelled nearly fifteen zigzagging miles each way to attend classes at ESF. His father had died the year before, and now his uncle had assumed some parental responsibilities. When I visited Fidel at his village (whose residents, with few exceptions, considered themselves mestizo

"Mexicans"), he took me to meet his uncle, who lived down the street and made wooden masks for the tourist trade. The mask business was going well, apparently. Fidel was learning the techniques as his uncle's apprentice, and said he often felt like working at the shop rather than attending school. Significantly, his uncle did not actively encourage Fidel's pursuit of further studies. When I asked Fidel in his uncle's presence whether he would go on to the *preparatoria*,[11] he hesitated, and the uncle intervened, "He sees that those who finish up their degrees a lot of times don't earn much, and they can't find work in their own field." After chatting further, I realized that it was, in fact, Fidel's uncle, a man with little formal education, who encouraged him to adopt this view.

It was not coincidental that the most forthright questioning of the value of continued schooling came from Fidel's uncle, an artisan from a historically peasant village. For it was here, outside most of the metropolitan circuits through which schooled cultural capital flows, that schooling meant less if it wasn't translated into tangible economic gain. Interestingly, Fidel's uncle had achieved some renown for his skills as an artisan precisely through his ability to exploit timely contacts. The previous year, he had been flown to Chicago to give a weeklong seminar on mask carving at a major museum. This experience, however, still didn't lead him to valorize the cultural knowledge which advanced schooling could impart. If anything, his uncle's relative fame proved to Fidel that it was possible to "become somebody" without further schooling. On the other hand, Franco's father, himself a part-time livestock veterinarian and an urban dweller, perceived the apparent disjuncture between schooling and economic gain in broader terms. He was more likely to see the present economic crisis as a temporary setback, and as a challenge to draw on the less immediately "economic" benefits of schooled cultural capital.

SCHOOLED IDENTITY AND EXCLUSIONARY DISTINCTIONS
WITHIN STUDENT CULTURE

Elsewhere (1993a, 1993b), I describe in detail the importance of the *grupo escolar*—the socio-academically heterogeneous classes, or cohorts, which facilitated students' passage through the secondary curriculum—as a site for the production of schooled identity. Upon arriving at the school, students were distributed into *grupos escolares* which would remain together for all three years. Virtually every organized activity within the school revolved around the *grupo escolar*. However, the social importance of the *grupo escolar* did not rest solely in its organizational function. Teachers and students alike invested the *grupo escolar* with meanings rooted in discourses of equality, cooperation, and solidarity. The *grupo escolar* was often explicitly modelled upon the Mexican nation itself. Indeed, the idea of creating a kind of diverse microcosm of the nation within each *grupo escolar* actually provided one of the key rationales for the heterogeneity of school grouping. Teachers deliberately formed each *grupo escolar* out of an assortment of academic aptitudes and social backgrounds. They hoped to create common national identifications across these differences by subjecting students to the same educational messages, and by exhorting them to unified endeavor within the *grupo escolar*. Students within the *grupo escolar* appropriated these context-specific discourses on solidarity and equality to construct collaborative practices and a shared, inclusive schooled identity.

Thus, while adults and older siblings provided important messages, the cultural production of schooled identity still took place largely in and through the realm of student culture, that is, in the informal domains of student-organized activities, in and out of school. This is where students eventually came to accept, reject, or modify their understanding of messages imparted by teachers and relatives. Significantly, this sense of schooled identity did not only assert itself within the confines of the school. Nor did it make sole reference to knowledges or skills normally associated with schooling. Often, the politics of schooled identity extended to areas of social affinity, and even sexual attraction, outside the immediate purview of the school. For example, and as I show elsewhere (Levinson 1993b:253-62), regardless of their class position or ethnicity, students at ESF by and large aligned themselves with youth who frequented the "plaza grande" (the larger of two central plazas). The small plaza, by contrast, was said to be a space occupied by *uneducated* people. Relatedly, ESF students, boys and girls alike, typically eschewed school dropouts or uneducated youth as potential romantic partners.

Another important focus for the production of a schooled identity consisted of students' ongoing attempts to contrast themselves with students who had dropped out of school to work, "loaf around" (*entregarse al vicio*), or marry. Students typically missed few opportunities to denigrate dropouts or the unschooled. They clearly dispensed such moral judgment in an effort to valorize their own educated status, thereby buttressing the foundations of a schooled identity.

Especially boys at ESF commented negatively on agemates who were no longer in school. While they acknowledged many agemates who worked hard and honestly, they also criticized most of these boys for squandering their earnings on frivolities, such as cigarettes, tape players, and weekend dances. Even though ESF students may themselves have worked weekend or afternoon jobs (and may indeed have purchased "frivolities"), they still characterized their counterparts as having given up—too lazy or easily distracted to continue their studies. According to the logic of the dominant schooled identity, agemates who no longer study have failed to become somebody in life. Saúl, an athletic 15-year-old who planned on enlisting in a "military college" after graduating, denounced his former buddy Ernesto:

> The thing is, that little freckle-face wants to be a rich guy (*se quiere hacer burgués*). . . . He started up with some vices, like smoking and drinking, and now you can't even take the cigarette out of his mouth . . . . He wants to sell

tacos, and the only thing that matters to him now is grabbing enough money to go to the dances.

Saúl had been very close to Ernesto when they were still attending the same primary school and living just down the street from one another in one of the poorer neighborhoods of San Pablo. However, the luck of the draw had placed Saúl in the afternoon shift at ESF, while Ernesto went in the morning, thus making it more difficult for them to play or work together. Then, Ernesto quit school after his second year in order to work full-time at a taco stand in the market. This was the move that Saúl so harshly judged. According to Saúl, Ernesto had too easily succumbed to the immediate pleasures of the emerging youth culture in San Pablo. He had forsaken the possibility of a higher social status in order to pursue the instant gratifications of money and leisure.

I happened to know Ernesto quite well also. I had befriended him the previous year on a shorter visit at ESF, and I often chatted with him at his taco stand. What struck me was the similarity between he and Saúl. Both came from poor families now headed by an abandoned or widowed mother. They had to work several hours a day in order to help provide for their younger siblings in the family. Moreover, both seemed to strike the tough masculine pose so common among the poorer urban youth. Saúl had channeled his energies into basketball and schoolwork, hoping to join the army and learn how to handle advanced weaponry. He felt the army would grant him a social status commensurate with his secondary education. Ernesto, on the other hand, failed to see the benefits of continued schooling. In his first and second years at the secundaria he had been hired to open up a refreshment stand in the market at 6:30 a.m., and to return at 2 p.m. to work until around eight o'clock. He complained of not having any time to do his schoolwork. Moreover, he had almost no time to spend what little money he retained after handing most of it over to his mother. After enduring numerous complaints from his teachers about tardiness, absence, and incomplete work, Ernesto simply dropped out. His mother urged him to continue, but she also knew she couldn't survive without his economic contribution. Ernesto made a strategic choice. By opting out of school, he could both contribute more to his family and have money and time left over to spend on dances and excursions.

Because he now only saw Ernesto at a distance, Saúl judged this strategic choice a copout, an abandonment of the premises of schooled identity. Ironically, he accused Ernesto of "bourgeois" pretensions, claiming that Ernesto's over-riding concern was to acquire money to support his many "vices." In light of the school-based production of identity, Saúl's use of the term for "bourgeois" to describe Ernesto's motivations was highly significant. Even though the continu-ation of schooling clearly promised Saúl himself a higher, possibly "bourgeois" status, he attributed Ernesto's sole interest in money to the bourgeois impulse for greater wealth and leisure. The term "bourgeois," appropriated from textbooks and teachers with a nationalist, socialist orientation, was applied to Ernesto in order to accentuate the distinction between the motivations of the schooled and the unschooled.

Gender Differences in the Bases of Exclusion

Perhaps since few secundaria-age girls work in paid and publicly visible jobs, only the boys tended to contrast themselves with workers. Girls at ESF often contrasted themselves with those who married young. To have a schooled identity was to abjure the prospects of an early marriage in order to focus on advanced schooling and a career. Here perhaps more than anywhere else the discourses of student culture mirrored parental imperatives. For among the vast majority of girls enrolled at ESF, parents issued strong warnings against serious involvement with boys. Parents had not invested in their child's development of a schooled identity only to watch it get squandered on a socially compromising marriage. In fact, many ESF mothers had been themselves obliged to marry young. Many had had their hearts set on some sort of a "career,"[12] only to have those hopes dashed by economic circumstance, or their parents' wish to have them marry within the community to keep them close at hand. But "times have changed," as San Pabloans often liked to note. In 1990, mothers whose aspirations were thwarted in this fashion emotionally invested in their daughters' schooling success. Moreover, fathers also encouraged their daughters to continue studying and avoid serious courtship with boys. The notorious possessiveness of most Mexican fathers, which has traditionally kept girls from openly pursuing their romantic/ sexual desires,[13] worked to favor their diligence in school. For the most part, and with some class variance, fathers would much rather have seen their daughters in a successful career than a successful marriage. Likewise, ESF students generally disparaged girls who had dropped out of school to marry. Thus, an important part of most girls' schooled identity was elaborated in opposition to those who married young.

For instance, Riki, the younger sister of a third-year student named Paco whom I will discuss shortly, was adamant about her continued schooling. This was especially significant, since Riki was the only daughter, and youngest sibling, in a poor village family which now survived largely by selling fish and straw hats in the San Pablo market. I had gone to Riki and Paco's home to meet their mother, Leticia, and conduct an interview. Riki stayed on to listen, so I involved her in the interview as well. During the interview, Leticia expressed ambivalence about Riki's prospects for finishing secundaria: On the one hand, she wanted to support her daughter's efforts, and felt a career would be a definite social and economic improvement. On the other hand, she was quite sure Riki's career would only serve to enrich her eventual husband, and might be a waste of time. Moreover, Leticia expressed doubt that Riki could complete her schooling, since she didn't have the right "head" for it. At this point in the interview, I turned to Riki and asked her why she thought she could keep doing well in school. Her reply revealed the way in which her own schooled identity was being constructed against the possibility of marriage:

> *Riki:* I don't know, I like studying . . . and I don't want to be like some [girls], like my friend who got married three days after we graduated from *primaria.* . . . Before she used to watch her appearance and go around nicely dressed, and now she wears *naguas* (traditional petticoats), she looks really ugly. I don't want to look like her, I'd rather have a career . . . .

> *BL:* So it doesn't seem right to you that the friends you had [in *primaria*] got married and don't study anymore?

> *Riki:* No, it doesn't seem fair to me. I don't want to end up like them. It looks really bad. . . .

> *BL:* Why?

> *Riki:* Because that way one begins to have a family and then with. . . . I don't know, that's just what I don't want. I want to have a career in order to support myself and have my own money.

Riki's case is interesting because she is one of the few girls who actively constructed this kind of schooled identity in the absence of obvious parental support. She clearly rejected marriage as an option, even while her mother did not give her wholehearted approval to continued schooling. Significantly, Riki singles out the "ugly" *naguas* worn by her former classmate, and associates them with marriage. The *naguas* signify traditional gendered comportment in her home village, and they are often the object of derision among the mostly mestizo, city-based schoolgirls at ESF. While I did not regularly observe Riki herself in school, her involvement in the student culture undoubtedly distanced her from indigenous cultural patterns, and fueled her resolve to stay the career course.

CONTESTING AND INVESTING: CONTRADICTIONS OF SCHOOLED IDENTITY

Mexican schools, like virtually all other public school systems in the modern era,[14] have been structured, in part, around the selective principle of liberal education—a principle which posits equality of opportunities while actually promoting a hierarchy of differential aptitude (see Alonso 1994:387). Practices of examination and selection have historically individualized educational strategies in Mexico as elsewhere. Most of the forms of Mexican educational practice structured by these liberal conceptions were already in place, in one form or another, by the end of the last century. It was not really until the outset of this century, with the explosion of social revolution in Mexico, that new forms of educational ideology and practice were grafted onto the liberal base. A new emphasis on cooperation, solidarity, and the collective good, oriented toward the construction of a national identity and national culture, in many ways superseded the liberal model of individualism. This new emphasis drew on already existing practices and discourses of solidarity in popular and indigenous cultures, articulating their local, community-oriented focus to a hegemonic national project.[15]

As the Mexican state has sought to use schools as a means of legitimating its rule and constructing a national identity, it has had to confront the contradictions generated by these coexisting orientations to individual and collective action. I argue (see especially Levinson 1993b:451–58) that the pattern and justification of Mexican educational expansion in this century largely reflects the tension between liberal individualism—with its imperative of selection through equal opportunities—and nationalist collectivism.[16] This tension, in turn, defines much of the ideological context of students' identity-work at ESF. Students attempt to navigate the variable emphases teachers and fellow students put on group solidarity and individual achievement, learning to resolve or reject the tension in a variety of ways. Importantly, the production of a common "schooled identity" allows students to situate individual and group endeavor within the same motivational rubric, while excluding those youth no longer in school.

Yet many students at ESF maintained only tenuous ties with the student culture and its associated schooled identity. Some came to develop an oppositional critique. Their stories help us to more clearly trace the way schooled identity was both contested and invested with meaning.

The Case of Andrea

We have already met Andrea, the daughter of poor mestizo artisans, who themselves had originally come from peasant *ranchos* (small agricultural settlements). Andrea's family had moved around to different parts of the country, engaging in wage labor in places as far afield as Mexico City and Ciudad Juárez (on the border with El Paso, Texas), before returning to San Pablo out of disgust with the dangers and uncertainties of big city life. Though Andrea's mother had managed to work a few years as a temporary rural schoolteacher, her husband's family would not let her continue this work after their marriage. In 1990, Andrea's family was engaged in a kind of petty commodity production, painting and adorning simple wooden craft products and marketing them at both regular local stalls and seasonal events throughout the state.

Andrea's parents considered themselves *gente humilde*, poor and modest people. They were concerned when Andrea, unlike her older sister, began to act as though she were of a different social class (*categoría*), taking an avid interest in boys and requesting a proper fifteen-year birthday party (*quinceañera*)—something completely beyond their means. Andrea's mother surmised that this behavior was due to the influence of her classmates, whom she believed (somewhat inaccurately) to be of uniformly higher social standing. Andrea's parents were especially concerned when she began to defy them to attend dances and visit her new boyfriend, staying out well beyond what they considered a reasonable hour. Moreover, at this time her grades began to fall steeply. Yet interestingly, her boyfriend was not of a higher social standing. On the contrary, he had dropped out of secundaria and begun to work as an apprentice at a tire repair shop (*vulcanizadora*).

Around the time Andrea began to see her new boyfriend, she also developed a critical attitude toward her female classmates. She came to oppose her own egalitarian orientation to romance and friendship—demonstrated by her relationships with an "unschooled" boyfriend and unschooled neighborhood playmates—to what she perceived as the hypocritical manipulation of egalitarian rhetoric by her female classmates.[17] Perhaps because her classmates began to chide her for dating the "unschooled," Andrea sought comfort in her relations outside the school. Though her mother claimed the school's elevated social atmosphere induced her inappropriate behavior, Andrea countered that it was her mother who insisted that she stick with friends of her own *categoría*, her own level of schooling. Andrea thought her parents were rather hypocritical for complaining about the negative effects of her classmates' higher social standing, while denigrating her boyfriend's unkempt appearance and lack of "educated" ambition. Indeed, while her mother praised Andrea's older sister (already in her second year of *preparatoria*) for her dedication to schoolwork and avoidance of "bad influences," she attributed Andrea's decline to precisely these peer influences.

One day I stopped to chat with Andrea as she tended her family's crafts stall in front of the main church. We came around to talking about her older sister (16), with whom she had not gotten along in recent months:

> *BL*: And why don't you get along?
>
> *Andrea*: Because she has another way of thinking from me. . . . I like to get along with everybody, and she doesn't. I like to have boy friends and girl friends, and she doesn't, she doesn't get along with boys, only girls . . . .
>
> *BL*: So would you say you're more comfortable now with your boy friends outside the school than with those you have in the school?
>
> *Andrea*: Yes, because [the ones at ESF] are stuck up (*sangrones*). . . . Outside of school it's like they respect me more, they respect me more because they know I study and so I don't just let them do whatever they please (*no me doy a llevar*). They'll grab other girls because [those girls] don't ask for any respect (*no se dan a respetar*), but they know full well that I like to have respect, just like I too give them their rightful place.

Despite this account of garnering respect for her schooled status, Andrea rejects the status altogether just a few minutes later:

> I think I'll keep studying, but sometimes when I see how everyone turns out over there by my house, I just lose all interest. Now my mother no, she thinks that one is better because one studies and others don't, but I don't like that, I like to get along with everybody even if I'm studying and they aren't. . . . [Some of my friends in the neighborhood] stopped talking to me because one day my mother shouted at me that I got together with good-for-nothings (*burros*), that I was hanging out with nothing but dropouts and that I was in another class (*categoría*), that I *do* study. That's when everyone stopped talking

to me. . . . But I still speak with a few, they don't study either, but I talk to them behind my mom's back because I like to get along with everybody. . . . I'm not like my sister, who sometimes doesn't talk to anybody, because she says they're not in her class. I say, "What do I lose, even if they're not in my class?" They're the same as me (*igual que uno*) I mean, not poor, but not rich either.

What fascinates me about Andrea is the way she positioned herself vis-à-vis the dominant construction of an exclusionary, schooled identity. On the one hand, she appropriated this identity as a means of gaining "respect" among the boys in her neighborhood. On the other hand, she rejected her mother's and sister's suggestion that she associate only with fellow students who were in her *categoría*. Indeed, while she perceived in her schoolmates' taunts and discrimination the fragility and hypocrisy of the school-based discourse on equality, she appropriated elements of the discourse to construct a kind of equality between herself and her relatively unschooled *barrio* friends. Clearly, Andrea felt more comfortable with her playmates in the neighborhood. She gravitated toward their friendship because they accepted and respected her the way none of her schoolmates did. Moreover, it was no accident that she insisted on getting along with "everybody" in her neighborhood because they were, despite differences in schooling, fundamentally "equal." Andrea resignified and recontextualized the school-based discourse on equality. Whereas the discourse pretended to erase or transcend differences among a diverse group of schoolkids, Andrea contested the basis of schooled identity by extending the discourse to include *all* youth, especially the unschooled. In the absence of other compelling discourses on equality,[18] Andrea took the construction of equality which normally operated on the terrain of the *grupo escolar* and the school, and extended it beyond the school, to defend and articulate a solidarity of neighborhood friendship which ran counter to the pretensions of an exclusionary schooled identity. Andrea challenged those elements of a schooled identity which would create antagonisms with the unschooled, yet she also drew on that identity selectively and contradictorily to make sense of her experience.

The Case of Paco and Fidel

Students from outside San Pablo, especially those from communities where an indigenous language was still spoken, developed different strategies for negotiating the social world at ESF. I got to know a couple of these boys from outside San Pablo quite well. Paco, whose sister Riki we've already met, came from one of the larger island villages which relied on a fishing and hatmaking economy. Like most of the village's adults, Paco's abandoned mother continued speaking the local language in the community, and Paco himself understood it well enough, though he claimed to be inept at speaking. Economically and culturally, the village was clearly undergoing a protracted crisis. By the late 1980s, young males, and in some cases entire families, began to migrate. Many, like Paco's older brother, made it to the fields and migrant ghettoes of California and Arizona. Still others migrated seasonally to pick fruits and vegetables on the coastal plain of Sinaloa, Mexico's most important agricultural region. In 1990, Paco recounted how the *enganchadores* (labor recruiters) still arrived each winter in their trucks and buses, taking whole families for months at a time.

Paco and his younger sister were the only students from his village attending ESF at the time of my study. Many students of secundaria age went to the *tele-secundaria*[19] on the island. Some went to a closer nearby town of about 5,000, while those who travelled to San Pablo typically attended one of the two vocational secundarias (*técnicas*). Since each village tended to develop a "tradition" of sending sons and daughters to one or another of San Pablo's secundarias, Paco's village had rarely patronized ESF. Paco ended up at ESF partly because his mother worked in the central San Pablo fishmarket and knew ESF's good reputation, and partly because his older brother had spoken poorly of his teachers at the nearby *secundaria técnica* he had attended.

During his first two years in secundaria Paco had remained mostly marginal to the life of his *grupo escolar*. Along with his classmate Fidel, Paco skipped classes a lot and hung out with other boys from villages. Both boys said they had felt "uncomfortable" from their very first days in school. However, despite the proximity of their respective home villages, Paco and Fidel did not become close friends at first. Fidel had arrived at ESF with five classmates from his village *primaria*, but each had been placed coincidentally in distinct *grupos escolares*. Nevertheless, the six boys reunited at every possible free moment, even cutting classes to do so. Paco formed a friendship group with several students from his own and other nearby villages, but not with Fidel's group.

From what Paco and other students have told me, and from what I've observed, it is not uncommon for first- and second-year students from the *pueblitos*, as San Pabloans call the villages, to forge social ties with one another across and within *grupos escolares*. The shared position which appears to bring them together is that of "country" or "village" dweller in relation to the school's predominantly urban culture. That Pablo and Fidel did not themselves become friends until the beginning of their third year would seem to refute this interpretation, if not for continual observations and reports which proved their situation an exception. Moreover, when most of the other *pueblito* students had dropped out or switched schools, Paco and Fidel finally came together at the outset of their third year. It is significant that they sought each other out at this point rather than develop closer ties to other San Pablo boys within their *grupo escolar*.

Since so many of the village students dropped out of school before graduating, by the third year the few that remained had to make a more concerted effort to incorporate themselves into the social life of their respective *grupos*. This is what appears to have happened in the case of Paco. Perhaps because his mother and older brother prompted him strongly to continue on to *preparatoria*, Paco gradually reduced his commitments to Fidel and sought to strengthen other friendships within the *grupo*. When I conducted a joint interview with them in November, the boys' brief friendship had already begun to weaken. Fidel, for his part, had become increasingly disaffected from the *grupo* and the school. His father had died the previous year, and though his teachers and classmates commented that Fidel seemed more motivated again this, his third year, Fidel confided that he'd rather spend his time in his home village. His older brothers, themselves secundaria dropouts, provided little incentive for him to continue. In the meantime, he was learning the trade of mask making from his uncle, and he knew that no secundaria certificate would be required for success in that endeavor. Thus, Paco was more actively participating in the intersubjective production of a schooled identity, while Fidel had developed a more ambivalent relation to it.

By his last year of secundaria, Paco was clearly beginning to distinguish himself from his villagemates, and he became more integrated into the *grupo*. Most of his previous friends had since dropped out, and he was obliged to seek the guidance and camaraderie of his classmates. By teachers' accounts, his grades and attendance began to improve. By classmates' accounts, he had become more sociable. He utilized his basketball skills to become one of the group's premier players, thus garnering more prestige for himself. Indeed, to the degree he became comfortably incorporated into the *grupo*, he began to feel distant from the ideas and practices in his home village. In one telling conversation, he ridiculed typical village musical tastes, such as *música ranchera* and "popular" groups like The Yonics or The Temerarios, extolling instead the virtues of contemporary rock and rap. These musical forms, clearly city-based and dominant within the school, had more recently captured his imagination. Fidel, on the other hand, sheepishly admitted his preference for the more traditional or "popular" Mexican music.

Negative discourse on ethnicity was clearly muted within the school (see Levinson 1993b), and Paco and Fidel claimed they were never made to feel rejected specifically as *indios* or *rancheros* (cf. Luykx, this volume). The way they told it, their earlier isolation had been self-imposed, a choice to be with other students from villages who, according to them, took the mistaken path of truancy rather than hard work. When I asked if they thought their fellow classmates had rejected or belittled them, they responded that, on the contrary, many had tried to help them improve their grades and join the *grupo*'s activities. If they had been rejected by some, it was not for being *indio*; it was for playing hookey so often that they no longer contributed to the solidarity of the *grupo*. Yet if Paco and Fidel didn't perceive any discrimination by their classmates, it was probably because their classmates largely kept derogatory remarks out of earshot. Importantly, the discourse of *grupo* solidarity strongly proscribed forthright expressions of conflict or discrimination—much less to a snooping anthropologist. Moreover, since several classmates *did* try to incorporate them into *grupo* life, Paco and Fidel only had recourse to notions of personal failure or weakness as a way of explaining their previous marginalization. While they acknowledged that a few classmates looked down on them, Paco and Fidel said it was for their lack of money, not their rural or indigenous roots. Social class was what really mattered, in their eyes.

Nevertheless, there was a price both the boys had to pay for being from the country. Whether or not Paco and Fidel recognized it as such, the friendship groups they had formed the first two years obviously drew on ethnic and rural identities. These identities were rather uneasily accommodated by the construction of equality in the *grupo escolar*. While Paco and Fidel attributed their discomfort at the outset to a vague sense of "not knowing anybody," it was clear that the process of "getting to know" their classmates was made considerably more difficult for them than for the average city student. Partly this was due to their relative isolation in home villages, but it was also because the dominant student discourse on equality was a discourse of sameness, of homogenization. In his final year, Paco had to adopt dominant, city-based tastes and skills (basketball, rock music, and urban slang Spanish) in order to succeed socially and academically on the terms the *grupo escolar* had set. Adopting a schooled identity presupposed this kind of adaptation. Fidel, still more bound to village life and the prospect of mask making, remained more marginal to the *grupo*. Notions of equality constructed largely in the *grupo* determined the arena within which Paco took on elements of a new schooled identity and against which Fidel had to define his school failure.

DISCUSSION AND CONCLUSION

In this final section, I want to suggest that the process by which students elaborate, or contest, a schooled identity at ESF helps us to understand how state schools' intervention in local social relations may partially succeed or fail in articulating forms of sociocultural difference to a hegemonic project.[20] I also want to argue that the symbolic identity "work" which students carry forth in secondary schooling is always shifting, always dependent upon both broader social movements and the idiosyncratic turns—often wrought by economic necessity—people's lives take.

I believe Lomnitz-Adler's (1992) work on regional class and ethnic differences can help us to understand what is happening when educational actors learn to consider themselves "equal" on the grounds of a schooled identity. Teachers' discourse on equality gets taken up by students, and becomes an important part of students' construction of an inclusionary/exclusionary schooled identity. In other words, both within the school and beyond it, in neighborhood networks, ESF students attempt to see each other as "equal" (inclusionary), while seeing the relatively unschooled as not quite "equal" (exclusionary). Following Lomnitz-Adler (1992), this process can be seen as a regional articulation of state hegemony, and thus an integral part of the state organization of what Lomnitz-Adler (1992:29) calls regional "cultures of social relations." According to Lomnitz-Adler, the "idioms" of regional cultures of social relations—the forms of talk by which different intimate cultures communicate—include "articulatory symbols" which cut across intimate cultures, and which can be drawn on to construct "shared" knowledges and orientations. However, while people from different intimate cultures within a region can understand and communicate with one another in the terms of this regional culture, they have different positions vis-à-vis that culture. Indeed, different intimate cultures are more, or less, "permeated" by it (1992:37).[21]

Lomnitz-Adler conceives of state action as responding in some sense to these regional cultures of social relations, intervening to articulate them to a state project: "Because the state represents national society, it is continuously cutting across intimate cultures and constructing an image of itself as a transcendental whole that fully encompasses each one of the nation's intimate cultures" (1992:306). Curiously, though, Lomnitz-Adler does not include state schools among those key interactional "frames," such as marketplaces and political rituals, through which the culture of social relations may bring intimate cultures into contact with one another. To be sure, schools are a part of "state culture," which is itself a "specific mode of the culture of social relations"; and "learning this hegemonic culture of class relations is one of (state culture's) main demands" (1992:104; cf Corrigan and Sayer 1985). Perhaps because most state schools do not bring virtually all of a region's intimate cultures into contact with one another, Lomnitz-Adler does not include them among the institutions which normally "frame" regional culture. At ESF, however, this is precisely what happened.

Ever since the Cardenista period of conflict and social reform, discourses on equality have formed an important of the regional "idiom" in San Pablo. This is reflected in the school. As Lomnitz-Adler suggests, regional intimate cultures will have developed different perspectives and positions regarding this idiom. Thus, students from more established professional and merchant classes in San Pablo tended to "euphemize" (Bourdieu 1977:196) their dominant position in the school and in local society by claiming that all students were equal, especially within what I call "officially structured informal domains," such as the *grupo escolar*.[22] As for students of less privileged backgrounds, from families of service workers, tradesmen, peasants, or from indigenous communities, the culture of equality came to signify a means of empowerment, of acquiring the same kind of cultural capital within an educational field (Bourdieu 1984). By wielding the discourses of the culture, these students could pursue their own strategies of educational and social mobility in a more congenial environment. Accordingly, their own expressions and understandings of class and ethnic domination in the school had to be modulated and downplayed. Moreover, with a greater investment in the culture of equality came subtle changes in identity and aspiration, as these students eventually saw themselves standing on common ground with more privileged students in the school. Those students who refused to adapt themselves to the dominant norms of the school, such as Andrea and Fidel, either contested the facade of equality itself, or learned to interpret their "failure" as a consequence of personal attributes and decisions.

The construction of a school*ed* identity thus involves an understanding of social self as educated person, as occupying a social position distinct from the *unschooled*. Parents, teachers, and students alike engage in an ongoing politics of the educated person, a discursive practice in which the value of schooling, a kind of cultural capital, is constantly circulated through the social "field" (Bourdieu 1984, 1989; Calhoun 1993). In plainer terms, people associated with the secundaria (students and parents, mainly) tend to distinguish those with a secundaria education from those without one. The "fact" of a general secundaria education, which holds the promise of future studies, gets elaborated into a series of cultural distinctions which signify the value of being properly schooled. This process magnifies the *difference* between schooled and unschooled, and thereby contributes further to the construction of a strong common culture, where students can identifiy with one another based on their allegiance to and active participation in the meanings of being secundaria-schooled. One could say that, unlike the working-class high school Wexler (1992:135) studied, identity-work at ESF primarily *reduced*, rather than exaggerated, class differences within the school. Ultimately, I would suggest, it is the sense of self as educated person which most powerfully articulates social difference into new configurations. Schooled identity not only emerges from the school-based culture of equality, but it also finds support and expression in myriad social spaces beyond the school. Significantly, it is an identity which for the most part accommodates the imperatives of family and school, of informal and formal domains, for it does not oppose itself to the goals of those institutions. Schooled identity and the category of educated person create new configurations of difference by bringing together and identifying previously opposed or antagonistic identities rooted in distinct intimate cultures.

To be sure, this reconfiguration has already begun to take place the moment students are placed in the secundaria by their parents. The commitment to public secundaria education (and often students are very active in this decision itself, vetoing the parents' choice of private school, for instance) already signals the family's social and cultural position, or their aspirations to a position. There is, in this sense, a kind of sociocultural levelling, or homogenization, which begins to occur from the very first day students set foot in the gate at ESF. However, the parental commitment, which the student may at first share, must then be filtered through the process of student cultural production, where new identities and identifications are created. In most cases at ESF, students strongly invested in the culture of equality and the schooled identity it provided, and this identity guided their conduct well beyond the school, into the two plazas and the pursuit of romance, for instance. Schooled identity thus created a perception of difference where there had been none before (between the schooled and the unschooled of the same intimate culture), thereby fracturing the potential solidarity of intimate cultures, and constituting new ones (Riki, you will remember, wanted no part of the *naguas* which her old schoolfriend now wore). Families in peasant communities or lower-class neighborhoods, for instance, often forbade their schooled children to continue interacting with the unschooled, even in the case of cousins and close neighbors. Often, too, these parental proscriptions were unnecessary, as students themselves internalized the distinctions. Andrea, and to a lesser degree Fidel, were among those few exceptions to the rule, but there were others. These students, for reasons I have already indicated, never fully adopted the schooled identity, choosing instead to find comfort and solidarity in their intimate cultures outside the school. Accordingly, their aspirations became more modestly defined in terms of the limited range of local economic and cultural options.

Thus, one of the interesting effects of the creation of a schooled identity is to produce a modest articulation of dominant and nondominant intimate cultures in the San Pablo region. Insofar as children from various intimate cultures begin to identify one another as sharing the same age interest and the same status as "educated person," their differences become less salient in their mutual perceptions of one another. Students from among dominant and subordinate groups in local society, who are positioned rather differently vis-à-vis the national economy and culture, and who have a rather different set of expectations and possibilities for the future, nevertheless come to share the same position within the nationalist construction of common citizenship. They are subject, in other words, to the same hegemonic construction, and their common forms of engagement with and resistance to that construction in the school constitute them as "equals" on the terrain of popular culture.

The school penetrates everyday life in a way few other state institutions can, provoking individuals, families and communities to structure expectations and practices according to new temporal patterns and socio-spatial horizons (cf. González 1988). The Mexican state has been ingenious at appropriating popular sensibilities and discourses to articulate a national culture and identity,[23] and schools have been a primary site for the cultural production of the national "educated person." At ESF, most students, through their own processes of cultural production, were "stated" as they were schooled.

EPILOGUE

This paper begs the question of the durability of "schooled identity" and its relation to state culture and national identity. Hegemony and identity-production are, after all, contingent processes, and the school, important as it may be, is only one force among many in students' lives. As I've kept up with some of these youth, there is some evidence that the social distinctions generated through schooling may strengthen or weaken according to economic fate and existential circumstance. By the summer of 1993, Paco had already gone to join his brother in the migrant ghettoes of southern California. I could not speak with him, but his mother claimed that he had all but abandoned his dreams of studying law. Fidel was making masks in his village. He had long ceased to dream about careers possible through schooling. Instead, he too was making plans for the long journey north. Saúl was doing odd jobs around town and attending high school classes desultorily. He still had hopes of joining the army or the federal police corps, and thus serving his country. But economic circumstance dictated that he help his mother raise the young ones. Andrea, as I mentioned, was living with relatives, taking occasional night classes, and waiting her turn to go north as well. The lure of economic salvation drew these kids to the north, while the press of economic necessity kept them busy at home. Their lives were converging in important ways.

NOTES

The field research reported here was made possible by a Fulbright Grant from the Institute of International Education, and the writing was enabled by grants from the Spencer Foundation and the Graduate School of the University of North Carolina—Chapel Hill. I thank these institutions, as well as the colleagues who helped me better formulate my arguments here: Gary Anderson, Douglas Foley, Dorothy Holland, and Elsie Rockwell.

1. The names of people and places have been changed to protect the interests of participants in this study.

2. The only significant industry in and around San Pablo would have to be considered "smallscale": there are several small saw mills, which employ from ten to fifteen employees; numerous furniture shops, which each employ from three to ten employees; and several textile shops, which also employ from five to ten people. The central marketplace is perhaps the single most important source of employment in San Pablo, providing a range of positions from small store or stall owner, to clerk, truck driver or "carrier" (*cargador*).

3. Most Mexican primary and secondary schools must institute morning and afternoon/evening shifts (*turnos*) in order to accommodate local educational demand.

4. My school survey of the morning shift in September 1990 brought back 667 completed questionnaires out of approximately 720 enrolled students. Of these 667, 303 (45 percent) indicated they lived in the city center or on a street not incorporated into one of the outlying *colonias populares* (lower-class neighborhoods). Some 237 (36 percent) lived in one of these *colonias*, while some 86 (13 percent) came from small towns or villages within or just beyond the boundaries of the San Pablo municipality (equivalent to our county). Forty-one questionnaires contained insufficient information to assign a residential location.

5. In 1990, approximately 55 percent of the students enrolled in the morning shift of ESF were girls. By contrast, only about 44 percent of the afternoon shift were girls.

6. Quiroz' (1987,1992) ethnographic studies of secundarias in Mexico City, among the few available in Mexico, have been immensely helpful to my own work.

7. For the school year 1987-88, the state where ESF is located had one of the lowest rates of secondary absorption (that is, the percentage of primary school graduates that

continue on to secundaria) in all of Mexico (70.6% versus the national average of 83.0%). More importantly, the state had by far the highest rate of secundaria desertion (that is, the percentage of students each year who discontinue their secondary studies before obtaining a certificate—12.7% per year, versus the national average of 8.9%) (Prawda 1987:51–52).

8. I arrived in San Pablo in early summer, 1990, and took up residence in the home of two teachers from ESF. Because of my familiarity with the community and my previous research clearance with school authorities, I was allowed virtually unconstrained access to all facets of school life, including classrooms, office dynamics, teacher union meetings, and parent-teacher conferences. I was also given access to all relevant school and individual student records, and I collected a number of site documents, such as exams, informational flyers, memos, and political pamphlets. For most of the school year, from late August to late June, I was engaged in classroom and playground observations, but I also participated in extracurricular activities, attending parties, dances, church services, sports events, civic ceremonies, and study groups. In addition to these observations, I chose *twenty focal students* who represented a full range of backgrounds, dispositions, and academic records in the school. Over the course of the year, I extensively interviewed each of these students at least twice, sometimes three times, and I paid special attention to them in my observations. I visited the homes of most of these focal students and interviewed one or more of their parents. I interviewed their teachers as well. Finally, I carried out several surveys of students at ESF and other local secondary schools. See Levinson (1993) for a fuller account of field methods and survey results.

9. Although revolutionary state rhetoric of this century has valorized the "Indian" contribution to national culture, and envisaged the mestizo as the main "protagonist of nationality" (Lomnitz-Adler 1992:279), the state has continued to incarnate the value of "whitening" the country as a whole (cf. Bonfil Batalla 1990).

10. The state of interethnic relations in the San Pablo region does not appear to be much different from the situation described by Friedlander (1975), Margolies (1975), Bonfil Batalla (1990), and others for different areas of Mexico.

11. College preparatory school equivalent to our high school.

12. In San Pablo, the term "career" (*carrera*) refers to employment which requires some kind of professional training, whether at the more modest high school level (*carrera corta*: technician, secretary, cosmetologist, nurse, mechanic, and the like), or at the university level.

13. See Levine 1993.

14. See Fuller (1991), Meyer et al. (1992), and Boli et al. (1985).

15. See Rockwell (this volume; 1994; in press).

16. Adler et al. (1993), in their study of Mexican political culture, describe this as a tension between the fundamentally "hierarchical and holistic" nature of the Mexican social formation, and the individualistic tenets of political liberalism.

17. The term *hipócrita* was very common in student discourse, and was used as a moral judgment against those who were perceived to violate the premises of the "culture of equality."

18. Other discourses available to Andrea, especially in the family, church, or mass media, may have important elements of equality, but these could not be discerned as readily as the school-based discourse.

19. Throughout the 1980s, the Secretariat of Education established numerous tele-vision-mediated secondary schools in smaller communities. In these schools, a single teacher typically supervises the instruction imparted by a centralized, televised curriculum.

20. The concept of articulation has become an important one in cultural studies. Other authors in this volume, such as Luykx, use it as well. Articulation is used in this context to mean an act of conjoining, of bringing elements together. See Hall (1986, 1988).

21. This in part accounts for Rockwell's (this volume; in press) and Mercado's (1985) insights into the negotiated character of "state" action in public schools. Rockwell emphasizes that the "state" in public schooling is represented by the contradictory alle-giances and frames of reference of local teachers, national teachers, zone inspectors, and other educational actors.

22. See my dissertation (Levinson 1993:414-423) for the distinction between formal, officially structured informal, and informal domains.

23. Bartra (1992), Joseph and Nugent (1994), Lomnitz-Adler (1992), and Rockwell (this volume).

REFERENCES

Adler Lomnitz, Larissa, Claudio Lomnitz-Adler, and Ilya Adler. 1993. The Function of the Form: Power Play and Ritual in the 1988 Mexican Presidential Campaign. *In* Constructing Culture and Power in Latin America. Daniel H. Levine, ed. Pp. 357–402. Ann Arbor: University of Michigan Press.

Alonso, Ana María. 1994. The Politics of Space, Time, and Substance: State Formation, Nationalism, and Ethnicity. Annual Reviews in Anthropology 23:379–405.

Bartra, Roger. 1992. The Cage of Melancholy: Identity and Metamorphosis in the Mexican Character. Christopher J. Hall, trans. New Brunswick, NJ: Rutgers University Press.

Becker, Marjorie. 1989. Lázaro Cárdenas and the Counter-Revolution: The Struggle over Culture in Michoacán, 1934–1940. Ph.D. Dissertation, Yale University.

Boli, John, Francisco O. Ramírez, and John W. Meyer. 1985. Explaining the Origins and Expansion of Mass Education. Comparative Education Review 29(2):145–190.

Bonfil Batalla, Guillermo. 1990. México Profundo: Una Civilización Negada. Mexico City: Grijalbo.

Bourdieu, Pierre. 1977. Outline of a Theory of Practice. Cambridge: Cambridge University Press.

————. 1984. Distinction: A Social Critique of the Judgment of Taste. Cambridge, MA: Harvard University Press.

————. 1989. Social Space and Symbolic Power. Sociological Theory 7(2):14–25.

Calhoun, Craig. 1993. Habitus, Field, and Capital: The Question of Historical Specificity. *In* Bourdieu: Critical Perspectives. Craig Calhoun, Edward LiPuma, and Moishe Postone, eds. Chicago: University of Chicago Press.

Corrigan, Philip and Derek Sayer. 1985. The Great Arch: English State Formation as Cultural Revolution. London: Basil Blackwell.

Dinerman, Ina. 1978. Economic Alliances in a Mexican Regional Economy. Ethnology 17(1):51–64.

Friedlander, Judith. 1975. Being Indian in Hueyapan: A Study of Forced Identity in Contemporary Mexico. New York: St. Martin's Press.

Fuller, Bruce. 1991. Growing-Up Modern: The Western State Builds Third World Schools. London: Routledge.

García Canclini, Néstor. 1981. Las Culturas Populares en el Capitalismo. Mexico City: Nueva Imagen.

————. 1990. Culturas Híbridas: Estrategias Para Entrar y Salir de la Modernidad. Mexico City: Grijalbo.

González Chávez, Humberto. 1988. The Centralization of Education in Mexico: Subordination and Autonomy. *In* State and Society: The Emergence and Development of Social Hierarchy and Political Centralization. John Gledhill, Barbara Bender, and Mogens Trole Larsen, eds. Pp. 320–343. London: Unwin Hyman.

Hall, Stuart. 1986. On Postmodernism and Articulation: An Interview with Stuart Hall. Lawrence Grossberg, ed. Journal of Communication Inquiry 10(2):45–60.

————. 1988. The Hard Road to Renewal: Thatcherism and the Crisis of the Left. London: Verso.

Holland, Dorothy, Carole Cain, William Lachicotte, Deborah Skinner, and Renee Prillaman, eds. in press. Emerging Selves: Identities Forming in and Against Cultural Worlds. Cambridge, MA: Harvard University Press.

Joseph Gilbert and Daniel Nugent. 1994. Introduction: Popular Culture and State Formation in Postrevolutionary Mexico. *In* Everyday Forms of State Formation: Revolution and the Negotiation of Rule in Modern Mexico. Gilbert Joseph and Daniel Nugent, eds. Durham: Duke University Press.

Levine, Sarah. 1993. Dolor y Alegría: Women and Social Change in Urban Mexico. Madison: University of Wisconsin Press.

Levinson, Bradley A. 1993a. School Groups and the Culture of Equality at a Mexican Secondary School. Working Paper No. 7, Duke-UNC Program in Latin American Studies.

―――. 1993b. Todos Somos Iguales: Cultural Production and Social Difference at a Mexican Secondary School. Ph.D. Dissertation, Department of Anthropology, University of North Carolina–Chapel Hill.

Lomnitz-Adler, Claudio. 1992. Exits From the Labyrinth: Culture and Ideology in the Mexican National Space. Berkeley: University of California Press.

Margolies, Barbara Luise. 1975. Princes of the Earth: Subcultural Diversity in a Mexican Municipality. Washington, DC: Special Publications of the American Anthropological Association, No. 2.

Mercado, Ruth. 1985. La Educación Primaria Gratuita: Una Lucha Popular Cotidiana. Cuadernos de Investigación #17. Mexico City: DIE.

Meyer, John W., David H. Kamens and Aaron Benavot. 1992. School Knowledge for the Masses: World Models and National Primary Curricular Categories in the Twentieth Century. London: Falmer.

Mir, Adolfo. 1979. Orígenes Socioeconómicos, Status de la Escuela y Expectativas Educativas de Estudiantes de Secundaria. *In* La Educación y Desarrollo Dependiente en América Latina. D. Morales, ed. Mexico City: Centro de Estudios Educativos.

Novelo, Victoria. 1976. Artesanías y Capitalismo en México. Mexico City: Secretaría de Educación Pública-INAH.

Prawda, Juan. 1987. Logros, Inequidades y Retos del Futuro del Sistema Educativo Mexicano. Mexico City: Grijalbo.

Quiroz, Rafael. 1987. El Maestro y el Saber Especializado. Mexico City: DIE.

―――. 1992. Obstáculos Para la Apropiación de los Contenidos Académicos en la Escuela Secundaria. Infancia y Aprendizaje.

Reichert, Joshua. 1982. A Town Divided: Economic Stratification and Social Relations in a Mexican Migrant Community. Social Problems 29:411–423.

Rockwell, Elsie. 1994. Schools of the Revolution: Enacting and Contesting State Forms in Tlaxcala, 1910–1930. *In* Everyday Forms of State Formation. Gilbert M. Joseph and Daniel Nugent, eds. Durham: Duke University Press.

―――. in press. Ethnography and the Commitment to Public Schooling: A Review of Research at the DIE. *In* Educational Ethnographic Research in Latin America: The Struggle for a New Paradigm. Gary Anderson and Martha Montero-Sieburth, eds. New York: Garland.

Vaughan, Mary Kay. 1982. The State, Education, and Social Class in Mexico, 1880–1928. Dekalb, IL: Northern Illinois University Press.

Wexler, Philip. 1992. Becoming Somebody: Toward a Social Psychology of School. London: Falmer.

Wiest, Raymond. 1973. Wage-Labor Migration and the Household in a Mexican Town. Journal of Anthropological Research 29:180–209.

10

Aurolyn Luykx _____

From *Indios* to *Profesionales*: Stereotypes and Student Resistance in Bolivian Teacher Training

Introduction

Urban Aymaras in the Multi-Ethnic State

At some point during the past decade, anthropologists and others realized that a reformulation of the relationship between indigenous groups and their corresponding nation-states was necessary, if not long overdue.[1] The effects of supranational systems continue to multiply, reaching even those "remotest people that anthropologists have made such a fetish of studying" (Gupta and Ferguson 1992:18). Long subject to external economic and environmental influences, indigenous groups are increasingly engaged in an expanding "intercontinental traffic in meaning" (Hannerz 1987:552) around the political ideologies and cultural products of the "developed" nations. When global capitalism and other belief systems penetrate daily practice in the remotest corners of the globe, indigenous groups can no longer be treated as closed social systems. Thus Thomas Abercrombie's claim that "'indigenous ethnic groups' and 'indigenous cosmologies' are unintelligible apart from their struggle with the state" (1991:111) is one we cannot dismiss.

Bolivia is the most "indigenous" of all Latin American countries, with nearly two thirds of its mostly rural population speaking Aymara or Quechua as their first language. Though certainly not the dominant group politically, indigenous people dominate Bolivia's cultural landscape, urban as well as rural, by sheer force of numbers and the cohesion of a distinctive complex of cultural traits. Nevertheless, urban *criollo* (Spanish-based) culture is far from irrelevant to the lives of indigenous Bolivians—partly because so much of national policy, resources, and debate is dedicated to "integrating" the largely rural, indigenous majority into the supposed "national culture." Consequently, questions of indigenous cultural legitimacy can arise in response to virtually any aspect of national policy. Furthermore, the discourse of indigenous rights is inevitably if uneasily yoked to that of class conflict, which seethes constantly in a country which, together with Haiti, is one of the poorest in the hemisphere (Klein 1992:279).

In Bolivian political discourse, the "problem" of cultural difference is frequently constructed as one of nationality. Indigenous people are seen as insufficiently nationalized;[2] they are inhabitants of Bolivia, but not quite "Bolivians." The rural school is a key institution in the attempted transformation of "Indians" into "Bolivians." Part of this process involves establishing dominant definitions of Bolivianness, Indianness, "national integration," and so on—concepts which the rapid social changes of the last four decades have shaken loose from their ideological moorings.

Before the popular revolution of 1952, the subject positions offered to indigenous people by the dominant *criollo* society were largely restricted to positions of servitude. There was an assumed identity between the terms *indígena* (a person of indigenous descent), *indio* (in the sense of a racist epithet), and *peón/pongo* (serf), which was virtually impossible to challenge within the racist hegemonic order of the era. In the postrevolutionary period, however, there emerged a national ideological project to disarticulate indigenous and peasant identities from the deeply entrenched stereotype of the despised *indio*, and rearticulate them to the revolutionary subject of the *campesino*, or peasant. This proposed isomorphism between *indígena* and *campesino* in turn became unwieldy, as increasing social mobility and urban migration produced significant numbers of Aymara and Quechua people who were not, in fact, peasants.[3] New subject positions were generated, into which indigenous people have moved in increasing numbers. These individuals now face the question of what it means to be indigenous within social categories which were previously incompatible with that status.

Rural education, and especially the rural "normal school" (teachers' college), are central to this shift in Bolivia's class/ethnic structure. Yet, while partially desegregating the middle class by providing social mobility to indigenous people, rural education has simultaneously stratified the indigenous community itself. First, access to primary schooling created a large stratum of literate rural dwellers, who are nevertheless still offset by a large stratum of illiterates. Secondly, the normal schools provided many rural dwellers with an avenue out of peasant life and into "the professions." However, this avenue is not only limited in the numbers it can accommodate, but also entails an at least partial and at times total rejection of the rural lifestyle which, until quite recently, was the unquestioned underpinning of Aymara cultural identity.

New alternatives for indigenous identity have emerged, accompanied by conflicts over which of these are desirable, advantageous, and morally acceptable. Now that "Aymara" does not automatically imply either *campesino* or *indio* (in the pejorative sense), many are left unsure as to what it does mean, and the resulting differences of opinion take on the bitterness characteristic of questions which threaten one's personal identity. Increased access to schooling, while lifting many rural dwellers out of society's lowest strata, has also thrown the solidarity of the indigenous community and the meaning of "indigenous culture" into uncertainty.

Socialization, Subjectivity, and the "Hidden Curriculum"

An axiom of most recent critical analyses of schooling is that schools reproduce macro-level structures via the minute, micro-level practices which permeate everyday life. These practices embody the subjectivities which students engage throughout their academic socialization. While "socialization" is traditionally thought of as that period of concentrated cultural learning through which the child is integrated into society—a universal phenomenon, though its specific content depends upon the society in question—this generalized view obscures the fact that "it is precisely the historical and class variations of 'socialization' which need to be studied" (Williams 1977:137).[4] The cultural learning which enables children to function as social beings is not distinct from that which fixes them in a particular position within society. Williams describes how the more abstract view of socialization conceals its role in the reproduction of hegemony:

> What is abstracted in orthodox sociology as "socialization" is in practice, in any actual society, a specific kind of incorporation. Its description as "socialization," the universal abstract process on which all human beings can be said to depend, is a way of avoiding or hiding this specific content and intention. Any process of socialization of course includes things that all human beings have to learn, but any specific process ties this necessary learning to a selected range of meanings, values, and practices which, in the very closeness of their association with the necessary learning, constitute the real foundations of the hegemonic. (1977:117)

Thus the need to reconceptualize socialization, not as "a set of transferred internal structures" unproblematically absorbed by the rising generation (Willis 1981:4), but rather as a dialogic process in which hegemonic forms are simultaneously absorbed, resisted and transformed in unpredictable ways. Walsh likewise conceives of "socialization" as explicitly historical, beginning but by no means ending with the child's positioning in the matrix of family and community relations; children are subjected to "not one socialization, but many" through their encounters with various institutions (1991:36–47). The influences of family, community, and school act simultaneously and at times contradictorily, mirroring the complex cross-currents of hegemony and the multiple subject-positions that social identity entails for each individual.

Emergence from childhood brings an increasing awareness of, and identification with, the various subject positions available in the adult world. Schools endeavor to interpellate students as particular types of subjects, via discourses and practices which position them in relation to their teachers, to "knowledge," to their own productive activity, and to various social groups within and beyond the nation. While a plethora of studies concerning this "hidden curriculum" have appeared during the last decade, few have addressed the world beyond the Western industrialized nations.[5] And yet, such investigation "is hardly any less relevant for an understanding of Third World education and its place in national cultures" (Hannerz 1987:554). With the growing scholarly and political interest in issues of nationalism and ethnicity, the hidden curricula of developing nations constitute fruitful territory for the investigation of how such identities and ideologies are constructed and contested.

Yet in much of Latin America, where schools are often overwhelmed by linguistic and cultural diversity, there is a temptation to view this diversity as fundamentally a technical and managerial problem. Proposed "solutions" usually fall within a narrow range, the most simplistic being to advocate more schools and increased access to schooling. While perhaps a worthy goal in itself, this approach fails to address what happens to students once they are in school. Others focus almost exclusively on bilingual education, with the implicit assumption that if the linguistic barriers faced by indigenous students can only be eliminated, their schooling will automatically "take" and the system will begin to "work." Questions of just what is being "taken," and precisely what the "work" of the system is, are raised with much less frequency. As noted by Henry Giroux:

> The rationality that dominates traditional views of schooling and curriculum is rooted in the narrow concerns for effectiveness, behavioral objectives, and principles of learning that treat knowledge as something to be consumed and schools as merely instructional sites designed to pass onto students a "common" culture and set of skills that will enable them to operate effectively in the wider society. . . . The issue of how teachers, students, and representatives from the wider society generate meaning tends to be obscured in favor of the issue of how people can master someone else's meaning, thus depoliticizing both the notion of school culture and the notion of classroom pedagogy. (1988:6)

Education is as much about the generation of meaning as it is about the transmission of academic skills. For indigenous students in Bolivia, many of the meanings generated in school are closely tied to their own developing sense of self. Through its intervention in the processes of students' identity formation, the school works to hegemonically create the types of social subjects conducive to the maintenance of a particular social order. When the foundations of that social order are shaken by other forces—changing demographics, economic crises, labor conflicts, external pressures from more powerful nations—the educational system is apt to find itself in crisis as well, as is presently the case in Bolivia.

A major concern of those occupying the upper echelons of Bolivian statecraft is the forging of a coherent and unified "nation" from a vastly diverse, frequently antagonistic mélange of social groups. Part of the difficulty is that the most formidable obstacles to national unity are some of Bolivia's most characteristic features: deep social inequalities, cultural and linguistic diversity, a conflictive history propelled by a strong working-class consciousness, and intense regional rivalries. While these factors define *lo boliviano* for many, they also represent the forces which constantly pull any notion of a unified "Bolivian society" away from a common center.

A crucial question faced by the school system, then, is how to define the Bolivian national subject broadly enough to resonate with all Bolivians, despite their conflicting interests and backgrounds. Clearly, any "authentic" Bolivian nationalism must take ethnicity into account; no articulation of ideological elements will find widespread acceptance if the indigenous element is not prominently included. Of course, the hegemonic response to such rival attachments for subjects' loyalties is not elimination, but incorporation; not "wish[ing] them out of existence by belittling them or even denying their reality, but domesticat[ing] them" (Geertz 1973b:277). So while Bolivia's *etnias* (indigenous ethnic groups) cannot be ignored, they may be encapsulated as a merely "cultural" phenomenon, in school curricula and elsewhere (see Rival, this volume, for an Ecuadorian example).

Nationalist ideologies are built from the cannibalized remains of other collective loyalties; to speak the national subject is to silence another. In the words of Corrigan and Sayer:

> To define "us" in national terms . . . has consequences. Such classifications are means for a project of social integration which is also, inseparably, an active disintegration of other focuses of identity and conceptions of subjectivity. They provide a basis for construction and organization of collective memory . . . which is inseparably an active organization of forgetting. (1985:195)

In the organization of collective memory and forgetfulness, there is perhaps no more crucial site of struggle than the school. The Bolivian "normal school" occupies a special place within this project, due to the geometric effect of the socialization that occurs there. Not only are students interpellated into particular subject positions (with varying degrees of success), they are also taught to carry out this same process with their future pupils. Correspondingly, extremely powerful messages delineating available subject positions are encountered both in and out of the classroom. The national, class, ethnic, and gender images which form part of the school curriculum are elements of the "practice producing subjects" (Mouffe 1981) of a key ideological site; they are "discourses predicating identities" (Mato 1992), constructed largely (though not exclusively) through language.

While it is essential that we critically analyze the school's role in producing subjects and predicating identities, we should not lose sight of students' own active participation in the processes of identity formation. The critical tradition referred to above, with its emphasis on the school as an instrument of social reproduction, has often presented students as passive subjects, "positioned" and "interpellated" with such efficiency that even their resistant impulses play into the reproduction of hegemonic forces. But a closer look at the creative interplay of meanings and practices within schools reveals another reality: one which is jointly constructed by students, teachers, and institutional constraints, where students are active agents in the formation of subjectivities, working and reworking the messages offered to them by the school (see also Giroux 1983b). As the following pages will show, the cultural production which occurs in schools is a dynamic blend of elements from inside and outside, above and below; the meanings which Bolivian students carry away from their school experience draw heavily on those which they have brought to it, as well as the fact of combining their experiences collectively within a specific institutional context. Every subject is also an agent, and thus cultural production by schools is simultaneously cultural production by students.

The Research Site and Subjects

The *Escuela Normal Rural "Kollasuyo"* is located on the edge of Los Pozos,[6] an agricultural town of about 500 inhabitants in the heart of the Aymara culture area. It provides a three-year program for rural schoolteachers specializing in primary education, with graduates guaranteed a teaching post by the government. During the research period, there were between 220 and 337 students, nearly half of whom were from Los Pozos or surrounding communities.[7] While most students were of rural origin, a significant proportion came from the urban working class.[8] Of those present throughout the entire research period, 135 were male and 85 female, ranging in age from eighteen to thirty-five, with most students around twenty years old. Nearly half of them lived in dormitories on the school grounds, thirty or forty students to each large room arranged barracks-fashion. Approximately half of those living off school grounds were from the surrounding area; others chose to live in town for reasons of privacy, comfort, or personal freedom. These *"externos"* were almost all male, since female students were strongly encouraged to live in the dormitories.

Faculty members were graduates of similar institutions, having subsequently taught school for several years and then completed a year of postgraduate study, specializing in a particular subject area. A few had some university training as well, usually in education or administration. All school personnel were male except for the librarian, the home economics teacher, the girls' dorm inspector, and the secretary. Several (including the rector) were from Los Pozos or the surrounding area, and most spoke Aymara as well as Spanish. Although most of teachers' contact with students took place in the classroom, the fact that they also lived on the school grounds made them accessible to students outside of class as well.

On weekends, most students and faculty travelled the three to four hours to La Paz, some catching other transportation in the city to return to their home communities. Many rural students had relatives or godparents in the city, and stayed with them on the weekends rather than making the long trip home. Students' parents occupied a wide range of working-class jobs, with 30 percent listing their father's occupation as agriculture. The next most common response was schoolteacher, with 18 percent.[9] Of those who listed an occupation for their mother, 73 percent answered "housewife."[10] Other responses included peasant farmer, schoolteacher, weaver, and market or street vendor. Two-thirds of responding students had themselves worked before entering the normal school, usually in domestic labor, the building trades, agriculture, vending, driving, or factory or office work. At least two students (both men in their early thirties) had worked as interim teachers before pursuing certification at the normal school.

Bolivian schools are divided into two parallel systems, rural and urban. The former are generally considered to be inferior in terms of both material resources and quality of instruction—one example of schooling's role in the stratification of Bolivian society. Normal schools are similarly divided (although graduates of rural normal schools can teach in urban schools, and vice versa). For rural youth seeking an avenue out of farming, mining, or the "informal economy"—in other words, a lifetime of manual labor—the rural normal school is the obvious and often the only choice. The university, while far from expensive by First World standards, is beyond the reach of most peasant or working-class families. Agricultural and technical institutes are virtually nonexistent in the countryside. The division between the normal schools and the universities reflects a system of higher education still largely segregated by class.

Correspondingly, the reasons my informants cited for choosing a teaching career were largely economic; primary among these was the normal school's status as the shortest, cheapest, and least demanding course of study. For many, the normal school represented a level of academic achievement unprecedented in their families, a step up the class ladder into the "professions"; for others, it was the continuation of a family tradition. However, students' reasons for entering seemed to have little bearing on their individual academic success, or even on what kind of teacher they would become. Some who freely admitted that they had entered with little interest in teaching later came to feel that they had found their true calling. Those most frustrated with the school program often seemed destined to become the best teachers, by virtue of the very intellectual restlessness which made them dissatisfied students.

CURRICULUM AND IDENTITY

Students' Expectations: The Ideology of Teaching and Teachers

Since Bolivia's 1952 revolution, social categories have been reformulated and new subject positions created, especially those constellating around indigenous identity. This process is accompanied by conflict, as individuals struggle to negotiate shifting social boundaries and promote their own demarcations of the cultural and political terrain such boundaries inscribe. These stresses were manifest in the micro-community of the normal school, where students were confronted daily with a variety of images relating to nationalism, ethnicity, class, gender, and professional identity. Some responded to these images by incorporating them, others by challenging them, others by privately withdrawing from the academic encounter.

Aside from having to construct and defend a sense of self amidst the antagonistic jostlings of class ambitions, ethnic loyalties, and gender stereotypes, students also had to contend with the ambiguity of their future role as rural schoolteachers. Part of their socialization involved coming to grips with the fact that the achievement of professional status would distance them from their ethnic and class origins, while simultaneously requiring them to live and work among those from whom they had differentiated themselves.[11] Furthermore, their transformation from captive subjects of the educational system into its active agents meant incorporating themselves within an institution which has traditionally threatened the integrity and value of indigenous culture. As future teachers, they would be called upon to disseminate a worldview opposed to the one they were encouraged to identify with as Aymaras. The only choice presented to them as legitimate was to maintain these two ideological loyalties simultaneously, despite their cultural and historical incompatibilities. It may not be an exaggeration to suggest that this dilemma constitutes a collective cultural-psychological crisis which indigenous teachers (and other upwardly mobile indigenous people) must traverse on their journey towards personal and professional identity.

The transformation of identity realized in the normal school, through discourse and other symbolic practices, was aimed at students' acceptance of a particular symbolic order and their own (and others') place in it. It constituted a move out of one symbolic construction (a subject position or set of subject positions) into another, entailing the adoption of the symbolic practices associated with the new identity. Within the normal school, "The Teacher" was seen as a civilizing and modernizing force, a leader (though not really a member) of the peasant community. He[12] was portrayed not only as classroom instructor, but also as mediator, translator, public health worker, and community organizer. As the center of the community, his behavior should reflect the highest moral standard, serving as a model for others. He should initiate and participate in community events, and should teach "enthusiasm, admiration, respect, and patriotism" for Bolivia's national culture, as well as understanding and regard for its regional cultures and customs.

Despite this romanticized image of the lone intellectual carrying the light of knowledge to an unschooled population, Bolivian teachers occupy an ambiguous position within the rural community. Supposedly the hub of community life, they are often occupational migrants without longstanding local ties, and may encounter difficulty in being considered fully integrated members (nor do all even desire such status). While education as an abstract institution is often idealized, the actual system and those it employs are subject to heavy criticism. The image of the rural schoolteacher as self-sacrificing advocate of the people is offset by that of the teacher as agent of cultural imperialism, exploiter of rural communities, and denigrator of their inhabitants.[13] Teachers' high status within the rural community may be all the more resented for being perceived as undeserved (see also Rockwell, this volume).

This dubious reputation is exacerbated by endemic corruption and the fact that, despite the numerous difficulties plaguing the school system, virtually all collective struggles waged by teachers over the last decade have focused not on the quality of training, curriculum, or materials, but on salaries.[14] The revolutionary rhetoric of the teachers' union notwithstanding, those who actually attempt radical changes in the classroom are very few. Students are quite aware of the resignation, cynicism, and lack of preparation with which many of their teachers approach their work, and the criticism to which they are subject from parents and the community. Cognizant of the inherent shortcomings of the mythos of the model teacher, and yet unwilling to abandon the ideals which led them into higher education, the normal school students rode a fine line between aspiration and disillusionment. Interviews revealed strong criticisms of teachers, both individually and collectively, offset by a profound idealism about the profession in the abstract:

> My idea is to add my little bit for the good of education. Education is the first priority, the basic foundation of any country, right? But unfortunately these days our education is turned upside down. . . . From what I've seen, sometimes I think "Lord, the people who get into teaching—." Sometimes I say to myself, "Damn it, I would die for the sake of education," but sometimes . . . it's like I'm going to be, pardon the expression, "one more *lunt"ata* [thief] working for the state," no? (*Laughs*) Yeah, like, sometimes I say, I ask myself, I say to my friends sometimes, "We're each just going to be one more *lunt"ata*, no?"[15]

While the teacher's attitude towards the community was ideally presented as democratic, participatory, and culturally sensitive, teachers were also supposed to command a healthy respect from those they served. This social distance was seen as a necessary element of the teacher's professional image, as explained by another student:

> Sure, we play around, have fun, but, for example when you talk with another person, or with a professor, you become a bit serious, responsible. And besides, you don't talk like that with just anybody, you know? You look for that quality, one who speaks well. You change . . . when you're a kid, you horse around, here among the guys we play but, when we graduate it's very different. You feel like, you're here in the normal school, "I'm going to be a teacher," you know. That always happens, I've really felt it. And that way, people are afraid of you. They're afraid, they talk to us with respect, with awe. Thinking that you really know, right? And then you have to reciprocate in the same manner.

The ideal relation between the teacher and the rural community was presented as one of solidarity and differentiation; the paternalistic terms in which it was frequently described left little doubt that the teacher was with and for the people, but no longer of them. As noted by Williams, hegemony consists of "no mere training or pressure," but rather "effective *self-identification* with the hegemonic forms: a specific and internalized 'socialization'" (1977:118). The disarticulation of students' identities from the peasant community, and their rearticulation to the cadre of professionals who supposedly lead it, was as crucial to their professional socialization as was their training in pedagogical methods, bureaucratic skills, and child psychology.

Uneasy Positionings on the Field of Race—or, "We Have Met El Hermano Campesino and He Is (not?) Us"

Students' notions of their place in the social universe factored heavily into their conceptions of teaching and their ideas of what they hoped to accomplish as teachers themselves. While questions of class, nationality, and gender presented their own problems, students' conceptions of their own ethnicity was perhaps the most complex factor in the evolution of a personal and professional identity. As future "agents of change" in rural communities, their orientation to both traditional Aymara culture and Bolivian "national culture" was key to their initiation into professional status and full citizenship. A large part of the curriculum was thus directly or indirectly dedicated to shaping this orientation.

Although the rhetoric of multiculturalism has largely replaced the openly racist ideology of the past, ethnic stereotypes are still conspicuously present in the normal school curriculum. Sweeping generalizations about the inherent characteristics of *campesinos* and *mestizos* appeared with discouraging frequency, from casual assertions of the "backwardness" and "primitiveness" of nonliterate societies, to more blatantly derogatory statements such as one professor's claim that *campesinos* habitually sleep late and go to their fields in the morning having hardly washed.[16]

The widely accepted notion that *altiplano* (highland) dwellers are reserved and timid, while those of the *oriente* (east) are more open and sociable, was repeated often in the classroom (a seemingly counterproductive move, given professors' frequent lamentations over the lack of student participation in class). In a lesson on reading, one professor linked the higher literacy rates among urbanites to a "linguistic and mental maturity" supposedly lacking in rural dwellers.

Classroom stereotypes which were superficially laudatory often dovetailed with more racist discourses in their narrow conception of indigenous character. Indians were described as honest, hardworking, introverted, long-suffering, and suspicious, while mestizos were considered more intelligent and sociable, but also opportunistic, idle, imitative (due to their lack of an essential racial character), and prone to decadence and degeneracy. Such images were sometimes accompanied by pseudo-scientific explanations of the peculiarities of race mixture, such as the assertion that the offspring of a white man and an indigenous woman will inherit the physical characteristics of the mother and the intelligence of the father (thus the craftiness of the mestizo). The professor who offered this statement qualified it by stating that such offspring "will retain the physical features of his mother, but not completely; he will be better-looking, although not as white as his father." Another professor told students that the central question in that week's reading was, "Which is more intelligent, the mestizo or the *indígena?*" (a few answered, *"el indígena,"* though this was not the "correct" answer). Yet he later asserted that "no one is incompetent, we all have the capacity to learn. . . . It's not a question of race." Occasional messages such as the latter could not negate the restricting effects of the discursive cage—constructed over so many similar lessons—whose bars sharply delimited the official view of Indianness.

In class discussions, a deficit model of indigenous culture predominated. Students as well as professors were likely to characterize indigenous people as conservative, superstitious, and introverted, and to ascribe their marginalization to a "lack of culture." Even when valorized, indigenous culture was usually spoken of in terms of a past "golden age," or positioned in remote historical time; there was little mention of Aymara culture as a contemporary phenomenon, or of its urban manifestations (except in the context of derogatory comments about *cholos*—Indians trying to "become" *mestizos*). When asked what "culture" was, students responded with "those customs that come from our ancestors" and references to the ancient civilization of Tiahuanaco. Aymara beliefs and customs were presented as anachronisms, no longer useful in contemporary Bolivian society. This perspective was brought home during a morning assembly after the holiday of Todos Santos (All Saints' Day, or the Day of the Dead), in which the rector reprimanded students who had left school on Thursday, when only Friday had been given as a holiday. He declared that the administration had been very understanding with regard to students' homesickness and ritual obligations toward their deceased, but insisted that "we're in a time of change; when there are responsibilities, one must leave behind . . . the customs of our grandparents." Those students who had left early were barred from their Monday exams as punishment.

It is not my intention to paint a black-and-white picture of racist professors imposing a reactionary worldview over the resistance of ethnically proud Aymara students. Many professors also strongly identified themselves as Aymara, and confusion over what this implied in the context of the contemporary nation-state was common to both groups. Positive images of indigenous culture were not totally absent from the curriculum; Native Languages class included assignments organized around Aymara proverbs and stories, while in (Spanish) Language class students analyzed books containing public health lessons embedded in culturally sensitive portrayals of rural life. Sometimes it was students themselves who seemed most ready to relegate Aymara culture to the dustbin of history. During the presentation of a sample elementary school lesson, in which the two themes were "Life and Customs of the Aymaras" and "Man's Voyage to the Moon" (themselves forming a rather provocative opposition), some wanted to correct the prepared materials to read "What *was* the name of the god of the Aymaras?" rather than "What *is* the name. . . ?" This was argued solely as a question of wording, not of the current viability of indigenous religion.[17]

The school's tendency, even when ostensibly glorifying indigenous culture, was to weaken rather than strengthen students' identification with it. This was accomplished by (1) presenting it as anachronistic—as a romanticized past with little (positive) bearing on students' present ambitions—and (2) presenting a stereotyped image of the indigenous subject from which students had to distance themselves in order to become true professionals. The inclusion of "Aymara culture" in the curriculum thus often constituted an exercise in contradiction, a superficial valorization of indigenous identity which cloaked a deeper discourse of denigration.

Self-Situating Discourses: Claiming a Place in the Bolivian Ethnoscape

Where do students and professors locate themselves within the unstable scaffolding of ethnic relations that is cobbled together in the classroom? As a relatively new entity on the social scene (indigenous rural professionals), their very existence throws the categories in which Bolivian society is conceived into sharp relief, and yet deep confusion. While the normal school students and (most) professors placed themselves firmly within the ethnic category of *los aymaras*, *los indios*, or *el pueblo indígena*,[18] the picture was complicated by the inclusion of the term *campesino*. As mentioned earlier, the term and its deployment in official discourses have had political and cultural implications which run far deeper than is immediately apparent from the simple gloss "peasant." Its use in the postrevolutionary period as a politically correct substitute for the epithet *indio* was an attempt not only to disallow a key marker of racism from legitimate public discourse, but also to de-emphasize ethnicity in favor of class. It can be viewed as part of a nationalist project of ethnic homogenization, the delegitimization of ethnicity as a basis for collective claims.

On the other hand, since the *ethnic* difference between Aymara/Quechua *campesinos* and white or mestizo urbanites was and is quite salient, this rhetorical drawing of attention towards class and away from ethnicity was not completely successful. Instead, the rather artless substitution of the term *campesino* for *indio* resulted in the former's partial disarticulation from a strictly class meaning, and its rearticulation with a particular image of ethnic identity. The normal school students constructed their adult identities precisely in this historical disjuncture between *indio*, *campesino*, and *aymara*, where class and ethnic subject positions which coincided in previous decades have since diverged, while others which were mutually exclusive now overlap.

The various ways in which the term *campesino* was used in class revealed the ambivalence it inspired, and its ambiguous relation to speakers themselves. Most often, the *campesino* was spoken of in laudatory but not self-identificatory terms, typically as *el hermano campesino* ("our peasant brother"). In one class discussion, a student spoke of discrimination as a question of "*nosotros mismos, nuestra raza*" ("we ourselves, our race"); another supported his view with a denunciation of how "*el hermano campesino*" is treated in city offices, while simultaneously making a subtle but definite shift away from the first-person pronoun. She asserted that without the *campesino* there would be no food for the cities, but also spoke of his deficiencies in language, education, and culture. She maintained that some *campesinos* have moved to the cities and improved their speech and education, but those who stay in the countryside are unable to change these characteristics. When I asked her where she and her classmates fit in this urban/rural scheme, she simply replied that not all were "from the provinces" (she herself was from a mining area).

Those students who *were* from the provinces tended to be less equivocal about their relation to the *campesino*. One girl, in a class presentation of rare eloquence for a rural female student, consistently spoke of the *campesinos* as "we," the ones who work and fight for the homeland while the whites avoid fulfilling their patriotic obligations. She indignantly recounted how "the politicians deceive the Indians in their campaigns, and then afterwards forget all about us." The professor's response, however, displayed the familiar mix of solidarity and distance, as he related how during the War of Independence the Indian's illiteracy made him incapable of analyzing the political situation, so that he ended up being utilized by forces on both sides.

Riding the line between the linked/opposed discourses of "*el **hermano** campesino*" and "***nuestro*** (our) *pueblo campesino*" was a touchy business, often provoking strong reactions from students when most other subjects failed to do so. One professor began a lesson on "factors impeding national development" with the question, "Why do the *campesinos* not pay their taxes?" This drew an immediate wave of protest, as students argued indignantly that it was a bad question, that the *campesinos* do pay, it's the upper class that doesn't. The professor, seemingly taken aback by the forcefulness of this reaction, hastily concurred, agreeing that "we have always paid, because they have always exploited us."

The "discourse of distance" remained present in a variety of guises, however. Sometimes it was wrapped in a progressive model of social change, informed by an awareness of the very real social barriers between peasant and teacher; thus advice for new teachers entering rural communities included: "With the peasant brother one never imposes, one should only suggest." On the other hand, the term *campesina* was sometimes employed for hurtful ends within the girls' dorm, and professors also occasionally fell into such usages, as did one who spent several minutes rebuking the class over the dirty state of the classroom and then exclaimed: "The *campesino* has just one room, with his cooking stove, etc.; he has no idea of what tidiness is, what organization is—but we are *high school graduates*."

Despite students' and professors' awareness that they constituted a new social phenomenon (as evidenced by comments like "Before, teachers were not of our race"), the topic of their problematic position in Bolivia's social structure remained submerged. In class discussions about discrimination, development, exploitation, and so on, the question of how they defined themselves in relation to such issues seemed frequently on the verge of being addressed, and yet never was. During Sociology class, one boy asked the difference between *indio* and *campesino*; the professor replied that it was merely a difference in terminology. Another student then asked if, when a *campesino* goes to the city, he stops being a *campesino* or goes on being one. The professor answered resolutely that he goes on being a *campesino*; the peasant cannot change his essence no matter how much he might imitate city dwellers. The first student objected, but the professor overruled him, reiterating that the *campesino* might live according to urban customs, but he remains a *campesino*. The implication for the students themselves—many of them children of peasants, supposedly in the process of being transformed into professionals—lingered in the realm of the unspoken, and the discussion ended there.

Language: The Golden Past and the Corrupt Present

Students' ambivalent position with regard to the *campesino* contrasted with their unequivocal identification of themselves as Aymara. One of the strongest markers of ethnic identity is language; correspondingly, it was largely because students spoke Aymara, or had grown up in homes where it was spoken, that they considered themselves natural members of this group. Attitudes toward the use of indigenous languages in school have greatly improved in recent decades, and Bolivia has thankfully left behind the days when children were physically punished for speaking their native language in class (often the only language they knew). Nevertheless, increased tolerance of Aymara does not mean that it now enjoys equal status with Spanish.

The normal school's treatment of Aymara, and of students as Aymara speakers, was fraught with contradictions. The rector chose to reprimand students the morning after their Independence Day parade through town because their banter during the supposedly silent procession had "not even been in Spanish!" He reminded them that they should be constantly practicing Spanish, since it was destined to become a universal language, whereas if they spoke Aymara when they travelled to other countries people wouldn't understand them. Whatever the validity of this last assertion, the unmistakable implication was that their horseplay had been even more vulgar and reprehensible for having utilized Aymara.

Students' Aymara identity received most of its official recognition in Native Languages class, where positive images of Aymara language and culture were regularly reinforced. Celebration of the Aymara language, however, was offset by the attitude toward students' own speech. The teacher, Professor Ramírez, had great respect for the Aymara language and was a stickler for it being spoken "correctly," that is, as it was spoken before the Spanish Conquest. He was fond of statements like "before the Spanish arrived, people spoke Aymara well," and "the Aymara language is becoming completely distorted," and frequently lamented that Aymara was losing its structure and "essence" in the mouths of speakers who corrupted it with Spanish borrowings.[19]

Thus a common practice of his was to ask students how to say something in Aymara—something which seemed deceptively easy to them, as native speakers—and then reject their responses as examples of Spanish influence. Not only were his "correct" forms often unfamiliar to students, but some of those he rejected were extremely common even among monolingual Aymara speakers.[20]

Though often frustrated and nonplussed at their professor's rejection of what seemed to them obviously correct Aymara, the students seldom challenged his pronouncements. But when he told them that the word for "potato" was not the familiar *ch'uqi*, but rather *amka*, some found this impossible to tolerate and insisted that in this region it was *ch'uqi*. Generally, however, this pedagogical technique made students reluctant to speak, feeling (with some justification) that the drills were designed to trip them up.

Students were frequently told, both in their classes and in their lives outside of school, that they spoke Spanish badly. It was true that many displayed a marked Aymara accent, and had trouble distinguishing between Spanish phonemes *d/t*, *k/g*, *e/i*, and *o/u* (which are not significant contrasts in Aymara). Even those who spoke Spanish fluently spoke a variety quite distinct from the standard, phonologically, morphologically, and grammatically. But students were given no systematic ear training or language drills to overcome this; they were simply reminded on an ongoing basis that their Spanish was deficient. Then, after years of being told that they spoke Spanish badly, students entered Native Languages class (instituted for the purpose of valorizing and legitimizing their native language), only to be told that they spoke Aymara badly as well. Code-switching was considered a result of linguistic deficiency or laziness, rather than creativity. Bilinguals were perceived not as versatile and linguistically skilled, but rather as lacking full competence in either language.[21] As evidenced by students' linguistic proficiency in a variety of contexts, this perception was due more to their use of nonstandard versions of both languages than to actual lack of communicative competence.

Even while Professor Ramírez extolled the beauty of Aymara and emphasized that it was in no way inferior to other languages, it always seemed to appear as the "deficit case" in his examples. He spoke of Spanish phonemic distinctions that do not exist in Aymara, but never of the Aymara ones that were lacking in Spanish; and it was always the hypothetical Aymara speaker who did not understand because of his lack of Spanish, never the converse. Aymara was presented as a noble and highly developed language whose contemporary speakers were incapable of doing it justice; on the contrary, they displayed "an anemic cognitive capacity, due to the limited linguistic conduct of the inferior social strata, where mothers pass their own inadequate speech habits on to their children, leaving them unprepared for the middle-class linguistic environment of the school."[22] In this context, the linguistic "shame" felt by some, as described by this male student, is hardly surprising:

The girls are ashamed to say they can speak Aymara. That is, in class they deny they can speak it well, or they just don't talk. But when they leave class, in the dorm, say, or in the street, they'll be talking with their friends, all in Aymara. I don't know, it's a big defect, one that hurts the person himself, hurts our own class, we're denying our own culture. If I know something, I have to say so. . . . But, I think it's also a product of how they've taught us ever since grade school . . . how they mold one's character to despise what is his own.

While Native Languages class provided official recognition of students' shared Aymara identity, it delegitimized their own linguistic expressions of that identity. Their dilemma recalls Clifford Geertz's observation that "[f]or any speaker of it, a given language is at once either more or less his own or more or less someone else's . . . a borrowing or a heritage; a passport or a citadel" (1973a:241). While Spanish was portrayed as a passport into a superior lifestyle and identity, students' own variety of Spanish was vulnerable to scrutiny and disapproval, likely to be rejected at the social border. Aymara, on the other hand, was offered as something "their own," but in the sense of a museum piece which could be admired but not touched; the reality of its use as a casual means of daily communication was viewed as a degradation of all that made it admirable. As a result, students were left with no form of linguistic expression which they could both own and use as a source of power.

The Bilingual as Neurotic

Central to the ideological environment of Native Languages class was a trope which I mentally entitled "The Bilingual as Neurotic," after the image repeatedly evoked in class lectures on bilingualism and its social and psychological consequences. While the effort to address language loyalty and related issues in class might be applauded, such attempts left the impression that bilingualism was an inherently pathological condition. Professor Ramírez would often cite various authors on how speakers' negative feelings toward their own language led them to reject their own identity and believe themselves inferior; while the references were to elementary pupils, they were disturbingly apropos to his own comments on the normal school students' defective language habits.

Encouraging the class to reflect on the dilemma of conflicting language loyalties, he asked them, "When we speak two languages, how do we feel? On the side of Spanish, or on the side of Aymara?" One girl whispered "Aymara," but most of the boys answered "Spanish," one adding, "because we do our school-work in Spanish" (a more appropriate answer might have been that it depends upon the context in which one happens to be speaking). Professor Ramírez explained that "this psychological complex affects the bilingual, while nothing happens to the monolingual. . . . Bilingualism is a kind of solution, a compromise, an alternating between situations, when there are conflicting loyalties in the individual." These "conflicting loyalties" could supposedly lead to "linguistic self-hatred," in which:

the individual rejects and detests his own language. There is a restructuring of the personality in accordance with the patterns of the new group into which he wishes to integrate himself. He will abandon the cultural values and ideas of his original culture. . . . That' s why we, being Aymara, no longer want to be Aymara, we want to be Spanish. . . . Similarly, the Spaniards want to be English. . . . An Aymara comes to exploit his fellow Aymaras, to hate his own language. (Excerpt from a class lecture)

Monolinguals, on the other hand, were portrayed as "*tranquilos*," free of the "psychological ruptures, tensions, and readjustments" suffered by bilinguals. And in the event of a race war, Professor Ramírez asked the class, where will the bilingual stand? With his own people, or with the oppressors? "He must define himself. . . . For this reason the bilingual exists in two worlds, he is unstable, he is in conflict."

Few would deny that bilinguals in a country like Bolivia do in fact confront social and psychological conflicts of the type described above. And yet, one must question the effects of such a one-sided portrayal. Aside from occasional references to teachers serving as translators between the rural community and the urban sphere, bilinguals were never portrayed as skilled, adaptive, versatile individuals whose broad range of linguistic resources provided access to a wide variety of social contexts. Bilingualism was never described as economically, socially, or intellectually advantageous, though one could enumerate myriad examples from Bolivian society. Instead, bilinguals were portrayed as conflicted, unstable, and potentially treacherous, though the bearing of such judgments on the existential condition of students themselves was never explicitly commented upon.

After one day's lengthy exposition on the bilingual malady, Professor Ramírez turned his attention to a girl in the second row and addressed her in Aymara, asking what she thought of this sad state of affairs. In response, he received the customary bashful silence. After a pause, the tension was broken by the laughter of the boy sitting next to her. "Self-hatred," he joked.

STUDENT RESISTANCE THROUGH EXPRESSIVE PRACTICES

Popular Parodies: The Satirical Performance of Ethnic Conflict

Expressions of humor often indicate points of social conflict; like turbulent eddies in the flow of discourse, they reveal the rocks and breaks under the surface. Certain kinds of humor can be read as popular critiques raised against the multiple oppressions of everyday life. The fact that such critiques are indirect and metaphorical rather than overtly oppositional does not invalidate their political significance. On the contrary, it demonstrates how such conflicts, far from being restricted to the strictly political realm, are regularly expressed—and, more importantly, are partially constructed—in everyday practice and discourse.

Popular satire comprises an amalgam of those two extremes that Gramsci (1971) termed "philosophy" and "common sense." Willis and Corrigan note how jokes about oppression, though often seen as trivial or passive responses, may highlight social contradictions in highly significant ways. A joke can be a knifeblade slipped into the interstices of an oppressive discourse; with a humorous twist, the discourse is (albeit momentarily) disarticulated, and possibly rearticulated toward other, more subversive ends. In seeking out these interstices, jokes resist certain kinds of discipline; "forms of 'discourse,' or patterns of control over others . . . can be unlocked or reinterpreted by the joke" (1983:96). In Bolivia, nationalist and ethnic ideologies are favored targets for this sort of unlocking.

Michael Apple (1983:ix) also notes the frequent tendency to overlook the degree to which individuals question and transform the mechanisms of ideological domination. Just as such domination can be subtle and largely unconscious, so can the challenges raised against it. The ways in which the ideological framework governing institutional life is reworked from below may not be perceived as "political" by actors themselves, but rather as "cultural" or even simply "recreational" (though the latter term itself hints at their transformative potential). The richest forms of student resistance are often found in these "cultural" challenges to dominant ideology.

In the normal school, official meanings were transmitted and contested not only in the classroom, but also in ceremonial contexts, where the organization of verbal and visual expression was often more amenable to semiotic challenge. Student performances were filled with subtle and not-so-subtle commentaries on the ethnic, class, gender, and nationalist discourses which made up the ideological environment of the school—commentaries which, in the classroom, were regularly stifled or frozen into rigid slogans. Students' extracurricular critiques relied heavily on the language of parody,[23] with images drawn not simply from indigenous culture, but rather from the disruptive interface where indigenous culture meets the dominant institutions of Bolivian society. The weekly *hora cívica* program presented by students was a frequent context for the ridicule of urban values and practices. Most often, the central performance would be an indigenous Bolivian dance, performed earnestly and with great attention to details of costume. Occasionally, however, students would present a dance favored by urban youth,[24] and this was always an opportunity for gleeful farce. Urban clothes and dance movements were exaggerated to the point of absurdity, in a wordless but pointed rejoinder to upper- and middle-class style.

In a similar vein was a dance called *Doctorcitos*,[25] featuring young men dressed in black trousers and waistcoat, fedora, spectacles, and a walking-stick, often with a florid pink paper nose (suggesting drunkenness) underlined by an imposing moustache of paper or ink. The normal school students' rendition included bespectacled young women as well, in severe white blouse and black skirt, city shoes and nylons, with their hair pulled back into a bun and carrying a clipboard in the manner of an executive secretary. The standard version of the dance features short, trotting steps punctuated every few seconds by an exaggerated bow and tipping of the fedora as pairs of dancers face one another. The overall effect is one of bumbling, drone-like businesspeople whose identical mannerisms and pompous gestures suggest the upper-class products of bureaucracy and overeducation.[26] The portrayal can be read as a potentially subversive de-naturalization of bourgeois norms; by turning them into a comic spectacle, the student performers shattered these norms' naturalized, invisible character, and with it their ideological power to define a social ideal. Borrowing Fiske's terminology, one might say that they weakened the credibility of such norms by foregrounding their discursivity (1989:94).

The richest vein for student satire was not the urban upper-class, however, but rather those with pretensions of upward mobility, especially the middle-class Aymara immigrants who practically define the cultural flavor of La Paz.[27] The practices and values of this group provided students with a bottomless trunk of humorous resource material. One well-received performance featured "The Imperial [Brass] Band of Oruro," a dozen male students in improvised silly versions of urban middle-class dress (complete with the ubiquitous fedora and dark glasses), soundlessly flailing away at their instruments while dancing to the strains of a recorded *morenada* in an unmistakable parody of urban immigrant style. As in much of Bolivia's popular literature, those attempting to cross class and ethnic boundaries drew even sharper ridicule than those who unambiguously occupy society's upper echelons.

In the repertoire of students' expressive practices, there were myriad forms for expressing indignation over both the past era of European conquest/colonialism and the current reality of institutionalized racism. The poems featured in *hora cívica* programs frequently had revolutionary or *indigenista* themes, whether recited in Spanish or in impassioned Aymara with the speaker in full traditional dress. The *tribuna libre* (open mike) periods occasionally showcased (male) students decrying racism, injustice, or the shortcomings of their own education, or eulogizing an indigenous martyr on the relevant historical anniversary. These poems and speeches constituted another channel for the contestation of dominant ethnic and class images, but they seldom provoked the enthusiastic response and full audience engagement that more humorous explorations of conflict did. This may be partly because the more serious performances usually dealt with historical themes, whereas the satirical ones addressed contemporary conflicts well within students' own experience. More importantly, however, the former did not allow the audience the pleasure of producing their own meanings; they were, in Fiske's terms, "readerly texts," providing ready-made meanings for audience members to passively receive. In contrast, students' satirical performances were "producerly texts" which invited the audience to participate in the construction of meaning (1989:103–104). By "showing" rather than "telling," such performances were left open to the multiple social connotations which audience members brought to them.

Student humor reached its highest pitch in the student-produced *veladas*, variety shows which included music, dance, skits, contests with prizes for audience participants, and a play (presented in several acts between the other performances). The mood for these nighttime events was playful and rowdy, in contrast to the (mostly) solemn daytime programs presented on patriotic holidays. The *veladas* presented by students for graduation and Mothers' Day were veritable banquets of ethnic and political satire. One skit lampooned candidates in the upcoming presidential election, gathered together for a television press conference. The boys playing the candidates strutted and pontificated in their best *caudillo* style, insulting each other, making outrageous campaign promises, pandering shamelessly to various groups, and elbowing each other for the most advantageous view of the camera until they were in a collective brawl on the floor.

The centerpiece of this program was the play, a modest little comedy about a working-class Aymara family who sends its oldest son abroad. Some of the play's funniest moments involved the convoluted negotiation of ethnic and linguistic boundaries. One scene featured the parents showing off their son's new passport, which listed its dark-skinned, obviously indigenous owner as "not even mestizo, but white!" as his mother exclaimed in an outburst of maternal pride. In another scene, the younger son attempted to write a letter to his brother, as dictated by his mother. The pair displayed remarkable wit and comic timing in their struggle to render orthographically the illiterate mother's vernacular terms of endearment for her son. The play drew an enthusiastic response from audience members, who were all too familiar with the problems entailed in negotiating two cultures. It spoke to their experience in a way that their sociology class never could.[28]

There are, of course, limits to this sort of cultural resistance. The plays were rehearsed during students' free time, under the direction of the Language professor; they were not integrated into the regular curriculum, nor were their social and political themes made the subject of class discussion (which would probably have ruined their humor value anyway, by making them into "readerly texts"). While fragments of Aymara speech gave them an authentically vernacular tone, and contributed greatly to the humor of the characters, there were no plays performed in Aymara. Moreover, despite the obvious pleasure students took in producing them, the plays were neither written nor chosen by students.

More autonomous expressions of student culture were found in those skits composed by students themselves. One of these (part of an *hora cívica* program) explicitly addressed the teacher/student conflict; it centered on a teacher's frantic efforts to control four oversized pupils, who instead of attending were entirely engrossed by the model cars and other toys they had brought to school with them. After several minutes of ineffective railing, the teacher finally managed to settle them down for a lesson. The lesson itself portrayed what is perhaps the quintessential classroom experience of the Aymara schoolchild: in a litany that every Bolivian student knows well, the teacher tried to teach his obstreperous pupils the five Spanish vowels.[29] However, he could not pronounce them correctly himself;

instead he would intone, loudly and deliberately, "aah—oo—ee—oo—ee!" and when the students repeated this faithfully, shouted "No, no! Aa—oo—ee—oo—ee!" After several repetitions of this exchange, the students finally gave up and went back to their play, eventually knocking over chairs and destroying any semblance of order in the "classroom." Understandably, students drew considerably more amusement from this portrayal of official linguistic hypocrisy and triumphant student intransigence than did faculty members.

In their exploration of the counter-hegemonic potential of playful or humorous public speech events, Bauman and Briggs note that "play frames . . . provide settings in which speech and society can be questioned and transformed" (1990:63). If "an authoritative text, by definition, is one that is maximally protected from compromising transformation" (1990:77), it follows that those texts whose protection is shattered by transformative, subversive satire are made vulnerable to the loss of their authority. In the above episode, the text of the lesson is challenged both by pupils' refusal to acknowledge its authority and by the implication that the teacher is incompetent. Furthermore, the teacher is portrayed as guilty of the very linguistic transgressions which it is his job to correct—a point which several students mentioned as being true of some teachers they had known.

Authoritative utterances are the most vulnerable to ironic reinterpretation, precisely because their authority derives from others' acceptance of it. For students to challenge this authority explicitly was beyond the pale; they could do so only outside the confines of the classroom, in "gossip" or interviews (both framed as confidential, private expression) or in humorous performance (framed as play). Such isolated, seemingly frivolous moments built up an accumulated context of subversive public discourse, functioning as links in an intertextual chain of oppositional meaning which spanned several speech events and held open a counter-hegemonic space over time (Bakhtin 1986). The sentiments engendered within play frames might also be carried over into other, more pragmatic activities; indeed, many of the serious concerns students raised in interviews—teacher incompetence, ethnic rivalries, linguistic difficulties, political corruption—were the very ones burlesqued in student skits.

Of course, not all popular forms are necessarily "progressive." Foley observes that some expressions of student culture not only fail to challenge the dominant ideology, but may actually reinforce it (1990:51). At the same time, any discourse which playfully inverts authoritative meanings strikes a blow against the hegemonic tendency to make the sign "uniaccentual," that is, to reduce it to a single possible reading (Volosinov 1976:23). From this perspective, even a skit whose "satire" consisted of little more than vulgar sexual puns could be considered significant, in its use of the sign's multivocality to express forbidden meanings and resistance to adult authority.

Everhart reasons that cultural forms which center on humor stand in contrast to the reified knowledge of the classroom because they are controlled by students themselves. In deciding "what is funny and what is not, what can be taken to be irreverent and what is sacred," students appropriate an area of school practice to their own purposes—unlike other domains in which their labor, time, and movements are externally controlled and their personal judgment counts for little (1983:162). Everhart celebrates such forms with little regard to their content, even claiming that "this resistance occurs in part . . . from [students'] lack of understanding" about their own role within the reproductive apparatus of the school (ibid.). I prefer to view such forms as evidence, not of students' ideological blindness, but of their capacity for critique (or in Willis' [1981] terms, as "penetrations" of the dominant ideology). The content of their popular expressions reflected the schisms and power relations that run through the larger society; even a seemingly casual practice like cheating on tests can be read as a commentary on the reification and commodification of knowledge and linguistic expression. There is more than indiscriminate defiance of authority at work here.

Folk Culture and Popular Culture

The foregoing arguments, while focusing on members of an ostensibly traditional, rural culture, draw heavily upon analyses of urban popular culture. Thus a clarification of the relationship between popular culture and folk culture would seem germane at this point. John Fiske's insightful analyses of the former have done much to both define the area of pop culture studies and suggest its possible articulation with other areas of social theory. Nevertheless, his oversimplified view of folk culture—indeed, his virtual dismissal of it—is clearly unsuitable to the analyses of a cultural scene like the one under consideration here.

Fiske spells out what he sees as the differences between folk and popular culture:

> Folk culture, unlike popular culture, is the product of a comparatively stable, traditional social order, in which social differences are not conflictual, and that is therefore characterized by social consensus rather than social conflict. . . . Popular culture, unlike folk culture, is produced by elaborated industrialized societies that are experienced in complex and often contradictory ways. . . . Folk cultures are much more homogeneous and do not have to encompass the variety of social allegiances formed by members of elaborated societies. (1989:169–170)

What Fiske fails to account for are those cases in which a traditional folk culture comprises one element *within* a heterogenous national culture, with the resultant conflicting claims on subjects' "social allegiances." In Bolivia, the category of "the folk" rivals that of the nation itself;[30] the folk collectivity which some refer to as "the Aymara nation" is spread across three countries and encompasses over three million people. Bolivian society is *more* complex and contradictory precisely because it is *not* a fully elaborated industrialized society, but rather one in which different modes of production (both material and symbolic) lurch along together in uneasy coexistence. If "popular culture is made at the interface between the cultural resources provided by capitalism and everyday life" (1989:129), then it must be recognized that the "everyday life" of a majority of Bolivians derives largely from folk culture, and that its location in a rural milieu does not exempt it from interfacing with the cultural resources provided by capitalism.

Does this mean that Bolivia's folk culture has simply been transformed into popular culture? Not if one accepts Fiske's assertion that "popular culture, unlike folk culture, is made out of cultural resources that are not produced by the social formation that is using them" (1989:170). A key characteristic of popular culture is that it draws upon forms generated by the dominant ideology to create its own oppositional meanings. But the expressive practices examined above, while resisting, inverting, and satirizing the dominant culture in ways characteristic of "the popular," clearly draw upon an indigenous cultural tradition (though not exclusively) for the resources to do so. This is partly a result of Bolivia's colonial history; many of the centuries-old dances which are most representative of Bolivia's folkloric tradition themselves arose as social commentaries on the realities of colonialism, often in the form of parodies of the powerful. Today, historical conflicts continue to be evoked, through the performance of folkloric forms, as implicit commentaries upon contemporary social ills.

The normal school students' creative use of tradition explicitly engages that tradition's interface with the urban belief systems that threaten it. Tradition is employed, not simply as a cultural refuge from the assault of modern forces, but as "the imaginative reconstruction of the past in the service of current interests" (Scott 1985:146). Parody is a crucial resource in this enterprise, a means of deflating the supposed superiority of urban cultural practices.

A historically situated interpretation of folk practices not only permits an exploration of how they are employed in modern struggles against modern forms of domination; it also provides a clearer picture of the processes of cultural transmission, one less vulnerable to the pitfalls of a theoretically static, romanticized "Andeanism" (Starn 1991). As Foley points out:

> An ethnic culture's cultural practices and forms are . . . whatever the group invent from their present struggle *and* from their past. . . . If "ethnic cultural forms" are produced or created in a historical class context rather than passively inherited, "cultural distinctiveness" becomes problematic and impossible to study without references to ongoing class struggles. (1990:166)[31]

Bolivian folk culture, although maintaining a strong continuity with precapitalist traditions, is hardly isolated from the conflicts of contemporary society. To further complicate the folk culture/popular culture distinction, the predominant resource material for Bolivia's urban popular culture is, precisely, rural folk culture, though considerably reworked by the forces of national and global capitalism. Conversely, in a city made up largely of rural migrants, popular culture achieves its resonances as much through its evocation of the folk aesthetic as from its relevance to life under urban capitalism. In a double-edged process of cultural revitalization and hegemonic incorporation, indigenous folklore has emerged as a defining feature of Bolivian nationalism. While partly a response to cultural pressure from below, this is also a result of the hegemonic mobilization of ethnic resources in the service of capitalism (i.e., tourism).

The mutual feedback between Bolivian rural folk culture and urban popular culture has considerable historical depth. The distinction between the two becomes blurred in such forms as the *Doctorcitos* dance, which comments on the pretensions of modern capitalism by recasting the objects of derision into a traditional form of parody. Not only does popular culture grow out of transplanted folk forms, but folk culture simultaneously incorporates images from popular culture in order to burlesque it.

In Bolivia, official culture, popular culture, and folk culture are tied up in an uneasy relationship which gives rise to conflicting allegiances within and across social groups. Urban aficionados of *el folklore* may eulogize "authentic" rural musical traditions while openly scorning the more popularized strains which draw upon them. Folk musical traditions are maintained in part by government-sponsored festivals and their popularization via the mass media.[32] Given that any large-scale contemporary folk culture becomes a "culture of conflict" simply by virtue of its relationship with the surrounding industrialized milieu, Fiske's assertion that "popular culture is a culture of conflict in a way that folk culture is not" (1989:171) is far too simplistic. In a national context like Bolivia, traditional expressive forms constitute a central site of symbolic struggle, not only for the folk culture's survival, but for control over its meanings and images against those who would appropriate them to hegemonic ends.

Thus we can see that a sharp distinction between folk culture and popular culture is no longer useful once "the folk" begin to participate in wider circles of signification, influencing and being influenced by them. Foley recommends abandoning such rigid dichotomies in favor of examining "the cultural politics surrounding shifting cultural forms and identities in a highly fluid cultural tradition" (1990:199). While Fiske argues that "[t]he idea of the people as an industrial equivalent of the folk is all too easily assimilated into a depoliticized liberal pluralism" (1989:170), a more productive approach might be to conceive of "the folk" as a rural equivalent of "the people," and of "folk culture" as just as conflictive, contradictory, and potentially progressive as popular culture in its penetrations of dominant ideologies.[33]

Teachers and students live out these contradictions in their everyday practice, though at what level of consciousness it is hard to say. Professors' oscillations between praise and denigration of the *campesino*, as well as students' difficulties in defining their own identities, would seem to reveal a certain ideological discomfort. But this is visible only in its social-interactional manifestations; what forms it takes within the "inner speech" of individuals is difficult if not impossible to discern. How much do Aymara students worry about whether seeking higher education really means "denying, abandoning, concealing their origins, their roots, betraying their own" (Oliart 1991:212)? To what degree can a Professor Ramírez distance himself from the psychological disorder he ascribes to the anonymous, generalized bilingual? Do rural schoolteachers privately question the heroic image that casts them as the saviors of the *hermano campesino*? Or their own capacity to fulfill such a role?

Part of the "ethnic identity crisis" students and teachers face can be ascribed to the necessity of cannibalizing old discourses in order to construct historically new subjectivities; as Caryl Emerson describes it: "One makes a self through the words one has learned, fashions one's own voice and inner speech by a selective appropriation of the voices of others" (1986:31). These voices may speak past realities better than present ones, making them less than ideal as materials for the construction of identity. Students must contend with the difficulty of constructing new subjectivities and challenging old ones via a language in which discursive categories are reified and subject positions assumed. As Bakhtin observed: "Language is not a neutral medium that passes freely and easily into the private property of the speaker's intentions; it is populated—overpopulated—with the intentions of others" (1981:249).

Though the focus here is not explicitly a linguistic one, it cannot be denied that expropriating and reshaping existing discourses to one's own purposes is even harder when the language in question is not one's own—when it carries the weight of colonialism, and speakers of nonstandard varieties are stigmatized. In such circumstances, "every linguistic interaction, no matter how personal and insignificant it may seem, bears the traces of the social structure that it both expresses and helps to reproduce" (Thompson 1991:2). Nevertheless, language serves more than a merely reproductive function; in Fiske's words, "language systems are complex and contradictory—their cultural work cannot be confined to the reproduction of the dominant ideological framework" (1989:180).

Clearly it takes more than individual gestures and performances of the type described above to change the structures of an entrenched system. Nevertheless, individual gestures (and small collective ones) reveal how subjects view themselves within such structures. Even when unable (or unwilling) to form explicit critiques of the dominant ideology, the forms of resistance in which students do engage serve as eloquent indicators of how they interpret their own alienation, and where they are able to discern weak points in the structures of hegemony.

Conclusions: Cultural Production and Ideological Articulation in Schooling

A primary function of public education, in Bolivia and elsewhere, is to foster in students a strong identification with the nation, transcending class or ethnic loyalties. But it has been shown that the school experience may strongly reinforce class and ethnic loyalties as well, though more often through the practices of students themselves than those of professors or the official curriculum. Recognition of this fact gives a more balanced and active picture of students' socialization; rather than simply being inculcated with a prefabricated ideology, students bring their own meanings, practices, and values to the pedagogic situation, and the outcome is a conflictive mixture of what they bring and what they encounter there. As Everhart observes, it is not simply the school and its formal organization that constitute the productive system of schooling; nonformalized aspects of student culture, outside the direct control of school officials, play a productive role as well (1983:22).

Students (especially "ethnically different" students) are disarticulated from particular social identities and rearticulated to others via their placement within selective discourses. This process of dis/rearticulation is aimed at producing "citizens"—at weakening those bonds of identity which challenge or compete with the claims of the nation-state, and creating in their place subjective bonds of self-identification as professionals and *bolivianos*. This process, and the naturalization that accompanies it, are manifestations of ideology, understood as "a practice of representation; a practice to produce a specific articulation, that is, producing specific meanings and necessitating certain subjects as their supports" (Coward and Ellis 1977:67).

If this were all there were to it, social reproduction would function easily and effortlessly. However, subjectivity is more than simply "an effect of language" (Giroux, in Walsh 1991:xxii). While social reproduction involves the creation of certain subject positions and subjects' interpellation into them, these positions are not constructed solely within the dominant ideology, to be simply imposed on subaltern groups. Rather, they arise in the space between the two, and their fixation within chains of signification is a never-ending struggle over meaning. Students are social agents as well as social subjects; they bring their own cultural forms into the school, and generate new ones from their contact with the institution itself. While absorbing to some degree the nationalist and ethnic meanings with which school ceremonies and curricula are suffused, students also challenge and rework these meanings within the public arenas allowed them. While holding fast to class solidarities, students also draw upon the meanings and practices of their home culture, valorizing Aymara ethnicity and subverting the urban orientation of the "national culture." Caught in a swirl of historical change, they attempt to forge a coherent identity from subject positions which recent shifts in their nation's class/race structure have brought into unprecedented conjunction.

Ethnographers studying cultural production and reproduction in schools (Willis 1981; Everhart 1983; MacLeod 1987; Foley 1990) have consistently reaffirmed the value of resistant cultural practices in strengthening bonds of collective identity and creating dignity and meaning in students' daily lives. Clearly, many aspects of institutional life act against students' personal dignity and private meanings; it can be argued that the entire ideological project of schooling is built upon a definition of the student as a socially deficient being, whose only chance of achieving full personhood depends upon the intervention of the school. As described by McLaren:

> Classroom lessons tacitly created dispositions toward certain student needs while simultaneously offering to fulfill those needs. For instance, students were made to feel inadequate due to their class and ethnic status and hence the school offered to help socialize them into the "appropriate" values and behaviors. (1986:215)

However, students do not invariably accept the school's implicit, pervasive assumption of their own inadequacy. In the practices described above, we see students taking at least partial control of the social arenas in which they are defined, both as Aymaras and as professionals. Utilizing the subversive strategies of satire, they deflate and de-naturalize official meanings around authority, class, and ethnicity, while simultaneously appropriating for themselves those empowering elements which can be found within the stereotype of "the Teacher." Having more or less voluntarily submitted themselves to the normal school's reworking of their personal identity, students make that reworking into a dialogic process, in which the achievement of professional status paradoxically involves participation in a student-generated culture of resistance.

Recent work in educational ethnography is notable for its recasting of students' resistant practices within a framework that "has little to do with the logic of deviance, individual pathology, [and] learned helplessness, and a great deal to do . . . with the logic of moral and political indignation" (Giroux 1983a:107). Such indignation is evident both in students' parodies of the powerful, and in their own rationalizations of other oppositional practices. Even where it is less explicit, the apparent absence of such "moral and political indignation" does not signify a neat division between those forms of resistance which are politically significant and those which are simply pathological, asocial, or even invisible. As noted by Colin Gordon:

> The existence of those who seem not to rebel is a warren of minute, individual, autonomous tactics and strategies which counter and inflect the visible facts of overall domination, and whose purposes and calculations, desires and choices resist any simple division into the political and the apolitical. (in Foucault 1980:251)

For such acts to enlarge the space of popular practice, rather than simply maintain it as a bulwark against hegemony's further encroachment, they must become collective, public, and informed by a collective awareness of their significance. We can see the glimmerings of such an awareness in the dissident delight which greets student burlesques of official pompousness, as well as in the umbrage provoked by classroom defamations of the *campesino*. The "truth" of such events lies in their potential—a term implying both possibility and the as-yet-unrealized nature of that possibility. Only a perspective which recognizes and accepts both the penetrations and the limitations of popular practice and subordinate ideology can theorize how that potential might be realized. Certainly not all indigenous or working-class practices are in themselves progressive; but the contradictory nature of such cultural expressions is itself a political resource. It makes the purposeful articulation between the theoretical and the popular—which was, for Gramsci, nothing more nor less than politics itself—not only necessary, but possible.

NOTES

Research on which this analysis is based was undertaken from June 1991 to June 1992, with support from the Fulbright Foundation, the National Science Foundation, and the University of Texas Institute of Latin American Studies (Austin). Aside from acknowledging the valuable support of these agencies, I would like to express my gratitude to the students and faculty of the Escuela Normal Rural "Kollasuyo" for their participation in the research.

1. Studies of nationalism and indigenous identity have been influenced by developments in ethnicity theory, and the corresponding move away from a conception of ethnicity as a static classification based on primordial characteristics, towards the realization that ethnicity is both relational and situational (Barth 1969; Williams 1989; among others). The recognition of ethnicity as something constructed in social intercourse and discourse opens it up to questions of ethnic mobility, state–ethnic group relations, and engagement with various theories of subjectivity.

2. Archondo summarizes this view as follows: "If the Indians have any rights that should be recognized, it is the right to stop being Indians so that they can finally belong to the national culture from which they have been separated" (1991:54).

3. Within the past twenty years, various Bolivian revitalization movements have argued that *campesino* is an inadequate term for referring to indigenous people in general. Aside from the demographic shift that has led many indigenous people out of agriculture, the term obscured, behind the reductionist rubric of class, the very cultural differences which such movements wished to emphasize and valorize. While the denomination "Aymara" was rarely used as an ethnic label thirty years ago (Albó 1988), its use has spread along with the growing "ethnic consciousness" among such sectors.

4. A key difficulty in such work is the need to theoretically connect collective phenomena such as nationalism, class conflict, sexism, and ethnic rivalries to the individual, subtle, and often unconscious psychological factors that enter into processes of identity formation. In the present work I focus on explicitly social processes, rather than psychological ones. Nevertheless, I believe that comprehension of the formation and articulation of ideologies in individuals, communities, and nations will ultimately depend upon the integration of socio-political, anthropological, and psychological approaches. For examples of bold efforts in this direction, see Stahr and Vega (1988) and Oliart (1991).

5. Notable exceptions include Masemann 1974 and Hornberger 1988.

6. Names of places, institutions and individuals have been changed to protect the anonymity of the subjects.

7. During the research period, the third-year students graduated, and due to a government moratorium on admissions no new students entered at the beginning of the 1992 school year. Statistical data is taken from a survey conducted during the second half of the research period, with 165 of the 220 students responding. While percentages are therefore not exact, they can be assumed to roughly reflect the composition of the student body as a whole.

8. Perhaps the most telling indicator of class, ethnic, and regional status in Bolivia is the use of the *pollera*: the full, multilayered skirt which is the characteristic dress of Aymara and Quechua women, both rural and urban. When asked whether their mothers wore the *pollera*, 93 percent of students responding answered affirmatively. Furthermore, more than half of female students said that they themselves wore the pollera when not at school.

9. In Bolivia, teaching tends to run in families. A full 56 percent of students responding counted at least one schoolteacher among their close relatives, and 15 percent had a relative or godparent on the faculty of the normal school itself. There were several sibling pairs among the student body, and several students had siblings at other normal schools as well.

10. As in so many surveys, the term "housewife" (*ama de casa*) served as a catch-all category for women not employed outside the home. Of course, in many families engaged primarily in agriculture, neither parent is employed outside the home; many of the mothers listed as "housewives" could clearly be considered "peasant farmers" as well. It is also common for Bolivians (urban as well as rural) to work at more than one job, combining fishing with agriculture and marketing, or teaching school during the day while driving a taxi at night. However, all responses to the question listed only one type of job for each parent.

11. Of course, this was more true for some than for others; for students from families in which teaching was already something of a tradition, their socialization constituted continuity with their origins rather than rupture.

12. This stereotyped image was almost invariably masculine.

13. While I did not witness personal mistreatment of community members by schoolteachers, students and parents regaled me with tales of such abuses.

14. The current conflict over the decentralization/privatization of the school system is an exception (although the threat to teachers' guaranteed employment accounts for much of their opposition), but significantly, even this wave of protest was sparked not by the abysmal conditions of the status quo, but by threats to change it.

15. All selections from interviews have been translated by the author.

16. This offhand defamation provoked a rare clamor of protest from the students, who claimed (many from personal experience) that *campesinos* must often rise at four or five in the morning. The professor refused to cede the point, however, arguing that the students didn't know all areas of the country.

17. This example displays a feature common throughout the curriculum: the taking for granted of ideological assumptions embedded in lessons whose purpose was the highlighting of other (often relatively trivial) points.

18. This was evident not only from markers like language, dress, and explicit affirmations of identity, but also from the innumerable casual usages of first-person pronouns when speaking of this group ("Before the arrival of the Spaniards, *we* were the masters. The Spaniards disinherited *us*"; "Before, there was no education for *us*") and frequent references to "*our* indigenous race," "*our* Aymara language," etc.

19. He was not alone in this estimation; other teachers also made pejorative comments about students' tendency to speak "Aymarañol." Hill has noted a similar tendency among Mexicano speakers, who express solidarity around the indigenous language through an attitude of "lexical purism" which views hispanicized Mexicano speech as spoiled and polluted. She also notes that "lexical purism is largely a losing battle, as precisely those speakers who are most concerned with it are also the most exposed to Spanish influence" (1987:130).

20. The Spanish borrowings he rejected were often centuries old, such as *nayax janiw puirkti* ("I can't"), which incorporates the (phonologically adapted) Spanish verb *poder*. This is essentially equivalent to rejecting as "incorrect English" expressions which incorporate French or Germanic roots no longer recognized as such by native English speakers.

21. Hill (1987) describes similar attitudes among Mexicano/Spanish bilinguals. Walsh (1991:62) also notes how in the United States, claims that bilingual students (and their parents) suffer from "semilingualism" (the inability to speak any language well) persist to the present day, despite an abundance of linguistic and educational research to the contrary.

22. Paraphrased from a class lecture.

23. Basso (1979) and Limón (1982, 1989) have also noted the use of "play frames" to put an ironic and critical twist on the dominant ethnic discourse. Within these performative frames, members of subordinated groups employ their shared knowledge of ethnic and class conflict to challenge the legitimacy of dominant norms and deflate the prestige of the dominant group. (The concept of "framing" performative and narrative events is taken from Goffman 1974.)

24. That is, as an urban pastime, in nightclubs and such. Bolivia's indigenous dances are an omnipresent part of school programs even in urban schools. There is a sharp contrast between the reverence in which even upper- and middle-class Bolivians hold "traditional" indigenous music (and its more modern interpretations), and their scorn for the (nonindigenous) dance music popular among rural youth.

25. A diminutive of "doctor," referring not to medical doctors but to the learned and urbane; it is the title commonly used in Bolivia to refer to lawyers.

26. *Doctorcitos* provides a fascinating modern parallel to the much older *awki-awki* dance, in which boys dress up as hunched old men of European appearance, with long white beards and canes, hobbling about in a hilarious parody of colonial-era elites. While

the accoutrements of upper-class identity have changed, it would seem that they are still mocked in ways remarkably similar to those of centuries ago.

27. This same target for popular humor is found in Peru: Oliart (1991:207) cites Vásquez and Vergara's description of carnival representations of "*la pakina*," a gum-chewing young woman of rural origin recently returned from a stay in Lima, dressed in too-tight, too-bright clothes, putting on airs and belittling her native culture, even denying any knowledge of Quechua (in "¡Chayraq! Carnaval ayacuchano," Lima, CEDAP/Tarea, 1988, p. 248).

28. As the research period came to an end, students were preparing another play, entitled *Miss Ch'ijini*. While I did not have an opportunity to find out much about the piece, the title (combining the high-prestige English term of feminine address with an Aymara word meaning a planted field) suggests a "Pygmalion" sort of theme.

29. Aymara has only three vowel phonemes; thus confusion of the Spanish vowels *e/i* and *o/u* is the shibboleth of the native Aymara speaker. Rural elementary school-teachers typically spend much time and effort trying to eradicate this and other features of their pupils' Aymara accents.

30. Bolivia's indigenous peoples are often referred to collectively as "the oppressed nationalities."

31. This may also serve as a critique of "cultural difference" explanations of minority school failure such as those embodied in Heath (1983) and Philips (1983).

32. On a related (if somewhat more sinister) note, Wara Céspedes mentions how a popular anthem by the *neo-folklorista* group "Los Kjarkas" was appropriated as the musical signature of the oppressive García Meza regime, which came to power via a violent military coup in 1980 (1993:79).

33. Scott argues that the blending and reinterpretation which occurs between those beliefs emanating "from above" and the pre-existing beliefs extant in agrarian societies makes it possible to speak of "folk socialism" and "folk nationalism" just as one speaks of "folk religion" (1985:319).

REFERENCES

Abercrombie, Thomas. 1991. To Be Indian, To Be Bolivian: "Ethnic" and "National" Discourses of Identity. *In* Nation-States and Indians in Latin America. Greg Urban and Joel Sherzer, eds. Austin: University of Texas Press.

Albó, Xavier. 1988. Introducción. *In* Raíces de Ameríca: El Mundo Aymara. Xavier Albó, ed. Madrid: UNESCO/Alianza Editorial.

Apple, Michael. 1983. Preface. *In* Reading, Writing and Resistance: Adolescence and Labor in a Junior High School. Robert B. Everhart. Boston: Routledge and Kegan Paul.

Archondo, Rafael. 1991. Compadres al Micrófono: La Resurrección Metropolitana del Ayllu. La Paz: HISBOL.

Bakhtin, M. M. 1981. The Dialogic Imagination. Caryl Emerson and Michael Holquist, trans. Michael Holquist, ed. Austin: University of Texas Press.

————. 1986. Speech Genres and Other Late Essays. Vern W. McGee, trans. Caryl Emerson and Michael Holquist, eds. Austin: University of Texas Press.

Barth, Fredrik, ed. 1969. Ethnic Groups and Boundaries: The Social Organization of Culture Difference. Boston: Little, Brown and Co.

Basso, Keith. 1979. Portraits of "The Whiteman": Linguistic Play and Cultural Symbols among the Western Apache. New York: Cambridge University Press.

Bauman, Richard and Charles Briggs. 1990. Poetics and Performance as Critical Perspectives on Language and Social Life. Annual Review of Anthropology 19:59–88.

Corrigan, Philip and Derek Sayer. 1985. The Great Arch: English State Formation as Cultural Revolution. New York: Basil Blackwell.

Coward, Rosalind and John Ellis. 1977. Language and Materialism: Developments in Semiology and the Theory of the Subject. New York: Routledge and Kegan Paul.

Emerson, Caryl. 1986. The Outer Word and Inner Speech: Bakhtin, Vygotsky, and the Internalization of Language. *In* Bakhtin: Essays and Dialogues on His Work. Gary Saul-Morson, ed. Chicago: University of Chicago Press.

Everhart, Robert B. 1983. Reading, Writing and Resistance: Adolescence and Labor in a Junior High School. Boston: Routledge and Kegan Paul.

Fiske, John. 1989. Understanding Popular Culture. Boston: Unwin Hyman.

Foley, Douglas. 1990. Learning Capitalist Culture: Deep in the Heart of Tejas. Foreword by Paul Willis. Philadelphia: University of Pennsylvania Press.

Foucault, Michel. 1980. Power/Knowledge: Selected Interviews and Other Writings, 1972–1977. Colin Gordon, ed. New York: Pantheon Books.

Geertz, Clifford. 1973a. After the Revolution: The Fate of Nationalism in the New States. *In* The Interpretation of Cultures. New York: Basic Books.

————. 1973b. The Integrative Revolution: Primordial Sentiments and Civil Politics in the New States. *In* The Interpretation of Cultures. New York: Basic Books.

Giroux, Henry A. 1983a. Theory and Resistance in Education: A Pedagogy for the Opposition. South Hadley, MA: Bergin and Garvey.

————. 1983b. Theories of Reproduction and Resistance in the New Sociology of Education: A Critical Analysis. Harvard Educational Review 53(3):257–293.

————. 1988. Teachers as Intellectuals: Toward a Critical Pedagogy of Learning. Granby, MA: Bergin and Garvey.

Goffman, Erving. 1974. Frame Analysis. New York: Harper & Row.

Gramsci, Antonio. 1971. Selections from the Prison Notebooks of Antonio Gramsci. Quintin Hoare and Geoffrey Nowell Smith, trans. and eds. New York: International Publishers.

Gupta, Akhil and James Ferguson. 1992. Beyond "Culture": Space, Identity, and the Politics of Difference. Cultural Anthropology 7(1):6–23.

Hannerz, Ulf. 1987. The World in Creolisation. Africa 57(4):546–559.

Heath, Shirley Brice. 1983. Ways With Words: Language, Life and Work in Communities and Classrooms. New York: Cambridge University Press.

Hill, Jane H. 1987. Women's Speech in Modern Mexicano. *In* Language, Gender, and Sex in Comparative Perspective. Susan Philips, Susan Steele, and Christine Tanz, eds. New York: Cambridge University Press.

Hornberger, Nancy. 1988. Iman Chay? Quechua Children in Peru's Schools. *In* School and Society: Learning Content through Culture. Henry Trueba and Conchita Delgado-Gaitan, eds. New York: Praeger.

Klein, Herbert S. 1992. Bolivia: The Evolution of a Multi-Ethnic Society (second edition). New York: Oxford University Press.

Limón, José. 1982. History, Chicano Joking, and the Varieties of Higher Education: Tradition and Performance as Critical Symbolic Action. Journal of the Folklore Institute 19(2):141–166.

————. 1989. Carne, Carnales, and the Carnivalesque: Bakhtinian Batos, Disorder, and Narrative Discourse. American Ethnologist 16(3):471–486.

MacLeod, Jay. 1987. Ain't No Makin' It: Leveled Aspirations in a Low-Income Neighborhood. Boulder: Westview Press.

McLaren, Peter. 1986. Schooling as a Ritual Performance: Towards a Political Economy of Educational Symbols and Gestures. Introduction by Henry Giroux. London: Routledge and Kegan Paul.

Masemann, Vandra. 1974. The "Hidden Curriculum" of a West African Girls' Boarding School. Canadian Journal of African Studies 8(3):479–494.

Mato, Daniel. 1992. A Provisional Map of Competing Discourses Predicating Pannational and Transnational Identities in "Latin America," in Times of Globalization. Paper presented at the 1992 Annual Meeting of the American Anthropological Association, San Francisco, 2–6 December.

Mouffe, Chantal. 1981. Hegemony and Ideology in Gramsci. *In* Culture, Ideology and Social Process: A Reader. Tony Bennett, Graham Martin, Colin Mercer, and Janet Woollacott, eds. London: Batsford Academic and Educational Ltd., in association with the Open University Press.

Oliart, Patricia. 1991. "Candadito de oro, llavecita filigrana . . .": Dominación Social y Autoestima Femenina en las Clases Populares. Márgenes: Encuentro y Debate (Lima) 4(7):201–220.

Philips, Susan U. 1983. The Invisible Culture: Communication in Classroom and Community on the Warm Springs Indian Reservation. New York: Longman.

Scott, James. 1985. Weapons of the Weak: Everyday Forms of Peasant Resistance. New Haven, CT: Yale University Press.

Stahr, Marga and Marisol Vega. 1988. El Conflicto Tradición-Modernidad en Mujeres de Sectores Populares. Márgenes: Encuentro y Debate (Lima) 4(3):47–62.

Starn, Orin. 1991. Missing the Revolution: Anthropologists and the War in Peru. Cultural Anthropology 6(1):63–91.

Thompson, John. 1991. Introduction. *In* Language and Symbolic Power. Pierre Bourdieu. Cambridge: Polity Press.

Volosinov, V. N. 1976. Marxism and the Philosophy of Language. Ladislav Matejka and I. R. Titunik, trans. Cambridge, MA: Harvard University Press.

Walsh, Catherine E. 1991. Pedagogy and the Struggle for Voice: Issues of Language, Power, and Schooling for Puerto Ricans. Introduction by Henry A. Giroux. New York: Bergin and Garvey.

Wara Céspedes, Gilka Wara. 1993. *Huayño, Saya,* and *Chuntuqui*: Bolivian Identity in the Music of "Los Kjarkas." Latin American Music Review 14:52–101.

Williams, Brackette F. 1989. A Class Act: Anthropology and the Race to Nation Across Ethnic Terrain. Annual Review of Anthropology 18:401–444.

Williams, Raymond. 1977. Marxism and Literature. Oxford: Oxford University Press.

Willis, Paul. 1981. Learning to Labor: How Working-Class Kids Get Working-Class Jobs. New York: Columbia University Press.

Willis, Paul and Philip Corrigan. 1983. Orders of Experience: The Differences of Working Class Cultural Forms. Social Text 7:85–103.

11

DEBRA SKINNER AND DOROTHY HOLLAND ⎯⎯⎯⎯⎯⎯⎯⎯⎯

Schools and the Cultural Production of the Educated Person in a Nepalese Hill Community

Public education is a fairly recent phenomenon in Nepal. The Rana regime, lasting from 1846 to 1951, purposely kept its subjects unschooled.[1] Only with the restoration of the Shah monarchy to full power in 1951 did the state begin to devote resources to the building and staffing of schools for the general populace. Even by the mid-1980s, the young Nepalis that Skinner followed from 1985 to 1993 were still some of the first in their area to experience state-provided schooling.

While the Rana government considered it easier to control uneducated subjects, and so refused to provide public schools, the government under the Shah kings wanted educated subjects who would work to "develop" Nepal. As we will soon recount, young Nepalis in their school and subsequent careers readily appropriated the development rhetoric presented to them in their textbooks and classroom lectures. In our frequent talks with them, the students passionately identified with the needs of their country and spoke of preparing themselves for a future of good works directed toward the development of their community in particular, and Nepal in general.

But these new schools should not be viewed simply as sites where Nepalis were being molded to the agenda of the state. As has been revealed through many studies largely beginning in the 1980s (see Levinson and Holland, this volume), schools, despite their overwhelming potential for shaping minds, bodies, and social futures, remain a paradoxical tool of control at best. In Nepal, school participants—teachers and students—were often struggling to turn the schools from a site of state control to a site of opposition not only to the state, but also to systems of caste and gender privilege hegemonic in the society. Certainly by the mid-1980s, the school had become a forum for the development of critical discourses on the government, as well as a space for alternative practices of caste relations and for the generation of alternative visions and discourses about caste privilege. Likewise, it had become an important site for the generation of new femininities, largely produced by female students.

Older transmission studies saw children and young people as passive receptacles of cultural values from the past. But here, in this ethnographic view of students in Naudada[2]—the place of our research in Central Nepal—we saw quite the opposite. We saw great activity, including efforts by at least some of the students and teachers, to turn the school against the hierarchies of privilege in Nepal.[3] In reproduction theory, children and young people were the passive objects of schooling, where they learned conformity to dominant relations and social structures (e.g., Althusser 1971; Bourdieu and Passeron 1977; Bowles and Gintis 1976; see Levinson and Holland, this volume, for more details). But this assumption of passivity cannot be maintained for the Naudadan schools. There, in support of the more recent emphasis on cultural production, we saw oppositional efforts against the state and against the mechanisms and legacies of caste and gender privilege.

Students' talk and actions, the foci of this chapter, suggest that schools in Nepal offered potent opportunities for liberation. Yet the story is incomplete without an examination of another side of this search for liberation. Paradoxically, with the advent of public schools and their turning toward what participants viewed as emancipation from oppression, we found new divisions, new distinctions of privilege, and new forms of disdain (what Bourdieu would call "symbolic violence," 1977a, 1977b). We saw an ever-increasing validation of formal education as a source of symbolic capital, giving those who possessed it claims to superior positions and statuses.

Particularly fueled by memories of repressive governments—their denial to the populace of education and free exchange of opinions, and the resultant "unawareness" of the people—students lauded the "educated person" (*paṛhnelekhekī, paṛhne mānche*),[4] and turned away from those left in the "dark." So convincing was the emblematic value of education as both a route to upward mobility and as a shedding of the hated oppressions of the past that we found this notion to be hardly contested by those who had been bypassed by schooling. Such was the valuation of schooling at the time of our studies that the "uneducated person" was someone to be pitied and scorned. Those persons who were not educated even held this attitude toward themselves. Uneducated women, especially, were constructed in political and development discourse as holding back the country. They were also constructing themselves and being constructed as less desirable wives than educated women.[5]

The school, in short, appeared in our studies to be a site of multiple agendas and multiple voices (Bakhtin's heteroglossia), alternative social spaces, and a new sort of person—a person whose knowledge and awareness were thought to contrast vividly with those of the older generations kept out of awareness and political consciousness by the state. Within this complex site that constituted the school, students were produced and produced themselves as "educated persons"; at the same time, they participated in the production of a person outside the school, the person who was uneducated and without awareness.

A Brief History of Public Education and "Educated Persons" in Nepal

The potency associated with formal education surely comes from the memories of past regimes of oppression. From 1846 to 1951, Nepal was ruled by a series of hereditary prime ministers, the Ranas. Naudadans and other Nepalis depicted the Rana era as the reign of a repressive autocracy. Stories abounded of the Ranas' oppressive domination and use of force to keep the populace poor, uneducated, and submissive. Although Nepal was never colonized, the Ranas "cooperated" with British India. By allowing British-Indian influence in foreign and trade policy, the Ranas were permitted to maintain power and extract the country's wealth for their own purposes.[6] Education for the people was not one of them.

Although they established a few Western-type schools in Kathmandu for the sons of elite families and set up one school for the training of lower-level government clerks, the Ranas deliberately prohibited education for the masses. The Rana leaders feared that an educated citizenry would pose a threat to their despotic rule, raising the aspirations of youth who would demand basic human rights and be the vanguard of a revolution (Sharma 1990:4). In the minds of the Ranas, as in the minds of contemporary Nepalis, to become educated was associated with becoming "conscious" (*cetanā*) or politically aware, a dangerous state for the repressed masses to attain. Those who did attempt to educate individuals outside of the narrow confines allowed by the Ranas were imprisoned or fined (Sharma 1990). At the end of 105 years of Rana rule, only 2 percent of Nepal's population was literate and only 0.9 percent of all 6–10-year-old children were enrolled in school (Sharma 1990:6).

In 1951, the Ranas were overthrown in a revolutionary movement to restore King Tribhuvan, of the Shah line of hereditary monarchs, to the throne. Although successive Shah kings banned political parties and repressed opposition to the divine monarchy and its one-party system of government (the panchayat system which lasted from 1962 to 1990), they did work for the expansion of public school facilities throughout Nepal. In the 1960s and early 1970s, with economic aid and encouragement from the U.S. Agency for International Development, the government established a series of educational commissions, boards, and committees to plan and implement a nationwide educational system (Seddon 1987:249–250; Aryal 1970). From the beginning of this process, education for the populace was tied to discourses of economic and social development, modernization, and national identity. Introductory statements in a report on education in Nepal exemplify the associations frequently made in political and everyday discourse among the concepts of education, development, modernization, and nationalization:

> Education is a critical foundation of economic and social development. Universal access, especially to primary education, is among those essential preconditions for any nation's modernization, and expanding that access has long been a priority of His Majesty's Government. (CERID/WEI 1984: foreword)

> Universalization of the first level education is a prerequisite for enabling the rural populace to participate effectively in development activities as well as forging national identity and integration. (CERID/WEI 1984:i)

Efforts at universal primary education resulted in a dramatic increase in basic literacy and schools. In 1950, only 8,500 students (less than 1 percent of the eligible population), were enrolled in primary schools; by 1989, there were well over a million students enrolled in the first through fifth grades.[7] The number of primary and secondary schools in the country also increased dramatically, from 332 in 1950 to 15,834 in 1989. Correspondingly, literacy rates increased during this same period from 5.3 percent in 1952/54 to an estimated 36 percent in 1989.[8]

In these government schools, *bikās* (development) became the new mantra, and education the means to bring Nepal into the modern age (*ādhunik kāl*). To this end, the educational system promoted by the Shahs in the largely agrarian nation was designed to improve people's technical and agricultural skills (Aryal 1970; Beach 1990), and to promote loyalty to the nation-state and the one-party panchayat system of government. It was not oriented toward producing a politically "aware" or "conscious" (*cetanā*) populace. As the Ranas before them, the Shahs repressed any open expression of ideas interpreted as subversive to their rule. In the early 1960s, King Mahendra banned political parties, portraying them as alien to Nepalese traditions, and denouncing them for disrupting the unity and harmony of the nation-state and the identity of its people (Burghart 1984:120). Political demonstrations, subversive media, and talk against the royal family and the panchayat government were suppressed through force.

Force notwithstanding, the government could not still all dissident voices and movements. College campuses became the sites of the most overt opposition to the panchayat system, and students the vanguard of a movement for democracy and a multiparty system. Throughout the panchayat era, students joined campus organizations associated with the banned Congress Party, pro-Chinese Communist Party, or pro-Soviet Communist Party, led political demonstrations, denounced government policies, and worked as activists in the rural areas, spreading their views among the people (Shaha 1990). Many of these student leaders were jailed and some killed. The panchayat system was maintained in the face of growing criticism and opposition until 1990, when hundreds of thousands of people joined together in the Pro-Democracy Movement that succeeded in overthrowing the panchayat government. The ban on political parties was lifted and multiparty elections were held in 1991. The coming of *bahudal* (the multiparty system) brought freedom of expression, a clamor for human rights and equality, and an anticipation of better things to come for all of Nepal's people.

Our research in Nepal made clear to us that the panchayat period, and the Rana era before that, were associated in people's minds with painful repression of dissent and numbing restriction of access to information crucial for the good of the people (Holland and Skinner 1995). With the rise of public schools, education had come to be seen as necessary for getting a good job and doing "good work" (*rāmro kām*) for the country and its people. Due to these memories of the past, however, it was also viewed as a means for people to gain access to knowledge and information, attain the "consciousness" necessary to overthrow repression, and reach parity with people under less oppressive governments. These meanings of being "educated" had consequences for the ways "educated persons" were being produced, and for the ways they in turn (re)produced other important discourses and practices such as those of caste and gender. It is at this point that we turn to an examination of the construction of educated persons in specific sites and activities in Naudada.

COMMUNITY AND THE ADVENT OF SCHOOLS IN NAUDADA

Naudada is the pseudonym we give to a subdistrict unit (formerly a panchayat) in central Nepal, some eight hours of travel west from Kathmandu. Naudada consisted of twenty square miles of rugged terrain, ranging in elevation from 800 feet in the low-lying river valleys to over 4,000 feet atop the highest ridge. It was located in the middle hills region of Nepal where, at the time of our studies from 1985 to 1993, subsistence agriculture on upland terraces and low-lying irrigated fields was the primary occupation of over 90 percent of the approximately 4,500 people who lived there.

Naudadans were predominantly Hindu and followed the many practices and rites associated with Hinduism in Nepal, including restrictions on caste interactions and on women's privileges vis-à-vis men.[9] There were approximately thirty hamlets or gaons (*gāũ*) in Naudada, most of which included inhabitants of only one caste.[10] These gaons were separated from one another by distance or distinct boundary markers. Although discrimination based on caste was banned in Nepal's Constitution, in local talk and practice, Naudadans divided themselves into *jāt* (caste/ethnic groups).[11] Of these the Bahun and Chetri maintained the highest ranking in the caste hierarchy, claiming a ritual and moral superiority based on Hindu notions of purity and pollution. Together these two groups constituted about 57 percent of the population of Naudada and held the majority of land and wealth. Ethnic groups of Tibeto-Burman origin (Newar, Gurung, Magar, Tamang) were thought to fall between these highest or "biggest" (*thulo*) castes and the ones ranked at the lowest rungs of the hierarchical ladder. These lowest-ranked castes were called "smaller" castes (*sāno jāt*) and were considered "untouchable" by many Naudadans. They included individuals who still followed the occupations historically associated with these castes: Damai (musicians and tailors), Sunar (goldsmiths), Kami (blacksmiths), and Sarki (leatherworkers). Caste restrictions on marriage, commensality, entering homes, and physical contact were practiced by many Naudadans in a number of contexts, but were relaxed in others.[12] Importantly, they were infrequent in places like the school.

Marriage patterns and gender relations were influenced by Brahmanical[13] and patriarchal ideas and practices. Because families of one gaon were often related through patrilineal ties, and because marriages were exogamous, a woman married out of her natal home (*māita*) and travelled hours or even days to reach her husband's house (*ghar*). Sons were entitled to stay with their parents, inheriting land and other property, while daughters had few rights over these posses-sions.[14] Due to these practices, parents tended to invest their scarce resources in the education of sons who were likely to stay with them after marriage, rather than daughters who were destined to leave.[15]

The effects of Nepal's economic development programs and foreign donor agencies' efforts could be seen in and near Naudada. In the 1980s, foreign aid helped build a large hydroelectric plant and factories not far from Naudada. Within a two-hour walk from the center of Naudada, roads were built in the last two decades to link trade between cities and towns in Nepal and India. Roads brought the type of "development" common to roadside bazaars: merchandise from foreign markets, teashops, electricity, cinema halls, "English boarding schools," buses and cars, news stalls. Within Naudada these accoutrements of development were not evident, but local development workers were present, actively encouraging Naudadans to practice "scientific" (*baigyānik*) approaches to health and to agriculture, livestock, and forest management.

Naudada received its first public schools some twenty years ago. In the last two decades, public schools have been established in Naudada with financial support from the government, Naudadans, and donor agencies. In 1947, some Naudadan families had established a Sanskrit language school (*bhāṣā pāṭhśālā*) for the purpose of religious and language instruction, but it was effectively restricted to sons of higher-caste families. Before the coming of public schools, some families hired Bahun priests to teach literacy and religion, and a few wealthy families sent their sons to Kathmandu to attend boarding school. But it was not until 1974, when the language school was converted to the first primary school, that both girls and boys of all castes had access to education. Nevertheless, children's equal access to school was effectively limited by many factors, including required travel time, parents' attitudes toward education, lack of money, and the family's need for children's labor, especially that of girls, in the home and fields.[16]

Over the next twenty years, eight more primary schools (grades 1–5), a lower secondary school (grades 6–7), and a secondary school (grades 8–10) were built with government and donor agency funds. Because of these schools and night literacy classes sponsored by donor agencies and the government, the overall literacy rate in Naudada increased, from 28 percent in 1979 to 39 percent in 1990. Correspondingly, the literacy rate among females during the same period rose from 4 percent to 20 percent.[17] Although comparable statistics do not exist on rates of literacy by caste, from observations and demographic data collected during our fieldwork, it seemed few men over twenty-five from the lower castes, and virtually no women that age and older were literate. In general, those who were literate were mostly under twenty-five, higher caste, and male. In the late 1970s and 1980s, however, an increasing number of girls and members of the lower castes enrolled in school and completed at least the primary grades.[18]

SCHOOL SPACES, TEXTS, AND DISCOURSES

From our perspective, Naudadan schools appeared sparsely furnished and austere. They were long buildings made of stone walls, concrete floors, and slate or tin roofs. Since there was no electricity, light came only from a few small windows. Some lower grades had no chairs or desks. Children in these classrooms sat on mats on the floor, rocking back and forth, reciting from their readers in the dim light. Higher grades had tables, benches, and blackboards.

The schools were located at some distance from any cluster of houses, physically and symbolically separated from the sphere of family and gaon relations. Although they provided another local arena for Naudadan political factions to play out their battles, schools also transcended local relations since they were the province of the state. Along with the meager furnishings were photographs of Nepal's king and queen, the flag of Nepal, posters of national cultural heroes, and emblems of development—all of which evoked a national identity and orientations beyond gaon life (see Cohen 1971; Johnson 1980, 1983).

The National Education System Plan of 1971 introduced a curriculum to be used throughout Nepal. In large part, this curriculum served to promote the hegemony of the Hindu nation-state, and its rule by members of elite Bahun and Chetri families. All school books were written in Nepali, the official national language. Through the national curriculum, schoolchildren of diverse ethnic groups, language backgrounds, and religions were introduced to Hindu folktales, rituals, and festivals. They read in Nepali stories about Hindu gods and epics. These same texts introduced the non-Hindu as well, in chapters that highlighted the religion, festivals, foods, customs, and ways of dress of various ethnic groups in Nepal. These depictions served mainly to construct these groups as "other" to Hindus of caste origin, and to circumscribe them in specific locales.

Although the texts in some ways (re)produced differences among Nepal's people, in other ways they worked to forge a national identity and feelings of unity. Stories detailed the history of Nepal's unification and the great kings and statesmen who led Nepal to its present status as a nation-state. Stories and poems evoked the beauty of "our Nepal," glorifying its magnificent rivers and mountains. Schoolbooks designed for "Moral Education" class proclaimed that all people in Nepal are one ("All people's blood is red") and "All religions follow God (Ishwar)."

National identity and nation-building efforts were tied to development and to religious merit. This merit could be earned by those individuals who did the "good work" of developing the country. Lessons exhorted students to perform "good works" for the sake of "our country" and "our society." Specific teachings urged them to practice good hygiene, go to health posts, reforest, have "happy families" (i.e., small families), build latrines, and otherwise work to develop Nepal and themselves as good citizens. Before the political revolution of 1990, students read of the glories of the one-party system and how it worked to benefit all of Nepal's people ("The panchayat works for everyone to get along and to give help to everyone").[19]

Even as these texts framed this vision of unity, diversity was again created through the ways they represented and juxtaposed rural and urban life. "Villagers" were idyllically depicted as working together cooperatively and without conflict, but this positive, though fictional, image of "the villager" faded in comparisons with urban dwellers. Certain pictures and lessons served to construct social differences between those living in the "developed" world and those residing in "the village" (Pigg 1992:499–503).[20] Classes in Nepali, science, moral education, social studies, and so forth, reinforced the association of the urban world of *bikās* (development) with "modern" (*ādhunik*) ways of thinking, and of the rural areas with "traditional" (*purāno bicār*, literally, "old ideas") ways of life. The "village," the setting for many stories, was often portrayed as peaceful and idyllic, but the final emphasis was generally on the ways in which the lives of rural dwellers could be improved through development and modernization.

The teachers at the school site, like the texts, did not present a single, homogeneous voice or perspective. Teachers at the primary schools in Naudada were upper-caste Naudadan men who had passed the tenth grade and the national examination which entitled them to the School Leaving Certificate (SLC). Teachers of the higher grades (grades 6–10) were males with college degrees. Many of them were from areas outside of Naudada, and boarded with Naudadan families when school was in session. Most Naudadan teachers who had attended college had been members of various student organizations at the campuses where they had studied. They often continued their political activism in Naudada by advocating at school and elsewhere for political and social change. They went beyond the idea of simple unity expressed in the school texts to promote more "progressive ideas" (*pragati śīl*) about equal rights, especially for people of different castes and gender. The teachers did not present a united voice to the students, however, as some disputed these aims and others were in contention about the political means to accomplish these goals. Although some teachers were critical of the government for its specific development policies, they did not call into question the notion of *bikās* itself. In their debates, they still reproduced the discourse of development and the distinction between the "modern" or "progressive" and the "traditional" or "superstitious." For example, they promoted the benefits of technology, and espoused biomedical models of health and treatment over local beliefs about disease causation and healing.

From the above account, we begin to see the truly heteroglossic nature of the school site. Bakhtin's (1981, 1984) view of heteroglossia goes beyond simple notions of one homogeneous, essentialized voice coexisting on an equal footing with other such static and monologic voices. Although the dominant discourse in the Naudadan schools was one of development and modernization, other perspectives and voices existed, even within the same text or person, and were intertwined and dialogized in complex ways. No single text or teacher or student gave voice to one consistent perspective. A "single" text contains several voices, some of which may be submerged, counterposed, or in contradiction to others. It is within this space of contested and dialogic encounters, within both its constraints and its sets of possibilities, that persons author notions of themselves and others, and (re)create meanings and relationships.[21] This heteroglossic space of the school site provided an important context for Naudadan schoolchildren's production of identities and (re)productions of notions of the "educated person."

SCHOOLS AS A SITE OF NEW RELATIONS AND ALTERNATIVE IDENTITIES

Over a thirteen month period in 1985–86, Skinner interviewed and observed thirty-two boys and girls, aged 8–17, from both high and low castes. She revisited them three more times over the next seven years, and listened to their stories about their ongoing lives: accounts of marriages, hardships, raising children, continuing education, seeking employment, participating in political meetings, and other events.[22] Our interpretations of their notions of themselves as "educated persons" or "uneducated persons" and the ways they (re)produced educated identities come primarily from this talk about their lives and from their songs,[23] as well as from observations of them in their home, school, and community contexts.

In 1986, the children who were in school made it clear that being a "student" (*bidyārthī*) was a very significant part of their (future) lives and self-understandings. For them, education was a major goal in life, and the necessary means to achieve their other goals: making their futures bright, developing the country, serving the people and king, "earning a big name" (i.e., becoming famous), and becoming a good citizen (*asal nagarik*). To questions about their future plans, students drew upon the discourses of nationalism and development predominant in school texts and pervasive in other media and talk. Shrawan, a sixteen-year-old Chetri boy stated, "In the future after getting an education, I would like to do development work and make my name well-known." Manohar related similar plans: "[After getting more knowledge (*gyān*)], my next duty will be to serve for the benefit of my motherland (*mātri bhūmi*), so I will spend most of my time developing my country." Several of them viewed development work as equivalent to religious work. For example, Maheswor, a student of sixteen who wanted to be a doctor, pilot, or engineer, stated: "For me, religious works are producing electricity, starting big factories by harnessing big rivers, and building irrigation facilities."

Female students' replies also emphasized the theme of service to the country. Most of them hoped to become doctors, teachers, or office workers. One Chetri girl of fourteen wanted to study diligently so she could become a doctor and "serve the sick people." (She also was determined to follow what she learned from "family planning," that two children and no more make a "happy family.") Another Chetri girl of fourteen wished to serve the poor people; her cousin hoped to become a scientist.

Both sites and selves can be contested and heteroglossic.[24] At times, students identified themselves as "villagers" (*gāūle*), noting their love for Naudada, respect for their parents, and reverence for certain traditions and customs (*riti*). When they were away from Naudada and rural ways of life, they expressed a romantic nostalgia for the gaon.[25] However, as reflected in other self-representations, many of these students also constructed themselves in line with the dominant school discourse of development and nationalism. They portrayed themselves as educated (*śikṣīt, paṛhne*), and located themselves within the "modern" (*ādhunik*), "developed" (*bikāsī*), "scientific" (*baigyānik*) world of "progress" (*unnati, pragati*). They spoke of the "traditional" (*purāno bicār*) or "superstitious" (*andhavisvās*),[26] or "conservative" (*rūṛhibadī*) world that many of them equated with their uneducated (*aśikṣīt, napaṛhne*) parents' way of life—one oriented more to farming and local affairs.[27] Male students, especially, aligned themselves in this way. Jit, a ten-year-old boy from the Gurung caste, stated:

> During their (parents') time, education was not important, but now there are many new schools everywhere, and these educated (*paṛhne*) people know a lot more things than do uneducated (*napaṛhne*) ones.

Another student told Skinner in 1986:

> There are some differences in my opinions from my parents'. Let me give some examples: I don't agree with them about religious things, about health, about education, and about conservative (*rūṛhibadī*) thinking.

Prajun, a Chetri boy who described himself as one "who wants to develop the gaon and who wants to give people their rights and serve them," made the distinction between himself and his parents in this way:

> My parents have old ideas (*purāno bicār*), and we search for new things. Yesterday is our parents' time. . . . The world was old yesterday. Now is the new world. That is why there are a lot of differences [between my parents and myself].

These kinds of distinctions were seldom disputed by Naudadan adults. The parents and grandparents of these children compared uneducated people to the "blind" who "sit in darkness." They spoke of educated persons as ones who had their "eyes opened" and a "bright future" before them. Bhim Bahadur, a Damai who earned his living by farming and tailoring, stated: "I am staying in darkness for not having studied. I didn't know anything. If I don't educate my sons and daughters, they will always be in darkness like me."[28] Although they did not always desire or could not always afford to send all of their children to school, most adults said they valued education. They recognized that an educated son could earn badly needed income, whereas an uneducated son could earn little to support the family. Where their daughters were concerned, parents had begun to see education as a prerequisite for being able to arrange a good marriage to a suitable man.

Not all about the "modern age" was viewed positively, however. Many adults lamented the bad habits (e.g., drinking, smoking, gambling) displayed by people "today," but they attributed it in part to the Kaliyug, the current era in the Hindu cycle associated with destruction and moral decay. They sometimes ridiculed "developed" livestock and vegetables, claiming the superiority of their own local stock and species. But all in all, adults had joined the quest for "development," and viewed education as leading to "brighter futures" for their children than they could have hoped for when they were young. They too took up the temporal idiom of "now and then" to locate the distinctions they saw emerging. Some parents observed that, "Times change, the system changes, people become different." They pointed out to us that since the time when they were young, caste restrictions and discriminations had lessened, the political system had changed, and women could now be educated and get jobs. Naudadan adults, along with the students, were co-constructing meanings of the "uneducated person," "tradition," and "village" in terms of a temporal idiom which associated these notions with the past. The "educated person" was associated and elaborated in tandem with notions of "the modern age," "development," and "urbanization" (see also Pigg 1992).[29]

ALTERNATIVE VISIONS OF CASTE AND GENDER

Schools did not only constitute a place for reading textbooks and listening to lectures by the teachers. They constituted a space in which different sorts of relations were possible and encouraged, different weights were placed on familiar forms of authority, and new identities were imagined. Yet students were not united in their vision of possible new worlds and identities. For girls, gender was the crucial focus of (re)creations and imaginings; for boys it was caste. In their talk and activities, female students drew upon notions of the educated person to produce novel forms of femininity that were in contest with older models. For boys, (re)constructions of the educated person intersected more with what it meant to be a male of a particular caste than with being male per se.

School was not the only arena for the production of novel views of gender and caste, but it was a significant one. Caste discrimination and segregation were not overtly practiced in school settings. At school, children ate and drank with members of other castes. Despite expectations outside the school, in school lower-caste children offered water to children from higher castes who accepted and drank it. Some higher-caste individuals purposely took water and food from lower-caste classmates to demonstrate their beliefs that "all men are alike."[30] Megh, a Chetri boy who wished to become a doctor, explained:

> Although people say not to drink water given by Damai, I do drink. All human beings are the same. If we cut a Chetri, blood comes, and in the same way, blood comes if we cut people of other castes.

In his explanation, Megh drew upon an idea reiterated in his textbook ("All people's blood is red," i.e., all people are the same). Disavowal of caste differences became one of the markers of an "educated person" as these children constructed it. Megh and other boys often employed the temporal idiom to talk about the caste system as belonging to their parents' time. In reply to our questions about caste relations, they would tell us that "today" educated persons or persons with progressive ideas (*pragati sīl*) do not believe in such things.

Lower-caste school boys looked to education as providing an escape from traditional caste occupations and restrictions that still existed in Naudada in 1993. Govinda, a Damai boy who was fourteen in 1986, had a strong emotional attachment to his view of himself as an educated person. He had resisted learning his caste's craft of tailoring. Instead, he struggled to remain in school and planned to use his education to obtain a good job that did not involve sewing. He also had developed a strategy to one day become a local politician who would serve the people and help develop Naudada. By 1993, Govinda had earned an intermediate (IA) college degree, obtained a salaried position as an overseer at a nearby factory (supervising some of his higher-caste neighbors), and was taking steps toward becoming a community leader.

Similarly Hari, a Damai adolescent in ninth grade in 1991, visualized how education could help him circumvent the caste restrictions he had experienced growing up in Naudada. He told stories of being angered and hurt when members of higher castes yelled at him to go away and refused him entry into their homes. He elaborated a plan to become educated and return to Naudada as a person who would work to transcend caste barriers and possibly redefine caste practices:

> Some people, especially the Newars, don't allow me to enter their house. I am a Sunar (caste of goldsmiths—considered "untouchable"), just a little above Babu Ram's (caste). But when I become a doctor, or an important man, I will be able to do some great works for this gaon. . . . I am a student also, but [these higher castes] have contempt for me. "Go away, don't come in our house," they say to me in the Newar's house, in the Bahun's house. . . . In front of these people, sister, [I say] I am also a student. I shouldn't do this [treat people differently because of their caste]. They hate me. [They say] "Don't go inside the house." . . . They say, "*napas!*" ("Don't enter!"). When tomorrow comes, I may be a teacher or doctor, or anything I want to be. Tomorrow I can be. I will study and do good deeds. . . . Later when I become a doctor, an important person, a powerful person, and bring money, I'll say to them, "Here, come, take some tea, have a cigarette." But I will not take myself [because I am a good man, without these bad habits]. After this, I'll go to their place to eat. This is necessary [to change the system].

Hari talked at length about the caste restrictions he had observed many Naudadan adults following, and the strategies he had for changing these practices. Like many other students in Naudada and elsewhere, he wanted to work to redefine the character of a man by his actions and deeds, not by his caste affiliation. During this same period, we heard reports of high caste students from another area in the district going in mass to a Sunar man's home and requesting to eat his cooked food. Like Hari, they too, hoped to break down constraints against intercaste commensality, and perhaps in so doing, make a symbolic statement against caste and for equality.[31]

Girls' understandings of the educated person and their vision of schooling as opportunity more explicitly intersected with their gender identity. In 1986, girls talked about education as a way of avoiding or postponing marriage, a fate that all but one of Skinner's female informants dreaded (Skinner 1990). They reasoned that their parents would not be so eager to marry them off if they were educated and capable of bringing in wages from a salaried job. Some girls had to drop out of school because their parents needed their labor at home or were unwilling or unable to pay the fees for books and tuition. But others strategized to remain in school in spite of opposition or lack of support from parents. For example, Sunita, a Bahun girl, was in the fifth grade in 1986, and at age ten, the youngest member of her class.[32] Sunita expressed a strong desire to continue in school. She wanted to learn new things and become a teacher, but her parents told her they could only afford to send her brother to school beyond the fifth grade, when books and tuition were no longer free. Sunita challenged her parents, saying, "You are sending boys (to school), why not girls?" Her mother finally agreed to Sunita's insistent demands. Sunita was allowed to attend school as long as she worked hard in the hours before and after school to finish her many household chores.

Those girls who could not attend school framed their experiences in the prevailing discourse that distinguished educated from uneducated females. They often portrayed themselves to us and to others as bearers of heavy loads in contrast to their school-going peers who only had to carry schoolbooks. Govinda's younger sister, Parbati, had to drop out of school in fifth grade to help her parents do the farmwork. In 1991, she explained that she was sad that she could not continue school. She spoke of herself as a *napaṛhne mānche* (uneducated person, one who has not studied) and contrasted herself to a *paṛhne mānche* (educated person, one who has studied).[33] She told Skinner: "Those who study have a happy life. They don't have to work hard all day long, going to work in the fields and carrying loads. Those who study only have to work on Friday afternoons and Saturdays." Annapurna, a Chetri girl whose parents kept her at home to do the chores after her older sister married, similarly noted that those who studied had happy (*sukha*) lives while those who did not study had hardship (*dukha*) and hard work.

A primary way in which Naudadan females constructed gendered self-understandings and identities as female was through song. They especially drew upon songs composed by groups of girls and young women for Tij, an annual festival for women. The songs were critical commentaries on women's positions in domestic life and the larger social and political world (Holland and Skinner 1995; Skinner et al. 1994).[34] In some of these songs, females gave voice to the sadness and anger they experienced because of being uneducated. A song composed for the 1991 Tij festival vividly expressed the distress girls felt when they were not allowed to go to school, and played upon the distinction between the girl who has to bear loads and the girl who gets to go to school. One of its composers gave it the title, "Lamentations of an Uneducated Daughter":[35]

> Far from here there is rice and corn and mustard in the garden.
> Listen to the lamentations of a daughter.
>
> I was very eager to go to school.
> I cried because I could not go to school.
>
> God, you fate (*bhābi*), you visited this sin on me.
> You caused me to be born in a poor family.
>
> My peers go to school, carrying books.
> It is difficult for me to even recognize the letter "*ka*" (first letter of Nepali alphabet).
>
> When my peers go to school,
> I feel that I am unlucky.
>
> When my friends carry schoolbooks and notebooks, they become happy,
> But I have to carry heavy loads.
>
> Unlucky people are not free from carrying heavy loads.
> I will spend my life wanting to study,
> But my life will be spent enslaved. . . .

These kinds of Tij songs were called *dukha* songs, or songs of hardship. *Dukha* song lyrics generally focused on household relations and were critical of the position allotted women. Composed for at least seventy years—the oldest women we could find sang us songs from their youth—these songs have been the collective products of groups of young, mostly illiterate women.[36] Yet beginning especially in the Tij festival of 1991, we heard a different type of song composed by educated girls. As with the *dukha* songs, these *rājnīti* (political) songs were critical, offering alternative views of women and feminine subjectivities. They differed in that they moved beyond the domestic arena, envisioning women in other spheres. In 1991, we discovered that Kamala, a thirteen-year-old Chetri in eighth grade, had a strong sense of herself as a student and a politically aware person. Kamala was recognized as an expert song composer, and used her skills to compose *rājnīti* Tij songs that were critical of how the poor and women were treated under Nepal's political and social system. In 1992, she composed the following Tij song that demanded equal rights and access to education not only for herself, but for women as a group.[37] She called her song "Tyranny over Women":

> Listen sisters, listen society,
> Today I am going to speak about tyranny over women.

The male and female born from the same womb,
Do not have equal rights.

The son gets the ancestral property at the age of fourteen,
Whereas the daughter has to get married when she is only twelve.

Parents engage in great trickery,
Sending their daughter weeping to her husband's house.

Parents send the son to school,
Whereas they are afraid to provide education for the daughter.

Father bought books and pens for my younger brother,
Whereas he wove a basket [for carrying loads] for me, the daughter.

My name is Kamala who has studied only to the 8th grade,
But who has a great desire for further education.

Parents, don't take me out of school,
See if I can study well or not!

Parents, if you provide me an education, I won't fail,
And after study, I can live by myself.

Parents, provide me an education at any cost,
And later when I hold a job, I will repay you.

We women are also energetic and want justice,
We also have the right to hold a job.

A red ribbon tied around black hair,
We women are always deprived in Nepal.

Women have even climbed Mt. Everest and reached the moon,
Women have done so many things in this world.

Women of other countries are pilots,
We Nepalese women will be happy if we get the chance to be great women.

Therefore, women of Nepal, this is not the time to be silent,
Let's fight to obtain our rights.

Kamala's song involved a different construction of being female than the *dukha* songs composed largely by "uneducated" groups of females. In her verses, women were depicted as capable of contributing their talents to the country. As females like Kamala produced these types of political songs, they reconceptualized themselves as politically aware actors and activists in a political world.

The division between educated and uneducated women was muted in most contexts in Naudada. Educated girls in many contexts identified with the lives of all gaon women. They were also gaon sisters and daughters. But the tensions and contradictions between being uneducated women of the gaon, and being educated women whose orientations were more toward school and the wider political arena, were emerging. Being an educated female was becoming a valued form of femininity, and uneducated women were expressing their sense that, perhaps, this valuation was justified (Holland and Skinner 1995).

THE EDUCATED PERSON AND POLITICAL MOVEMENTS

Schools were fashioned by the monarchy and the panchayat government to be instruments for promoting loyalty to the nation-state and producing the basic skills necessary for developing the country. In actuality, schools in Naudada did not provide the harmonious and homogeneous march toward nation-building and unity that those in power envisioned. Schools offered contested and heterogeneous sites for identity formation. Drawing on Bakhtin's (1981, 1984) idea of voice, we can distinguish multiple social positions and perspectives in dialogue and in contention at the school site. The dominant "voice" of school textbooks and national symbols promoted loyalty to the panchayat system of government and its policies, and promoted Hindu hegemony. But other voices existed as well, even within these same texts. For example, these texts constructed Nepal's people as distinct and ranked, but also constituted them as equal and one.

Several Naudadan teachers had been active in student organizations and movements at the campuses where they had studied. These student campus organizations were aligned with various political parties, parties that were banned until the fall of the panchayat government. Teachers often carried their political views to the schools where they subsequently taught. Sometimes in class and often outside of the classroom, teachers discussed politics with students and other Naudadans. They openly challenged what they saw as the corruption and oppressive practices of the panchayat government, and after its fall, the corruption and abuses of the Congress Party which won the majority of seats in the 1991 elections.

Within this heteroglossic milieu, students developed and orchestrated their own views. While not challenging "development" per se, they began to question the ways *bikās* was being carried out by those in power. They debated among themselves what kind of political system could bring about development for the poor and rural populace, development which could free them from oppression by wealthier landowners and from a conservative social system which placed women and lower castes in a relatively powerless position.

In the 1991 Tij festival, female students led their song group in the following verses:

Oh dominated sisters of Nepal.
We have so much tyranny.

The panchas (officials of the former government) ate the flesh and also the blood [of the people].
At last we have the multiparty system.

> The thirty-year panchayat reign gave so much trouble to women.
> They [the panchas] drank liquor by selling young girls.
>
> They sold our innocent sisters. . . .
> The panchas dominated women.
>
> Now this type of rule cannot be tolerated.
> Women will no longer tolerate what they did in the past. . . .

Various renditions of this song, some of which supported the Congress Party and others which endorsed one of the communist parties, were widely sung after the Pro-Democracy Movement. Their verses chronicled the abuses women had suffered under the previous system, and called for women to move forward against any political party that would perpetuate these injustices.

Yet even before the Pro-Democracy Movement and the multiparty system it reinstated, students raised a collective voice against the abuses they saw in the political and social system. In a cultural performance (*nāṭak*) held several years before the Movement, students banded together to perform skits and songs that they created as a group with little guidance from, and sometimes in direct opposition to, the headmaster and some of the teachers.[38] In front of a crowd of about 500 Naudadans, students enacted satirical skits of the ways people in high positions treated rural dwellers. They performed songs that drew upon their experience of being hill farmers. Some songs portrayed the problems women face in their roles as daughters, daughters-in-law, and wives.

In a song entitled "Our Sister," female students advocated equal rights for women and an end to the bad treatment they received at the hands of others:

> Being enslaved and repressed, don't remain in isolation.
> We have to tear and throw out this net of exploitation.
> If a husband keeps a co-wife, it is all right.
> But if a woman takes another man, she must pay a price.
>
> Even to eat, you have to fight hard.
> Even to survive, you have to sell your very life.
> Wake up, O sister, and recognize this sinner man.
> Let's unite together to destroy this tradition.

Adolescent boys chose songs that opposed the system of labor existing in Naudada:

> Carrying other people's loads, we travel up and down Naudada,
> Sometimes across rivers and sometimes across hills,
> To feed a handful [of food] to my old father during festivals.
> To cover my wife's nakedness with a piece of cloth. . . .
>
> The wishes of a poor man's son could never be fulfilled.
> [Even] depositing the blood in my heart,
> The moneylender's debt could not be paid.

In verse, these students detailed the hardships faced by poor villagers. As farmers' sons they had to carry loads through monsoon rains and hot sun. If they had not experienced it in their own family, they had seen fellow Naudadans struggle to earn scant wages though bearing heavy loads, wages which often had to go to pay the steep interest on loans that ensnared many farmers in a web of never-ending debt.[39] Their verses expressed criticisms against moneylenders and wealthy landlords, and more subtly, of the political and economic system that engendered and allowed such exploitation.[40]

In the *nāṭak*, students contested systems of gender and class privileges. They worked together to create criticisms of these privileges, and called for transformations in systems of gender and class relations. When asked how they could create such songs and skits that could be perceived as criticisms against those in power, one student explained:

> The students are united at school. The students sing about how to get rid of the exploiters and how to achieve equality. The students are united. Therefore, the headmaster can't do anything.

In their verses and skits, students portrayed the poor and women as laboring under exploitative and repressive systems. Their call for action against abuses prefigured the 1990 revolution and its call for equal rights for women and the poor. Their sense of themselves as educated and progressive students, their agency in redefining gender, class, and caste relations, and the world of political revolution, were developing together.[41]

SUMMARY AND CONCLUSION

Public schools in Nepal provide access to the status of "educated person," and supposedly to the jobs that are available to such persons.[42] Through a nationalized curriculum and textbooks, the schools have promoted a specific model of what being an educated person entails. As expressed in school texts and the pervasive discourse on social and economic development (*bikās*), an educated citizen is one who serves the people, works toward the development of the country, recognizes that all of Nepal's diverse peoples are one, and is loyal to the sovereign nation of Nepal and its government. These national discourses, as well as memories of the historical denial of schooling and associated oppression, constitute the context for the present study of "on the ground" appropriations of schooling. We have looked indepth at students' constructions of schools and found that they treated the schools as sites for the opposition of systems of gender and caste privilege in Nepal, the formation of critical commentary on governmental policies and practices, and their own constructions of the *paṛhne mānche*, the educated person.

Naudadan students took up the discourse of nationalism and development, but they were not solely the mouthpieces and vehicles of it. They were not "interpellated" by its ideology, nor were they determined by its texts. They valued the image of being educated which was promoted by official school discourse, but the active role that students have taken in political and social movements suggest that this discourse was not powerful enough to form them completely in the mold which the former panchayat government had in mind when it first established public education. Neither did nationalist and development agendas dictate efforts by the students to dismantle the caste and gender hierarchies that shaped their lives.[43] Schools, school participants, and school texts in Naudada were contested and heteroglossic. There was not a single homogeneous message students could draw on for (re)creating themselves as moral persons and social selves. Within this heteroglossic site, students had to orchestrate different voices for their understandings of themselves and the world. The ways in which these children and adolescents were constructing their identities had implications, not only for their continued educational participation and future goals, but also for potential changes in dominant ideologies and structures. Schoolchildren were creating new identities and self-understandings that resisted older forms of privilege.

At the same time, they, too, were engaged in the creation of a new form of symbolic capital—the capital associated with formal education—and in the process produced the "other" of the educated world—the uneducated person. While students have so far gone beyond the bounds of state agendas for schools, and seen liberatory potential as regards caste and gender restrictions, they have participated in the constitution of a new social distinction.

NOTES

We wish to thank Stacy Pigg, Pratyoush Onta, and Al Pach for their insightful comments on an earlier draft of this paper. The material for this chapter comes from Skinner's research in Nepal in 1985 and 1986, which was supported by a Fulbright grant, and from Skinner and Holland's joint research supported in 1991 by the National Science Foundation (BNS-9110010). We thank our research associates and friends in Nepal, especially Sapana Sharma, G. B. Adhikari, Renu Lama, and Maheswor Pahari, for their assistance and their dialogues with us over the years. We continue to remember the people of Naudada who have been very kind and helpful to us. Although we have tried, in our turn, to contribute to community projects and help in other ways, their gift to us has been by far the greater.

1. Vedic and Buddhist traditions of religious teachings, in existence since at least the second century, were not seen as threats to the government and were not prohibited (Beach 1990).

2. Naudada is a pseudonym, as are the names we use for individuals from Naudada.

3. We cannot say with any certainty to what extent these kinds of activities were present in other schools throughout Nepal. We heard reports of similar efforts of schoolchildren in places both to the east and west of our field site. Although children and adolescents from the higher grades (grades 6–10) were the most active in the generation of alternative discourses and visions in Naudada, primary schoolchildren were learning to participate, alongside their older siblings and cousins, in these activities.

4. The reader should keep in mind that the Nepali words given in this chapter have multiple meanings. The translations we provide should be not be taken as direct and unproblematic equivalents of the Nepali terms. As with any word or utterance in a dialogic and heteroglossic world, these terms evoke and are imbued with multiple and dialogic threads of meaning (see Bakhtin 1981, 1984; Vološinov 1973). A full-scale exposition of the many nuances of these Nepali terms as informed by the context and history of their use, the intentions of the speaker, and the positions of the hearers would no doubt inform us more of the complex ways identities and meanings are constructed, but this task is beyond us in this paper. Here we merely provide the Nepali terms that Naudadans employed along with the English translations that Nepalis who were fluent in English most often associated with these terms.

5. Women were more likely to be uneducated than were men.

6. See Husain (1970), Des Chene (1991), and Seddon et al. (1979), for accounts of Nepal's relationship with British India and its "semi-colony" status.

7. During both periods, schooling was much more available to males than females. In 1950, 1 percent of the student population was female; in 1989, 28 percent was female.

8. These rates vary slightly from source to source. Statistics given here are taken from CERID/WEI (1984) and the *Statistical Yearbook of Nepal*, 1991.

9. Although we are fairly certain that many of the demographics and practices noted here are descriptive of the situation in Naudada at the time of this writing, because of the concern in anthropology about writing in the "ethnographic present" and hence freezing people in time and out of history, we employ the past tense throughout this account.

10. Naudada is best described as having gaons or neighborhoods, rather than villages. Despite the widespread use of the term "village" in development policies and political rhetoric, Benjamin (1989) has convincingly argued that many areas in Nepal lack the organization implied by the concept of "village." Naudada is one such area. Furthermore, Pigg (1982) demonstrates how "villages" and "village traditions" are not natural categories, but recent constructions formed in part through the discourse of development and modernization.

11. For the history of the construction of caste and ethnic divisions in Nepal, see Gaborieau (1982), Höfer (1979), and Levine (1987).

12. Besides school, one arena where some higher-caste males ate together with males of lower castes occurred after dark during the illicit activity of gambling and drinking homemade liquor (*raksi*). The frequency of this practice produced a new proverb in Nepal: "By day a Bahun, by night a drunkard."

13. We use the term "Brahmanical" to refer to ideologies and practices promoted by Vedic literature and by most Bahun priests, many of which place women in less powerful and less esteemed positions vis-à-vis men. The texts and practices of the "Brahmanical" are also multivoiced and complex, but refer to a narrower field than the more encompassing term, "Hindu."

14. See Bennett (1979) and Gilbert (1992) for thorough accounts of Nepalese women and family and inheritance law.

15. For more details on Brahmanical and patriarchal practices in Nepal, see Bennett (1983), Skinner (1990), and Stone (1978).

16. See CERID/WEI (1984) and Skinner (1990) for the factors that constrain and enable children's participation in school.

17. These figures are estimates based on data from Save the Children Federation (SCF: 1979, 1990). Male literacy rates for the country as a whole increased from 9.5% in 1952 to 51.8% in 1986, compared to 0.7% to 18% for females.

18. In 1986, 42% of the children enrolled in grades 1–5 in Naudada were female. This percentage of female enrollment dropped to 31% for grades 6–10. The number of females enrolled represented roughly 50% of all school-aged girls in Naudada. Approximately 70% of all eligible boys were enrolled. From 1979 to 1986, there was a 59% increase in enrollment of girls in grades 1–3. UNICEF (1992) statistics showed that nationwide, only 36% of the total school age population was enrolled in grades 1–5. Other national statistics indicated problematic areas for universal primary education: high retention rates for first-graders (64%), high dropout rates (48%), irregular attendance by students (71%) and by teachers (70%), and the number of days schools were actually in session (120 days) (UNICEF 1992). Pratyoush Onta (personal communication) makes the point that despite the great increase in school enrollment, educational quality remains low, secondary school dropout rates are high, and 67% of those who attempt to pass the SLC fail. According to Onta, in some areas of Nepal, students who dropped out or failed the SLC have questioned the equation between education, upward mobility, and modernization. As of 1993, students in Naudada were not yet making this critique, although it is likely to emerge in the fixture.

19. After *bahudal* (the multiparty system), the textbooks did not change, but teachers skipped over (or ripped out) the sections that contained descriptions of the defeated panchayat system.

20. Pigg (1992) presents a cogent analysis of the ways the discourse of development works to represent and produce these divisions. She examines how the urban elite and some rural dwellers claim a more modern and transnational identity by aligning themselves with *bikās* (development), thereby distinguishing themselves from "less educated" or "traditional persons." In a more recent account relevant to our conceptualization of "heteroglossic selves," Pigg (1994) notes that this identity might not be as fixed and durable for some as it first appears.

21. How persons author themselves within heteroglossic sites, how voices come to be recognized as voices and linked to identities—are the processes addressed in theoretical and ethnographic detail in Skinner and Valsiner (n.d.) and Holland et al. (in press; see especially Chapter 8).

22. Skinner began her research in Naudada in 1982 on women's roles in forestry use. In 1985, she began a longitudinal study of children's developing understandings of gender, caste, and other identities (see Skinner 1989, 1990). In 1986, 1990, and 1991,

Skinner and Holland conducted joint research projects in Naudada and elsewhere in Nepal, primarily on women's production of critical commentary and gendered identities in the arena of the Tij festival (see Holland et al. in press; Holland and Skinner 1995, in press; Skinner and Holland 1990; Skinner et al. 1994).

23. Songs were an important medium in Naudada and elsewhere in Nepal for expression of inner emotions and thoughts (*manko kurā*) and for a collective critical commentary on domestic and political worlds (see Holland and Skinner 1995; Skinner et al. 1991; Skinner et al. 1994; Enslin 1992; see also Raheja and Gold 1994, for women's songs from India.)

24. For elaboration of this point, see Holland and Skinner (1995), Skinner and Holland (1990), and Ewing (1990).

25. Throughout the years, Skinner has encountered many of these children and adolescents, mostly the boys, in Kathmandu and other urban areas where they have come for further education or employment. As of 1993, they had not taken up the type of urban identities that Liechty (1994) describes for Kathmandu teenagers. Instead, they contrasted themselves to these types.

26. See Pigg (1994) for a discussion of the multiple meanings of *andhavisvās* (glossed here as "superstition") that she detected in a region in eastern Nepal, and the significance of these meanings for the construction of "modern" and "traditional" persons and places.

27. These Nepali terms were the ones the students most often used in their verbatim statements, but the reader should keep in mind the caution noted above in note 4.

28. Some Damai parents, however, anticipated continuing prejudice and so believed that good jobs were not available for their sons. They were reluctant to commit their limited resources toward an education for which they believed there would be no payoff. Kali, a Damai mother, asked Skinner how a son of a Damai could get a salaried job. She stated, "Small castes have small knowledge. We can't let our oldest son study and spend all that money just to open his eyes. If he sews, he can easily rear a family. . . . This is all we ask of our children in the hills. What else do we know than this? How can one milk and keep the milk in a bamboo basket even if he has the fate to do so?" In spite of these beliefs, however, many Damai boys had convinced their parents to allow them to continue school. Kali's oldest son was "first boy" (highest rank) in grade six in 1986 and was very proud of his academic achievements. He was hoping to one day become a teacher. In 1993, Skinner learned that he had earned an IA (intermediate) college degree and was earning a good income trading goods internationally.

29. Pigg (personal communication) notes that the temporality of these notions seems "natural" at this point because of the generational changes in access to education and the political system. She reminds us that Naudadans are speaking of a very specific "then and now"—one that is historically constructed and, therefore, a distinction that might not be as marked in ten years.

30. Taking water or food from a lower-caste person was interpreted, outside the school, as opening one's self and, by extension, one's family to pollution.

31. These kinds of actions were more common, or perhaps more discussed, during and after the Pro-Democracy Movement in the Spring of 1990, and with the coming of the multiparty system. But they were not absent before.

32. In her school in 1986, there were 225 students enrolled in grades 1–5. Of these, 79 (35%) were girls, most of whom (87%) were concentrated in grades 1–3.

33. Even though she was literate, she was not "educated." In most people's understandings, "educated" means having completed at least the eighth grade.

34. See also Skinner et al. (1991) and Skinner (1990) for girls' constructions of self-understandings through other genres of folksongs.

35. For complete versions of this and other Tij songs and the transliteration of the original Nepali words into romanized Nepali, see Skinner et al. (1994).

36. *Rājnīti* (political) songs were sung before 1991, but infrequently (Holland and Skinner 1995).

37. Some of Kamala's lines were taken from published Tij songbooks that greatly increased in number in 1991. However, the way she altered and combined them with her own verses was novel (see Skinner et al. 1994, for notes on the authorship of songs).

38. Students may have borrowed parts of some of the songs from published songbooks. As with Kamala's song described above, this possibility does not negate the creative aspect of the verses. Skinner and co-workers (1994) found that lines from songs are often recombined and altered in ever-emerging renditions.

39. A common saying in Naudada was "A farmer is born in debt, lives in debt, dies in debt, and bequeaths debt to his sons." In Naudada in 1979, fully 83% of the households had received money from gaon moneylenders who were most often the wealthier Bahun and Chetri landowners (SCF 1979).

40. At the time of the *nāṭak* several years past, the headmaster of the school requested that Skinner not tape the songs. Students later explained that he was worried about reprisals from government officials. His fears were not unfounded. In January of 1984, police opened fire at a *nāṭak* in the village of Piskar, killing two people (Amnesty International 1987:15–17). Varying accounts of this incident circulated in Naudada and elsewhere, but the basic story was that police were called because the songs performed in the *nāṭak* denounced the practices of local landowners, and were interpreted by some in power as insulting the monarchy. Since the Pro-Democracy Movement and the restoration of a multiparty system, people have spoken more openly in public and in the press about political issues.

41. For an elaboration of a model of the co-development of identity, agency, and cultural worlds, see Holland and Skinner (in press).

42. The availability of good salaried jobs was extremely questionable at the time of our study. Owing to a number of different factors, including Nepal's relationship with India, the country lacked much in the way of jobs relating to industry. Government positions were available in insufficient numbers for those who sought them, and often did not

pay enough to support the employee and his or her family. Work provided by non-governmental organizations (NGOs) was valued, but again insufficient in number for those seeking such jobs.

43. For another example of students' and communities' productions that turned the educational goals of the New Education System Plan to their own agenda, see the case described by Ragsdale (1989).

REFERENCES

Althusser, Louis. 1971. Ideology and Ideological State Apparatuses. *In* Lenin and Philosophy. London: New Left Books.

Amnesty International. 1987. Nepal: A Pattern of Human Rights Violations. New York: Amnesty International.

Aryal, K. R. 1970. Education for the Development of Nepal. Kathmandu: Shanti Prakashan.

Bakhtin, Mikhail M. 1981. The Dialogic Imagination. Michael Holquist, ed. Austin: University of Texas Press.

―――. 1984. Problems of Dostoevsky's Poetics. Caryl Emerson, ed. and trans. Minneapolis: University of Minnesota Press.

Beach, King. 1990. From School to Work: A Social and Psychological History of Math in a Nepali Village. Himalayan Research Bulletin 10:18–23.

Benjamin, Paul. 1989. Local Organization for Development in Nepal. Ph.D. dissertation. Anthropology Department, University of North Carolina at Chapel Hill.

Bennett, Lynn. 1979. Tradition and Change in the Legal Status of Nepalese Women: The Status of Women in Nepal, volume I, part 2. Centre for Economic Development and Administration. Kathmandu: Tribhuvan University Press.

Bourdieu, Pierre. 1977a. Outline of a Theory of Practice. Cambridge: Cambridge University Press.

―――. 1977b. The Economics of Linguistic Exchanges. Social Science Information 16:645–668.

Bourdieu, Pierre, and Jean-Claude Passeron. 1977. Reproduction in Education, Society, and Culture. London: Sage.

Bowles, Samuel, and Herbert Gintis. 1976. Schooling in Capitalist America: Educational Reform and the Contradictions of Economic Life. London: Routledge and Kegan Paul.

Burghart, Richard. 1984. The Formation of the Concept of Nation-State in Nepal. Journal of Asian Studies 44:101–125.

CERID/WEI. 1984. Determinants of Educational Participation in Rural Nepal: Research Centre for Educational Innovation and Development. Kathmandu: Tribhuvan University Press.

Cohen, Yehudi A. 1971. The Shaping of Men's Minds: Adaptations to Imperatives of Culture. *In* Anthropological Perspectives on Education. Murray L. Wax, Stanley Diamond, and Fred O. Gearing, eds. Pp. 19–50. New York: Basic Books.

Des Chene, Mary. 1991. Relics of Empire: A Cultural History of the Gurkhas, 1815–1987 Ph.D dissertation. Anthropology Department, Stanford University.

Enslin, Elizabeth. 1992. Collective Powers in Common Places: The Politics of Gender and Space in a Woman's Struggle for a Meeting Center in Chitwan, Nepal. Himalayan Research Bulletin 12:11–26.

Ewing, Katherine P. 1990. The Illusion of Wholeness: Culture, Self, and the Experience of Inconsistency. Ethos 18:251–278.

Gaborieau, Marc. 1982. Les Rapports de Classe dans l'Idéologie Officielle du Népal. Collection Purushartha 6:251–290.

Gilbert, Kate. 1992. Women and Family Law in Modern Nepal: Statutory Rights and Social Implications. New York University Journal of International Law and Politics 24:729–758.

Höfer, András. 1979. The Caste Hierarchy and the State in Nepal: A Study of the Muluki Ain of 1854. Innsbruck: Universitätsverlag Wagner.

Holland, Dorothy, Carole Cain, Debra Skinner, William Lachicotte, and Renee Prillaman. in press. Emerging Selves: Identities Forming in and against Cultural Worlds. Cambridge, MA: Harvard University Press.

Holland, Dorothy and Debra Skinner. 1995. Contested Ritual, Contested Femininities: (Re)forming Self and Society in a Nepali Women's Festival. American Ethnologist 22(2):279–305.

―――. in press. The Co-Development of Identity, Agency, and Lived Worlds. *In* Comparisons in Human Development: Understanding Time and Context. J. Tudge, S. Shanahan, and J. Valsiner, eds. Cambridge: Cambridge University Press.

Husain, Asad. 1970. British India's Relations with the Kingdom of Nepal, 1857–1947. London: George, Allen & Unwin.

Johnson, Norris. 1980. The Material Culture of Public School Classrooms: The Symbolic Integration of Local School and National Culture. Anthropology and Education Quarterly 11:173–190.

―――. 1983. School Spaces and Architecture: The Social and Cultural Landscape of Educational Environments. Journal of American Culture 5:77–87.

Levine, Nancy. 1987. Caste, State, and Ethnic Boundaries in Nepal. Journal of Asian Studies 46:71–88.

Liechty, Mark. 1994. Consumer Culture and the Construction of Modern Youth: "Teenagers" in Kathmandu, Nepal. Paper presented at the American Anthropological Association Meetings, Atlanta, Georgia, December.

Pigg, Stacy. 1992. Inventing Social Categories through Place: Social Representations and Development in Nepal. Comparative Studies in Society and History 34:491–513.

———. 1994. The Credible and the Credulous: The Question of "Villagers' Beliefs" in Nepal. Paper presented to the Program in Agrarian Studies, Yale University, April 1994.

Ragsdale, Todd. 1989. Once a Hermit Kingdom. Delhi: Manohar.

Raheja, Gloria Goodwin and Ann Grodzins Gold. 1994. Listen to the Heron's Words: Reimagining Gender and Kinship in North India. Berkeley: University of California Press.

SCF (Save the Children Federation, USA). 1979. Baseline Survey Report. Nepal Field Office.

———. 1990. Nonformal Education Baseline Survey Report Ilaka No. 1, Gorkha District, Nepal. Kathmandu: SCF Nepal Field Office.

Seddon, David. 1987. Nepal: A State of Poverty. New Delhi: Vikas Publishing House.

Seddon, David, with P. Blaikie and J. Cameron, eds. 1979. Peasants and Workers in Nepal. New Delhi: Vikas Publishing House Pvt Ltd.

Shaha, Rishikesh. 1990. Politics in Nepal 1980–1990: Referendum, Stalemate, and Triumph of People Power. Columbia, MO: South Asian Publications.

Sharma, Gopi Nath. 1990. The Impact of Education During the Rana Period in Nepal. Himalayan Research Bulletin 10:3–7.

Skinner, Debra. 1989. The Socialization of Gender Identity: Observations from Nepal. *In* Child Development in Cultural Context. Jaan Valsiner. ed. Pp. 181–192. Toronto: Hogrefe and Huber Publishers.

———. 1990. Nepalese Children's Understanding of Themselves and Their Social World. Ph.D. dissertation. Anthropology Department, University of North Carolina at Chapel Hill.

Skinner, Debra and Dorothy Holland. 1990. Good Selves, Angry Selves; Formation of Gender Identities in a Hindu Mixed Caste Community in Nepal. Paper presented at the 19th Annual South Asia Meetings, Madison, WI. November 2–4.

Skinner, Debra, Dorothy Holland, and G. B. Adhikari. 1994. The Songs of Tij: A Genre of Critical Commentary for Women in Nepal. Asian Folklore Studies 53:259–305.

Skinner, Debra and Jaan Valsiner. n.d. Voices and the Orchestration of Self. Unpublished manuscript.

Skinner, Debra, Jaan Valsiner, and Bidur Basnet. 1991. Singing One's Life: An Orchestration of Personal Experiences and Cultural Forms. Journal of South Asian Literature 26:15–43.

UNICEF/National Planning Commission. 1992. Children and Women of Nepal: A Situational Analysis. Kathmandu: HMG National Planning Commission/UNICEF.

Vološinov, V. N. 1973. Marxism and the Philosophy of Language. Cambridge, MA: Harvard University Press.

12

ELSIE ROCKWELL

Keys to Appropriation: Rural Schooling in Mexico

Rural schooling in Mexico during the 1920s and early 1930s offers a privileged context for studying the complex cultural processes that shape formal education. Postrevolutionary regimes—such as the one that came to power in Mexico at the time—often respond to the demand for education by creating new transcripts for educating "the people." They adopt popular schooling as a favored means for disseminating images of the "educated person" that break with those associated with the immediate past. When directed to peasants, these programs tend to incorporate rural themes, while simultaneously seeking to transform village life. Yet rural people have their own agendas for schooling, which often preserve prior values and contest the new models put forth by authorities.[1] Far from constituting simple instruments used by the state to mold hearts and minds, schools become sites where diverse representations of the educated person come into play, are advanced, withdrawn, or elaborated. This process of cultural production is evident in the configuration of the Mexican rural schools, which I will examine in this chapter. The particular history of this program also poses significant conceptual problems for the ongoing discussion about the nature of schooling as a cultural process.

Current analyses of cultural production must acknowledge the intersection between "the purposive, reasoning behavior of agents" and "the constraining and enabling features of the social and material contexts" (Giddens 1984:177) that has been at the center of much theoretical discussion during the past two decades. Studies in this field that explore how cultural practices fabricate multiple social identities have contributed greatly to our understanding of this complex relationship.[2] However, the term cultural production lends itself to opposing interpretations. When the phrase is understood as "culture producing persons," the "dull compulsion" of culture tends to overpower human agency. When cast as "persons producing culture," on the other hand, the concept risks discounting the cultural matter out of which new meanings and practices are produced. This dual reading often blurs the interaction between human agency and cultural context.

I would like to draw into this discussion another concept: *appropriation*. In this case too, there are several possible interpretations. In the reproduction paradigm, appropriation has referred to the concentration of symbolic capital by dominant social groups.[3] In other conceptual frameworks, however, appropriation has been linked to multiple social actors. This broader usage suggests that the appropriation of cultural meanings and practices can occur in several directions, and is not necessarily patterned after the unidirectional appropriation of surplus value in capitalist production. In this sense, cultural appropriation, while constrained by material conditions, can be substantially different from appropriation in the economic cycle of production/reproduction.

Unlike the term production, appropriation *simultaneously* conveys a sense of the active/transforming nature of human agency, and the constraining/enabling character of culture. The term unambiguously situates agency in the person, as s/he takes possession of and *uses* available cultural resources.[4] At the same time, it alludes to the sort of culture embedded in everyday life—in objects, tools, practices, words and the like, as they are experienced by persons. This notion of appropriation is thus consonant with an emerging anthropological concept of culture as multiple, situated, historical and clearly not an agent.[5] While this meaning of appropriation has a long history, and has been appearing increasingly in studies of cultural and educational processes,[6] it has not been fully incorporated into mainstream theoretical discourse.

One formulation of the concept that may help shape a new usage is that offered by French cultural historian Roger Chartier. Chartier distinguishes his understanding of the notion from various other uses (1993:7). He considers, for example, that Foucault restricts the meaning of "social appropriation" to procedures for controlling and denying popular access to public discourse. In contrast, Chartier proposes a notion of appropriation which "accentuates plural uses and diverse understandings." This perspective requires "a social history of the various uses (which are not necessarily interpretations) of discourses and models, brought back to their fundamental social and institutional determinants, and lodged in the specific practices that produce them" (1993:7).[7] However, wary of reducing culture to a variety of practices considered to be "diverse but equivalent," Chartier further locates cultural appropriation within "the social conflicts over [the] classification, hierarchization and consecration or disqualification" of cultural goods (1993:7).

In Chartier's perspective, any essential *correspondence* between social groups and univocal cultural identities fades, as the dynamic *relationship* between diverse social groups and particular cultural practices comes into focus. Accordingly, Chartier studies the relationship between popular classes and elite or literate culture. Thus, in approaching popular culture, he attempts to identify "not cultural sets defined in themselves as popular, but rather the ways in which common cultural sets are appropriated differently" (1993:7). In this view, cultural appropriation becomes a fundamentally collective achievement, which occurs only when resources are taken over and put to use within particular social situations. Chartier further argues that appropriation always "transforms, reformulates and exceeds what it receives" (1991:19).

When used to explain the transformation of cultural representations, including social identities, the concept of appropriation takes on other connotations. When these representations are studied over a period of time, the contested nature of appropriation becomes evident. Cycles of appropriation are generated as dominant groups confiscate popular traditions and alter their use and meaning, while subordinate groups occupy spaces and claim symbols formerly restricted to elites. Those in power often create new forms of authoritarian rule by using the resources of popular classes, while insurgent groups may turn to their advantage cultural means originally destined to do the work of domination. Struggles in this sphere are expressed through an array of mechanisms, including control, distinction, exclusion, defiance, resistance, abandonment, and even parody.[8]

The history of the *Escuela Rural Mexicana* (the Mexican Rural School) is particularly illustrative of the reciprocal appropriation that occurs in any politicized arena. In trying to capture some of the outcomes—and ironies—of this process, I will center my present discussion on two separate analyses of historiographical data from central Tlaxcala.[9] One examines the training of rural teachers, at a time when schooling was practically synonymous with becoming a teacher. The other recounts the controversies that arose over the use of space, as schools expanded into the rural communities of the region. Both accounts attempt to convey the sense of appropriation that I have outlined above. However, as the process under study has a historical specificity not easily transferred to other times and places, I will first briefly describe how rural schooling fit into the hegemonic project of postrevolutionary Mexico, and sketch in the social landscape of rural Tlaxcala.

RURAL SCHOOLS IN THE POSTREVOLUTIONARY CONTEXT

The Mexican revolution, initiated in 1910 to depose eight-term dictator Porfirio Díaz, generated numerous relatively autonomous regional struggles. The insurrection claimed many rural provinces and mobilized the then predominantly agrarian population of Mexico. Remote sierra settlers, pueblo-based peasants, ranchers, hacienda peons, and sheer adventurers, took to arms to either change or preserve their ways of life, and were subsequently caught up in the conflicts and alliances that ensued among regional chiefs and military strongmen. Historians currently stress the "demise of the autonomous revolutionary movement" (Buve 1990:237) after the victory of Venustiano Carranza's Constitutionalist army in 1916, as the initial rebellion was interrupted and co-opted by those who came to power in its name. Yet many agree with Knight (1994) that the multifaceted popular upheaval that dismantled the Porfirian state and generated fundamental shifts in the social order of the country, was indeed a revolution, albeit one that poses serious problems of interpretation.

As has often occurred, those who emerged victorious from the armed revolution "created a more coercive and hegemonic state apparatus" (Scott 1985:29).[10] When the Northern faction, led by Alvaro Obregón, defeated or neutralized its contenders and came to power in 1920, it began to forge an increasingly strong central state. To this end, it availed itself of a selective implementation of the mandates for social change that had been inserted into the Constitution of 1917 by the more radical revolutionary forces. Obregón appropriated the legacy of agrarian leader Emiliano Zapata[11] and incorporated it into the hegemonic project; the regime thus gained—for some time—a degree of legitimacy that had been denied to Carranza. During the administrations of Plutarco Elías Calles (1924-28) and of Lázaro Cárdenas (1934-40), the federal government further strengthened its control over local politics through the central organization of peasant, worker, and teacher sectors. These postrevolutionary regimes found in both agrarian reform and the extension of rural schools a way to counter the remaining regional forces, by setting up alternative networks and clientelist alliances with peasant constituencies.

In 1921, José Vasconcelos convinced President Obregón to reestablish the Secretary of Education, which had been suppressed by Carranza, and vest it with authority to establish elementary schools throughout the country. He argued that local governments had neglected rural education, and only federal action could actually raise the nation's cultural level. As the federal government began to send teachers to the furthest confines of the country, training them to subordinate the three Rs to the betterment of rural life, a new image of the school was created. The educators and anthropologists of the 1920s who articulated the ideal of the *Escuela Rural Mexicana* proposed a "civilizing mission" to transform rural society. Their explicit intention was to preserve the country's "plurality of cultures" while integrating them into a unified nation.[12]

Educators involved in the federal project drew on their training in the renowned Porfirian Normal Schools and on their own experience in rural schools. As they charted the new program, they had in mind an agrarian way of life that differed radically from the prerevolutionary hacienda arrangement and the indigenous tradition, both considered to be incompatible with progress. The notion of restructuring the rural world by fostering literate, self-sufficient farmers, fully knowledgeable of their civil rights and obligations, had long been favored by liberal educators in Mexico, and was taken up again with force during this period. Radical educators further hoped to create "a cooperative, class-conscious, solidary peasantry" (Knight 1994:63). This notion of an "educated rural person" was disseminated through the practical training of rural teachers, and through readers (such as *Simiente*) written for peasant children.

The federal initiative led to diverse outcomes in particular settings.[13] Rural life as projected from above did not always accord with the demands of the townspeople. Many of the pueblo-based peasants who had participated in the revolutionary struggle had for decades demanded schools commensurate in quality, ritual and orientation with those serving the urban elite.[14] While federal educators proffered a radically different, and presumably more relevant, rural agenda, literate peasant leaders and traditional authorities often defended the precepts and contents of education they had appropriated during previous years.[15] Beneath the controversies over the content of schooling, a structural issue—the intersection between central control and local autonomy—was also at stake. The federal system tended to restructure school governance in order to counter local powers and brace central rule, while the local population attempted to preserve its control over the school—a control symbolized by its possession of the keys.

The encounter did not necessarily end in confrontation, but was played out according to the conditions of each locality. In some cases, groups that traditionally controlled the towns succeeded in blocking or redefining the federal teachers' work, or in preserving the prerevolutionary educational arrangements. In other cases, sectors of the local population welcomed the implicit alliance with federal authorities and supported the teachers' attempts to organize productive social projects. Over the years, federal teachers became a fundamental link in the political reconfiguration of the central government. They connected disaffected peasant groups with federal agrarian dependencies, while promoting local organizations that were eventually integrated into the national confederations and the "official" political party[16] that shaped the Mexican postrevolutionary state.

The new rural schools were thus neither the pure expression of a popular revolutionary program nor a unilateral instrument of state co-optation and control. They were the result of negotiations between an expanding, though initially tenuous, central power and a rural population intent on gaining access to resources previously denied them. The official transcript[17] for rural education was taken up, transformed and reenacted under different guises, by those who actually built and worked in the schools.

SCHOOLS IN THE SOCIAL LANDSCAPE OF TLAXCALA

The small state of Tlaxcala is situated due east of Mexico City, directly on the strategic route to the Gulf of Mexico. Its southwestern region, surrounding the Malintzi volcano, owes its basic configuration to the Mesoamerican cultural matrix which Guillermo Bonfil (1987) has called *México profundo*. During the years preceding the insurrection, the Indian population of the region was still largely organized around political and religious traditions forged during the colonial period. The Tlaxcalan government, headed for twenty-six years by Próspero Cahuanzti, was intermeshed with both the indigenous hierarchies and the local oligarchies. These groups gave way during the Revolution to a succession of local factions whose destinies were mandated by the increasingly centralized federal government (Buve 1990; Ramírez Rancaño 1991).

At the time of the revolution, Tlaxcala was predominantly agrarian.[18] A patchwork of clusters of small households with adjacent cornfields, separated by communal lands and steep ravines, covered the central valleys and Malintzi foothills. Large market-oriented haciendas, with extensive agricultural fields and settlements of several hundred workers, bordered the fertile river banks. While residents of the state's few cities or *villas* took pride in their Spanish descent, most Tlaxcalans of the southwestern region were of Nahua ancestry and many still spoke *Mexicano*.[19] For the great majority, rural lifestyles—indexed in the census by the use of *huaraches* (sandals) and a maize-based diet—continued well into the century.

In the densely populated central region most of the villages had over several centuries achieved the relatively autonomous status of *pueblo*. Becoming a pueblo involved long-term struggles to assert a degree of independence from the municipal and district authorities. In order to aspire to this higher rank, the *vecinos* (adult male residents) had to establish a proper center for the town, build a church and schoolroom, and count on a literate elite capable of organizing local political and religious life. Though they continued cultivating *milpas* (subsistence cornfields), in many ways these town-dwellers considered themselves distinctly more "civilized" than the residents of the surrounding barrios and agrarian colonies that had not yet become pueblos.

The various social environments of the region were interrelated, so there was no clear distinction between the rural and urban spheres. The elites of the towns emulated the lifestyles, and demanded the services, of the *villas*. Conversely, the cities yielded to rural traditions, as villagers congregated in their central squares on market days and during religious festivities. Trains connecting Mexico City and the port of Veracruz could be seen or heard from any point in the valleys. The state's human resources had attracted textile mills, as the local knowledge of weaving, a legacy of colonial times, was easily transferred to operating modern machinery. Both hacienda and factory production depended on the villagers' labor, and peasants in turn relied on wages to complement the produce from their small fields.

During the prerevolutionary period, central Tlaxcala had become a land of peasant-workers, with that mixture of indigenous traditions and modern conditions that sustained insurrection. In the process, a long series of grievances in both the agricultural and industrial domains had contributed to "a vigorous peasant tradition of protest" (Buve 1990:239). Classic forms of labor exploitation were denounced by reformers and activists of the region. On the eve of the Revolution, both economic crises and political exclusion contributed to the discontent and tension which further linked the rural population with the urban-based liberal movement.

Schools had not been absent from this scene. During the Porfirian regime, massive stone classrooms had been built adjoining the municipal buildings or facing the colonial churches on the central squares of the *cabeceras* (municipal seats), as well as in many pueblos. These schools embodied a sense of cultural progress which had been strictly separated from the Catholic Church since Benito Juárez's mid-nineteenth-century liberal reforms. For decades, the Tlaxcalan government had paid teacher salaries in all of the pueblos, and regularly distributed textbooks and supplies. Though most schools taught a uniform elementary (1-4) curriculum, the "superior" schools (1-6) in the cities offered additional courses, including music, history, and the sciences. These became model centers emulated by teachers in the town schools. Public schooling had given pueblo-based peasants access to certain cultural elements—literacy, numeracy and patriotic civic ceremony—which had been effectively, though selectively, integrated into the indigenous life of the region.

On the eve of the Revolution, half of the population of the region had spent some time in school, and about a third had learned to read and write. Schooling was not for all, however. The children of the poorer hacienda workers found it difficult to share a bench with the overseer's kids, and town children often chose—despite regulations to the contrary—to become unpaid apprentices to relatives working in factories. Some local authorities kept enrollments low, arguing, as did one committee member, that if all children were to attend classes, "the teacher—unable to work with so many—would just have them stored away."[20] In the more populous indigenous municipalities,[21] there was room in the school for only one out of ten children—enough to form the local elites from which emerged both conservative *caciques* (local bosses) and revolutionary leaders. Practically no state-paid teachers were sent to the haciendas and barrios. Nevertheless, some hacienda-owners and remote villages had hired teachers for their own "rural schools," as required by law.

During the crucial years between 1913 and 1916, the revolutionary confrontations disrupted communication, production, and administration, as contending factions controlled roads and railways, redistributed hacienda lands, and levied taxes. When Carranza's army took control of the region, incorporating or eliminating forces that had been loyal to Emiliano Zapata, it dissolved what remained of the former administrative structure (Buve 1990). Although the schools initially faced only isolated assaults, by 1915 many had been closed or converted to garrisons. As civil government was slowly rebuilt after 1916, it was forced to respond to constant petitions for reopening town schools or establishing new ones. Barrios and new agrarian colonies solicited official state-paid teachers while committing local resources to building schoolrooms. The Tlaxcalan government was unable to fund all pre-existing schools, and cut many down to one teacher. When the federal government began to strengthen its control over regional forces during the 1920s, it responded to the demand for education and found in the rural schools a key to constructing new forms of rule (Rockwell 1994).

As federal inspectors entered the region, they encountered the long-term struggle for local autonomy which Tlaxcalans had resumed during the Revolution. They negotiated with town assemblies to transfer existing services to the federal budget. In some cases, town-dwellers insisted on retaining the state-paid teacher, over whom they had greater control. In others, they allied with federal authorities to gain independence from municipal authorities. Federal teachers were also sent to the outlying barrios and newly formed agrarian colonies, where peasant groups were eager to support a school as a first step towards autonomy. Although some villagers mistrusted the federal scheme and turned to the governor for funding, others found the new system advantageous, as it allowed them to suspend contributions to the distant pueblo school. The federal system thus grew following an irregular pattern that mapped on to underlying political allegiances in the region. The innovative programs for the new rural schools were channeled through this federalized structure. As the reforms entered the region, they were put in practice by teachers trained in the prerevolutionary period who had to contend with preexisting canons of schooling.

THE APPROPRIATION OF TEACHING

Schooling in the prerevolutionary days in rural Tlaxcala was intimately related to becoming a teacher. The local representation of the "educated person" (literally, *persona educada*) was strengthened through the various specialized tasks associated with teaching in rural regions. For decades, the mastery of literacy had been the privileged domain of a select group of citizens who cultivated a highly legible and graceful handwriting. These persons often dedicated at least some years to teaching, and then became scribes or secretaries in the governing and military spheres. While apprenticeship produced knowledgeable individuals in many trades and professions, a fourth-grade education, which at the time was more selective and exacting than in later years, generally led to this specialized career requiring skill in writing. Indeed, becoming a "preceptor" seemed to townsfolk practically the only valid reason for continuing a formal education beyond third grade.[22]

Parents at the time had formed a clear image of a teacher's capacities and obligations. The script, honored by both rural and urban inhabitants, had been influenced by the prestigious Instituto Científico y Literario (ICL), Tlaxcala city's primary and postprimary school for boys, and its counterpart for girls, Educación y Patria.[23] For years, these schools had recruited young scholars from each municipality to finish the upper primary grades (5–6) and become teachers. The institute had also certified many in-service teachers who lacked formal training but had been hired by the pueblos on the basis of their literacy skills and honorable conduct.

Throughout the later Porfirian years (1895–1910), professors at the capital's schools had inculcated the mores and disseminated the notions of science considered obligatory for civilized men and women at the time. The institutes' inventoried supplies are indicative of the curriculum: geometry sets and up-to-date laboratory equipment, hundreds of desiccated animals, dozens of maps and charts, pianos and other instruments, and for the girls, a fully equipped sewing room and kitchen. A well-stocked library included literary, scientific, and legal works, plus special titles on the proper upbringing of young women. Ironically, programs for the upper grades at this urban school included the new agricultural science which educators hoped would boost hacienda production, but which had not yet been associated with rural schooling.

After the Revolution, the institutes were converted into two primary schools and an underfunded normal school. The ICL's material legacy was in a sorry state; it was scarcely used and never to be renewed. The old guard professors, still in charge at the normal school, continued to train and certify teachers, testing them on principles of discipline and didactics and mastery of orthography, applied math, and zoology. Furthermore, a former headmaster of the ICL, Justiniano Aguillón de los Ríos, continued to influence teachers and parents as director of the state school system during the 1920s. Noted for his degrees in both education and agronomy, his eccentric tastes, and his fine multilingual library, Aguillón was a prototype of the educated man of prerevolutionary years.

Thus, the Porfirian model was perpetuated and disseminated during the postrevolutionary years, and its imprint can be discerned in the smaller town schools, despite their meager resources.[24] *Vecinos* continued to insist on separate schools, with a woman teacher in charge of all the girls. Teachers continued to request wall charts and maps, geometry sets, globes, and musical instruments. Parents were particularly grateful to instructors who organized elaborate civic or literary ceremonies, such as those practiced in the cities, or who trained students to read musical scores and play band instruments. These practices had been appropriated and integrated into the towns' ritual calendar, and were a significant element of rural life. The generally strict older teachers guaranteed that at least some students would achieve full competency in writing, and could eventually meet local needs for translating and drawing up official documents. The ICL tradition was still the touchstone for quality schooling during the years when teachers began to hear about the experimental "new Mexican school" proposed by the federal government.

In 1926, a call went out to the towns announcing the opening of a federal normal school at Xocoyucan,[25] a stately hacienda expropriated for the cause. Some sixty youths enrolled in the boarding school, most from literate rural families, and several from the new ruling elite that emerged after the revolutionary movement. The class included twenty women from families progressive enough to allow daughters to live at a coeducational boarding school. Many students had tried other trades, doing a turn at carpentry or commerce; some had even taught for a year or two, or had transferred from the state normal school. The few who were not accustomed to working in the fields were dubbed, by their fellow students, *catrines*, a derisive term referring to the urban upper class. The rest not only were accustomed to such work, but in some cases even felt more knowledgeable about cultivating and animal-breeding than their teachers.

The boarding regime forged life-long ties among youths and contributed to an indelible sense of belonging to the *magisterio* (teacher corps). When old-timers get together,[26] they recall the hard work at Xocoyucan. They had apparently spent much of the time renewing the hacienda building, cleaning vegetable gardens and chicken coops, building shelves for the library, and generally taking charge of everyday life on the farm. In numerous workshops, the future teachers learned to make soap, tan hides, tend to bees, raise silkworms, preserve fruit and work at a dozen other domestic industries. They then taught these skills to the adults of nearby communities, while summoning them to night literacy classes. Their social work entailed organizing a growing list of civic celebrations, as well as promoting reforestation, vaccination, and sobriety. Xocoyucan students were also allowed to govern their own community, and often imposed their conditions upon the headmasters.

Graduates of the first class had vivid memories of the founder, Professor Amezcua, who turned Xocoyucan into a functioning model of the "school of action" that the future teachers were to establish in the communities. The second headmaster, the solemn Professor Gómez, had been a disciple of John Dewey, yet he left a dimmer impression. Teachers mention that they often received visiting educators at Xocoyucan, as Mexico City was but a few hours away. Two recall having mimicked Dewey's unintelligible English as he conversed with Gómez. Only years later, when the myth of the Mexican Rural School had taken shape, did they learn that the American educator had inspired much of their training. At the time, Dewey's texts were apparently not widely read at Xocoyucan. Nevertheless, many of the progressive educational ideas in vogue at the time filtered through their everyday life or were rediscovered through practical experience.

A certain mistrust of books seems to have been one of the lessons of Xocoyucan, as former students remember few significant titles. Vasconcelos' initial thrust toward a classical education had apparently not taken root, though copies of his popular editions of literary texts were in the library. Most professors lectured, and students relied on their notes rather than reading textbooks. Nor did the agricultural brochures sent from the U.S. guide the everyday work on the farm. Yet despite the explicit criticism of "bookish knowledge," literacy was taken on as a serious mission. The debates on ways of teaching reading and writing were lively, as the *natural* method promoted by the Ministry lost ground to the *onomatopoeic* (phonetic) method of the elder educator, Torres Quintero. The written word was also present in other, perhaps more vital, ways, as Xocoyucan students wrote theatrical pieces, published a small periodical, *The New Light*, and consulted the new legal codes on numerous agrarian issues.

Once assigned to schools, the rural teachers from Xocoyucan set out to prove their worth. As they left the normal school, teachers recall with pride, they felt they "owned the world." Their stance is evident in the official photo of the graduation. For the occasion all had purchased, with considerable difficulty, their first urban attire: coats and ties, stylish dresses and high-heeled shoes. Two intensive-years of postprimary training were much more than most teachers in Tlaxcala at the time had received. Xocoyucan graduates were hired to replace "empirical" or uncertified state teachers.[27] Dressed in the proper garb for their profession, they referred to the older teachers, many of whom had settled down to a meager semi-rural style of life, as "barefoot teachers."[28] In turn, many state teachers considered their new colleagues to be *catrines*, an ironic epithet for those trained to teach rural industries. This judgment was borne out by villagers quick to denounce some federal teachers as *altaneros* (haughty), contending that the Revolution had abolished these Porfirian attitudes.[29]

Though wearing *huaraches* and living off the land, the old guard teachers were convinced that a proper elementary education consisted of knowing the arts and sciences taught at the ICL, plus mastering calligraphy and declamation through hours of practice. Some shared the view held by many parents that school was for learning literacy, and that there was little sense in having school children plant vegetable gardens. The Xocoyucan graduates, on the other hand, sought to go beyond the "rudiments" as they restated the criteria for schoolwork in rural environments.[30] Given ample leeway in planning their own syllabi within four domains—physical, social, artistic and intellectual—many new teachers broadened the rather fixed contents characteristic of the prerevolutionary schools. They offered children the opportunity to produce a variety of goods and services, as part of their formal education. Many of the rural teachers also won over the most indigenous communities by their willingness to speak Mexicano[31] and adapt to local custom.

For all of its impact, Xocoyucan did not totally determine the new teachers' practice. One graduate, Narciso Pérez, claims he faced his class the first day "as though he knew nothing." To begin working, he recalled the lessons of his elementary schoolteacher, Ismael Bello, a cultured individual from one of the pueblos who had a passion for music and silkworm production, and a strict view of academic discipline.[32] Narciso also used his hometown experience in theater, and pretraining skill as a carpenter, to mold his own version of the school of action. Yet other lessons of the Xocoyucan boarding days—such as those learned through student government—became useful to his career. Narciso soon entered the turbulent political life of the early 1930s, organizing teachers to protest a six-month paycheck delay and resist doing the required community work on weekends. His trajectory is indicative of the growing consciousness of labor rights among teachers, which eventually limited federal attempts to erase the boundaries between school time and community life.

The federal school program appropriated a rural knowledge base through teachers who drew on local experience and molded their practice to village resources and preferences. Teachers in Tlaxcala had experienced both rural life and the revolutionary movement from different vantage points. Those who had learned about agriculture as children in the pueblos often shared their knowledge with peasants of the poorer barrios and the newly founded colonies. Others had little to offer that local producers did not already know. On the other hand, many adults wanted to learn to write, "with a sort of desperation, as though it were indispensable for being a citizen."[33] During these years, *vecinos* increasingly wrote their own petitions, as the position of scribe gradually became obsolete. In this context, rural teachers intensified their efforts toward adult literacy, often linking it to political organization. As one veteran rural teacher expressed it, rural schools "grew conditioned and molded by the social forces of the rural community" (Castillo 1965:249).

APPROPRIATIONS OF THE SPACE OF SCHOOLING

In the official rhetoric, rural schools were first named *casas del pueblo* (houses of the pueblo), while the pueblos, appropriately, were to become the "houses of the school." In reality, conflicting claims emerged in the pueblos over the spaces allotted to formal education. By reconstructing these encounters, through documents produced to report rather than to norm,[34] it is possible to uncover the intermeshing popular and official representations of schooling.

As the federal system entered Tlaxcala, it began by incorporating state schools, in effect appropriating the local history of public education. Pre-existing installations and dispositions toward schooling benefited the undertaking. The official pueblo schools, which were the proud achievement of town-dwellers who had progressed toward an urban lifestyle by Porfirian standards, were renamed "Rural Schools" in the process. As only the unofficial hacienda schools had previously been considered "rural," this implicit downgrading occasioned some resistance to federalization. The new authorities also requisitioned existing schoolrooms, a measure which entailed potential conflicts. Some teachers, especially those in charge of the girls, had worked in municipal buildings or on church premises, which nominally belonged to the state[35] but served locally for other purposes as well. Other schools were established in rooms loaned or donated by private citizens, or were built on communal land. Yet the main source of resistance was the townspeople's strong sense of possession of the official schools they had built and maintained over the years (Mercado 1992; Rockwell 1994).

Communities were legally responsible for providing a locale for the school. For decades, they had subsidized state-financed public schooling, through the customary rules for collecting funds, contributing labor, and donating material that applied for all public works (Rockwell 1994). As villagers took it upon themselves to provide proper schoolrooms for the federal teachers, they favored the Porfirian model: one long room with high ceilings and a raised dais at one end, designed to accommodate boys of all grades under one headmaster and to double as town hall. The costs and time required to purchase wooden beams and build with stone, rather than with the adobe used in most local constructions, did not hinder these long-term projects. Most villages did not heed the official recommendation to build a less expensive model, with several classrooms, adapted to the new coeducational, graded arrangement. Local committees provided furniture, watched over classrooms and equipment, asked arriving teachers to sign a detailed inventory as they turned over the school to them, and checked everything again at the end of year. They also guarded the school keys.

A different use of space emerged as the new educational program was disseminated during the late 1920s. When a team of federal educators, the Misión Cultural, arrived at Natívitas in 1929 to train in-service teachers from surrounding schools, it set to work in all available areas.[36] The *misioneros* used the schoolroom for only an hour a day, to teach the Palmer writing system which promised to free time for other activities. The rest of the course was centered on community projects: tanning skins by the riverside, setting up workshops under trees, planting vegetables on available plots, practicing new ways of building ovens, or preparing meals in peasant homes. Open lots were taken over for promoting new sports with English names. Makeshift stages served for the evening entertainment, which featured skits with revolutionary themes. Volunteers were gathered together to take part in demonstration classes. As the teachers began working, children peeked through windows and sat upon stone walls to watch.

Teachers returned from the month-long course to face complaints that schoolchildren were behind in reading, writing and 'rithmetic. Over the years, some were able to muster enthusiasm for the new rural program. A young teacher at the small colony of Analco, Lorenza García,[37] delivered her report aloud—in the conventional style—to the local population at the end-of-year ceremony. She had set up a veritable farm, which had been tended by the children rather than by sharecroppers, as in other schools. Her strongest argument was that she had "not sacrificed the fragile local economy," since all the crops and animals—"except for the pigeons that adorned the school"—had been sold to cover costs. At the same time, she claimed that the children had learned to read and write, and furthermore to draw, recite, and sing, as the old urban curriculum demanded. Her school had an open air theater and a sports field, but as yet no library—a trend that was typical of the rural schools at the time.

Federal educators prescribed a growing number of "annexes" to complete the space of the rural schools. The full list, as formalized in a 1934 circular,[38] included: a library, a science section, a meteorological station, and a museum; workshops for carpentry, ceramics, ironwork, soapmaking, tailoring and sewing, printing, and shoemaking; cabinets for hairdressing, hygiene and first-aid supplies; a vegetable garden and orchard and, if possible, a larger agricultural field; beehives, a fishpond, and cages for birds, pigeons, chickens, and rabbits; a desk for public writing, an outdoor or indoor theater, and a sports field. Inspectors checked off each school's resources on printed formats and reported statistics annually.

These yearly tallies show the distribution of annexes in actual schools.[39] Most communities had set aside a field for the new sports. Over half had built open-air theaters, a sign of the positive reception of the renewed civic calendar. Though not on the list, musical instruments continued to be in great demand, even if the requests were generally frowned upon by federal inspectors.[40] About one out of four reported libraries consisting of assorted textbooks, many from former times, and the periodicals and brochures sent by the federal government. Teachers promoted various domestic industries as their own repertoires and the local resources allowed. Many formed cooperatives to build the required annexes and tend to the animals. Over a hundred workshops and productive projects were reported in 1930, yet five years later only half had survived. Several rural schools were selected as models to be emulated by other teachers, on the merit of particular projects.[41]

Arrangements for managing school plots show how new dispositions were often assimilated to old uses. Agricultural parcels were available in about a third of the schools of the region. In some cases, teachers simply planted a vegetable garden on the public grounds next to the schoolroom. In *ejido* settlements (postrevolutionary communal farms), land for the school was specified in the federal land grants. In the pueblos, the agricultural plot often belonged to the century-old communal "public instruction fund." In most cases, parents collectively cultivated the land or rented it out to defray school expenses. Indeed, inspectors lamented that, because of this practice, children were not learning to "love the earth," as the program recommended. Traditional messages, such as the value of communal work, were thus asserted over the official rural themes.

Rural teachers convened adults and children in town squares, theaters and communal kitchens, and staged many activities outside the classroom. In some cases, these activities competed with traditional and religious activities. In others, the school gave the village its first outline of a truly public space (often bordered with pine trees), even before a chapel or town square had been projected. In many communities, teachers inaugurated a ceremonial life previously restricted to the cities and the sanctuaries, and thus supported the thrust toward autonomy. Yet underneath these new practices, something else was going on as well: confrontations occurred over the possession of the school, as appears in the occasional reports of conflicts over the school keys.

Keys are particularly telling indices to the appropriation of space. When villagers completed schoolrooms, they often considered securing the doors, even though in rural schools, unlike urban ones, thievery was rarely a problem, and latecomers were admitted to classes. Purchasing the lock was a project in itself, generally undertaken by parents. Local committees safeguarded the keys and controlled the uses of the locale, which ranged from classes to town meetings to fund-raising dances. Many schools served for storage, and one even doubled as a jail, with an additional lock, during the evenings. Teachers had their own claims on the space of schooling, however. They had to save supplies, and many actually lived in the schoolroom, at least during weekdays. In these cases, they often decided to install the locks or replace keys.

Controversies over the control of school premises were common during the postrevolutionary years.[42] The governors received accusations from local authorities charging particular teachers of leaving without turning over the keys, or of denying them access to the schoolroom. Teachers in turn complained that committees did not open classrooms on time, or accused local authorities of breaking into the school. An agent of Ixcotla responded to one such complaint by saying that he had "ventured to force open the school doors early one morning, to hold a meeting of utmost importance; at about eight-thirty, the teachers arrived and without waiting a moment, departed. The following day they came late, as they have often done."[43] Committee members of Tizostoc, having complained of their teacher to the governor, "took the key away from him," pending a change in personnel.[44] Local control over space implied control over teachers; nevertheless, the teachers were increasingly backed by higher authorities, and held the school keys ever more firmly in their own hands.

As a more radical educational discourse gathered force in the 1930s,[45] opposition to federal teachers was spurred by town priests and landowners, causing division in many communities. Tactics on both sides could involve the keys. For example, in conservative Tepeyanco,[46] town elders who mistrusted the new socialist form of education asked the head teacher to turn over the keys and leave. The inspector recommended that the teachers "leave their school and their materials well-locked and retreat to the district office, until the conflict was resolved." Certain women and children had backed the teachers[47] manifesting generation and gender differences that often affected local alignments. The following year, the teachers agreed not to attack the local religious customs nor back the agrarian groups' demands for land, and thus were allowed to continue their program of social activities in Tepeyanco.

Over a period of three decades, the keys, formerly a rare item of school inventories, became a matter of contestation; then they slowly receded again into the undocumented everyday life of schools. The fate of the school keys marked a fundamental shift, as professional administrators gained a measure of control previously held by local authorities (Rockwell 1994). However, villagers continued to use the leverage they had won by building schoolrooms to strengthen their demands. Teachers thus learned to yield in order to maintain the delicate balance with the local *vecinos* whose contributions sustained the school. In the process, the spaces designated for schooling did not totally merge with the community, as envisioned by the federal educators. Nevertheless, the cumulative effect of the program did alter the notion of educational space.

As the 1930s came to a close, the social landscape in central Tlaxcala showed signs of change,[48] though certain deeper patterns persist to this day. A network of new roads exposed communication and consumer patterns to further external influence. Where the Nahuatl language persisted, it generally receded into ritual and domestic spheres. The locus of production shifted away from the haciendas and the textile factories, as out-of-state urban centers began to attract a migrant labor force. A few activities initiated by the rural schools—such as baseball and silkworm breeding—had enjoyed a temporary success, though they were not permanently incorporated into local culture. In some pueblos, the rural teachers influenced ways of life, leaving traces of their work to the present day.[49] In others, they broke down the subtle social barriers to schooling that had excluded children of outlying barrios. As the image of the educated person was transformed, it became more inclusive, allowing children to use their local knowledge in school activities. Significant changes in the social relationship to literacy in rural areas also added a new dimension to schooling. Towards the end of the period, though enrollment had not kept up with population growth, overall literacy rates had nearly reached the 50 percent mark in the state.[50]

After 1940, the Mexican Rural School was mentioned as something of the past. Yet for years, many rural schools continued to be set in open spaces, and had paths cutting across their unfenced grounds to adjacent fields. Classrooms continued to be used for civic meetings and community storage. As youths of this period grew to be parents and teachers, they reenacted the scripts experienced in the federal schools they had attended, just as previous generations had preserved the ICL model. Parents continued to evaluate the practical value of school contents in varying contexts, long after official policy had erased the rural/urban distinction.[51] Teachers continued to dedicate personal time to social work, long after the union had won them the right to a limited workday.[52] Practices appropriated during those years became weapons of everyday resistance, used against the modernizing projects of later years which enclosed the space of schooling and reinstated a unified curriculum.[53] Thus, the intergenerational appropriation of a different notion of the educated person had consequences for many years to come.

APPROPRIATION AND THE EDUCATED PERSON

The historical perspective used in this study uncovers some of the uses, practices, and spaces that were appropriated by different social actors to construct schools in central Tlaxcala during the postrevolutionary years. These elements shaped the everyday environments within which rural children "taught themselves," as Tlaxcalan elders usually say. In this sense, I have argued, the process of *appropriation* sustained local cultures of schooling and transformed representations of the educated person. In my initial discussion, I concurred with Roger Chartier's understanding of appropriation as multiple, relational, transformative, and embedded in social struggles. In concluding, I will relate each of these attributes to instances of appropriation I have described above.

First, authorities, parents and teachers each selectively appropriated the cultural resources allotted to schooling. Federal educators made use of the knowledge possessed by rural teachers and incorporated communal spaces as they projected the schools of the Revolution. As the federal government took over public schooling, it displaced local powers and strengthened central rule. Many rural towns, in turn, appropriated the federal program and used it to secure their own autonomy in relation to municipal authorities. While defending their right to assess the quality of teaching by urban standards, villagers selectively endorsed the novel activities introduced by rural schools. Rural teachers, moved by their own interests, yet alert to parental demands, used an assortment of tools of the trade, acquired in a variety of contexts. Each of these groups limited the others' power to "mold" the lives of schoolchildren.

Second, none of the various transcripts of schooling—those preserved by town authorities, conceived by central educators, or enacted by rural teachers—corresponded to some essential "rural" quality. The interplay among them was constant, and was grounded in changing relationships among social forces. Thus, in defending local autonomy, peasants often resisted ruralization and emulated the style of urban schooling. In legitimizing central rule, on the other hand, federal educators advocated teaching agrarian laws and domestic industries. Nor did the image of persons educated in schools always correspond to the identities they constructed in other situations: many literate preceptors continued to till the earth, while teachers trained in agrarian matters ascended in political organizations. Despite these changing relations, as the rural themes wove in and out of the culture of schooling they opened spaces and validated abilities not previously connected with the notion of an educated person. Though rural education did not produce the ideal farmers that educators had imagined, through schooling townspeople altered their relation to literacy and created strategies to face changing political and economic conditions.

Third, the appropriated resources were reinterpreted and transformed. Federal educators changed pueblo schools into rural schools, and communal lands into children's farms. Pueblo residents assimilated federal dispositions to local custom—for example in building classrooms—and thus molded the rural schools to fit their own standards. Teachers fashioned a practice that did not wholly resemble official mandate. Rather, it was a blend of their knowledge of local custom and language, the pedagogical common sense they had inherited from their childhood mentors, and a progressive outlook they had absorbed during official training. The mixture of these educational uses and meanings was what actually shaped the local cultures of schooling.

Finally, social struggles conditioned the appropriation of school practices and spaces. The issue of the school keys is indicative of the confrontations which occurred as professional educators and local authorities attempted to control schoolgrounds and to extend the schools' influence. Several fundamental tendencies—such as the villagers' defense of autonomy and the teachers' struggle for labor rights—countered the federal endeavor to promote an idealized rural life through schooling. State action—then and thereafter—always encounters local forces which transform educational plans in unpredictable ways. Other forces were also at work. Educators at the time did not foresee the gradual conversion of labor as it was appropriated by a modern industrial sector. This development soon rendered obsolete not only the calligraphy taught in Porfirian schools, but also many of the rural industries taught at Xocoyucan. At the same time, it ushered in a new use for elementary schooling, as credentials were soon to be required even for manual work.

How do these intersecting appropriations account for the educated rural person? Whatever the pedagogical discourse of the time prescribed, children could only appropriate the culture actually embedded in school practices. The tacit images of an educated person found in laboratory practices or in animal husbandry had no immanent power to mold subjectivities. Nevertheless, these images did influence the layout of schools, the purchase of supplies, and the performance of everyday rituals. Acts which enlarged or enclosed educational spaces circumscribed the situated experience of schooling. Cultural scripts reenacted by teachers became models for proper learning. Yet as children appropriated the available culture, they further transformed it; they fashioned their own schooled identities out of stuff picked up during class time. If one were able to look into the rural classrooms of the past,[54] one would surely find, there too, "the specific logics at work in the customs, practices and ways of making one's own that which is imposed" (Chartier 1993:7).

Schooled persons carry past experience into future ventures and continue to reproduce practices that may seem out of phase with contemporary trends. They also construct, often beyond any explicit intention, the physical and symbolic environments which characterize further schooling. New generations appropriate, that is select and use, particular pieces of culture found in a school's radius of action. In the process, they make them their own, reorder them, adapt them to new tasks, and otherwise transform them. Vertical socialization or cultural transmission models rarely capture the complexity of this relationship. In this sense, the concept of appropriation offers a persuasive alternative for rethinking schooling as a process of cultural production.

NOTES

I wish to thank Bradley Levinson, Douglas Foley, Katie Anderson-Levitt, and my colleagues Antonia Candela, Ruth Mercado, and Ruth Paradise for helpful comments on earlier versions of this paper.

1. Recent studies showing this include Furet and Ozouf 1982, Ansión 1988, Eklof 1990, Reed-Danahay 1987, Anderson-Levitt and Reed-Danahay 1991, Mercado 1992, Vaughan 1994, Rockwell 1994, Luykx (in this volume).

2. See the introduction by Levinson and Holland (this volume).

3. This sense of the term comes from the writings of Karl Marx and Max Weber, with reference to the economic sphere. Bourdieu (1980) occasionally used the term in this sense, though it was not a central concept in his theory.

4. Agnes Heller (1977:239) links appropriation to the active use of cultural resources. Paul Willis (1977:175) likewise views social agents as "active appropriators." Both perspectives contrast with classical socialization and reproduction theories, which focus on "internalization" and "inculcation." Nevertheless, see Luykx (in this volume) for a parallel discussion within socialization theory.

5. For example Ortner 1984, Quinn and Holland 1987, Roseberry 1989, Rosaldo 1989, Hannerz 1992, and Keesing 1994.

6. *Appropriation* in this sense is used colloquially in Romance languages with reference to social or political vindications. It has been an integral part of Marxist scholarship, used by such authors as Leontiev (1981), Bakhtin (1968), and Heller (1977). See similar uses by Willis (1977), Ansión (1988), Bonfil (1987), Scott (1990), Foley (1990), Rogoff (1990), and several authors in this volume.

7. Chartier draws on Bourdieu (1980) in his emphasis on practice, yet his general view is perhaps more indebted to Norbert Elias.

8. See, for example, Thompson (1966), Bakhtin (1968), and Scott (1985, 1990).

9. Documentary evidence is primarily from the Archivo General del Estado de Tlaxcala (AGET), Fondo de la Revolución y del Régimen Obregonista (FRRO), and Fondo de Educación Pública (EP), as well as from the Archivo Histórico de la Secretaría de Educación Pública (AHSEP). Research was supported by grants from the Consejo Nacional para la Cultura y las Artes, and from the Instituto Nacional de Estudios Históricos de la Revolución Mexicana, both in Mexico.

10. On the formation of the postrevolutionary Mexican state as a cultural process, see Joseph and Nugent (1994).

11. Zapata had fought against presidents Díaz, Madero, Huerta, and Carranza, and was assassinated by orders of Carranza in 1919.

12. Sáenz (1976) summarizes the ideology of the rural school program.

13. Regional response to the federal program was extremely diverse, as has been shown by Vaughan (1994).

14. As Scott puts it (1985:318, also cited in Anderson-Levitt and Reed-Danahay, 1991:556), "subordinate classes . . . [defend] their own interpretation of an earlier dominant ideology against new and painful arrangements imposed by elites and/or the state."

15. Others (e.g., Ansión 1988; Foley 1990) have noted the popular rejection of "special" programs in defense of the appropriation of the cultural resources of the elite through schooling.

16. The Partido Nacional Revolucionario, founded in 1929, was precursor to the current Partido Revolucionario Institucional (PRI).

17. See Scott 1990 on the notion of "official transcripts."

18. The following section is based on census data from 1910 to 1940 and on Ramírez Rancaño (1991), among other sources.

19. Mexicano is the local name for the Nahuatl language. In the 1921 census, 54 percent of the population was classed as "Indian race" and 42 percent as "mixed race." Statewide census figures underestimated native language speakers at 16 percent for that year.

20. Report from Teacalco, AGET/EP 266-21, 1930.

21. Three predominantly Indian pueblos were larger than the state capital. Each had over 4,000 inhabitants, distributed in a large central sector and several surrounding barrios.

22. Interviews with Cleofas Galicia and Lucía Galicia, Tlaxcala, 1992.

23. Information on these institutions is based on documents in AGET/FRRO, cajas 300, 303, 304, 309, 313, 321, 323, 1910 to 1915.

24. Examples can be found in school reports in AGET/FRRO 346-13 1917; AGET/EP 246-15 1929; 266-21 1930; 369-14 and 369-18 1933.

25. Information on Xocoyucan is based on documents from AHSEP, Fondo Departamento de Educación Agrícola y Normales Rurales, files 158-23, 162-2, 167-27, 168-16, 171-8, 178-3, 1928–1933, as well as on extensive interviews with four former graduates.

26. Based on joint interviews with Lucia Galicia and Narciso Pérez, and with Narciso Pérez and Cándido Zamora, Tlaxcala, 1992.

27. Documented in AGET/EP 369-15 1933.

28. Many probably wore sandals, as a 1917 circular orders teachers to wear shoes AGET/FRRO 341-56 1917.

29. References to this sort of attitude are found in various village complaints, in AGET/EP 414 Legajo 11 1935; 369-14 1933; 398 Legajo 1 1935.

30. For example, report by Professor Villeda, AHSEP/DER 794-14 1925, and circular #8 to teachers from Director E. López, AGET/EP 261-1 1930.

31. Though the use of the native language was not part of official educational policy at the time, bilingual teachers did use it to communicate with villagers. See Hernández (1987).

32. Bello later became a model rural teacher, winning over parents through a range of social projects that benefited the towns AGET/EP 120-16 1925 and interviews with former students.

33. Interview with Lucía Galicia, Tlaxcala, 1992.

34. Numerous inspector's reports from both AGET and AHSEP guide the following account, including those in: AGET/EP 250-28 1929; 404-9 1935; 414, Legajo 11 1935; AHSEP/DEP 1-745 1929; 888-29 1932; 14-4335 1937–39.

35. The state had expropriated all church property during the previous century.

36. The following is based on report in AHSEP/DENR 178-3 1929.

37. Based on information in AGET/EP 374-26 and 388-12 1934, and 11-27 (provisional) 1937.

38. Circular 18, 1V-7-34, published in *Memoria relativa al estado que guarda el Ramo de Educación Pública*. Tomo II. Documentos. Mexico: Talleres Gráficos de la Nación, 1934, pp. 95-97.

39. Annexes are reported by Inspector G. Pérez, AGET/EP 369-15 1933, and in Gov. A. Bonilla's *Informe de Gobierno*, 1934.

40. For example, report from San Isidro, AHSEP/DEP 888-29 1932.

41. Director of Federal Education in Tlaxcala, E. López, circular #8 to teachers, AGET-EP 261-1 1930.

42. Examples in AGET/FRRO 334-38 1915; AGET/EP 110-24 1924; AGET/EP 145-70 1926; AHSEP/DGEPET 3-127 1928; AGET/EP 251-8 1929; 414-13 1935; AGET/EP Legajo 8 10-10 (provisional) 1936.

43. Letter to the Director of Education, AGET/EP, Legajo 3, 2-33 (provisional) 1936.

44. Letter from *vecinos* of Tizostoc, AGET/EP 414-3 1935.

45. In 1934, the federal government adopted a socialist educational policy, which was opposed by the Catholic Church and other sectors of society. See Vaughan (1994).

46. Information on the Tepeyanco incident is found in AGET/EP 398 Legajo 1 1935.

47. This also happened in other communities, as new teachers challenged traditional powers. See Hernández (1987).

48. See González Jácome (1991) and Ramírez Rancaño (1991).

49. For example, a few towns still noted for producing barbers or tailors trace these skills back to rural schools.

50. Between 1920 and 1940, about fifty new schools were founded in the state, half federal- and half state-funded. Statewide literacy, which had been 30 percent in 1910, reached 47 percent in 1940.

51. After this period, educators in Mexico began to construct a new transcript, based on a "culture of equality" (see Levinson, in this volume), which, among other things, erased the explicit distinction between the urban and the rural curricula in primary schools.

52. See examples in the autobiographical account of Claudio Hernández (1987), for the 1940s.

53. Several examples from the 1980s are included in our ethnographic research done in the same region (Rockwell 1995).

54. One of the restrictions of historiographical research is the paucity of documented accounts of life in classrooms; in this aspect, ethnography has the last say.

REFERENCES

Anderson-Levitt, Kathryn and Deborah Reed-Danahay. 1991. Backward Countryside, Troubled City: French Teachers' Images of Rural and Working-Class Families. American Ethnologist 18(3):546–564.

Ansión, Juan. 1988. La escuela en la comunidad campesina. Lima: Proyecto Escuela, Ecologia y Comunidad Campesina.

Bakhtin, Michael. 1968. Rabelais and His World. Cambridge, MA: MIT Press.

Bonfil Batalla, Guillermo. 1987. México profundo: Una civilización negada. Mexico City: Secretaría de Educación Pública.

Bourdieu, Pierre. 1980. Le sens pratique. Paris: Les Editions de Minuit.

Bourdieu, Pierre and Jean-Claude Passeron. 1977. Reproduction: In Education, Society, and Culture. Beverly Hills: Sage.

Buve, Raymond. 1990. Consolidating a Cacicazgo. *In* Provinces of the Revolution: Essays on Regional Mexican History, 1910–1929. T. Benjamin and M. Wasserman, eds. Pp. 237–272. Albuquerque: University of New Mexico Press.

Castillo, Isidro. 1966. México y su revolución educativa. Mexico: Pax México.

Chartier, Roger. 1991. The Cultural Origins of the French Revolution. Durham: Duke University Press.

————. 1993. Popular Culture: A Concept Revisited. Intellectual History Newsletter 15:3–13. To appear also *In* Forms and Meanings: Texts, Performances, and Audiences in Early Modern Europe. Philadelphia: University of Pennsylvania Press.

Eklof, Ben. 1990. Peasants and Schools. *In* The World of the Russian Peasant. B. Eklof and S. P. Frank, eds. Pp. 115–132. Boston: Unwin Hyman.

Foley, Douglas. 1990. Learning Capitalist Culture. Philadelphia: University of Pennsylvania Press.

Furet, François and Jacques Ozouf. 1982. Reading and Writing: Literacy in France from Calvin to Jules Ferry. Cambridge: Cambridge University Press.

Giddens, Anthony. 1984. The Constitution of Society. Berkeley: University of California Press.

González Jácome, Alba, ed. 1991. La economía desgastada. Historia de la producción textil en Tlaxcala. Mexico: Universidad Iberoamericana.

Hannerz, Ulf. 1992. Cultural Complexity: Studies in the Social Organization of Meaning. New York: Columbia University Press.

Heller, Agnes. 1977. La sociología de la vida cotidiana. Barcelona: Península.

Hernández, Claudio. 1987. El trabajo escolar de un maestro rural. *In* Los Maestros y la Cultura Nacional, 1920–1950, vol. 3. Pp. 51–90. Mexico: Dirección General de Culturas Populares, Secretaría de Educación Pública.

Joseph, Gilbert and Daniel Nugent, eds. 1994. Everyday Forms of State Formation: Revolution and the Negotiation of Rule in Modern Mexico. Durham: Duke University Press.

Katz, Friedrich, ed. 1988. Riot, Rebellion, and Revolution: Rural Social Conflict in Mexico. Princeton: Princeton University Press.

Keesing, Roger. 1994. Theories of Culture Revisited. *In* Assessing Cultural Anthropology. R. Borofsky, ed. Pp. 301–311. New York: McGraw-Hill.

Knight, Alan. 1994. Weapons and Arches in the Mexican Revolutionary Landscape. *In* Everyday Forms of State Formation: Revolution and the Negotiation of Rule in Modern Mexico. G. Joseph and D. Nugent, eds. Pp. 24–66. Durham: Duke University Press.

Leontiev, A. N. 1981. Problems of the Development of Mind. Moscow: Progress Publishers.

Mercado, Ruth. 1992. La escuela en la memoria histórica local: una construcción colectiva. Nueva Antropología 42:73–87.

Ortner, Sherry. 1984. Theory in Anthropology since the Sixties: Comparative Studies in Society and History 26:126–166.

Quinn, Naomi and Dorothy Holland, eds. 1987. Cultural Models in Language and Thought. Cambridge: Cambridge University Press.

Ramírez Rancaño, Mario, ed. 1991. Tlaxcala: Una historia compartida. Volume 16. Tlaxcala: Gobierno del Estado de Tlaxcala.

Reed-Danahay, Deborah. 1987. Farm Children at School: Educational Strategies in Rural France. Anthropological Quarterly 60(2):83–89.

Rockwell, Elsie. 1994. Schools of the Revolution: Enacting and Contesting State Forms in Tlaxcala, 1910–1930. In Everyday Forms of State Formation: Revolution and the Negotiation of Rule in Modern Mexico. G. Joseph and D. Nugent, eds. Pp. 170–208. Durham: Duke University Press.

Rockwell, Elsie, ed. 1995. La escuela cotidiana. Mexico: Fondo de Cultura Económica.

Rogoff, Barbara. 1990. Apprenticeship in Thinking. New York: Oxford University Press.

Rosaldo, Renato. 1989. Culture and Truth: The Remaking of Social Analysis. Boston: Beacon Press.

Roseberry, William. 1989. Anthropologies and Histories: Essays in Culture, History, and Political Economy. New Brunswick, NJ: Rutgers University Press.

Sáenz, Moisés. 1976 [1939]. La escuela y la cultura. *In* México íntegro. Pp. 63–71. Mexico City: Secretaría de Educación Pública.

Scott, James. 1985. Weapons of the Weak: Everyday Forms of Peasant Resistance. New Haven: Yale University Press.

Scott, James. 1990. Domination and the Arts of Resistance: Hidden Transcripts. New Haven: Yale University Press.

Thompson, E. P. 1966. The Making of the English Working Class. New York: Vintage.

Vaughan, Mary Kay. 1994. The Educational Project of the Mexican Revolution: The Response of Local Societies (1934–1940). *In* Molding the Hearts and Minds:

Education, Communication and Social Change in Latin America. J. Britton, ed. Pp. 105–127. Wilmington, DE: Scholarly Resources.

Weber, Max. 1978. Economy and Society. 2 Volumes. Berkeley: University of California Press.

Willis, Paul. 1977. Learning to Labour. London: Gower.

NOTES ON CONTRIBUTORS

KATHRYN M. ANDERSON-LEVITT is Associate Professor of Anthropology at the University of Michigan–Dearborn. In addition to her numerous publications on schools in France, she has recently completed research on girls' schooling in Guinea, West Africa. She is presently editor of the *Anthropology and Education Quarterly*.

MARGARET EISENHART is Professor of Educational Anthropology and Research Methodology in the School of Education at the University of Colorado–Boulder. She is the author (with Dorothy Holland) of *Educated in Romance*. Her interests include: the anthropology of learning, the meanings of gender in schools and workplaces, and the applications of ethnographic methods in educational research.

DOUGLAS E. FOLEY is Professor of Education and of Anthropology at the University of Texas–Austin. His publications include *From Peones to Políticos, Learning Capitalist Culture, The Heartland Chronicles* and numerous articles on education and ethnicity. He is presently editor of the *International Journal of Qualitative Studies in Education*.

DOROTHY HOLLAND received her Ph.D. in Anthropology from the University of California–Irvine, and is now J. Ross Macdonald Professor of Anthropology at the University of North Carolina, Chapel Hill. She is a social and cultural anthropologist whose research has contributed primarily to theory in cognitive anthropology (see, for example, *Cultural Models in Language and Thought*, Holland and Quinn, eds., Cambridge University Press, 1987, and *Mind in Society/Society in Mind: A Critical Anthropology of Cognition*, Holland and Strauss, in preparation), to the extension of neo-Vygotskian theory into social theories of practice (see "Symbols, Cognition and Vygotsky's Developmental Psychology" in *Ethos* 16(3):247–272, 1988 and *Emerging Selves: Identities Forming in and against Cultural Worlds*, Holland et al., forthcoming from Harvard University Press), and to the anthropology of schooling and studies of social reproduction and cultural production (see, for example, *Educated in Romance: Women, Achievement, and College Culture*, Holland and Eisenhart, University of Chicago Press, 1990).

BRADLEY A. LEVINSON is Assistant Professor of Anthropology at Augustana College, Rock Island, Illinois. His dissertation (University of North Carolina, 1993), "Todos Somos Iguales: Cultural Production and Social Difference at a Mexican Secondary School," won the Outstanding Dissertation Award from the Council on Anthropology and Education. His interests include popular culture, schooling, and nationalism in Latin

America; the ethnography of transnational migration and schooling; and Mexican tour books as informal pedagogy.

WENDY LUTTRELL is Assistant Professor of the Practice in Cultural Anthropology and Sociology, and Assistant Director of the Center for Teaching and Learning, at Duke University. Her forthcoming book, *School Smart and Mother Wise: Women's Selves, Voices, and Values in School,* compares two groups of women literacy learners and their educational views and experiences. She writes about how gender, race, class, and sexual identities are formed and transformed through schooling, and she has translated much of her research findings into adult basic education curriculum materials.

AUROLYN LUYKX completed her Ph.D. in Anthropology at the University of Texas–Austin in 1993, and is currently living in Cochabamba, Bolivia, where she teaches school-teachers at the Universidad Mayor de San Simón. She is also an invited researcher at the Instituto de Investigación en las Humanidades y Ciencias de la Educación, where she is working on her forthcoming book, *The Citizen Factory: Language, Labor, and Identity in Bolivian Rural Schooling.*

ELSIE ROCKWELL is professor and senior researcher at the Department of Educational Research, Center for Advanced Studies of the National Polytechnic Institute (DIE-CINVESTAV/IPN), Mexico City, Mexico. Trained in both history and social anthropology, she helped initiate educational ethnography in Mexico. In addition to her new edited collection, *La Escuela Cotidiana (The Everyday School),* she has published extensively, in English and in Spanish, on educational ethnography, school culture and teachers' practice, critical theory, literacy, and the history of rural schooling.

LAURA RIVAL is Lecturer in Social Anthropology at the University of Kent, England. Her Ph.D. dissertation (University of London, 1992) examined the impact of Ecuadorian state education and nationalism on the Huaorani, a small group of Amazonian hunter-gatherers. She has carried out research in Ecuador since 1987, and has written on bilingual education, processes of modernization and development, and indigenous conceptualizations of the rainforest.

DEBRA SKINNER is a Research Investigator at the Frank Porter Graham Child Development Center, and a Research Assistant Professor in the Department of Anthropology, at the University of North Carolina–Chapel Hill. Her publications and research interests center on children's culture, and children as cultural co-creators. She is carrying out three longitudinal research projects in Nepal and the southeastern United States on this topic, focusing specifically on the ways children and adolescents form identities within changing sociohistorical and cultural contexts.

THOMAS A. SHAW is an Assistant Professor at the Harvard Graduate School of Education. Trained as a cultural anthropologist at Columbia University, his research interests include youth culture, adolescence across cultures, the life course, modernization, and constructions of self, person, and individual. He has done research in Taiwan, Japan, and the United States.

ARMANDO L. TRUJILLO is Assistant Professor in the Division of Bicultural/Bilingual Studies at the University of Texas–San Antonio. He completed his Ph.D. in anthropology at the University of Texas–Austin in 1993, with a dissertation entitled, "Community Empowerment and Bilingual/Bicultural Education: A Study of the Movimiento in a South Texas Community." He has extensive experience in education, and has taught in both the public schools and at the university level. Currently he is also a Research Associate for a Ford Foundation project called "Cultures of Success: A Study of Community Colleges with High Transfer Rates."

INDEX